Fodor's 15th Edition

Vienna and the Danube Valley

The Guide
for All Budgets

Completely
Updated

Where to Stay, Eat,
and Explore

On and Off
the Beaten Path

When to Go,
What to Pack

Maps, Travel Tips,
and Web Sites

Excerpted from *Fodor's Austria*

Fodor's Travel Publications • New York, Toronto, London, Sydney, Auckland
www.fodors.com

Fodor's Vienna and the Danube Valley

EDITORS: Robert I. C. Fisher, Tom Mercer

Editorial Contributors: Bonnie Dodson, Gary Dodson
Editorial Production: Kristin Milavec
Maps: David Lindroth, *cartographer;* Rebecca Baer and Robert Blake, *map editors*
Design: Fabrizio La Rocca, *creative director;* Guido Caroti, *art director;* Jolie Novak, *senior picture editor;* Melanie Marin, *photo editor*
Cover Design: Pentagram
Production/Manufacturing: Colleen Ziemba
Cover Photo (Naiad's Fountain, Schönbrunn Palace): Shaun Egan/Stone

Copyright

Fifteenth Edition

ISBN 1–4000–1109–4

ISSN 1095–3922

Important Tip

Although all prices, opening times, and other details in this book are based on information supplied to us at press time, changes occur all the time in the travel world, and Fodor's cannot accept responsibility for facts that become outdated or for inadvertent errors or omissions. So **always confirm information when it matters,** especially if you're making a detour to visit a specific place.

Special Sales

Fodor's Travel Publications are available at special discounts for bulk purchases for sales promotions or premiums. Special editions, including personalized covers, excerpts of existing guides, and corporate imprints, can be created in large quantities for special needs. For more information, contact your local bookseller or write to Special Markets, Fodor's Travel Publications, 1745 Broadway, New York, NY 10019. Inquiries from Canada should be directed to your local Canadian bookseller or sent to Random House of Canada, Ltd., Marketing Department, 2775 Matheson Boulevard East, Mississauga, Ontario L4W 4P7. Inquiries from the United Kingdom should be sent to Fodor's Travel Publications, 20 Vauxhall Bridge Road, London SW1V 2SA, England.

PRINTED IN THE UNITED STATES OF AMERICA

10 9 8 7 6 5 4 3 2 1

CONTENTS

ON THE ROAD WITH FODOR'S

Taking a trip completely takes you out of yourself. Concerns of life at home are quickly driven away by more immediate thoughts—about, say, what marvels will beguile the next day or where you'll have dinner. That's where Fodor's comes in. We make sure that you have all the right choices and that you don't knowingly miss out on something that's around the next bend just because you didn't know it was there. Always mindful that it's often the things that you didn't come to Vienna expecting to see that end up meaning the most, we guide you to sights large and small all over the city. You might set out to discover the famed Kunsthistorisches Museum, smothered in priceless works of art, but back home you'll be unable to forget that idyllic afternoon when you yielded to the whispered temptation of wind-stirred leaves in Vienna's wine villages and savored an *achtel* (one-eighth) of the fall vintage at a terrace café. With Fodor's at your side, serendipitous discoveries are never far away.

Our success in showing you every corner of Austria is a credit to our extraordinary writers. Although there's no substitute for travel advice from a good friend who knows your style, our contributors are the next best thing—the kind of people you would poll for travel advice if you knew them.

Just when **Bonnie Dodson** thinks she's seen everything Austria has to offer, she makes another discovery. That's one of the happy results of her work on several editions of this book (for this edition, she updated the Vienna, Side Trips from Vienna, Danube Valley, and Smart Travel Tips chapters). A native of Minneapolis with a graduate degree in writing, Bonnie moved to Vienna 10 years ago with her husband and still gets a thrill every time she walks around the cobblestone streets of the historic First District. Like a true Viennese, she believes that coffee drinking is a life's work. Updating our section on Vienna's cafés, she rarely could resist stopping into her favorite coffeehouses for a *Mazagran*—a Mélange with a dollop of whipped cream—and, of course, for the latest city news and gossip. Doing research for this edition also involved lots of driving, making the best of snowy mountain roads, and lots of good eating. Bonnie's husband, **Gary Dodson,** has worked around the globe and speaks five languages. His passions are travel, wine, movies, and Mozart (he wrote our CLOSE-UP boxes on the great composer and Vienna's new architecture), and he enjoys partaking of all four in Austria.

"To the age, its art; to art, its freedom" was the motto of the famous Vienna Secession group, and **George Sullivan** firmly believes in this maxim, as any reader of our magisterial Exploring Vienna tours (in Chapter 2) can vouch. A native of Virginia, he gets to Europe as often as he can (he's also written about Florence for Fodor's) and is working on an architectural guide to Rome.

Robert I. C. Fisher—editor of *Fodor's Austria,* art history buff, and Mozart-worshiper—toasts the Austria team with a hearty *"Prosit"* (cheers). He urges readers to discover the perfect antidote for the high sugar content of Rodgers and Hammerstein's *The Sound of Music*: the inspiring book, written by Baroness von Trapp (the real Maria) that served as the basis for the film. *The Story of the Trapp Family Singers,* first published in the 1950s, is filled with great good nature and wit, and for travelers there could be no better introduction to the endearing qualities of the Austrian people.

Danke, vielen Dank (many thanks) to **Satu Hummasti**—sterling for matter of our Essential Information section—and the directors of the Austrian National Tourist Offices in Vienna and in New York for their generous and considerable assistance in preparing this new edition. Ulrike Weichselbaum of the Upper Austria Tourist Office in Linz and Susanne Bedits and Eva Oswald of the Graz Tourist Office were particularly helpful.

Rest assured that you're in good hands and that no property mentioned in the book has paid to be included—each has been selected strictly on its merits, as the best of its type in its price range.

How to Use This Book

Up front is Smart Travel Tips A to Z, arranged alphabetically by topic and loaded with tips plus Web sites and contact information for the companies and organizations we recommend. Our introductory chapter, Destination: Vienna and the Danube Valley, helps get you in the mood for your trip. Subsequent chapters are arranged regionally. The Vienna chapter begins with Exploring information, with a section for each neighborhood (each recommending a walking tour and listing sights alphabetically). The two regional chapters that follow are divided geographically; within each area, towns are covered in logical geographical order. To help you decide what you'll have time to visit in the days available, all chapters begin with our writers' favorite itineraries. The A to Z section that ends every chapter covers getting there and getting around and provides more helpful contacts and resources. At the end of the book you'll find a helpful list of German vocabulary and an Austrian menu guide.

Icons and Symbols

★   Our special recommendations
✕   Restaurant
▦   Lodging establishment
✕▦   Lodging establishment whose restaurant warrants a special trip
🐤   Good for kids (rubber duckie)
☞   Sends you to another section of the guide for more information
✉   Address
☎   Telephone number
🕐   Opening and closing times
💴   Admission prices (those we give apply to adults; substantially reduced fees are almost always available for children, students, and senior citizens)

Numbers in white and black circles ③ ❸ that appear on the maps, in the margins, and within the tours correspond to one another.

Don't Forget to Write

Your experiences—positive and negative—matter to us. If we have missed or misstated something, we want to hear about it. We follow up on all suggestions. Contact the Vienna editor at editors@fodors.com or c/o Fodor's at 1745 Broadway, New York, New York 10019. And have a fabulous trip!

Karen Cure

Karen Cure
Editorial Director

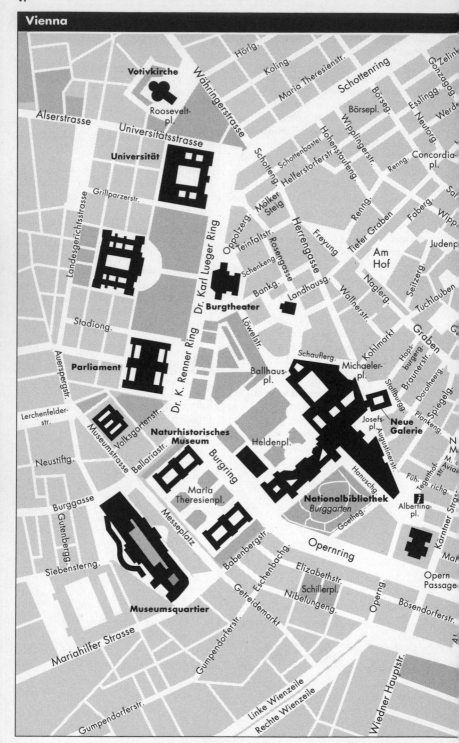

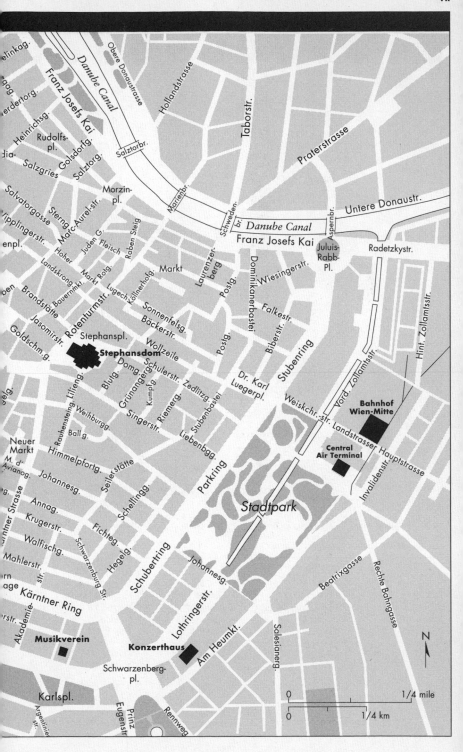

World Time Zones

-9

MONDAY
SUNDAY

+12   +13

-3

-1

25   0

International Date Line

-10

3

7

-5   -4

4

-7

14 15

-3:30

5   -8

8

9   13

-11

6

-6

10

17 16

-10

2

11

18

12

-4

-5

19

22

+11

-5

-4   -3

20

+12

1

-4

23

-3

21   24

+11   +12 -   -11   -10   -9   -8   -7   -6   -5   -4   -3   -2

Numbers below vertical bands relate each zone to Greenwich Mean Time (0 hrs).
Local times frequently differ from these general indications,
as indicated by light-face numbers on map.

Algiers, **29**	Berlin, **34**	Delhi, **48**	Jerusalem, **42**
Anchorage, **3**	Bogotá, **19**	Denver, **8**	Johannesburg, **44**
Athens, **41**	Budapest, **37**	Dublin, **26**	Lima, **20**
Auckland, **1**	Buenos Aires, **24**	Edmonton, **7**	Lisbon, **28**
Baghdad, **46**	Caracas, **22**	Hong Kong, **56**	London
Bangkok, **50**	Chicago, **9**	Honolulu, **2**	(Greenwich), **27**
Beijing, **54**	Copenhagen, **33**	Istanbul, **40**	Los Angeles, **6**
	Dallas, **10**	Jakarta, **53**	Madrid, **38**
			Manila, **57**

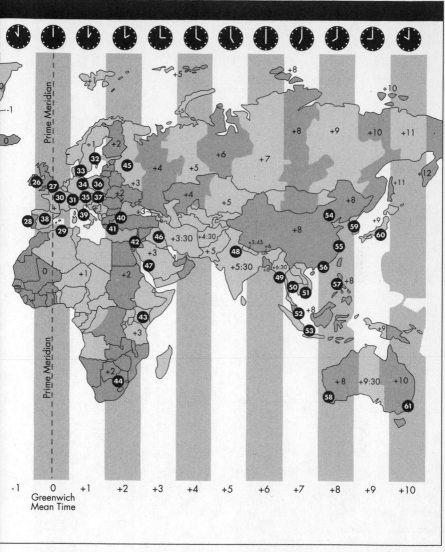

-1   0   +1   +2   +3   +4   +5   +6   +7   +8   +9   +10

Greenwich
Mean Time

x

Austria

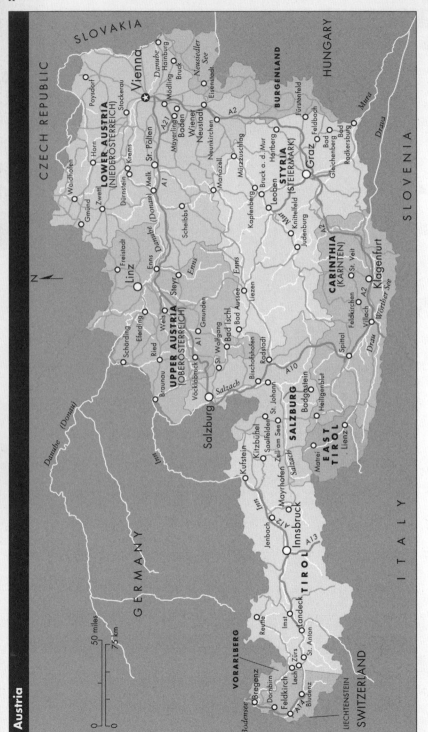

SLOVAKIA

CZECH REPUBLIC

HUNGARY

SLOVENIA

GERMANY

ITALY

SWITZERLAND

LIECHTENSTEIN

Poysdorf
Hollabrunn
Danube
Hainburg
Bruck
Neusiedler See
Stockerau
Vienna
Mödling
Eisenstadt
BURGENLAND
Mur
Horn
Waidhofen
LOWER AUSTRIA
(NIEDERÖSTERREICH)
Krems
A21
A2
St. Pölten
Mayerling
Baden
Wiener Neustadt
Feldbach
Gmünd
Zwettl
Dürnstein
Melk
A1
Neunkirchen
Mürzzuschlag
Harberg
Radkersburg
Graz
Bad
Gleichenberg
STYRIA
(STEIERMARK)
Freistadt
Danube (Donau)
Scheibbs
Mariazell
Bruck a. d. Mur
Leoben
Bad
Feldkirch
Drava
Enns
Kapfenberg
Knittelfeld
Judenburg
A2
Linz
Steyr
Enns
Liezen
SLOVENIA
Schärding
Eferding
Ried
Wels
A1
Gmunden
Bad Ischl
Bad Aussee
Radstadt
St. Veit
Feldkirchen
Klagenfurt
UPPER AUSTRIA
(OBERÖSTERREICH)
Vöcklabruck
St. Wolfgang
CARINTHIA
(KÄRNTEN)
A2
Wörther See
Braunau
Salzach
Bischofshofen
A10
Villach
Spittal
Drau
Danube (Donau)
Inn
Salzburg
Kitzbühel
St. Johann
Badgastein
Heiligenblut
EAST TIROL
Kufstein
Saalfelden
Zell am See
SALZBURG
Matrei
Lienz
Salzach
Mayrhofen
A12
Jenbach
Innsbruck
A13
TIROL
Reutte
Imst
Landeck
St. Anton
VORARLBERG
Bregenz
Dornbirn
Feldkirch
Bludenz
Lech
Zürs
A14
Bodensee

50 miles
75 km
0
0

N

ESSENTIAL INFORMATION

Half the fun of traveling is looking forward to your trip—but when you look forward, don't just daydream. There are plans to be made and things to learn about, and there is serious work to be done. The following information will give you helpful pointers on many of the questions that arise when planning your trip and when you are on the road. In addition, the organizations listed in this section will supplement the information in this guidebook. Note that additional essential information is provided in the A to Z sections found at the end of each regional chapter of this book. Many trips begin by first contacting the Austrian tourist bureau: consult the Austrian National Tourist Offices listed under Visitor Information. Happy landings!

AIR TRAVEL

BOOKING

Price is just one factor to consider when booking a flight: frequency of service and even a carrier's safety record are often just as important. Major airlines offer the greatest number of departures. Smaller airlines—including regional and no-frills airlines—usually have a limited number of flights daily. On the other hand, so-called low-cost airlines are certainly cheaper, and their fares impose fewer restrictions, such as advance-purchase requirements. Safety-wise, low-cost carriers as a group have a good history—about equal to that of major carriers.

When you book **look for nonstop flights** and **remember that "direct" flights stop at least once.** Try to avoid connecting flights, which require a change of plane. Two airlines may jointly operate a connecting flight, so ask if your airline operates every segment—you may find that your preferred carrier flies you only part of the way. International flights on a country's flag carrier are almost always nonstop; U.S. airlines often fly direct.

Ask your airline if it offers electronic ticketing, which eliminates all paperwork. There's no ticket to pick up or misplace.

CARRIERS

When flying internationally, you must usually choose between a domestic carrier, the national flag carrier of the country you are visiting, and a foreign carrier from a third country. You may, for example, choose to fly Austrian Airlines to Austria. National flag carriers have the greatest number of nonstops. Domestic carriers may have better connections to your hometown and serve a greater number of gateway cities. Third-party carriers may have a price advantage.

Austrian Airlines is the only air carrier that flies nonstop to Vienna from various points in the United States. There are no longer any American or Canadian carriers who fly directly to Vienna. Many major American carriers—such as American, Northwest, and United—instead fly passengers to major European hubs, such as London, Amsterdam, or Frankfurt, for transfers to flights with other airlines. Austrian Airlines is currently in partnership with United Airlines. Austrian Airlines also has many routes connecting Vienna with many European capitals, including Paris, London, and Munich.

Travelers from North America should note that many international carriers do service Vienna after stopovers at major European airports. For instance, Lufthansa flies from the United States to Frankfurt, Düsseldorf, and Munich, then can offer you connections to Vienna. British Airways (which has 15 gateways from the United States alone) offers many direct flights to

Vienna from London's Heathrow and Gatwick airports.

Within Austria, Austrian Airlines and its subsidiary, Tyrolean, offer service from Vienna to Linz and Innsbruck; they also provide routes to and from points outside Austria. In addition, Rheintalflug has service between Vienna and Altenrhein (Switzerland, near Bregenz), and Welcome is now providing some nice air links between Innsbruck and other European cities. Winter schedules on all domestic lines depend on snow conditions.

➤ MAJOR AIRLINES: **Austrian Airlines** (☎ 800/843–0002). **British Airways** (☎ 800/247–9297; 020/8897–4000 London; 0345/222–111 outside London). **Lufthansa** (☎ 800/645–3880).

➤ FROM THE U.K.: **Austrian Airlines** (☎ 020/7434–7300). **British Airways** (☎ 020/8897–4000; 0345/222–111 outside London).

➤ WITHIN AUSTRIA: **Austrian Airlines/Tyrolean** (☎ 05/1789 from all over Austria; main Austrian office at Kärntner Ring 18, A–1010 Vienna). **Rheintalflug** (☎ 00800–48800–000 in Vorarlberg). **Welcome** (☎ 0512/ 295–296 in Innsbruck, WEB www. welcomeair.at).

CHARTER

Charters usually have the lowest fares but are the least dependable. Departures are infrequent and seldom on time. Flights can be delayed for up to 48 hours, or can be canceled for any reason up to 10 days before you're scheduled to leave. Also, itineraries and prices can change after you've booked your flight.

In the United States, the Department of Transportation's Aviation Consumer Protection Division has jurisdiction over charters, which provides a certain degree of protection. The DOT requires that money paid to charter operators be held in escrow, so if you can't pay with a credit card, **always make your check payable to a charter carrier's escrow account.** The name of the bank should be in the charter contract. If you have any problems with a charter operator, contact the DOT. If you buy a charter package that includes both air and land arrangements, remember that the

escrow requirement applies only to the air component.

CHECK-IN AND BOARDING

Assuming that not everyone with a ticket will show up, airlines routinely overbook planes. When everyone does, airlines ask for volunteers to give up their seats. In return, these volunteers usually get a certificate for a free flight and are rebooked on the next flight out. If there are not enough volunteers, the airline must choose who will be denied boarding. The first to get bumped are passengers who checked in late and those flying on discounted tickets, so **get to the gate and check in as early as possible,** especially during peak periods.

Although the trend on international flights is to drop reconfirmation requirements, many airlines still ask you to reconfirm each leg of your international itinerary. Failure to do so may result in your reservation's being canceled. Always **bring a government-issued photo I.D. to the airport.** You will be asked to show it before you are allowed to check in.

CUTTING COSTS

The least expensive airfares to Austria must usually be purchased in advance and are nonrefundable. It's smart to **call a number of airlines, and when you are quoted a good price, book it on the spot**—the same fare may not be available the next day.

Airlines generally allow you to change your return date for a fee. If you don't use your ticket, you can apply the cost toward the purchase of a new ticket, again for a small charge. However, most low-fare tickets are nonrefundable. To get the lowest airfare, **check different routings.** Compare prices of flights to and from different airports if your destination or home city has more than one gateway. Also price off-peak flights, which may be significantly less expensive.

Travel agents, especially those who specialize in finding the lowest fares, can be especially helpful when booking a plane ticket. When you're quoted a price, **ask your agent if the price is likely to get any lower.** Good agents know the seasonal fluctuations of airfares and can usually anticipate a sale or fare war. However, waiting can be risky: the fare could go *up* as seats become scarce, and you may wait so long that your preferred flight sells out. A wait-and-see strategy works best if your plans are flexible. If you must arrive and depart on certain dates, don't delay.

Consolidators are another good source. They buy tickets for scheduled international flights at reduced rates from the airlines, then sell them at prices that beat the best fare available directly from the airlines, usually without restrictions. Sometimes you can even get your money back if you need to return the ticket. Carefully read the fine print detailing penalties for changes and cancellations, and **confirm your consolidator reservation with the airline.**

When you **fly as a courier,** you trade your checked-luggage space for a ticket deeply subsidized by a courier service. There are restrictions on when you can book and how long you can stay.

➤ CONSOLIDATORS: **Cheap Tickets** (☎ 800/377–1000). **Discount Airline Ticket Service** (☎ 800/576–1600). **Unitravel** (☎ 800/325–2222). **Up & Away Travel** (☎ 212/889–2345, WEB www.upandaway.com). **World Travel Network** (☎ 800/409–6753).

ENJOYING THE FLIGHT

State your seat preference when purchasing your ticket, and then repeat it when you confirm and when you check in. For more legroom, you can request one of the few emergency-aisle seats at check-in, if you are capable of lifting at least 50 pounds— a Federal Aviation Administration requirement of passengers in these seats. Seats behind a bulkhead also offer more legroom, but they don't have underseat storage. Don't sit in the row in front of the emergency aisle or in front of a bulkhead, where seats may not recline.

Ask the airline whether a snack or meal is served on the flight. If you have dietary concerns, **request special meals when booking.** These can be vegetarian, low-cholesterol, or kosher, for example. It's a good idea to pack some healthful snacks and a small (plastic) bottle of water in your carry-on bag. On long flights, try to maintain a normal routine, to help fight jet lag. At night, **get some sleep.** By day, **eat light meals, drink water** (not alcohol), and **move around the cabin** to stretch your legs. For additional jet-lag tips consult *Fodor's FYI: Travel Fit & Healthy* (available at bookstores everywhere).

Austrian Airlines does not permit smoking on board its flights. Meal options include kosher, vegetarian, vegan, and nondairy.

FLYING TIMES

Flying time is 8 hours to Vienna from New York, 9 hours from Washington, and 90 minutes from London.

HOW TO COMPLAIN

If your baggage goes astray or your flight goes awry, complain right away. Most carriers require that you **file a claim immediately.**

➤ AIRLINE COMPLAINTS: U.S. Department of Transportation **Aviation Consumer Protection Division** (✉ C-75, Room 4107, Washington, DC 20590, ☎ 202/366–2220, aironsumer@ost.dot.gov, WEB www.dot.gov/airconsumer). **Federal Aviation Administration Consumer Hotline** (☎ 800/322–7873).

RECONFIRMING

It is not necessary to reconfirm flights on Austrian, but it's still a good idea to do so by phone a day before departure.

AIRPORTS

The major airport is Vienna's Schwechat Airport, about 19 km (12 mi) southeast of the city. The Linz Airport is 12 km (7½ mi) southwest of Linz.

➤ AIRPORT INFORMATION: **Schwechat Airport (Vienna)** (☎ 01/7007–0). **Linz Airport** (☎ 07221/600–123).

BIKE TRAVEL

Biking is a popular sport in Austria. In central Vienna, special bike lanes make transportation fast, easy and safe. Throughout Austria there are several cycling trails, including the well-known Passau (Germany) to Vienna route, which follows the Danube across the country, passing through the spectacular Danube Valley (☞ Outdoors and Sports).

Mountain biking is increasingly popular, with "mountain bike hotels" welcoming enthusiasts, along with rigorous guided tours.

➤ INFORMATION: **Mountain Bike Hotels and Reverie** (✉ Glemmerstr. 21, A–5751 Maishofen, ☎ 06542/ 804–8022, FAX 06542/804804, WEB www.bike-holidays.com).

BIKES IN FLIGHT

Most airlines accommodate bikes as luggage, provided they are dismantled and boxed. For bike boxes, often free at bike shops, you'll pay about $5 from airlines (at least $100 for bike bags). International travelers can sometimes substitute a bike for a piece of checked luggage at no charge; otherwise, the cost is about $100. Domestic and Canadian airlines charge $25–$50.

BOAT AND FERRY TRAVEL

For leisurely travel between Vienna and Linz or eastward across the border into Slovakia or Hungary, consider taking a Danube boat. More than 300 km (187 mi) of Austria's most beautiful scenery awaits you as you glide past castles and ruins, medieval monasteries and abbeys, and lush vineyards. One of the lovelier sections, particularly in spring, is the *Wachau* (Danube Valley) west of Vienna.

Blue Danube Schiffahrt offers a diverse selection of pleasant cruises, including trips to Melk Abbey and Dürnstein in the Wachau, a grand tour of Vienna's architectural sights from the river, and a dinner cruise, featuring Johann Strauss waltzes as background music.

Most of the immaculate white-painted craft carry about 1,000 passengers each on their three decks. As soon as you get on board, give the steward a good tip for a deck chair and ask him to place it where you will get the best views. Be sure to book cabins in advance. Day trips are also possible on the Danube. You can use boats to move from one riverside community to the next, and along some sections, notably the Wachau,

the only way to cross the river is to use the little shuttles (in the Wachau, these are special motorless boats that use the current to cross).

Hydrofoils run daily from Vienna to Bratislava in Slovakia and to Budapest in Hungary from mid-April through October. One-way or round-trip tickets are available. It takes about 90 minutes from Vienna to Bratislava and more than 6 hours from Vienna to Budapest.

➤ BOAT AND FERRY INFORMATION: **Blue Danube Schiffahrt** (✉ Friedrich-str. 7, A–1043 Vienna, ☎ 01/588–800, FAX 01/588–8044–0, WEB www. ddsg-blue-danube.at).

BUS TRAVEL

BUS LINES

Austria features extensive national networks of buses run by post offices and railroads. Where Austrian trains don't go, buses do, and you'll find the railroad and post-office buses (bright yellow for easy recognition) in even remote regions carrying passengers as well as mail. You can get tickets on the bus, and in the off-season there is no problem getting a seat, but on routes to favored ski areas during holiday periods reservations are essential. Bookings can be handled at the ticket office (there's one in most towns with bus service) or by travel agents. In most communities, bus routes begin and end at or near the railroad station, making transfers easy. Increasingly, coordination of bus service with railroads means that many of the discounts and special tickets available for trains also apply to buses. There are private bus companies in Austria as well. Buses in Austria run like clockwork, typically departing and arriving on time. Smoking is generally allowed.

➤ PRIVATE BUS LINES: **Columbus** (☎ 01/53411–0). **Blaguss Reisen** (☎ 01/ 50180–0). **Post und Bahn** (☎ 01/ 71101). **Dr. Richard** (☎ 01/33100–0).

BUSINESS HOURS

BANKS AND OFFICES

In most cities, banks are open weekdays 8 to 3, Thursday until 5:30 PM. Lunch hour is from 12:30 to 1:30. All banks are closed on Saturday, but you can change money at various locations (such as American Express offices on Saturday morning and major railroad stations around the clock), and changing machines are also found here and there in the larger cities.

GAS STATIONS

Gas stations on the major autobahns are open 24 hours a day, but in smaller towns and villages you can expect them to close early in the evening and on Sundays. You can usually count on at least one station to stay open on Sundays and holidays in most medium-size towns, and buying gas in larger cities is never a problem.

MUSEUMS AND SIGHTS

Museum hours vary from city to city and museum to museum; if museums are closed one day, it is usually Monday. Few Austrian museums are open at night.

PHARMACIES

Pharmacies (called *Apotheken* in German) are usually open from 9 to 6, with a midday break between 12 and 2. In each area of the city one pharmacy stays open 24 hours; if a pharmacy is closed, a sign on the door will tell you the address of the nearest one that is open. Call 01/1550 for names and addresses (in German) of the pharmacies open that night.

You may find over-the-counter remedies for headaches and colds much less effective than those sold in the United States. Austrians are firm believers in natural remedies, such as herbal teas. Vitamins are generally scoffed at, and though available, are expensive.

SHOPS

In general, you'll find shops open weekdays from 8:30 or 9 until 6, with a lunchtime closing from noon to 1 or 1:30. In smaller villages, the midday break may run until 3. Many food stores, bakeries, and small grocery shops open at 7 or 7:30 and, aside from the noontime break, stay open until 7 or 7:30 PM. Shops in large city centers forgo the noon break. On Saturday, most shops stay open until 5 or 6 PM, though a few follow the old rules and close by 1 PM. Food stores stay open until 5 on Saturdays. Barbers and hairdressers traditionally take Monday off, but there are exceptions. It is fashionable these days for hairdressers to work evenings and nights on certain "good-for-haircutting" moon days! Also in the country, many shops close on Wednesday afternoon, and in parts of Burgenland they may also close on Thursday afternoon.

CAMERAS AND PHOTOGRAPHY

➤ PHOTO HELP: Kodak Information Center (☎ 800/242–2424). *Kodak Guide to Shooting Great Travel Pictures,* available in bookstores or from Fodor's Travel Publications (☎ 800/533–6478; $18 plus $5.50 shipping).

EQUIPMENT PRECAUTIONS

Always **keep your film and tape out of the sun.** Carry an extra supply of batteries, and **be prepared to turn on your camera or camcorder** to prove to security personnel that the device is real. Always **ask for hand inspection of film,** which becomes clouded after repeated exposure to airport X-ray machines, and **keep videotapes away from metal detectors.**

FILM AND DEVELOPING

All kinds of film are available for purchase in Austria, with the best prices at grocery and drugstores. Developing is very expensive, especially for one-hour service.

VIDEOS

Austrian videotapes use the PAL system, which is not compatible with NTSC players in the United States.

CAR RENTAL

Rates in Vienna begin at €73 a day and €208 a weekend for an economy car with manual transmission and unlimited mileage. This includes a 21% tax on car rentals. Renting a car may be cheaper in Germany, but make sure the rental agency knows you are driving into Austria and that the car is equipped with an autobahn sticker (☞ Car Travel) for Austria. When renting an RV be sure to compare prices and reserve early. It's

Smart Travel Tips A to Z

cheaper to arrange your rental car from the United States, but **be sure to get a confirmation of your quoted rate in writing.**

➤ MAJOR AGENCIES: **Alamo** (☎ 800/522–9696; WEB www.alamo.com). **Avis** (☎ 800/331–1084; 800/879–2847 in Canada; 0870/606–0100 in the U.K.; 02/9353–9000 in Australia; 09/526–2847 in New Zealand; WEB www.avis.com). **Budget** (☎ 800/527–0700; 0870/156–5656 in the U.K.; WEB www.budget.com). **Dollar** (☎ 800/800–6000; 0124/622–0111 in the U.K., where it's affiliated with Sixt; 02/9223–1444 in Australia; WEB www.dollar.com). **Hertz** (☎ 800/654–3001; 800/263–0600 in Canada; 020/8897–2072 in the U.K.; 02/9669–2444 in Australia; 09/256–8690 in New Zealand; WEB www.hertz.com). **National Car Rental** (☎ 800/227–7368; 020/8680–4800 in the U.K.; WEB www.nationalcar.com).

➤ LOCAL AGENCIES: **Europcar** (✉ Erdberg Center/U-Bahn [U3], A–1110 Vienna, ☎ 01/740-500). **Autoverleih Buchbinder** (✉ Schlachthausg. 38, A–1030 Vienna, ☎ 01/717–50–0, FAX 01/717–5022, with offices throughout Austria).

CUTTING COSTS

To get the best deal, **book through a travel agent who will shop around.** Also **ask your travel agent about a company's customer-service record.** How has the company responded to delayed plane arrivals and vehicle mishaps? Are there often lines at the rental counter? If you're traveling during a holiday period, does a confirmed reservation guarantee you a car?

Do **look into wholesalers,** companies that do not own fleets but rent in bulk from those that do at often better rates than traditional car-rental operations. Prices are best during off-peak periods. Payment must be made before you leave home.

➤ WHOLESALERS: **Auto Europe** (☎ 207/842–2000 or 800/223–5555, FAX 800–235–6321, WEB www.autoeurope.com). **Europe by Car** (☎ 212/581–3040 or 800/223–1516, FAX 212/246–1458, WEB www.europebycar.com). **DER Travel Services** (✉ 9501 W. Devon Ave., Rosemont, IL 60018,

☎ 800/782–2424, FAX 800/282–7474 for information; 800/860–9944 for brochures, WEB www.dertravel.com). **Kemwel Holiday Autos** (☎ 800/678–0678, FAX 914/825–3160, WEB www.kemwel.com).

INSURANCE

When driving a rented car you are generally responsible for any damage to or loss of the vehicle. Before you rent, see what coverage your personal auto-insurance policy and credit cards already provide.

Collision policies that car-rental companies sell for European rentals usually do not include stolen-vehicle coverage. Before you buy it, check your existing policies—you may already be covered.

REQUIREMENTS AND RESTRICTIONS

In Austria, your own driver's license is acceptable. An International Driver's Permit is a good idea; it's available from the American or Canadian automobile association, and, in the United Kingdom, from the Automobile Association or Royal Automobile Club. These international permits are universally recognized, and having one in your wallet may save you a problem with the local authorities.

There is no age limit to renting a car at most agencies in Austria. However, you must have had a valid driver's license for one year. For some of the more expensive car models, drivers must be at least 25 years of age. There is also usually an extra charge to drive over the border into Italy, Slovakia, Slovenia, Hungary, and the Czech Republic, but no extra charge to drive to Germany.

SURCHARGES

Before you pick up a car in one city and leave it in another, **ask about drop-off charges or one-way service fees,** which can be substantial. Note, too, that some rental agencies charge extra if you return the car before the time specified in your contract. To avoid a hefty refueling fee, **fill the tank just before you turn in the car,** but be aware that gas stations near the rental outlet may overcharge.

CAR TRAVEL

Make absolutely sure your car is equipped with the *Autobahnvignette*, as it is called, a little trapezoidal sticker with a highway icon and the Austrian eagle, or with a calendar marked with an M or a W. This sticker allows use of the autobahn. It costs €72.76 for a year and is available at gas stations, tobacconists, and automobile-club outlets in neighboring countries or near the border. You can also purchase a two-month Vignette for €28.80, or a 10-day one for €7.63. Prices are for vehicles up to 3.5 tons and RVs. For motorcycles it is €29 for one year, €10.90 for two months, and €4.36 for 10 days. Not having a Vignette (which is generally called the *Pickerl*) can lead to extremely high fines if you're caught. Get your Pickerl before driving to Austria!

Besides the Pickerl, if you are planning to drive around a lot, budget in a great deal of toll money: for example, the tunnels on the A10 autobahn cost €7 apiece, the Grossglockner Pass road will cost €25.50, and passing through the Arlberg Tunnel costs about €11. Driving up some especially beautiful valleys, such as the Kaunertal in Tirol, or up to the Tauplitzalm in Styria, also costs money, around €11.

The Austrian highway network is excellent, and roads are well maintained and well marked. Secondary roads may be narrow and winding. The main highway routes (autobahns), especially the A2 down to Carinthia and Italy, are packed during both Austrian and German school holidays, as well as on weekends in summer. As a nod to the environment, less salt is being used on highways in winter, but few drivers seem to take heed of the greater hazard. Remember that in winter you will need snow tires and often chains, even on well-traveled roads. It's wise to check with the automobile clubs for weather conditions, since mountain roads are often blocked, and ice and fog are hazards.

AUTO CLUBS

Austria has two automobile clubs, OAMTC and ARBO, both of which operate motorist service patrols. You'll find emergency (orange-colored) phones along all the highways. If you break down along the autobahn, a small arrow on the guardrail will direct you to the nearest phone. Otherwise, if you have problems, call **ARBO** (☎ 123) or OAMTC (☎ 120) from anywhere in the country. No area or other code is needed for either number. Both clubs charge nonmembers for emergency service. Remember to get proper coverage from your home club.

➤ IN AUSTRIA: **Austrian Automobile Club/ÖAMTC** (✉ Schubertring 1–3, A–1010 Vienna, ☎ 01/711–99–55, WEB www.oemtc.at).

➤ IN AUSTRALIA: **Australian Automobile Association** (☎ 06/247–7311).

➤ IN CANADA: **Canadian Automobile Association** (CAA, ☎ 613/247–0117).

➤ IN NEW ZEALAND: **New Zealand Automobile Association** (☎ 09/377–4660).

➤ IN THE U.K.: **Automobile Association** (AA, ☎ 0990/500–600), **Royal Automobile Club** (RAC, ☎ 0990/722–722 for membership; 0345/121–345 for insurance).

➤ IN THE UNITED STATES: **American Automobile Association** (☎ 800/564–6222).

FROM THE U.K.

The best way to reach Austria by car from England is to take North Sea/Cross Channel ferries to Oostende or Zeebrugge in Belgium or Dunkirk in northern France. An alternative is the Channel Tunnel; motoring clubs can give you the best routing to tie into the continental motorway network. Then take the toll-free Belgian motorway (E5) to Aachen, and head via Stuttgart to Innsbruck and the Tirol (A61, A67, A5, E11, A7), or east by way of Nürnberg and Munich, crossing into Austria at Walserberg and then on to Salzburg and Vienna. Total distance to Innsbruck from London is about 1,100 km (650 mi); to Vienna, about 1,600 km (1,000 mi). The most direct way to Vienna is virtually all on the autobahn via Nürnberg, Regensburg, and Passau, entering Austria at Schärding. In summer, border delays are much shorter at Schärding than at

Salzburg. The trip to Innsbruck via this route will take two–three days.

If this seems like too much driving, in summer you can **put the car on a train** in s'Hertogenbosch in central southern Netherlands on Thursday, or in Schaerbeek (Brussels) on Friday, for an overnight trip, arriving in Salzburg early the following morning and in Villach three hours later.

➤ AGENCIES: **DER Travel Service** (✉ 18 Conduit St., London W1R 9TD, ☎ 020/7290–0111, FAX 020/7629–7442) has details on fares and schedules.

EMERGENCY SERVICES

See Auto Clubs.

GASOLINE

Gasoline and diesel are readily available, but on Sunday stations in the more out-of-the-way areas may be closed. Stations carry only unleaded (*bleifrei*) gas, both regular and premium (super), and diesel. If you're in the mountains in winter with a diesel, and there is a cold snap (with temperatures threatening to drop below -4°F [-20°C]), add a few liters of gasoline to your diesel, about 1:4 parts, to prevent it from freezing. Gasoline prices are the same throughout the country, slightly lower at discount and self-service stations. Expect to pay about €0.94 per liter for regular, €0.98 for premium, and €0.78 for diesel. If you are driving to Italy, fill up before crossing the border because gas in Italy is even more expensive. Oil in Austria is expensive, retailing at €9 upward per liter. If need be, purchase oil, windshield wipers, and other paraphernalia at big hardware stores.

ROAD CONDITIONS

Roads in Austria are excellent and well maintained—perhaps a bit too well maintained, judging by the frequently encountered construction zones on the autobahns.

ROAD MAPS

A set of eight excellent, detailed road maps is available from the Austrian Automobile Club/ÖAMTC (☞ Auto Clubs), at most service stations, and at many bookstores. The maps supplied without charge by the Austrian National Tourist Office are adequate for most needs, but if you will be covering much territory, the better ÖAMTC maps are a worthwhile investment.

RULES OF THE ROAD

Tourists from EU countries may bring their cars to Austria with no documentation other than the normal registration papers and their regular driver's license. A Green Card, the international certificate of insurance, is recommended for EU drivers and compulsory for others. All cars must carry a first-aid kit (including rubber gloves) and a red warning triangle to use in case of accident or breakdown. These are available at gas stations along the road, or at any automotive supply store or large hardware store.

The minimum driving age in Austria is 18, and children under 12 years of age must ride in the back seat; smaller children require a restraining seat. Note that all passengers must use seat belts.

Drive on the right side of the street in Austria. Vehicles coming from the right have the right of way, except that at unregulated intersections streetcars coming from either direction have the right of way. No turns are allowed on red. In residential areas, the right of way can be switched around; the rule is, be careful at any intersection.

Drinking and driving: since 1998, the maximum blood-alcohol content allowed is 0.5 parts per thousand, which in real terms means very little to drink. Remember when driving in Europe that the police can stop you anywhere at any time for no particular reason.

Unless otherwise marked, the speed limit on autobahns is 130 kph (80 mph), although this is not always strictly enforced. But if you're pulled over for speeding, fines are payable on the spot, and can be heavy. On other highways and roads, the limit is 100 kph (62 mph), 80 kph (49 mph) for RVs or cars pulling a trailer weighing more than 750 kilos (about 1,650 lb). In built-up areas, a 50 kph (31 mph) limit applies and is likely to be taken seriously. In some towns, special 30 kph (20 mph) limits apply.

More and more towns have radar cameras to catch speeders. Remember that insurance does not necessarily pay if it can be proved you were going above the limit when involved in an accident.

Sometimes the signs at exits and entrances on the autobahns are not clear—a reason why Austria has a special problem, called the *"Geister- fahrer,"* which means a driver going the wrong way in traffic. Efforts are being made to correct this problem with clearer signage.

CHILDREN IN AUSTRIA

Be sure to plan ahead and **involve your youngsters** as you outline your trip. When packing, include things to keep them busy en route. On sightsee- ing days try to schedule activities of special interest to your children. If you are renting a car, don't forget to **arrange for a car seat** when you reserve. Austria is filled with wonders and delights for children, ranging from the performing Lipizzaner horses at the Spanish Riding School in Vienna to the Salzburg Marionet- tentheater and the rural delights of farm vacations.

➤ BABY-SITTING: In Vienna, the cen- tral baby-sitting service is **Kinder- drehscheibe** (✉ Wehrg. 26, A–1050, ☎ 01/581–0660, FAX 01/585–7432). It's best to have your hotel call to make the arrangements, unless you speak German.

DINING

The best restaurants in Vienna do not welcome small children; fine dining is considered an adult pastime. With kids, **you're best off taking them to more casual restaurants and cafés.** *Heurige* are perfect for family dining, and they usually open by 4 PM. To accommodate flexible meal times, look for signs that say *Durchgehend warme Küche,* which means warm meals are available all afternoon. Cafés offer light meals all day, and you can always get a sausage from a *Würstelstand.*

Several chain restaurants have high chairs (*Hochstühle*), and a few serve children's portions *(Für den kleinen Hunger),* usually *Wienerschnitzel,* a thin slice of veal, breaded and fried.

FLYING

If your children are two or older, **ask about children's airfares.** As a general rule, infants under two not occupying a seat fly at greatly reduced fares or even for free.

In general the adult baggage allowance applies to children paying half or more of the adult fare. When booking, **confirm carry-on allowances** if you're traveling with infants. In general, for babies charged 10% of the adult fare you are allowed one carry-on bag and a collapsible stroller; if the flight is full, the stroller may have to be checked or you may be limited to less.

Experts agree that it's a good idea to use safety seats aloft for children weighing less than 40 pounds. Air- lines set their own policies: U.S. carriers usually require that the child be ticketed, even if he or she is young enough to ride free, since the seats must be strapped into regular seats. Do **check your airline's policy about using safety seats during takeoff and landing.** And since safety seats are not allowed just everywhere in the plane, get your seat assignments early.

When reserving, **request children's meals or a freestanding bassinet** if you need them. But note that bulk- head seats, where you must sit to use the bassinet, may lack an overhead bin or storage space on the floor.

GROUP TRAVEL

When planning to take your kids on a tour, look for companies that special- ize in family travel.

➤ FAMILY-FRIENDLY TOUR OPERATORS: **Families Welcome!** (✉ 92 N. Main St., Ashland, OR 97520, ☎ 541/482– 6121 or 800/326–0724, FAX 541/482– 0660). **Grandtravel** (✉ 6900 Wiscon- sin Ave., Suite 706, Chevy Chase, MD 20815, ☎ 301/986–0790 or 800/ 247–7651) for people traveling with grandchildren ages 7–17.

LODGING

Most hotels in Austria allow children under a certain age to stay in their parents' room at no extra charge, but others charge for them as extra adults; be sure to **find out the cutoff age for children's discounts.**

SIGHTS AND ATTRACTIONS

Places that are especially appealing to children are indicated by a rubber duckie icon in the margin.

SUPPLIES AND EQUIPMENT

Supermarkets and drugstores (look for *DM Drogerie* and *Bipa*) carry *Windeln* (diapers), universally referred to as Pampers. Remember that weight is given in kilos (2.2 pounds equals 1 kilo). Baby formula is available in grocery stores, drugstores, or pharmacies. There are two brands of formula: Milupa and Nestlé, for infants and children up to three years old. Austrian formulas come in powder form and can be mixed with tap water.

COMPUTERS ON THE ROAD

If you use a major Internet provider, getting on-line in Vienna shouldn't be difficult. Call your Internet provider to get the local access number in Austria. Many hotels have business services with Internet access and even in-room modem lines. You may, however, need an adapter for your computer for the European-style plugs. As always, if you're traveling with a laptop, carry a spare battery and adapter. Never plug your computer into any socket before asking about surge protection. IBM sells a pen-size modem tester that plugs into a telephone jack to check whether the line is safe to use.

➤ ACCESS NUMBERS IN AUSTRIA: **AOL** (☎ 01/585–8483). For **Compuserve**, you must call Germany (☎ 0049/1805–7040–70).

CONSUMER PROTECTION

Whenever shopping or buying travel services in Austria, **pay with a major credit card** so you can cancel payment or get reimbursed if there's a problem. If you're doing business with a particular company for the first time, **contact your local Better Business Bureau and the attorney general's offices** in your own state and the company's home state as well. Have any complaints been filed? Finally, if you're buying a package or tour, always **consider travel insurance** that includes default coverage.

➤ BBBs: **Council of Better Business Bureaus** (✉ 4200 Wilson Blvd.,

Suite 800, Arlington, VA 22203, ☎ 703/276–0100, FAX 703/525–8277 WEB www.bbb.org).

CUSTOMS AND DUTIES

When shopping, **keep receipts** for all purchases. Upon reentering the country, **be ready to show customs officials what you've bought.** If you feel a duty is incorrect or object to the way your clearance was handled, note the inspector's badge number and ask to see a supervisor. If the problem isn't resolved, write to the appropriate authorities, beginning with the port director at your point of entry.

IN AUSTRIA

Travelers over 17 who are residents of European countries—regardless of citizenship—may bring in, duty free, 200 cigarettes or 50 cigars or 250 grams of tobacco, 2 liters of wine and 2 liters of 22% spirits or 1 liter of more than 22% spirits, and 50 ml of perfume. These limits may be liberalized or eliminated under terms of the European Union agreement. Travelers from all other countries (such as those coming directly from the United States or Canada) may bring in twice these amounts. All visitors may bring gifts or other purchases valued at up to €175 (about $175), although in practice you'll seldom be asked.

IN AUSTRALIA

Australian residents who are 18 or older may bring home $A400 worth of souvenirs and gifts (including jewelry), 250 cigarettes or 250 grams of tobacco, and 1,125 ml of alcohol (including wine, beer, and spirits). Residents under 18 may bring back $A200 worth of goods. Prohibited items include meat products. Seeds, plants, and fruits need to be declared upon arrival.

➤ INFORMATION: **Australian Customs Service** (Regional Director, ✉ Box 8, Sydney, NSW 2001; ☎ 02/9213–2000 or 1300/363263; 1800/020504 quarantine-inquiry line; FAX 02/9213–4043; WEB www.customs.gov.au).

IN CANADA

Canadian residents who have been out of Canada for at least 7 days may bring home C$500 worth of goods duty free. If you've been away less than 7 days but more than 48 hours, the duty-free allowance drops to C$200; if your trip lasts 24–48 hours, the allowance is C$50. You may not pool allowances with family members. Goods claimed under the C$500 exemption may follow you by mail; those claimed under the lesser exemptions must accompany you. Alcohol and tobacco products may be included in the 7-day and 48-hour exemptions but not in the 24-hour exemption. If you meet the age requirements of the province or territory through which you reenter Canada, you may bring in, duty free, 1.14 liters (40 imperial ounces) of wine or liquor *or* 24 12-ounce cans or bottles of beer or ale. If you are 16 or older you may bring in, duty free, 200 cigarettes and 50 cigars. Check ahead of time with Revenue Canada or the Department of Agriculture for policies regarding meat products, seeds, plants, and fruits.

You may send an unlimited number of gifts worth up to C$60 each duty free to Canada. Label the package UNSOLICITED GIFT—VALUE UNDER $60. Alcohol and tobacco are excluded.

➤ INFORMATION: **Revenue Canada** (✉ 2265 St. Laurent Blvd. S, Ottawa, Ontario K1G 4K3, ☎ 613/993–0534; 800/461–9999 in Canada, WEB www. ccra-adrc.gc.ca).

IN NEW ZEALAND

Homeward-bound residents 17 or older may bring back $700 worth of souvenirs and gifts. Your duty-free allowance also includes 4.5 liters of wine or beer; one 1,125-ml bottle of spirits; and either 200 cigarettes, 250 grams of tobacco, 50 cigars, or a combination of the three up to 250 grams. Prohibited items include meat products, seeds, plants, and fruits.

➤ INFORMATION: **New Zealand Customs** (Head office: ✉ The Customhouse, 17–21 Whitmore St., Box 2218, Wellington, ☎ 09/300–5399 or 0800/428–786, WEB www.customs. govt.nz).

IN THE UNITED KINGDOM

If you are a U.K. resident and your journey was wholly within the European Union (EU), you won't have to pass through customs when you return to the United Kingdom. If you plan to bring back large quantities of alcohol or tobacco, check EU limits beforehand. In most cases, if you bring back more than 200 cigars, 800 cigarettes, 10 liters of spirits, and/or 90 liters of wine, you have to declare the goods upon return.

➤ INFORMATION: **HM Customs and Excise** (✉ Portcullis House, 21 Cowbridge Rd. E, Cardiff CF11 9SS, ☎ 029/2038–6423 or 0845/010–9000, WEB www.hmce.gov.uk).

IN THE UNITED STATES

U.S. residents who have been out of the country for at least 48 hours may bring home, for personal use, $800 worth of foreign goods duty free, as long as they haven't used the $800 allowance or any part of it in the past 30 days. This exemption may include 1 liter of alcohol (for travelers 21 and older), 200 cigarettes, and 100 non-Cuban cigars. Family members from the same household who are traveling together may pool their $800 personal exemptions. For fewer than 48 hours, the duty-free allowance drops to $200, which may include 50 cigarettes, 10 non-Cuban cigars, and 150 ml of alcohol (or perfume containing alcohol). The $200 allowance cannot be combined with other individuals' exemptions, and if you exceed it, the full value of all the goods will be taxed. Antiques, which the U.S. Customs Service defines as objects more than 100 years old, enter duty free, as do original works of art done entirely by hand, including paintings, drawings, and sculptures.

U.S. residents 21 and older may bring back 1 liter of alcohol duty free. In addition, regardless of your age, you are allowed 200 cigarettes and 100 non-Cuban cigars.

You may also send packages home duty free: up to $200 worth of goods for personal use, with a limit of one parcel per addressee per day (except alcohol or tobacco products or perfume worth more than $5); label the package PERSONAL USE and attach a list of its contents and their retail value. Do not label the package UNSOLICITED GIFT or your duty-free exemption will drop to $100. Mailed items do not affect your duty-free allowance on your return.

➤ INFORMATION: **U.S. Customs Service** (✉ 1300 Pennsylvania Ave. NW, Washington, DC 20229, WEB www. customs.gov; inquiries ☎ 202/354–1000; complaints c/o ✉ Office of Regulations and Rulings; registration of equipment c/o ✉ Resource Management, ☎ 202/927–0540).

DINING

Austria has the largest number of organic farms in Europe, as well as the most stringent food quality standards. (Finland comes in second, followed by Italy and Sweden, though they all fall far behind Austria; France, Spain, and the U.K. are at the bottom of the list.) An increasing number of restaurants use food and produce from local farmers, ensuring the freshest ingredients for their guests.

When dining out, you'll get the best value at simpler restaurants. Most post menus with prices outside. If you begin with the *Würstelstand* (sausage vendor) on the street, the next category would be the *Imbiss-Stube,* for simple, quick snacks. Many meat stores serve soups and a daily special at noon; a blackboard menu will be posted outside. A number of cafés also offer lunch, but watch the prices; some can turn out to be more expensive than restaurants. *Gasthäuser* are simple restaurants or country inns. Austrian hotels have some of the best restaurants in the country, often with outstanding chefs. In the past few years the restaurants along the autobahns have developed into very good places to eat (besides being, in many cases, architecturally interesting).

Some Austrian chain restaurants offer excellent value for the money, such as Wienerwald, which specializes in chicken dishes, and Nordsee, which has a wide selection of fish.

In all restaurants, be aware that the basket of bread put on your table isn't free. Most of the older-style Viennese restaurants charge €0.70–€1.25 for each roll that is eaten, but more and more establishments are beginning to charge a per person cover charge—anywhere from €1.50 to €4—which includes all the bread you want, plus usually an herb spread and butter. Tap water (*Leitungswasser*) in Austria comes straight from the Alps and is among the purest in the world. Be aware, however, that a few restaurants in touristy areas are beginning to charge for tap water.

The restaurants we list are the cream of the crop in each price category.

For a discussion of the delights of Austrian cuisine, *see* "Schnitzels, Strudels, and Sachertortes" *in* Pleasures and Pastimes *in* Chapter 1.

MEALTIMES

Besides the normal three meals, Austrians sometimes throw in a few snacks in between, or forgo one meal for a snack. The day begins with a very early Continental breakfast of rolls and coffee. *Gabelfrühstück* is a slightly more substantial breakfast with eggs or cold meat. A main meal is usually served between noon and 2, and an afternoon *Jause* (coffee with cake) is taken at teatime. Unless dining out, a light supper ends the day, usually between 6 and 9, but tending toward the later hour. Many restaurant kitchens close in the afternoon, but some post a notice saying DURCHGEHEND WARME KÜCHE, meaning that hot food is available even between regular mealtimes. In Vienna, some restaurants go on serving until 1 and 2 AM, a tiny number also through the night. The rest of Austria is more conservative.

Unless otherwise noted, the restaurants listed in this guide are open daily for lunch and dinner.

RESERVATIONS AND DRESS

Reservations are always a good idea: we mention them only when they're essential or not accepted. Book as far ahead as you can, and reconfirm as soon as you arrive. We mention dress only when men are required to wear a jacket or a jacket and tie.

WINE, BEER, AND SPIRITS

Austrian wines range from unpretentious *Heurige* whites to world-class varietals. For a proper rundown of regional specialties, *see* the Austrian Wine Regions box *in* Chapter 1. Austrian beer rivals that of Germany for quality. Each area has its own brewery and local beer that people are loyal to. A specialty unique to Austria is the dark, sweet *Dunkles* beer. Look for *Kaiser Doppelmalz* in Vienna. Schnapps is an after-dinner tradition in Austria, with many restaurants offering several varieties to choose from.

DISABILITIES
AND ACCESSIBILITY

The Austrian National Tourist Office in New York has a guide to Vienna for people with disabilities (including hotels with special facilities) and a special map of the city's accessible sights. As a general guideline, the Hilton, InterContinental, and Marriott chain hotels, plus a number of smaller ones, are usually accessible. Once in Austria, check with the Österreichischer Zivilinvalidenverband; the Vienna Tourist Office also has a booklet on Vienna hotels and a city guide for travelers with disabilities.

➤ LOCAL RESOURCES: The **Austrian National Tourist Office** (☞ Visitor Information). **Österreichischer Zivilinvalidenverband** (✉ Stubenring 2, A–1010 Vienna, ☎ 01/513–1535). For phone inquiries, call the **Vienna Tourist Office** (✉ Obere Augartenstr. 40, A–1025, ☎ 01/211–140). For walk-in information, go to the **Vienna Tourist Office** (✉ Albertinapl., A–1010) near the Opera.

RESERVATIONS

When discussing accessibility with an operator or reservations agent, **ask hard questions.** Are there any stairs, inside *or* out? Are there grab bars next to the toilet *and* in the shower/tub? How wide is the doorway to the room? To the bathroom? For the most extensive facilities meeting the latest legal specifications, **opt for newer accommodations,** which are more likely to have been designed with access in mind. Older buildings or ships may have more limited facilities. Be sure to **discuss your needs before booking.**

TRANSPORTATION

The railroads are both understanding and helpful. If prior arrangements have been made, taxis and private vehicles are allowed to drive right to the train platform; railway personnel will help with boarding and leaving trains; and with three days' notice, a special wheelchair can be provided for getting around train corridors. If you're traveling by plane, ask in advance for assistance or a wheelchair at your destination. A number of stations in the Vienna subway system have only stairs or escalators, but elevators are being added at major stations.

➤ COMPLAINTS: **Disability Rights Section** (✉ U.S. Department of Justice, Civil Rights Division, Box 66738, Washington, DC 20035-6738, ☎ 202/514–0301 or 800/514–0301; TTY 202/514–0301 or 800/514–0301, FAX 202/307–1198) for general complaints. **Aviation Consumer Protection Division** (☞ Air Travel) for airline-related problems. **Civil Rights Office** (✉ U.S. Department of Transportation, Departmental Office of Civil Rights, S-30, 400 7th St. SW, Room 10215, Washington, DC 20590, ☎ 202/366–4648, FAX 202/366–9371) for problems with surface transportation.

TRAVEL AGENCIES
AND TOUR OPERATORS

As a whole, the travel industry has become more aware of the needs of travelers with disabilities. In the United States, the Americans with Disabilities Act requires that travel firms serve the needs of all travelers. Some agencies specialize in working with people with disabilities.

➤ TRAVELERS WITH MOBILITY PROBLEMS: **Access Adventures** (✉ 206 Chestnut Ridge Rd., Rochester, NY 14624, ☎ 716/889–9096, dltravel@prodigy.net), run by a former physical-rehabilitation counselor. **CareVacations** (✉ 5-5110 50th Ave., Leduc, Alberta T9E 6V4, ☎ 780/986–6404 or 877/478–7827, FAX 780/986–8332, WEB www.carevacations. com), for group tours and cruise vacations. **Flying Wheels Travel** (✉ 143 W. Bridge St., Box 382, Owatonna, MN 55060, ☎ 507/451–5005 or 800/535–6790, FAX 507/451–1685, thq@ll.net, WEB www.flyingwheels. com). **Hinsdale Travel Service** (✉ 201 E. Ogden Ave., Suite 100, Hinsdale, IL 60521, ☎ 630/325–1335, FAX 630/325–1342, hinstrvl@interaccess.com).

DISCOUNTS AND DEALS

Be a smart shopper and **compare all your options** before making decisions. A plane ticket bought with a promotional coupon from travel clubs, coupon books, and direct-mail offers may not be cheaper than the least expensive fare from a discount ticket agency. And always keep in mind that what you get is just as important as what you save.

CLUBS AND COUPONS

Many companies sell discounts in the form of travel clubs and coupon books, but these cost money. You must use participating advertisers to get a deal, and only after you recoup the initial membership cost or book price do you begin to save. If you plan to use the club or coupons frequently, you may save considerably. Before signing up, find out what discounts you get for free.

➤ DISCOUNT CLUBS: **Entertainment Travel Editions** (✉ 2125 Butterfield Rd., Troy, MI 48084, ☎ 800/445–4137; $20–$51, depending on destination). **Great American Traveler** (✉ Box 27965, Salt Lake City, UT 84127, ☎ 801/974–3033 or 800/548–2812; $49.95 per year). **Moment's Notice Discount Travel Club** (✉ 7301 New Utrecht Ave., Brooklyn, NY 11204, ☎ 718/234–6295; $25 per year, single or family). **Privilege Card International** (✉ 237 E. Front St., Youngstown, OH 44503, ☎ 330/746–5211 or 800/236–9732; $74.95 per year). **Sears's Mature Outlook** (✉ Box 9390, Des Moines, IA 50306, ☎ 800/336–6330; $19.95 per year). **Travelers Advantage** (✉ CUC Travel Service, 3033 S. Parker Rd., Suite 1000, Aurora, CO 80014, ☎ 800/548–1116 or 800/648–4037; $59.95 per year, single or family). **Worldwide Discount Travel Club** (✉ 1674 Meridian Ave., Miami Beach, FL 33139, ☎ 305/534–2082; $50 per year family, $40 single).

CREDIT-CARD BENEFITS

When you use your credit card to make travel purchases you may get free travel-accident insurance, collision-damage insurance, and medical or legal assistance, depending on the card and the bank that issued it. American Express, MasterCard, and Visa provide one or more of these services, so **get a copy of your credit card's travel-benefits policy.** If you are a member of an auto club, always **ask hotel and car-rental reservations agents about auto-club discounts.** Some clubs offer additional discounts on tours, cruises, and admission to attractions.

DISCOUNT RESERVATIONS

To save money, **look into discount reservations services** with toll-free numbers, which use their buying power to get a better price on hotels, airline tickets, even car rentals. When booking a room, always **call the hotel's local toll-free number** (if one is available) rather than the central reservations number—you'll often get a better price. Always ask about special packages or corporate rates.

When shopping for the best deal on hotels and car rentals, **look for guaranteed exchange rates,** which protect you against a falling dollar. With your rate locked in, you won't pay more, even if the price goes up in the local currency.

➤ AIRLINE TICKETS: ☎ **800/359–4537** or **800/359–2727.**

➤ HOTEL ROOMS: **Hotel Reservations Network** (☎ 800/964–6835, WEB www.hoteldiscount.com). **International Marketing & Travel Concepts** (☎ 800/790–4682, imtc@mindspring.com). **Steigenberger Reservation Service** (☎ 800/223–5652, WEB www.srs-worldhotels.com). **Travel Interlink** (☎ 800/888–5898, WEB www.travelinterlink.com).

PACKAGE DEALS

Don't confuse travel packages with guided tours. When you buy a package, you travel on your own, just as though you had planned the trip yourself. Fly/drive packages, which combine airfare and car rental, are often a good deal. If you **buy a rail/drive pass,** you may save on train tickets and car rentals. All Eurail- and Europass holders get a discount on Eurostar fares through the Channel Tunnel.

ECOTOURISM

Austria is a popular vacation spot for those who want to experience nature—many rural hotels offer idyllic bases for hiking in the mountains or lake areas. There are an increasing number of *Urlaub am Bauernhof* (farm vacations) offered throughout Austria, where families can stay on a working farm and children can help take care of farm animals. Contact the associations below for information on these increasingly popular accommodation options.

There are numerous outfitters who can provide information on basic as well as specialty farms, such as organic farms or farms for children, for the disabled, and for horseback riders.

➤ GENERAL INFORMATION: **Landidyll-Hotels in Österreich** (⊠ WEB www.landidyll.at). **Austrian Tourist Board** (⊠ Margaretenstr. 1, A–1040 Vienna, ☎ 01/587–2000, FAX 01/588–6620).

➤ INFORMATION ON FARM HOLIDAYS: **Farmhouse Holidays in Austria** (⊠ Gabelsbergerstr. 19, A–5020 Salzburg, ☎ 0662/880202, FAX 0662/880202–3). **Kärnten/Landesverband Urlaub auf dem Bauernhof** (⊠ Viktringer Ring 5, A–9020 Klagenfurt, ☎ 0463/330099, FAX 0463/330099–33, WEB www.urlaubambauernhof.com). **Oberösterreich/Das Land vor den Alpen** (Upper Austria) (⊠ Auf der Gugl 3, A–4021 Linz, ☎ 0732/6902–1248, FAX 0732/6902–48, WEB www.upperaustria.farmholidays.com).

ELECTRICITY

To use your U.S.-purchased electric-powered equipment, **bring a converter and adapter.** The electrical current in Austria is 220 volts, 50 cycles alternating current (AC); wall outlets take Continental-type plugs, with two round prongs.

If your appliances are dual-voltage, you'll need only an adapter. Don't use 110-volt outlets marked FOR SHAVERS ONLY for high-wattage appliances such as blow-dryers. Most laptops operate equally well on 110 and 220 volts and so require only an adapter.

EMBASSIES

➤ AUSTRALIA: **Embassy of Australia** (⊠ Mattiellistr. 2–3, 4th District, Vienna, ☎ 01/50674).

➤ CANADA: **Embassy of Canada** (⊠ Laurenzerberg 2, on the 3rd floor of

Hauptpost building complex, 1st District, Vienna, ☎ 01/53138–3000).

➤ NEW ZEALAND: **Mission of New Zealand** (⊠ Mattiellistr. 2–4, 4th District, Vienna, ☎ 505–3021).

➤ UNITED KINGDOM: **Embassy of United Kingdom** (⊠ Jauresg. 12, 3rd District, Vienna, ☎ 01/71613–5151).

➤ UNITED STATES: **Embassy of the United States** (⊠ Boltzmanng. 16, A–1090, 9th District, Vienna, ☎ 313–39). **Consulate of the U.S./Passport Division** (⊠ Gartenbaupromenade 2–4, A–1010, 1st District, Vienna, ☎ 313–39).

EMERGENCIES

On the street, some German phrases that may be needed in an emergency are *Zur Hilfe!* (Help!), *Notfall* (emergency), *Rettungswagen* (ambulance), *Feuerwehr* (fire department), *Polizei* (police), *Arzt* (doctor), and *Krankenhaus* (hospital).

➤ CONTACTS: **Police** (☎ 133). **Fire** (☎ 122). **Ambulance** (☎ 144).

ENGLISH-LANGUAGE
AND LOCAL MEDIA

The *International Herald Tribune, The Wall Street Journal,* and *USA Today* are readily available in Vienna. For local Austria-specific information in English, the choice is more limited. For a vast selection of American magazines, go to the bookstore *Morawa* (⊠ Wollzeile 11, Vienna). There is no longer an exclusive English-language radio station in Austria. You can hear short English news broadcasts at 103.8 Mhz from early morning until 6 PM.

BOOKS

In Vienna, it's fairly easy to find English-language bookstores. Bookstores in smaller towns sometimes have an English section or rack.

➤ LOCAL RESOURCES: **British Bookstore** (⊠ Weihburgg. 24–26, 1st District, Vienna, ☎ 01/512–1945–0), and (⊠ Mariahilferstr. 4, 7th District, Vienna, ☎ 01/522–6730). **Shakespeare & Co.** (⊠ Sterng. 2, 1st District, Vienna, ☎ 01/535–5053).

AUSTRIAN NEWSPAPERS
AND MAGAZINES

The most widely read Austrian German-language newspaper is the *Kro-*

nen Zeitung, with a culture section on Fridays, but the most comprehensive section on the culture scene in Vienna can be found in the liberal weekly newsmagazine *Falter,* with a new edition every Wednesday. Even though the listings are in German, it's easy to understand. Popular magazines are readily available at Tabak shops and newspaper stands and include the international weekly editions of *Time* and *Newsweek,* European editions of the fashion magazines *Marie-Claire,* and *Elle* (in German), and *Cosmopolitan,* also in German.

RADIO AND TELEVISION

For news and weather broadcasts in English on the hour from early morning until 6 PM, go to the eclectic rock music station U4 at 103.8 Mhz. For classical music interrupted with a lot of German poetry readings, tune into Radio Stephansdom at 107.4 Mhz. RTL and Radio Wien offer American and British soft rock music at 92.9 Mhz and 89.9 Mhz respectively. British and American pop can be found at Energy, 104.2 Mhz, and Neue Antenne, 102.5 Mhz. There are two noncable television stations in Austria, the state-owned ORF 1 and ORF 2. Service is entirely in German, and American and English movies are dubbed in German. ORF 1 leans more toward sports events and children's shows, whereas ORF 2 schedules documentaries and Austrian and American TV series and films. A new private television station, ATV (Austrian TV) was recently granted a license and should start broadcasting before the end of 2002.

ETIQUETTE AND BEHAVIOR

The most common form of greeting in Austria is *Grüss Gott,* which literally means "God greets you." When it comes to table manners, there are some surprising differences from American usage: Austrians eat hamburgers, french fries, and pizza with a knife and fork—and even sometimes ribs. Corn on the cob is seldom found on restaurant menus; it's regarded as animal feed. It's proper to bring flowers to your hostess if you're invited to someone's home for dinner, but never red roses (which are re-

served for lovers). Note that if you bring wine to your hostess, it's considered a gift and is usually not served. Austrians are comfortable with nudity, and public and hotel saunas are used by both sexes; in such facilities, people are seldom clothed (though this is an option).

BUSINESS ETIQUETTE

Punctuality is a virtue in Austria. Austrians are very courteous and rather formal in business situations. Business luncheons and dinners are generally paid for by the person who arranges the meeting.

GAY AND LESBIAN TRAVEL

Austria is a gay-tolerant country in general. In Vienna, the twice-monthly free magazine *Xtra!* runs a calendar of daily events and addresses. Also look for the *Vienna Gay Guide,* a map showing locations of gay-friendly bars, restaurants, hotels, and saunas. For additional information, check the Web site www.gayguide.at.

➤ GAY- AND LESBIAN-FRIENDLY TRAVEL AGENCIES: **Different Roads Travel** (✉ 8383 Wilshire Blvd., Suite 902, Beverly Hills, CA 90211, ☎ 323/651–5557 or 800/429–8747, FAX 323/651–3678, leigh@west.tzell.com). **Kennedy Travel** (✉ 314 Jericho Turnpike, Floral Park, NY 11001, ☎ 516/352–4888 or 800/237–7433, FAX 516/354–8849, main@kennedy-travel.com, WEB www.kennedytravel.com). **Now Voyager** (✉ 4406 18th St., San Francisco, CA 94114, ☎ 415/626–1169 or 800/255–6951, FAX 415/626–8626). **Skylink Travel and Tour** (✉ 1006 Mendocino Ave., Santa Rosa, CA 95401, ☎ 707/546–9888 or 800/225–5759, FAX 707/546–9891, skylinktvl@aol.com) serves lesbian travelers.

➤ LOCAL RESOURCES: **Homosexuelle Initiative (HOSI)** (✉ Novarag. 40, A–1020 Vienna, ☎ 01/216–6604, WEB www.hosi.at; ✉ Schubertstr. 36, A–4020 Linz, ☎ 0732/609898).

The **Rosa Lila Villa** in Vienna is a boardinghouse with a restaurant catering to gay men and lesbians, with separate floors for men and women. For information, women should call ☎ 01/586–8150 (FAX 01/585–4159). Men can call ☎ 01/585–

4343 (FAX 01/587–1778). (✉ Linke Wienzeile 102, A–1060 Vienna).

HEALTH

MEDICAL PLANS

No one plans to get sick while traveling, but it happens, so **consider signing up with a medical-assistance company.** Members get doctor referrals, emergency evacuation or repatriation, 24-hour telephone hot lines for medical consultation, cash for emergencies, and other personal and legal assistance. Coverage varies by plan, so **review the benefits of each carefully.**

English-speaking doctors are readily available, and health care in Austria is usually excellent.

OVER-THE-COUNTER REMEDIES

You must buy over-the-counter remedies in an *Apotheken,* and most personnel speak enough English to understand what you need. Pain relievers are much milder than those available in the United States.

SHOTS AND MEDICATIONS

No special shots are required before visiting Austria, but if you will be cycling or hiking through the eastern or southeastern parts of the country, get inoculated against encephalitis; it can be carried by ticks.

HOLIDAYS

All banks and shops are closed on national holidays: New Year's Day; Jan. 6, Epiphany; Easter Sunday and Monday; May 1, May Day; Ascension Day; Pentecost Sunday and Monday; Corpus Christi; Aug. 15, Assumption; Oct. 26, National Holiday; Nov. 1, All Saints' Day; Dec. 8, Immaculate Conception; Dec. 25–26, Christmas. Museums are open on most holidays but closed on Good Friday, on Dec. 24 and 25, and New Year's Day. Banks and offices are closed on Dec. 8, but most shops are open.

INSURANCE

Travel insurance is the best way to **protect yourself against financial loss.** The most useful travel insurance plan is a comprehensive policy that includes coverage for trip cancellation and interruption, default, trip delay, and medical expenses (with a waiver for preexisting conditions).

Without insurance you will lose all or most of your money if you cancel your trip, regardless of the reason. Default insurance covers you if your tour operator, airline, or cruise line goes out of business. Trip-delay covers expenses that arise because of bad weather or mechanical delays. Study the fine print when comparing policies.

For overseas travel, one of the most important components of travel insurance is its medical coverage. Supplemental health insurance will pick up the cost of your medical bills should you get sick or injured while traveling. U.S. residents should note that Medicare generally does not cover health-care costs outside the United States, nor do many privately issued policies. Residents of the United Kingdom can buy an annual travel-insurance policy valid for most vacations taken during the year in which the coverage is purchased. If you are pregnant or have a pre-existing condition, make sure you're covered. British citizens should buy extra medical coverage when traveling overseas, according to the Association of British Insurers. Australian travelers should buy travel insurance, including extra medical coverage, whenever they go abroad, according to the Insurance Council of Australia.

Always **buy travel policies directly from the insurance company;** if you buy them from a cruise line, airline, or tour operator that goes out of business you probably will not be covered for the agency or operator's default, a major risk. Before making any purchase, **review your existing health and home-owner's policies** to find what they cover away from home.

➤ TRAVEL INSURERS: In the United States: **Access America** (✉ 6600 W. Broad St., Richmond, VA 23230, ☎ 804/285–3300 or 800/284–8300, FAX 804/673–1583, WEB www.accessamerica.com). **Travel Guard International** (✉ 1145 Clark St., Stevens Point, WI 54481, ☎ 715/345–0505 or 800/826–1300, FAX 800/955–8785, WEB www.noelgroup.com).

In Canada: **Voyager Insurance** (✉ 44 Peel Center Dr., Brampton, Ontario L6T 4M8, ☎ 905/791–8700; 800/ 668–4342 in Canada).

➤ INSURANCE INFORMATION: In the U.K.: **Association of British Insurers** (✉ 51–55 Gresham St., London EC2V 7HQ, ☎ 020/7600–3333, FAX 020/7696–8999, info@abi.org.uk, WEB www.abi.org.uk). In Australia: **Insurance Council of Australia** (☎ 03/9614–1077, FAX 03/9614–7924).

LANGUAGE

German is the official national language in Austria. In Vienna and in most resort areas you will usually have no problem finding people who speak English; hotel staffs in particular speak it reasonably well, and many young Austrians speak it at least passably. However, travelers do report that they often find themselves in stores, restaurants, and railway and bus stations where it's hard to find someone who speaks English—so it's best to have some native phrases up your sleeve. Note that all public announcements on trams, subways, and buses are in German. Train announcements are usually given in English as well, but if you have any questions, try to get answers before boarding.

LANGUAGES FOR TRAVELERS

A phrase book and language-tape set can help get you started.

➤ PHRASE BOOK AND LANGUAGE-TAPE SET: *Fodor's German for Travelers* (☎ 800/733–3000 in the U.S.; 800/ 668–4247 in Canada; $7 for phrase book, $16.95 for audio set).

LODGING

You can live like a king in a real castle in Austria or get by on a modest budget. Starting at the lower end, you can find a room in a private house or on a farm, or dormitory space in a youth hostel. Next up the line come the simpler pensions, many of them identified as a *Frühstückspension* (bed-and-breakfast). Then come the Gasthäuser, the simpler country inns. The fancier pensions in the cities can often cost as much as hotels; the difference lies in the services they offer. Most pensions, for example, do

not staff the front desk around the clock. Among the hotels, you can find accommodations ranging from the most modest, with a shower and toilet down the hall, to the most elegant, with every possible amenity.

The lodgings we list are the cream of the crop in each price category. We always list the facilities that are available—but we don't specify whether they cost extra: when pricing accommodations, always ask what's included and what costs extra (two items that occasionally fall into the latter category are parking and breakfast). Properties marked ✕🗓 are lodging establishments whose restaurants warrant a special trip.

Assume that hotels operate on the **European Plan** (EP, with no meals) unless we specify otherwise. Increasingly, more and more hotels are including breakfast with the basic room charge, but check when booking. In addition, the room rates for many hotels in the rural countryside often include breakfast and one other meal. Therefore, outside of the main urban centers, you should **inquire if the quoted room rate includes Half Board,** as this plan is called (in rare cases, Full Board, or all three meals, is included). Happily, many of these lodgings will also offer a breakfast buffet–only rate if requested.

Faxing is the easiest way to contact the hotel (the staff is probably more likely to read English than to understand it over the phone long-distance), though calling also works, and using e-mail messages is increasingly popular. In your fax (or over the phone), specify the exact dates you want to stay at the hotel (when you will arrive and when you will check out); the size of the room you want and how many people will be sleeping there; what kind of bed you want (single or double, twin beds or double, etc.); and whether you want a bathroom with a shower or bathtub (or both). You might also ask if a deposit (or your credit card number) is required and, if so, what happens if you cancel. Request that the hotel fax you back so that you have a written confirmation of your reservation in hand when you arrive at the hotel.

Here is a list of German words that can come in handy when booking a room: air-conditioning (*Klimaanlage*); private bath (*privat Bad*); bathtub (*Badewanne*); shower (*Dusche*); double bed (*Doppelbett*); twin beds (*Einzelbetten*).

APARTMENT AND CHALET RENTALS

If you want a home base that's roomy enough for a family and comes with cooking facilities, **consider a furnished rental.** These can save you money, especially if you're traveling with a large group of people. Home-exchange directories list rentals (often second homes owned by prospective house swappers), and some services search for a house or apartment for you (even a castle, if that's your fancy) and handle the paperwork. Some send an illustrated catalog; others send photographs only of specific properties, sometimes at a charge. Up-front registration fees may apply.

➤ INTERNATIONAL AGENTS: **Drawbridge to Europe** (✉ 5456 Adams Rd., Talent, OR 97540, ☎ 541/512–8927 or 888/268–1148, FAX 541/512–0978, requests@drawbridgetoeurope. com, WEB www.drawbridgetoeurope. com). **Hometours International** (✉ Box 11503, Knoxville, TN 37939, ☎ 865/690–8484 or 800/367–4668, hometours@aol.com, WEB http: thor.he.net/~hometour). **Interhome** (✉ 1990 N.E. 163rd St., Suite 110, North Miami Beach, FL 33162, ☎ 305/940–2299 or 800/882–6864, FAX 305/940–2911, WEB www.interhome.com). **Villas International** (✉ 4340 Redwood Hwy., Suite D309, San Rafael, CA 94903, ☎ 415/499–9490 or 800/221–2260, FAX 415/499–9491, WEB www.villasintl. com).

CASTLES

➤ INFORMATION: **Schlosshotels und Herrenhäuser in Österreich** (✉ Moosstr. 60, A–5020 Salzburg, ☎ 0662/8306–8141, FAX 0662/8306–8161, WEB www.schlosshotels.co.at).

HOME EXCHANGES

If you would like to exchange your home for someone else's, **join a home-exchange organization,** which will

send you its updated listings of available exchanges for a year and will include your own listing in at least one of them. It's up to you to make specific arrangements.

➤ EXCHANGE CLUBS: **HomeLink International** (✉ Box 650, Key West, FL 33041, ☎ 305/294–7766 or 800/638–3841, FAX 305/294–1448, usa@homelink.org, WEB www. homelink.org; $98 per year). **Intervac U.S.** (✉ Box 590504, San Francisco, CA 94159, ☎ 800/756–4663, FAX 415/435–7440, WEB www.intervac. com; $89 per year includes two catalogs).

HOSTELS

No matter what your age, you can **save on lodging costs by staying at hostels.** In some 5,000 locations in more than 70 countries around the world, Hostelling International (HI), the umbrella group for a number of national youth-hostel associations, offers single-sex, dorm-style beds and, at many hostels, rooms for couples and family accommodations. Membership in any HI national hostel association, open to travelers of all ages, allows you to stay in HI-affiliated hostels at member rates; one-year membership is about $25 for adults (C$35 for a two-year minimum membership in Canada, £13 in the U.K., A$52 in Australia, and NZ$40 in New Zealand); hostels run about $10–$30 per night. Members have priority if the hostel is full; they're also eligible for discounts around the world, even on rail and bus travel in some countries.

Austria has more than 100 government-sponsored youth hostels, for which you need an International Youth Hostel Federation membership card. Inexpensively priced, these hostels are run by the Österreichischer Jugendherbergsverband and are popular with the backpack crowd, so be sure to reserve in advance.

➤ IN AUSTRIA: **Österreichischer Jugendherbergsverband** (✉ Schottenring 28, A-1010 Vienna, ☎ 01/533–53–53).

➤ ORGANIZATIONS: **Hostelling International—American Youth Hostels** (✉ 733 15th St. NW, Suite 840, Washington, DC 20005, ☎ 202/783–

6161, FAX 202/783–6171). **Hostelling International—Canada** (✉ 400-205 Catherine St., Ottawa, Ontario K2P 1C3, ☎ 613/237–7884 or 800/663–5777, FAX 613/237–7868). **Youth Hostel Association of England and Wales** (✉ Trevelyan House, Dimple Rd., Matlock, Derbyshire DE4 3YH, U.K., ☎ 0870/870–8808, FAX 0169/592–702, WEB www.yha.org.uk).

HOTELS

All hotels listed have private bath unless otherwise noted.

➤ TOLL-FREE NUMBERS: **Best Western** (☎ 800/528–1234, WEB www.bestwestern.com). **Choice** (☎ 800/221–2222, WEB www.hotelchoice.com). **Hilton** (☎ 800/445–8667, WEB www.hiltons.com). **Holiday Inn** (☎ 800/465–4329, WEB www.sixcontinentshotels.com). **Inter-Continental** (☎ 800/327–0200, WEB www.intercontinental.com). **Marriott** (☎ 800/228–9290, WEB www.marriott.com). **Ramada** (☎ 800/228–2828. WEB www.ramada.com). **Renaissance Hotels & Resorts** (☎ 800/468–3571, WEB www.hotels.com). **Sheraton** (☎ 800/325–3535, WEB www.sheraton.com).

MAIL AND SHIPPING

Post offices are scattered throughout every district in Vienna and are recognizable by a square yellow sign that says "Post." They are usually open weekdays 9–12 and 2–6, Saturday 8–10 AM. The main post office near Schwedenplatz is open 24 hours daily. For overnight services, Federal Express, DHL, and UPS service Vienna and Austria; check with your hotel concierge for the nearest address and telephone number.

➤ CONTACT: **Main Post Office** (✉ Fleischmarkt 19, A–1010 Vienna).

POSTAL RATES

All mail goes by air, so there's no supplement on letters or postcards. Within Europe, a letter or postcard of up to 20 grams (about ¾ ounce) costs €0.51. To the United States or Canada, a letter of up to 20 grams takes €1.09 for airmail. If in doubt, mail your letters from a post office and have the weight checked. The Austrian post office also adheres strictly to a size standard; if your letter or card is outside the norm, you'll have to pay a surcharge. Postcards via airmail to the United States or Canada need €1.09. Always place an airmail sticker on your letters or cards. Shipping packages from Austria to destinations outside the country is extremely expensive.

RECEIVING MAIL

When you don't know where you'll be staying, American Express mail service is a great convenience, with no charge to anyone either holding an American Express credit card or carrying American Express traveler's checks. Pick up your mail at the local offices. You can also have mail held at any Austrian post office; letters should be marked *Poste Restante* or *Postlagernd*. You will be asked for identification when you collect mail. In Vienna, if not addressed to a specific district post office, this service is handled through the main post office.

➤ CONTACTS: **American Express** (✉ Kärntnerstr. 21–23, A–1015 Vienna, ☎ 01/515–40–0 and ✉ Bürgerstr. 14, A–4021 Linz, ☎ 0732/669013). **Austrian post office** (✉ Fleischmarkt 19, A–1010 Vienna, ☎ 01/515–09–0).

MONEY MATTERS

Prices throughout this guide are given for adults. Substantially reduced fees are almost always available for children, students, and senior citizens. For information on taxes, *see* Taxes.

ATMS

➤ ATM LOCATIONS: **Cirrus** (☎ 800/424–7787). **Plus** (☎ 800/843–7587).

Fairly common throughout Austria, **ATMs are one of the easiest ways to get euros.** Although ATM transaction fees may be higher abroad than at home, banks usually offer excellent wholesale exchange rates through ATMs. Cirrus and Plus locations are easily found throughout large city centers, and even in small towns. If you have any trouble finding one, ask your hotel concierge. Note, too, that you may have better luck with ATMs if you're using a credit card or debit card that is also a Visa or MasterCard rather than just your bank card.

To get cash at ATMs in Austria, **your personal identification number (PIN) must be four digits long.** Note, too, that you may be charged by your bank for using ATMs overseas; inquire at your bank about charges.

COSTS

A cup of coffee in a café will cost about €3–€4; a half liter of draft beer, €3–€4; a glass of wine, €4–€8; a Coca-Cola, €3; an open-face sandwich, €3.50; a midrange theater ticket €20; a concert ticket €30–€50; an opera ticket €40 upward; a 1-mi taxi ride, €4. Outside the hotels, laundering a shirt costs about €4; dry–cleaning a suit costs around €12–€18; a dress, €9–€12. A shampoo and set for a woman will cost around €25–€35, a manicure about €12–€15; a man's haircut about €25–€35.

CREDIT AND DEBIT CARDS

In the last couple of years credit cards have been gaining broad acceptance, but still try to have traveler's checks and cash available. Most grocery stores do not accept credit cards. Some establishments have a minimum sum for use of credit cards; others may accept cards grudgingly.

Should you use a credit card or a debit card when traveling? Both have benefits. A credit card allows you to delay payment and gives you certain rights as a consumer. A debit card, also known as a check card, deducts funds directly from your checking account and helps you stay within your budget. When you want to rent a car, though, you may still need an old-fashioned credit card. Although you can always *pay* for your car with a debit card, some agencies will not allow you to *reserve* a car with a debit card.

Otherwise, the two types of plastic are virtually the same. Both will get you cash advances at ATMs worldwide if your card is properly programmed with your personal identification number (PIN). Both offer excellent wholesale exchange rates. And both protect you against unauthorized use if the card is lost or stolen. Your liability is limited to $50 as long as you report the card missing.

Be aware that several U.S. credit card companies are now adding a 2%–3% conversion surcharge on all charges made in Europe. This can really add up on big purchases and hotel charges. Check with your credit card company so you'll know in advance.

Throughout this guide, the following abbreviations are used: **AE**, American Express; **DC**, Diner's Club; **MC**, MasterCard; and **V**, Visa.

➤ REPORTING LOST CARDS: **American Express** (☎ 336/939–1111 or 336/668–5309) call collect. **Diner's Club** (☎ 303/799–1504) call collect. **MasterCard** (☎ 0800/90–1387). **Visa** (☎ 0800/90–1179; 410/581–9994 collect).

CURRENCY

Because it is a member of the European Union (EU), Austria's unit of currency is the euro. Under the euro system there are eight coins: 1 and 2 euros, plus 1, 2, 5, 10, 20, and 50 euro cent, or cents of the euro. All coins have the value of the euro on one side and each country's own unique national symbol on the other. There are seven banknotes: 5, 10, 20, 50, 100, 200, and 500 euros. Banknotes are the same for all EU countries.

Please note that prices in euros correspond generally to the U.S. dollar, as their current values are relatively close—at least at press time (fall 2002). At press time, the exchange rate was about €1.02 to the U.S dollar, €1.56 to the British pound, €0.66 to the Canadian dollar, €0.55 to the Australian dollar, and €0.47 to the New Zealand dollar. These rates can and will vary.

CURRENCY EXCHANGE

Generally, exchange rates are far less favorable outside of Austria, and there is no need to exchange money prior to your arrival. ATMs are conveniently located in city centers. Although fees charged for ATM transactions may be higher abroad than at home, Cirrus and Plus exchange rates are excellent, because they are based on wholesale rates offered only by major banks. Otherwise, the most favorable rates are through a bank. You won't do as well at exchange booths in airports or rail and bus stations, in hotels, in restaurants, or in stores, although you may find their hours more convenient than at a bank.

➤ EXCHANGE SERVICES: **Chase *Currency to Go*** (☎ 800/935–9935; 935–9935 in NY, NJ, and CT). **International Currency Express** (☎ 888/278–6628 for orders). **Thomas Cook Currency Services** (☎ 800/287–7362 for telephone orders and retail locations, WEB www.us.thomascook.com).

TRAVELER'S CHECKS

Do you need traveler's checks? It depends on where you're headed. If you're going to rural areas and small towns, go with cash; traveler's checks are best used in cities. Lost or stolen checks can usually be replaced within 24 hours. To ensure a speedy refund, buy your own traveler's checks—don't let someone else pay for them; irregularities like this can cause delays. The person who bought the checks should make the call to request a refund.

OUTDOORS AND SPORTS

The Austrians are great sports lovers and go in for a greater variety of sports than any other European nation.

BICYCLING

Cyclists couldn't ask for much more than the cycle track that runs the length of the Danube or the many cycling routes that crisscross the country, major cities included. Just about every lake is surrounded by bike paths, and there are other rivers, too, such as the Drau, that have trails. You can no longer rent a bike at train stations in Austria. The cost of renting a bike (21-gear) from a local agency is around €27 a day.

Tourist offices have details (in German), including maps and hints for trip planning and mealtime and overnight stops that cater especially to cyclists. Ask for the booklet "Radtouren in Österreich."

➤ CONTACTS: **Austria Radreisen** (✉ Joseph-Haydn-Str. 8, A–4780 Schärding, ☎ 07712/5511–0, FAX 07712/4811). **Pedal Power** (✉ Ausstellungsstr. 3, A–1020 Vienna, ☎ 01/729–7234, FAX 01/729–7235).

BOATING AND SAILING

Rowboats can be rented on almost all of Austria's lakes and on the side arms of the Danube (Alte Donau and the Donauinsel) in Vienna.

Windsurfing (*Windsegeln*) is extremely popular, particularly on the Neusiedler See in Burgenland, on the Attersee in Upper Austria, and on the side arms of the Danube in Vienna. There are schools at all these locations with lessons and rentals.

➤ CONTACT: **Österreichischer Segel-Verband, the Austrian Yachting Club** (✉ Zetscheg. 21, A–1230 Vienna, ☎ 01/662–4462, FAX 01/662–1558, WEB www.sailing.or.at).

CAMPING

If your idea of a good holiday is the "great outdoors" and if your purse is a slender one, a camping holiday may be just the thing for you. Austrians love the idea and there are practically as many tourists under canvas as in hotels and Gasthäuser. You'll find more than 450 campsites throughout the country, usually run by regional organizations, a few private. Most have full facilities, often including swimming pools and snack bars or grocery shops. Charges average about €20 per day for a family of three, depending on the location and the range and quality of services offered. Many campsites have a fixed basic fee for three adults and one child, parking included. Camping is not restricted to the summer season; some sites are open year-round, with about 155 specifically set up for winter camping. For details, check with the tourist offices of the individual Austrian provinces.

➤ CONTACT: **Österreichischer Camping Club** (✉ Schubertring 1–3, A–1010 Vienna, ☎ 01/71199–1272, FAX 01/71199–2754).

FISHING

Among Austria's well-stocked lakes are the Traunsee, Attersee, Hallstätter See, and Mondsee in Upper Austria; the Danube, Steyr, Traun, Enns, Krems, and Alm rivers also provide good fishing. Carinthian lakes and the streams in Lower Austria also abound in fish. Ask the Austrian National Tourist Office for the guidebook "Austrian Fishing Waters"; it includes licensing details. The separate provinces also have detailed brochures on waters and licensing. Unfortunately, the rights along many of the best streams have been given, meaning that no additional licenses will be issued, but ask at the local tourist office. Some hotels have fishing rights; we note these throughout the book.

GLIDING

From May to September you can glide solo or learn to glide at one of Austria's schools, at Zell am See (Salzburg Province); Niederöblarn and Graz-Thalerhof (Styria); and in Wiener Neustadt and Spitzberg bei Hainberg (Lower Austria). In Zell am See and at Wien-Donauwiese (Vienna) there are two-seater gliders, for instructor and passenger; at the other airfields you're on your own.

➤ CONTACT: **Austrian Aero-Club** (✉ Prinz Eugen-Str. 12, A–1040 Vienna, ☎ 01/505–1028–74, 𝔽𝔸𝕏 01/505–7923).

GOLF

Austria now has more than 50 courses. Most are private, but for a greens fee you can arrange a temporary membership. Many courses are associated with hotels, so package arrangements can be made. Austrian National Tourist Offices have golfing brochures.

➤ CONTACTS: **Johann Ruisz Hotelnetzwerk Betriebsfuehrung** (✉ Fürbergstr. 44, A–5020 Salzburg, ☎ 0662/645–143, 𝔽𝔸𝕏 0662/648–206). **Österreichischer Golfverband** (✉ Prinz Eugen-Str. 12, A–1040 Vienna, ☎ 01/505–3245–0, 𝔽𝔸𝕏 01/505–4962, 𝕎𝔼𝔹 www.golf.at).

HIKING AND CLIMBING

With more than 50,000 km (about 35,000 mi) of well-maintained mountain paths through Europe's largest reserve of unspoiled landscape, the country is a hiker's paradise. Three long-distance routes traverse Austria: E4, the Pyrenees–Jura–Neusiedler See route, ending in Burgenland on the Hungarian border; E5 from Lake Constance in Vorarlberg to the Adriatic; and E6 from the Baltic, cutting across mid-Austria via the Wachau

valley region of the Danube and on to the Adriatic. Wherever you are in Austria, you will find shorter hiking trails requiring varying degrees of ability. Routes are well marked, and maps are readily available from bookstores, the Österreichischer Alpenverein/OAV, and the automobile clubs.

➤ CONTACT: **Österreichischer Alpenverein** (✉ Wilhelm-Greil-Str. 15, A–6020 Innsbruck, ☎ 0512/59547–19, 𝔽𝔸𝕏 0512/575528, 𝕎𝔼𝔹 www.alpenverein.at. In the U.K., ✉ 13 Longcroft House, Fretherne Rd., Welwyn Garden City, Hertfordshire AL8 6PQ, ☎ 01707/324835).

HORSEBACK RIDING

Whether you want to head off cross-country or just canter around a paddock, Austria offers many kinds of equestrian holidays, and some hotels have their own riding schools. Ask for the booklet "Riding Arena Austria" from the tourist office. The provinces of Upper and Lower Austria are particularly popular with riders.

SPECTATOR SPORTS

Soccer is a national favorite. Every town has at least one team, and rivalries are fierce; matches are held regularly in Vienna and Innsbruck. When Austrians aren't skiing, they like to watch the national sport; downhill and slalom races are held regularly in Innsbruck, Kitzbühel, Seefeld, and St. Anton. There's horse racing with pari-mutuel betting at the track in the Prater in Vienna. Tennis matches are held in Vienna, Linz, and Innsbruck.

WATER SPORTS AND SWIMMING

In the Vienna area, the Alte Donau and Donauinsel arms of the Danube are accessible by public transportation and are suitable for families. It's best to go early to avoid the crowds on hot summer weekends. The Alte Donau beaches have changing rooms and checkrooms. Swimming in the Neusiedler See in Burgenland is an experience; you can touch bottom at virtually any place in this vast brackish lake. Swimming naked or at least partly so is fairly common.

PACKING

CHECKING LUGGAGE

How many carry-on bags you can bring with you is up to the airline. Most allow only one, so make sure that everything you carry aboard will fit under your seat or in the overhead bin, and get to the gate early. Note that if you have a seat at the back of the plane, you'll probably board first, while the overhead bins are still empty.

If you are flying internationally, note that baggage allowances may be determined not by piece but by weight—generally 88 pounds (40 kilograms) in first class, 66 pounds (30 kilograms) in business class, and 44 pounds (20 kilograms) in economy.

Airline liability for baggage is limited to $1,250 per person on flights within the United States. On international flights it amounts to $9.07 per pound or $20 per kilogram for checked baggage (roughly $640 per 70-pound bag) and $400 per passenger for unchecked baggage. You can buy additional coverage at check-in for about $10 per $1,000 of coverage, but it excludes a rather extensive list of items, shown on your airline ticket.

Before departure, **itemize your bags' contents** and their worth, and label the bags with your name, address, and phone number. (If you use your home address, cover it so potential thieves can't see it readily.) Inside each bag, **pack a copy of your itinerary.** At check-in, **make sure that each bag is correctly tagged** with the destination airport's three-letter code. If your bags arrive damaged or fail to arrive at all, file a written report with the airline before leaving the airport.

PACKING LIST

Dressing in Austria ranges from conservative to casual, and is somewhat dependent on age. Older people tend to dress conservatively; slacks on women are as rare as loud sport shirts are on men. Young people tend to be very trendy, and the trend is basically United States, with kids in baseball caps, baggy trousers, and loud shirts with all kinds of things written on them in (sometimes poor) English. In the country or more rural areas of, say, Styria or Burgenland, things are a little less loud. Jeans are ubiquitous in Austria as elsewhere, but are considered inappropriate at concerts (other than pop) or formal restaurants. For concerts and opera, women may want a skirt or dress, and men a jacket; even in summer, gala performances at small festivals tend to be dressy. And since an evening outside at a Heuriger (wine garden) may be on your agenda, be sure to take a sweater or light wrap. Unless you're staying in an expensive hotel or will be in one place for more than a day or two, take hand-washables; laundry service gets complicated. Austria is a walking country, in cities and mountains alike. If you intend to hike in the mountains, bring boots that rise above the ankle and have sturdy soles. For lots of city walking a good pair of sports shoes is needed.

Consider packing a small folding umbrella for the odd deluge, or a waterproof windbreaker of sorts. Sunglasses are a must as well. Mosquitoes can become quite a bother in summer around the lakes and along the rivers, especially the Danube and the swampy regions created by its old arms. Bring some good insect repellent.

In your carry-on luggage, **pack an extra pair of eyeglasses or contact lenses** and **enough of any medication you take** to last a few days longer than the entire trip. You may also ask your doctor to write a spare prescription using the drug's generic name, since brand names may vary from country to country. In luggage to be checked, **never pack prescription drugs or valuables.** To avoid customs delays, carry medications in their original packaging. And don't forget to carry with you the addresses of offices that handle refunds of lost traveler's checks.

PASSPORTS AND VISAS

When traveling internationally, **carry your passport even if you don't need one** (it's always the best form of I.D.) and **make two photocopies of the data page** (one for someone at home and another for you, carried separately from your passport). If you lose your passport, promptly call the nearest embassy or consulate and the local police.

ENTERING AUSTRIA

United States, Australian, Canadian, New Zealand, and U.K. citizens need only a valid passport to enter Austria for stays of up to three months.

PASSPORT OFFICES

The best time to apply for a passport or to renew is in fall and winter. Before any trip, check your passport's expiration date, and, if necessary, renew it as soon as possible. (Some countries won't allow you to enter on a passport that's due to expire in six months or less.)

➤ AUSTRALIAN CITIZENS: **Australian Passport Office** (☎ 131–232, WEB www.passports.gov.au).

➤ CANADIAN CITIZENS: **Passport Office** (to mail in applications: ✉ Department of Foreign Affairs and International Trade, Ottawa, Ontario K1A 0G3; ☎ 800/567–6868 toll free in Canada or 819/994–3500, WEB www.dfait-maeci.gc.ca/passport).

➤ NEW ZEALAND CITIZENS: **New Zealand Passport Office** (☎ 0800/ 22–5050 or 04/474–8100, WEB www. passports.govt.nz).

➤ U.K. CITIZENS: **London Passport Office** (☎ 0990/210–410, WEB www. passport.gov.uk) for fees and documentation requirements and to request an emergency passport.

➤ U.S. CITIZENS: **National Passport Information Center** (☎ 900/225–5674; 35¢ per minute for automated service or $1.05 per minute for operator service, WEB www.travel.state.gov).

SENIOR-CITIZEN TRAVEL

To qualify for age-related discounts, **mention your senior-citizen status up front** when booking hotel reservations (not when checking out) and before you're seated in restaurants (not when paying the bill). When renting a car, ask about promotional car-rental discounts, which can be cheaper than senior-citizen rates.

Austria has so many senior citizens that facilities almost everywhere cater to the needs of older travelers, with discounts for rail travel and museum entry. Check with the Austrian National Tourist Office to find what

form of identification is required, but generally if you're 65 or over (women 60), once you're in Austria the railroads will issue you a *Seniorenpass* (you'll need a passport photo and passport or other proof of age) entitling you to the senior-citizen discounts, regardless of nationality.

➤ EDUCATIONAL PROGRAMS: **Elderhostel** (✉ 75 Federal St., 3rd floor, Boston, MA 02110, ☎ 877/426–8056, FAX 877/426–2166, WEB www. elderhostel.org). **Interhostel** (✉ University of New Hampshire, 6 Garrison Ave., Durham, NH 03824, ☎ 603/862–1147 or 800/733–9753, FAX 603/862–1113, WEB www.learn. unh.edu).

STUDENTS IN AUSTRIA

To save money, **look into deals available through student-oriented travel agencies.** To qualify you'll need a bona fide student ID card. Members of international student groups are also eligible. Information on student tickets, fares, and lodgings is available from Jugend Info Wien (Youth Information Center) in Vienna.

➤ I.D.s AND SERVICES: **STA Travel** (CIEE; ✉ 205 E. 42nd St., 14th floor, New York, NY 10017, ☎ 212/ 822–2700 or 888/268–6245, FAX 212/ 822–2699, info@councilexchanges. org, WEB www.councilexchanges.org) for mail orders only, in the United States. **Travel Cuts** (✉ 187 College St., Toronto, Ontario M5T 1P7, Canada, ☎ 416/979–2406 or 888/838–2887, FAX 416/979–8167, WEB www.travelcuts.com).

➤ LOCAL RESOURCES: **Jugend Info Wien** (✉ Babenbergerstr. 1, Vienna, ☎ 01/1799, FAX 01/585–2499), open Monday–Saturday, noon–7 PM.

➤ STUDENT TOURS: **AESU Travel** (✉ 2 Hamill Rd., Suite 248, Baltimore, MD 21210-1807, ☎ 410/323–4416 or 800/638–7640, FAX 410/323–4498), **Contiki Holidays** (✉ 300 Plaza Alicante, Suite 900, Garden Grove, CA 92840, ☎ 714/740–0808 or 800/266–8454, FAX 714/740–2034).

TAXES

VALUE-ADDED TAX

The Value Added Tax (VAT) in Austria is 20% generally but only 10% on food and clothing. If you are planning to take your purchases with you when you leave Austria (export them), you can get a refund. The shop will give you a form or a receipt, which must be presented at the border, where the wares are inspected. The Austrian government will send you your refund, minus a processing fee.

Wine and spirits are heavily taxed—nearly half of the sale price goes to taxes. For every contract signed in Austria (for example, car-rental agreements), you pay an extra 1% tax to the government, so tax on a rental car is 21%.

Global Refund is a VAT refund service that makes getting your money back hassle free. The service is available Europe-wide at 130,000 affiliated stores. In participating stores, **ask for the Global Refund form** (called a Shopping Cheque). Have it stamped like any customs form by customs officials when you leave the European Union. Then take the form to one of the more than 700 Global Refund counters—conveniently located at every major airport and border crossing—and your money will be refunded on the spot in the form of cash, check, or a refund to your credit-card account (minus a small percentage for processing).

Global Refund (✉ 707 Summer St., Stamford, CT 06901, ☎ 800/566-9828, 𝔽𝔸𝕏 203/674-8709, taxfree@us. globalrefund.com, 𝕎𝔼𝔹 www. globalrefund.com).

TELEPHONES

AREA AND COUNTRY CODES

The country code for Austria is 43. When dialing an Austrian number from abroad, drop the initial 0 from the local area code.

Austria's telephone service is in a state of change as the country converts to a digital system. We make every effort to keep numbers up to date, but do recheck the number—particularly in Linz and Vienna—if you have problems getting the connection you want (a sharp tone indicates no connection or that the number has been changed). All numbers given in this guide include the city or town area code; if you are

calling within that city or town, dial the local number only.

DIRECTORY AND OPERATOR INFORMATION

For international information dial 118200 for numbers in Germany and Austria, 118202 for numbers in other European countries and overseas numbers. Most operators speak English; if yours doesn't, you'll be passed along to one who does.

INTERNATIONAL CALLS

You can dial direct to almost any point on the globe from Austria. However, it costs more to telephone from Austria than it does to telephone to Austria. Calls from post offices are always the least expensive and you can get helpful assistance in placing a long-distance call; in large cities, these centers at main post offices are open around the clock.

To make a collect call—you can't do this from pay phones—dial the operator and ask for an *R-Gespräch* (pronounced air-ga-*shprayk*). Most operators speak English; if yours doesn't, you'll be passed to one who does.

The international access code for the United States and Canada is 001, followed by the area code and number. For Great Britain, first dial 0044, then the city code without the usual "0" (171 or 181 for London), and the number. Other country and many city codes are given in the front of telephone books (in Vienna, in the A-H book).

LOCAL CALLS

When making a local call in Vienna, **dial the number without the city prefix.** A local call costs €0.20 for the first minute, and €0.20 for every three minutes thereafter.

LONG-DISTANCE CALLS

When placing a long-distance call to a destination within Austria, you'll need to know the local area codes, which can be found by consulting the telephone numbers that are listed in this guide's regional chapters. The following are area codes for Austria's major cities: Vienna, 01; Graz, 0316; Salzburg, 0662; Innsbruck, 0512; Linz, 0732. When dialing from out-

side Austria, the 0 should be left out.
Note that calls within Austria are
one-third cheaper between 6 PM and
8 AM on weekdays and from 1 PM on
Saturday to 8 AM on Monday.

LONG-DISTANCE SERVICES

AT&T and MCI access codes make
calling long-distance relatively convenient, but you may find the local
access number blocked in many hotel
rooms. First ask the hotel operator to
connect you. If the hotel operator
balks, ask for an international operator, or dial the international operator
yourself. One way to improve your
odds of getting connected to your
long-distance carrier is to travel with
more than one company's calling card
(a hotel may block Sprint, for example, but not MCI). If all else fails, call
from a pay phone.

➤ ACCESS CODES: **AT&T Direct** (☎
01/0800–200–288; 800/435–0812 for
other areas). **MCI WorldPhone** (☎
0800–200–235; 800/444–4141 for
other areas).

PHONE CARDS

If you plan to make calls from pay
phones, a *Telephon Wertkarte* is a
convenience. You can buy this electronic phone card at any post office
for €7.20 or €3.60, which allows
you to use the card at any SOS, or
credit-card phone booth. You simply
insert the card and dial; the cost of
the call is automatically deducted
from the card, and a digital window
on the phone tells you how many
units you have left (these are not
minutes). A few public phones in the
cities also take American Express,
Diner's Club, MasterCard, and Visa
credit cards.

PUBLIC PHONES

Coin-operated pay telephones are
dwindling in number. A local call
costs €0.20 for the first minute. At
the oldest coin-operated machines,
pick up the receiver and dial; when
the party answers, push the indicated
button and the connection will be
made. If there is no response, your
coin will be returned into the bin to
the lower left. The smaller machines
are more recent and don't have the
button to connect. If your party has
an answering machine you'll have to

pay a little something. Most pay
phones have instructions in English
on them. Add €0.20 when the time is
up to continue the connection.

Faxes can be sent from post offices
and received as well, but neither
service is very cheap.

TIME

The time difference between New
York and Austria is 6 hours (so when
it's 1 PM in New York, it's 7 PM in
Vienna). The time difference between
London and Vienna is 1 hour; between Sydney and Vienna, 14 hours;
and between Auckland and Vienna,
13 hours.

TIPPING

Although virtually all hotels and
restaurants include service charges in
their rates, tipping is still customary,
but at a level lower than in the United
States. Tip the hotel doorman €1 per
bag, and the porter who brings your
bags to the room another €1 per bag.
In very small country inns such tips
are not expected but are appreciated.
In family-run establishments, tips are
generally not given to immediate
family members, only to employees.
Tip the hotel concierge only for
special services or in response to
special requests. Room service gets
€1 for snacks or ice, €2 for full
meals. Maids normally get no tip
unless your stay is a week or more or
service has been special.

In restaurants, tip about 5%. You can
tip a little more if you've received
exceptional service. Big tips are not
usual in Austrian restaurants, since
10% has already been included in the
prices. Checkroom attendants get
€1–€2, depending on the locale.
Washroom attendants get about
€0.50. Wandering musicians and the
piano player get €2, €5 if they've
filled a number of requests.

Round up taxi fares to the next
€0.50; a minimum €0.50 tip is
customary. If the driver offers (or you
ask for) special assistance, such as
carrying your bags beyond the curb,
an added tip of €0.50–€1 is in order.

TOURS AND PACKAGES

Buying a prepackaged tour or inde-
pendent vacation can make your trip

to Austria less expensive and more hassle free. Because everything is prearranged, you'll spend less time planning.

Operators that handle several hundred thousand travelers per year can use their purchasing power to give you a good price. Their high volume may also indicate financial stability. But some small companies provide more personalized service; because they tend to specialize, they may also be more knowledgeable about a given area.

BOOKING WITH AN AGENT

Travel agents are excellent resources. But it's a good idea to collect brochures from several agencies, as some agents' suggestions may be influenced by relationships with tour and package firms that reward them for volume sales. If you have a special interest, **find an agent with expertise in that area**; ASTA (☞ Travel Agencies) has a database of specialists worldwide.

Make sure your travel agent knows the accommodations and other services of the place they're recommending. Ask about the hotel's location, room size, beds, and whether it has a pool, room service, or programs for children, if you care about these. Has your agent been there in person or sent others whom you can contact?

Do some homework on your own, too: local tourism boards can provide information about lesser-known and small-niche operators, some of which may sell only direct.

BUYER BEWARE

Every year consumers are stranded or lose their money when tour operators—even large ones with excellent reputations—go out of business. So **check out the operator.** Ask several travel agents about its reputation, and try to **book with a company that has a consumer-protection program.** (Look for information in the company's brochure.)

In the United States, members of the National Tour Association and the United States Tour Operators Association are required to set aside funds to cover your payments and travel

arrangements in the event that the company defaults. It's also a good idea to choose a company that participates in the American Society of Travel Agents' Tour Operator Program (TOP); ASTA will act as mediator in any disputes between you and your tour operator.

➤ TOUR-OPERATOR RECOMMENDATIONS: **American Society of Travel Agents** (☞ Travel Agencies). **National Tour Association** (NTA; ✉ 546 E. Main St., Lexington, KY 40508, ☎ 606/226–4444 or 800/682–8886, WEB www.ntaonline.com). **United States Tour Operators Association** (USTOA; ✉ 342 Madison Ave., Suite 1522, New York, NY 10173, ☎ 212/599–6599 or 800/468–7862, FAX 212/599–6744, ustoa@aol.com, WEB www.ustoa.com).

COSTS

The more your package or tour includes, the better you can predict the ultimate cost of your vacation. Make sure you know exactly what is covered, and **beware of hidden costs.** Are taxes, tips, and service charges included? Transfers and baggage handling? Entertainment and excursions? These can add up.

Prices for packages and tours are usually quoted per person, based on two sharing a room. If traveling solo, you may be required to pay the full double-occupancy rate. Some operators eliminate this surcharge if you agree to be matched with a roommate of the same sex, even if one is not found by departure time.

GROUP TOURS

Among companies that sell tours to Austria, the following are nationally known, have a proven reputation, and offer plenty of options. The classifications used below represent different price categories, and you'll probably encounter these terms when talking to a travel agent or tour operator. The key difference is usually in accommodations, which run from budget to better, and better-yet to best. Note that each company doesn't schedule tours to Austria every year; check by calling.

➤ SUPER-DELUXE: **Abercrombie & Kent** (✉ 1520 Kensington Rd., Oak

Brook, IL 60521-2141, ☎ 630/954–2944 or 800/323–7308, FAX 630/954–3324). **Travcoa** (✉ Box 2630, 2350 S.E. Bristol St., Newport Beach, CA 92660, ☎ 714/476–2800 or 800/992–2003, FAX 714/476–2538).

➤ DELUXE: **Globus** (✉ 5301 S. Federal Circle, Littleton, CO 80123-2980, ☎ 303/797–2800 or 800/221–0090, FAX 303/347–2080). **Maupintour** (✉ 1515 St. Andrews Dr., Lawrence, KS 66047, ☎ 785/843–1211 or 800/255–4266, FAX 785/843–8351). **Tauck Tours** (✉ Box 5027, 276 Post Rd. W, Westport, CT 06881-5027, ☎ 203/226–6911 or 800/468–2825, FAX 203/221–6866).

➤ FIRST-CLASS: **Brendan Tours** (✉ 15137 Califa St., Van Nuys, CA 91411, ☎ 818/785–9696 or 800/421–8446, FAX 818/902–9876). **Caravan Tours** (✉ 401 N. Michigan Ave., Chicago, IL 60611, ☎ 312/321–9800 or 800/227–2826, FAX 312/321–9845). **Collette Tours** (✉ 162 Middle St., Pawtucket, RI 02860, ☎ 401/728–3805 or 800/340–5158, FAX 401/728–4745). **DER Travel Services** (✉ 9501 W. Devon Ave., Rosemont, IL 60018, ☎ 800/937–1235, FAX 847/692–4141; 800/282–7474; 800/860–9944 for brochures). **Gadabout Tours** (✉ 700 E. Tahquitz Canyon Way, Palm Springs, CA 92262-6767, ☎ 619/325–5556 or 800/952–5068). **Trafalgar Tours** (✉ 11 E. 26th St., New York, NY 10010, ☎ 212/689–8977 or 800/854–0103, FAX 800/457–6644).

➤ BUDGET: **Cosmos** (Globus: ✉ 5301 S. Federal Circle, Littleton, CO 80123-2980, ☎ 303/797–2800 or 800/221–0090, FAX 303/347–2080). **Trafalgar Tours** (☞ First Class).

THEME TRIPS

➤ BARGE/RIVER CRUISES: **Abercrombie & Kent** (☞ Group Tours). **KD River Cruises of Europe** (✉ 2500 Westchester Ave., Purchase, NY 10577, ☎ 914/696–3600 or 800/346–6525, FAX 914/696–0833).

➤ BICYCLING: **Backroads** (✉ 801 Cedar St., Berkeley, CA 94710-1800, ☎ 510/527–1555 or 800/462–2848, FAX 510-527–1444). **Butterfield & Robinson** (✉ 70 Bond St., Toronto, Ontario, Canada M5B 1X3, ☎ 416/864–1354 or 800/678–1147, FAX 416/864–0541). **Euro-Bike Tours** (✉ Box

990, De Kalb, IL 60115, ☎ 800/321–6060, FAX 815/758–8851).

➤ CHRISTMAS/NEW YEAR'S: **Annemarie Victory Organization** (✉ 136 E. 64th St., New York, NY 10021, ☎ 212/486–0353, FAX 212/751–3149) is known for its spectacular "New Year's Eve Ball in Vienna" excursion. This highly respected organization has been selling out this tour—which includes deluxe rooms at the Bristol, the Imperial Palace Ball, and a Konzerthaus New Year's Day concert—for 10 years running. In 1996, Annemarie Victory premiered a "Christmas in Salzburg" trip, with rooms at the Goldener Hirsch and a side trip to the Silent Night Chapel in Oberndorf. **Smolka Tours** (✉ 82 Riveredge Rd., Tinton Falls, NJ 07724, ☎ 732/576–8813 or 800/722–0057) has also conducted festive holiday-season tours that included concerts and gala balls.

➤ HIKING/WALKING: **Alpine Adventure Trails Tours** (✉ 322 Pio Nono Ave., Macon, GA 31204, ☎ 912/478–4007). **Mountain Travel-Sobek** (✉ 6420 Fairmount Ave., El Cerrito, CA 94530, ☎ 510/527–8100 or 800/227–2384, FAX 510/525–7710).

➤ MOUNTAIN CLIMBING: **Mountain Travel-Sobek** (☞ Hiking/Walking).

➤ MUSIC: **Dailey-Thorp Travel** (✉ 330 W. 58th St., #610, New York, NY 10019-1817, ☎ 212/307–1555 or 800/998–4677, FAX 212/974–1420). **Smolka Tours** (☞ Christmas/New Year's).

TRAIN TRAVEL

Austrian train service is excellent: it's fast and, for Western Europe, relatively inexpensive, particularly if you take advantage of the discount fares. Trains on the mountainous routes are slow, but no slower than driving, and the scenery is gorgeous!

Austrian Federal Railways trains are identifiable by the letters that precede the train number on the timetables and posters. The IC (InterCity) or EC (EuroCity) trains are fastest, and a supplement of about €5 is included in the price of the ticket. EN trains have sleeping facilities. All tickets are valid without supplement on D (express), E (*Eilzug;* semi-fast), and local trains. You can reserve a seat for €3.40 up until a few hours before departure. Be sure to do this on the main-line trains (Vienna–Innsbruck or Vienna–Graz, for example) at peak holiday times. The EC trains usually have a dining car with fairly good food. The trains originating in Budapest have good Hungarian cooking. Otherwise there is usually a fellow with a cart serving snacks and hot and cold drinks. Most trains are equipped with a card telephone in or near the restaurant car.

Make certain that you inquire about possible supplements payable on-board trains traveling to destinations outside Austria **when you are purchasing your ticket.** Austrians are not generally forthcoming with information, and you might be required to pay a supplement in cash to the conductor while you are on the train. For information, call 05/1717 from anywhere in Austria. Unless you speak German, it's a good idea to have your hotel call for you.

Railroad enthusiasts and those with plenty of time can treat themselves to rides on narrow-gauge lines found all over Austria that amble through Alpine meadows; some even make flower-picking stops in season. A few lines still run under steam power, and steam excursions are increasingly easy to find. Local stations have descriptive brochures with dates, points of origin, and fares.

CLASSES

The difference between first and second class on Austrian trains is mainly a matter of space. First- and second-class sleepers, and couchettes (six to a compartment), are available on international runs, as well as on long trips within Austria. If you're driving and would rather watch the scenery than the traffic, you can put your car on a train in Vienna and accompany it to Salzburg, Innsbruck, Feldkirch, or Villach. You relax in a compartment or sleeper for the trip, and the car is unloaded when you arrive.

DISCOUNT PASSES

To save money, **look into rail passes.** But be aware that if you don't plan to cover many miles you may come out ahead by buying individual tickets.

Austria is one of 17 countries in which you can **use Eurailpasses,** which provide unlimited first-class rail travel, in all of the participating countries, for the duration of the pass. If you plan to rack up the miles, get a standard pass. These are available for 15 days ($572), 21 days ($740), one month ($918), two months ($1,298), and three months ($1,606).

In addition to standard Eurailpasses, **ask about special rail-pass plans.** Among these are the Eurail Youthpass (for those under age 26), the Eurail Saverpass (which gives a discount for two or more people traveling together), a Eurail Flexipass (which allows a certain number of travel days within a set period), the Euraildrive Pass, and the Europass Drive (which combines travel by train and rental car). Whichever pass you choose, remember that you must **purchase your pass before you leave** for Europe.

Many travelers assume that rail passes guarantee them seats on the trains they wish to ride. Not so. You need to **book seats ahead even if you are using a rail pass**; seat reservations are required on some European trains, particularly high-speed trains, and are a good idea on trains that may be crowded—particularly in summer on popular routes. You will also need a reservation if you purchase sleeping accommodations.

Another option that gives you discount travel through various countries is the European East Pass, good for travel within Austria, the Czech Republic, Hungary, Poland, and Slovakia: cost is about $154 for any five days unlimited travel within a one-month period.

The ÖBB, the Austrian rail service, offers a large number of discounts for various travel constellations. If you are traveling with a group of people, even small, there are percentages taken off for each member. Families can also get discounts. Schoolchildren and students also get good deals. The Vorteilscard is valid for a year and costs €94, allowing 45% fare reduction on all rail travel. If you are planning lots of travel in Austria, it could be a good deal. Ask for other special deals, and check travel agencies. Children between 6 and 15 travel at half price, under 6 years of age for free.

You can buy an Austrian Rail Pass in the United States for travel within Austria for 15 days ($154 first class, $104 second class). It's available for purchase in Austria also, but only at travel agencies.

For €25.40 and a passport photo, women over 60 and men over 65 can obtain a Seniorenpass, which carries a 45% discount on rail tickets. The pass also has a host of other benefits, including reduced-price entry into museums. Most rail stations can give you information.

Travelers under 26 should inquire about discount fares under the Billet International Jeune (BIJ). The special one-trip tickets are sold by Eurotrain International, travel agents, and youth-travel specialists, and at rail stations.

➤ INFORMATION AND PASSES: **CIT Tours Corp** (⊠ 15 W. 44th St., 10th floor, New York, NY 10036, ☎ 212/730–2400; 800/248–7245 in the United States; 800/387–0711; 800/361–7799 in Canada). **DER Travel Services** (⊠ 9501 W. Devon Ave., Rosemont, IL 60018, ☎ 800/782–2424, ℻ 800/282–7474 for information). **Rail Europe** (⊠ 500 Mamaroneck Ave., Harrison, NY 10528, ☎ 914/682–5172 or 800/438–7245, ℻ 800/432–1329; ⊠ 2087 Dundas E, Suite 106, Mississauga, Ontario L4X 1M2, ☎ 800/361–7245, ℻ 905/602–4198).

FARES AND SCHEDULES

For train schedules, ask at your hotel or stop in at the train station and look for large posters labeled ABFAHRT (departures) and ANKUNFT (arrivals). In the Abfahrt listing you'll find the departure time in the main left-hand block of the listing and, under the train name, details of where it stops en route and the time of each arrival. There is also information about connecting trains and buses, with departure details. Workdays are symbolized by two crossed hammers, which means that the same schedule might not apply on weekends or holidays. A

little rocking horse means that a special playpen has been set up for children in the train. Women traveling alone may book special compartments on night trains or long-distance rides (ask for a *Damenabteilung*).

FROM THE UNITED KINGDOM

There's a choice of rail routes to Austria, but check services first; long-distance passenger service across the Continent is undergoing considerable reduction. There is daily service from London to Vienna via the *Austria Nachtexpress*. Check other services such as the *Orient Express*. If you don't mind changing trains, you can travel via Paris, where you change stations to board the overnight *Arlberg Express* via Innsbruck and Salzburg to Vienna. First- and second-class sleepers and second-class couchettes are available as far as Innsbruck.

When you have the time, a strikingly scenic route to Austria is via Cologne and Munich; after an overnight stop in Cologne you take the *EuroCity Express Johann Strauss* to Vienna.

➤ INFORMATION AND RESERVATIONS: Contact **Eurotrain** (⊠ 52 Grosvenor Gardens, London SW1W OAG, ☎ 020/7730–3402), which offers excellent deals for those under 26, or **British Rail Travel Centers** (☎ 020/7834–2345). For additional information, call **DER Travel Service** (☎ 020/7408–0111) or the **Austrian National Tourist Office** (☞ Visitor Information).

TRAVEL AGENCIES

A good travel agent puts your needs first. Look for an agency that has been in business at least five years, emphasizes customer service, and has someone on staff who specializes in your destination. In addition, **make sure the agency belongs to a professional trade organization.** The American Society of Travel Agents (ASTA), with more than 24,000 members in some 140 countries, is the largest and most influential in the field. Operating under the motto "Integrity in Travel," it maintains and enforces a strict code of ethics and will step in to help mediate any agent-client disputes if necessary. ASTA also maintains a Web site that includes a directory of agents. (If a travel agency is also acting as your tour operator, *see* Buyer Beware *in* Tours and Packages.)

➤ LOCAL AGENT REFERRALS: **American Society of Travel Agents** (ASTA; ☎ 800/965–2782 24-hr hot line, FAX 703/739–3268, WEB www.astanet. com). **Association of British Travel Agents** (✉ 68–71 Newman St., London W1P 4AH, ☎ 020/7637–2444, FAX 020/7637–0713, information@abta.co.uk, WEB www. abtanet.com). **Association of Canadian Travel Agents** (✉ 1729 Bank St., Suite 201, Ottawa, Ontario K1V 7Z5, ☎ 613/521–0474, FAX 613/521–0805, acta.ntl@sympatico.ca, WEB www.acta.ca). **Australian Federation of Travel Agents** (✉ Level 3, 309 Pitt St., Sydney 2000, ☎ 02/9264–3299, FAX 02/9264–1085, WEB www.afta.com. au). **Travel Agents' Association of New Zealand** (✉ Box 1888, Wellington 6001, ☎ 04/499–0104, FAX 04/499–0827, taanz@tiasnet.co.nz).

VISITOR INFORMATION

➤ AUSTRIAN NATIONAL TOURIST OFFICES: **In the United States:** (✉ 500 5th Ave., 20th floor, New York, NY 10110, ☎ 212/944–6880, FAX 212/730–4568, or write to ✉ Box 1142, New York, NY 10108). **In Canada:** (✉ 2 Bloor St. E, Suite 3330, Toronto, Ontario M4W 1A8, ☎ 416/967–3381, FAX 416/967–4101; ✉ 1010 Sherbrooke St. W, Suite 1410, Montréal, Québec H3A 2R7, ☎ 514/849–3709, FAX 514/849–9577; ✉ 200 Granville St., Suite 1380, Granville Sq., Vancouver, BC V6C 1S4, ☎ 604/683–5808 or 604/683–8695, FAX 604/662–8528). **In the U.K.:** (✉ 30 St. George St., London W1R 0AL, ☎ 020/7629–0461; WEB www.anto.com).

➤ U.S. GOVERNMENT ADVISORIES: **U.S. Department of State** (✉ Overseas Citizens Services Office, Room 4811 N.S., 2201 C St. NW, Washington, DC 20520, ☎ 202/647–5225 interactive hot line or 888/407–4747, WEB www.travel.state.gov); enclose a business-size SASE.

WEB SITES

Do check out the World Wide Web when you're planning. You'll find everything from up-to-date weather forecasts to virtual tours of famous cities. Fodor's Web site, www.fodors. com, is a great place to start your on-line travels—just search for the Vienna miniguide, then search for "Links." For basic information: Vienna (info.wien.at); Burgenland (www.burgenland-tourism.co.at); and Upper Austria (www.tiscover. com/upperaustria). For train information: (www.oebb.at).

For Vienna, here are some top Web sites: Wien Online—the city's official Web site (www.magwien.gv.at); Vienna Scene—the Vienna Tourist Board Web site (www.austria-tourism.com); Wienerzeitung—the city's leading newspaper Web site (www. wienerzeitung.at); Time Out Vienna (www.timeout.com/vienna/index. html); Vienna tickets (www. viennaticket.at/english).

WHEN TO GO

Austria has two main tourist seasons. The weather usually turns glorious around Easter to mark the start of the summer season and holds until about mid-October, sometimes later. Because much of the country remains "undiscovered," you will usually find crowds only in the major cities and resorts. May and early June, September, and October are the most pleasant months for travel; there is less demand for restaurant tables, and hotel prices tend to be lower.

A foreign invasion takes place between Christmas and New Year's Day, at which time many Viennese are already on the slopes of western Austria, and over the long Easter weekend, and hotel rooms in Vienna are at a premium. July and August and the main festivals are crowded times, but again, the Viennese head out for their vacations, so the city itself is relatively calm.

CLIMATE

Austria has four distinct seasons, all fairly mild. But because of altitudes and the Alpine divide, temperatures and dampness vary considerably from one part of the country to another; for example, northern Austria's winter is often overcast and dreary, while the southern half of the country basks in sunshine. The eastern part of the country, especially Vienna and the areas near the Czech border, can become bitterly cold in winter thanks to Continental influence.

The *Föhn* is a wind that makes the country as a whole go haywire. It comes from the south, is warm, and announces itself by very clear air, blue skies, and long wisps of cloud. Whatever the reason, the Alpine people (all the way to Vienna) begin acting up; some become obnoxiously aggressive, others depressive, many people have headaches, and (allegedly) accident rates rise. The Föhn breaks with clouds and rain.

➤ FORECASTS: **Weather Channel Connection** (☎ 900/932–8437), 95¢ per minute from a Touch-Tone phone.

The following are average monthly maximum and minimum temperatures for Vienna:

Jan.	34F	1C	May	66F	19C	Sept.	68F	20C
	25	− 4		50	10		52	11
Feb.	37F	3C	June	73F	23C	Oct.	57F	14C
	27	− 3		57	14		45	7
Mar.	46F	8C	July	77F	25C	Nov.	45F	7C
	34	1		59	15		37	3
Apr.	59F	15C	Aug.	75F	24C	Dec.	37F	3C
	43	6		59	15		30	− 1

1 DESTINATION: VIENNA AND THE DANUBE VALLEY

BEYOND THE SCHLAG

TODAY'S AUSTRIA—AND IN PARTIC-
ULAR its capital, Vienna—reminds
some observers of a formerly fat
man who is now at least as gaunt as the
rest of us but still allows himself a lot of
room and expects doors to open wide
when he goes through them. After losing
two world wars and surviving amputation,
annexation, and occupation, a nation that
once ruled Europe now endures as a tourist
mecca and a neutralized, somewhat balka-
nized republic.

Still, there are oases of perfection, such as
those Sunday mornings from September
to June when—if you've reserved months
in advance—you can hear (but not see)
those "voices from heaven," the Vienna
Boys Choir, sing mass in the marble-and-
velvet royal chapel of the Hofburg. Lads
of 8 to 13 in sailor suits, they peal out an-
gelic notes from the topmost gallery, and
you might catch a glimpse of them after
mass as you cut across the Renaissance
courtyard for the 10:45 performance of
the Lipizzaner stallions in the Spanish
Riding School around the corner. Beneath
crystal chandeliers in a lofty white hall,
expert riders in brown uniforms with gold
buttons and black hats with gold braid put
these aristocrats of the equine world
through their classic paces.

Just past noon, when the Spanish Riding
School lets out, cross the Michaelerplatz
and stroll up the Kohlmarkt to No. 14:
Demel's, the renowned and lavish pastry
shop founded shortly after 1848 by the
court confectioner. It was an instant success with those privileged to dine with
the emperor, for not only was Franz Josef
a notoriously stodgy and paltry eater, but,
when he stopped eating, protocol dic-
tated that all others stop, too. Dessert at
Demel's became a must for hungry higher-
ups. Today's Demel's features a flawless
midday buffet offering venison en croûte,
chicken in pastry shells, beef Wellington,
meat tarts, and frequent warnings to
"leave room for the desserts."

Closer to the less costly level of everyday
existence, my family and I would lay on
a welcoming meal for visitors just off

plane or train: a freshly baked slab of
Krusti Brot to be spread with *Liptauer,* a
piquant paprika cream cheese, and *Kräuter
Gervais,* Austria's answer to cream cheese
and chives, all washed down by a youngish
white wine. Such simple pleasures as a jug
of wine, a loaf of bread, and a spicy cheese
or two are what we treasure as Austrian
excellence in democratic days. And if our
visitors really carried on about our wine,
we would take them on the weekend to
the farm it was from, for going to the
source is one of the virtues of living in this
small, unhomogenized land of 7.5 million
people that is modern Austria.

"Is it safe to drink the water?" is still a
question I hear sometimes from visitors
to Vienna. "It's not only safe," I reply, "but
it's recommended." Sometimes they call
back to thank me for the tip. Piped cold
and clean via Roman aqueducts from a
couple of Alpine springs, the city's water
has been rated the best in the world by con-
noisseurs as well as by authorities such as
the Austrian Academy of Sciences and an
international association of solid-waste-
management engineers. Often on a summer evening, when our guests looked as
though a cognac after dinner might be too
heavy, I brought out a pitcher of iced tap
water, and even our Viennese visitors
smacked their lips upon tasting this re-
freshing novelty. But don't bother to try
it in a tavern; except for a few radical
thinkers and the converts I've made, virtually all Viennese drink bottled mineral
water, and few waiters will condescend to
serve you any other kind.

People say that after two decades in Vienna one must feel very Viennese, and
maybe they're right, because here I am chat-
ting about food and drink, which is the
principal topic of Viennese conversation.
So, before leaving the capital for the
provinces, let me call your attention to three
major culinary inventions that were all introduced to Western civilization in Vienna in the watershed year of 1683: coffee,
the croissant, and the bagel.

That was the year the second Turkish
siege of Vienna was at last repelled, when
King Jan Sobieski of Poland and Duke

Charles of Lorraine rode to the rescue, thereby saving the West for Christianity. The sultan's armies left behind their silken tents and banners, some 25,000 dead, and hundreds of huge sacks filled with a mysterious brownish bean. The victorious Viennese didn't know what to make of it—whether to bake, boil, or fry it. But one of their spies, Franz George Kolschitzky, a wheeler-dealer merchant who had traveled in Turkey and spoke the language, had sampled in Constantinople the thick black brew of roasted coffee beans that the Turks called *Kahve*. Though he could have had almost as many sacks of gold, he settled for beans—and opened history's first Viennese coffeehouse. Business was bad, however, until Kolschitzky tinkered with the recipe and experimented with milk, thus inventing the *Mélange*: taste sensation of the 1680s and still the most popular local coffee drink.

While Kolschitzky was roasting his reward, Viennese bakers were celebrating with two new creations that enabled their customers truly to taste victory over the Muslims: a bun curved like a crescent, the emblem of Islam (what Charles of Lorraine might have called *croissant* Austrians call *Kipferl*), and a roll shaped like Sobieski's stirrup, for which the German word was *Bügel*. The invention of the bagel, however, proved less significant, for it disappeared swiftly and totally, only to resurface in America centuries later, along with Sunday brunch.

One would be hard put to tell the sometimes smug and self-satisfied Viennese that Wien (the German name for the capital) is not the navel of the universe, let alone of Austria, but the person who could tell it to him best would be a Vorarlberger. The 305,600 citizens of Austria's westernmost province live as close to Paris as they do to Vienna, which tries to govern them; their capital, Bregenz, is barely an hour's drive from Zürich, but eight or more from Vienna, and the natives sometimes seem more Swiss than Austrian.

The northern reaches of Tirol and the western parts of Upper Austria border on Germany and have a heartier, beerier character than the eastern and southern provinces. (There are nine provinces in all; Vienna, the capital, counts as a state, too, and its mayor is also a governor.) Al-

though the glittering city of Salzburg, capital of rugged Salzburg Province, perches right on the German border, 26 km (16 mi) from Berchtesgaden, Austrian traditions, folk customs and costumes, and the music of native son Mozart flourish there as nowhere else in the country—revered and cherished, revived and embroidered.

Austria borders not just on Germany and Switzerland but also on Liechtenstein, Italy, Slovenia, the Czech Republic, Slovakia, and Hungary. In Austria's greenest province, Styria, one side of the road is sometimes in Slovenia, and you're never far from Hungary or Italy. Styria is so prickly about its independence, even from Austria, that it maintains its own embassies in Vienna and Washington. It is the source of Schilcher, Austria's best rosé wine, which you almost never see in Viennese restaurants. A few years ago, at a farmhouse near Graz, the Styrian capital, I was sipping some Schilcher that went with some wonderful lamb. "Where is this lamb from?" I asked my host.

"Right here," he replied. "Styrian lamb wins all kinds of prizes."

"Then why can't we find it in Vienna?" I wondered. "When we do get lamb, it comes all the way from New Zealand and costs a fortune."

"That's because we don't grow lambs or Schilcher for export," he replied, dead serious.

The influx and tastes of Balkan and Turkish workers have made lamb cheaper and plentiful all over Austria, and now, since the crumbling of the Iron Curtain, Austria is reluctantly becoming even more of a melting pot than it was in the days of the Habsburg empire. The province of Burgenland used to be part of Hungary, and it retains much of its Magyar character in villages where you open a door and find, instead of a courtyard, a whole street full of steep-roofed houses, people, and life. Burgenland also boasts a culturally active Croatian minority, while Carinthia, Austria's southernmost province, has a proud Slovenian minority that is still fighting for the legal right not to Germanize the names of its villages.

The ultimate identity problem, however, belonged until recently to the province of Lower Austria, which is neither low nor south but takes its name from the part of the Danube it dominates on the map. Before 1986, Lower Austria had no capital city; its state offices were scattered around Vienna, the metropolis it envelops with forest. Upon its selection as the provincial seat, the small city of St. Pölten, with a core of lovely churches and cloisters that swirl around you like a baroque ballet, danced onto the map of tourist destinations.

Any day of the year, you can take an express train at Vienna's Westbahnhof for an 8-hour, 770-km (480-mi) east–west crossing of most of the country. One thing remains certain, however. Travel to as many towns as you wish and you will "see" Austria, but you won't fully understand it. To do that, you must get to know Vienna itself.

— Alan Levy

WHAT'S WHERE

Poised in the heart of the continent, Austria is as topographically diverse as it is historically wealthy. Although it is one of Europe's smallest countries, Austria manages to pack within its borders as many mountains, lakes, and picturesque cities as countries five times its size. Happily, many of Austria's most memorable destinations are centered in Vienna province and the Danube Valley.

Vienna

Think of Vienna and you think of operettas and psychoanalysis, Apfelstrudel and marble staircases, Strauss waltzes and Schubert melodies. Baroque and imperial, it goes without saying that the city has an old-world charm—a fact that the natives are both ready to acknowledge and yet hate being reminded of. Today, Vienna is a white-gloved yet modern metropolis, a place where Andrew Lloyd Webber's *Phantom of the Opera* plays in the same theater that premiered Mozart's *Magic Flute*. A walk through the city's neighborhoods—many dotted with masterpieces of Gothic, baroque, and Secessionist architecture—offers a fascinating journey thick with history and peopled by the spirits of Empress Maria Theresa, Haydn, Beethoven, Metternich, Mozart, and Klimt.

Most visitors start along the Ringstrasse, the grand boulevard that surrounds the inner city, whose broad sweep grandly evokes the imperial era of Strauss, Metternich, and emperor Franz Josef during the cultural heyday of the Austro Hungarian empire. Here you'll find great art treasures, magnificent spectacles at Austria's finest opera house, and the Hofburg, Vienna's gigantic Imperial Palace. Even within the shadow of the city's spiritual heart—the great Stephansdom cathedral (which leads off the massive roll call of dazzling Gothic and baroque churches in the city)—Vienna comes alive during the "Merry Season"—the first two months of the year—when raised trumpets and opera capes adorn its great Fasching balls; then more than ever, Vienna moves in three-quarter time. Café Hawelka and the city's other famous coffeehouses—of which Vienna is said to have more than Switzerland has banks—are havens in which to share gossip, read, and conduct a little business, but most of all to engage in the age-old coffee drinking ritual that every dutiful Viennese observes daily.

Pomp, circumstance, and no small amount of innovation hold sway in Vienna's 90 museums and its hundreds of houses of worship and other landmarks. The city's vast holdings range from the Brueghels, Rembrandts, Vermeers, and other treasures in the Kunsthistorisches Museum to the magnificent National Library, where rare manuscripts are as lovingly showcased as the rooms' splendid frescoes. Travelers in search of Imperial Vienna will find no dearth of Habsburgian opulence throughout the city: there's Schönbrunn Palace, in whose Grand Salon the Congress of Vienna celebrated the defeat of Napoléon; there's the Imperial Palace known as the Hofburg, where the Lipizzaner horses of Spanish Riding School fame still prance to a measured cadence, just as they did when pulling emperor Franz Josef's royal carriage; and then there's the Karlskirche. This baroquely ornate church looks, especially when illuminated at night, like a magical vision, although, to the architectural purists who first denounced its Trajan columns, it seemed a bad dream. The baroque love of ornament for ornament's sake hit a chord with the Viennese—almost two centuries later, they embraced the Jugendstil style. Top visionary in this group was Gustav Klimt, among the first to shock turn-of-the-20th-century Vienna with his luxuriously nontraditional paintings. His greatest masterpiece, *The Kiss* is today housed in truly regal splendor in the Belvedere Palace museum—a masterwork witness to an artistic bravado soon emulated by legions of other painters and architects. In our own age, that honor has been bestowed on Friedensreich Hundertwasser, whose Hundertwasserhaus has, until recently, become the city's most outrageous, antitraditional structure. Today, the modernist laurels have been shifted to the gigantic new Museums-Quartier complex, home to several fabled modern art collections and housed in a striking combination of baroque and minimalist structures.

Thanks to the great musicians and composers who, at times, made Vienna their own, travelers are quite likely to approach the city with a song in their heart. The Vienna of the past has inspired some of the world's most beautiful music, from Beethoven's *Pastoral Symphony* to Johann Strauss the Younger's "Blue Danube Waltz." As a traveler soon discovers, these and other ineffable strains are heard nonstop in the Vienna of the present as well. In fact, monuments commemorating many of the musical geniuses who have lived here are to be found throughout the city in various forms. Check out the bust of Mozart in the Figarohaus, one of the composer's many residences in the city, where he wrote some of his most famous works; pay your respects at the Pasqualatihaus, which was Beethoven's address when he composed *Fidelio,* his only opera; and tip your hat to the merrily gilded statue of Johann Strauss II in the Stadtpark. Chances are that somewhere nearby an orchestra or an opera company or a church organist will be performing the works of these great men; the city is, after all, home to two of the world's greatest symphony orchestras (the Vienna Philharmonic and the Vienna Symphony) and is graced with a top opera house (the Staatsoper) as well as a world-renowned concert hall (the Musikverein). Head for the Theater an der Wien to hear beloved operettas (*Die Fledermaus* and *The Merry Widow* both premiered here) or to the Volksoper. Amble into the Gothic interior of the Augustinerkirche any Sunday morning and you may have the pleasure of hearing its mighty organ accompany a high mass oratorio by Mozart or Haydn.

Unfortunately, a seat at the Philharmonic's famous New Year's Eve concert is harder to come by, much. Equally prized is a ticket to the annual Opernball at the Staatsoper; if you do manage to snag one, and if you are one of those romantic souls for whom the mere mention of Vienna conjures up images of hand kissing, deep bows, and white-tied men twirling white-gloved women across the floor, you may think you've died and ascended into heaven—to the accompaniment of a waltz, of course.

Vienna Environs

The Viennese take their leisure seriously. Fortunately, there is a plethora of opportunities for them to indulge their pleasure-seeking natures, for they live in a city surrounded with enticing places to hike, plunge into natural thermal baths, and, perhaps best of all, sip a glass of Riesling wine. The Vienna Woods—the Wienerwald—march right from the city's outskirts south to the Alps and across rolling hills sprinkled with dense woods, vineyards, and the occasional palace. The only dark patch in this otherwise blessed terrain is Mayerling, where emperor Franz Josef built a Carmelite convent on the site where Rudolf, his only son, and Marie Vetsera met an untimely end (lovers' pact or political intrigue—to this day, no one really knows). Of more interest to the Viennese out for an idyllic getaway is Gumpoldskirchen, the tiny village with the big reputation for producing one of Europe's most famous white wines. Tempting as it may be to linger over a glass or two at one of its vintners' houses, press on into the romantic countryside north and west of Vienna. The vines are even thicker in the Weinviertel (the Wine District), and the forests even denser in the Waldviertel (the Forest District).

The Danube Valley

The famously blue Danube courses through Austria on its way from the Black Forest to the Black Sea, past medieval abbeys, fanciful baroque monasteries, verdant pastures, and compact riverside villages. Though the river's hue is now somewhat less than pristine, this is still one of Europe's most important waterways, and to traverse its scenic length is to immerse yourself with a heady dose of history and culture, and, of course, to enjoy some pleasant scenery while doing so. Hereabouts, legends and myths stoke the imagination. In enchantingly picturesque Dürnstein, Richard the Lion-Hearted spent a spell locked in a dungeon. Not far away, the Nibelungs—immortalized by Wagner—caroused at the top of their lungs in battlemented forts. The Danube is liquid history, and you can enjoy drifting eight hours downriver in a steamer or—even better—traveling 18 hours upriver against the current.

Along the way you discover the the storybook Gothic market town of Steyr, where Anton Bruckner composed his Sixth Symphony. For 10 years he was the organist at the neighboring Abbey of St. Florian, where he is buried; his organ still fills the high-ceilinged church with its rich, sorrowful notes. Krems, founded just over 1,000 years ago, is another delightful spot, where wine is the main business of the day. For nonpareil splendor, head to nearby Melk Abbey, best appreciated in the late afternoon when the setting sun lights the twin towers cradling its baroque dome. Inside, its magnificent library was the real-life setting of Umberto Eco's novel *The Name of the Rose*. In addition to Melk, the Wachau valley—"crown jewel of the Austrian landscape"—includes the robber castles of Studen and Werfenstein. A convenient base point is Linz, Austria's third-largest city (and its most underrated): its Old Town is filled with architectural treasures, glockenspiel chimes, and pastry shops that offer the best Linzertortes around. The town is right on the Danube, which, if you catch it on a bright summer day, takes on the proper shade of Johann Strauss *blau*.

PLEASURES AND PASTIMES

Mozart Mania

Had you been in Innsbruck on August 13, 1993, you would have had a most graphic illustration of what music is to Austria. Suddenly all 23 church spires of the city started pealing away. It was a "city concert" for all the town's bells by the Spanish composer Llorenc Barber. It can happen in Austria: you're walking along thinking of nothing special, and you are suddenly hearing a concert, a recital, an orchestra rehearsing, a soprano going through her

scales. You can sit in the Mirabellgarten in Salzburg enjoying coffee and cake, and listen to the opera singers rehearsing. You can be swimming in the Wörther See in Carinthia and 20 minutes later attending a Brahms recital in Pörtschach, where the great romantic composer spent time (and wrote his Fourth Symphony). That's musical Austria.

It's not only Mozart whose music pours from churches and concert halls, even from the instruments of street musicians—it's music in general that seems to be the spiritual fuel of the country. Wherever you go in Austria, you'll be confronted with classical, jazz, pop, folk, techno, punk, you name it. In summer, if you can't afford the prices of Salzburg and have not packed your best threads, then go to the more congenial Bregenz music festival, or explore the innumerable offerings of the Carinthian Summer in Ossiach.

As for Vienna itself, no city can boast such a roster of fine composers and performers. From the huge empire and beyond, they poured in in droves (assuming they were not born there)—the better known being Mozart (naturally), Beethoven, Schubert, Haydn, Johannes Brahms, Mahler, Richard Strauss, Johann Strauss the Younger (no relation), and Arnold Schönberg.

Schnitzels, Strudels, and Sachertortes

Food in Austria is extremely varied. All the gastronomic traditions of the old empire have left their mark here, so be prepared for genuine Hungarian *pörkölt* (what we call goulash) and *lecsó* (red pepper and tomato stew), and for divine Bohemian desserts. The *Palatschinken* are originally Hungarian as well, thin pancakes that can be stuffed around chocolate, marmalade, or a farmer's-cheese stuffing (*Topfen*). Serb *cevapcici* (kebabs) and *rasnici* also appear on menus with fair frequency, even in Austrian establishments, as does *Serbische Bohnensuppe,* a mighty Serb bean soup.

The national gastronomy itself includes lean spareribs and heavy-caliber bread or potato dumplings (also a Bohemian legacy) mixed with bacon or liver or stuffed with anything from cracklings (*Grammel*) to apricots (*Marillen*). In Carinthia (and to an extent in Burgenland), you should try

Sterz (also called polenta), filling and healthful cornmeal dishes that have roots in Italy and Slovenia as well. From western Austria comes *Kaiserschmarrn,* the "emperor's nonsense" eaten with cranberry jam. The Styrians have their salads, goat's and sheep's cheeses, their various soups, garlic soup, pumpkin soup (*Kürbiskremsuppe*), and a basic soup of meat and root vegetables (*Wurzelfleisch*). In some friendly country *Heuriger* in Lower Austria you can try blood sausage; *Blunz'n,* with mashed potatoes; or the standard *Schweinsbraten,* pork roast. And there is more: the famous *Wienerschnitzel* (veal scallop, breaded, deep-fried in fresh oil); *Schinkenfleckerl* (broad flat noodles with ham—a Bohemian recipe), and the cheap but delicious *Beuschl* (lung and heart of beef in a thick sauce always served with a giant Knödel). *Tafelspitz mit Kren* is boiled beef fillet with horseradish.

Venison (*Wild*) is a specialty that crosses restaurant class boundaries. A nice *Rehrücken mit Serviettenknödel* (saddle of deer with a bread dumpling cooked wrapped in cloth) at a four-star establishment is something to write home about. By the same token, you may find a robust *Gamsgulasch* (chamois goulash) in a rustic little hut near the summit of a Styrian mountain, or excellent smoked sausages and hams being offered by a Carinthian *Almbauer* at a few tables outside his summer farm in the mountains.

You need not go thirsty on your travels either. Austria has excellent water, which can be drunk from the tap or straight from the spring at times, and that, good brewers will tell you, makes for excellent beer. Murau in Styria has a top brewery, with a fine restaurant attached. Some swear by Vienna's own Ottakringer. All the orchards in the country also make for terrific fruit juices. The new kid on the block for the past few years is elderberry (*Hollunder*), which comes in dry reds or whites and which—like wine—can be *gespritzt,* mixed with either tap water (*stilles Wasser*) or mineral water (*Mineral*). The *Sommergespritzter* is one-third wine, two-thirds water.

Austria's wines range from good to outstanding. Don't hesitate to ask waiters for advice, even in the simpler restaurants, and as with the food, go for the local wine, if possible. A novelty, if you happen to be traveling around Heiligenbrunn

in Burgenland, is the powerful Uhudler, made of ungrafted vines that originally came from the United States to make European vines resistant to devastating phylloxera. The Austrian government prohibited making it because of its high alcohol content, but after Austria joined the EU in 1995, the prohibition was lifted for fear other European nations would catch on and turn a good penny making this quintessential Austrian wine. For a detailed treatment of regional wine production, *see* the Austrian Wine Regions box, *below.*

Souvenirs, Austrian-Style

Not so long ago, almost any store on Vienna's Kärntnerstrasse could boast that it once created its exquisite jewelry, fine leather goods, or petit-point handbags (as Viennese as St. Stephen's Cathedral) for the imperial Habsburgs. The court has vanished, but the *Hoflieferanten* (court suppliers) still maintain their name and at times the old-fashioned grace, slightly fawning touch, and lots of *Gnä Frau* and *der Herr* thrown in for good measure.

There are various types of souvenirs to take home and enjoy, of course: fine glassware from Riedel's in Kufstein (founded 1756); Swarovski crystal; ceramics from a variety of manufacturers, including Gmunder (from Traun near Salzburg); and Augarten porcelain, Europe's oldest china after Meissen. These wares are distributed throughout the country in large and loud shops in the pedestrian zones of Vienna, Salzburg, Graz, Innsbruck, Klagenfurt, and so on. The same applies to traditional clothing: *Trachten, Lederhosen, Dirndls,* and the like can be purchased at such places as Lanz (Vienna and Salzburg), Geiger (in Salzburg), Giesswein (in Vienna) or by keeping a sharp eye out for the magic word *Trachten* while driving about. You may accidentally stumble over some treasures in small towns such as Tamsweg or Feldkirchen in Carinthia, or run across a farmer's market where honest-to-goodness handmade traditional clothing and ornamentations are being sold alongside sheep, boar, or deer skins, leatherware of all sorts, the best plum schnapps, and elderberry and wild raspberry syrups. As for pottery and crockery, you may prefer to take home some of the cottage-industry ware from Stoob in Burgenland or a set of wooden plates that simply get better by the year. Of course,

AUSTRIAN WINE REGIONS

AUSTRIAN VINTNERS ARE beginning to be taken seriously in the world market after successfully rebounding from the scandal of the mid-1980s, when a few unscrupulous merchants added antifreeze to their wines. And they've gone a long way toward changing the outdated image of the simple, undemanding white of the *Heurige* (wine taverns), usually served *gespritzt* (mixed with seltzer water) and drunk at a picnic table on a hot summer day.

The majority of grapes grown in Austria are still traditional varieties, with 80% of these used for white wines like Grüner Veltliner and Welschriesling. Of the reds, Zweigelt is the most widely grown; Blaufränkisch is capable of greater complexity; and Blauer Portugieser produces pleasant, softer wines. But wine growers are becoming more venturesome and are experimenting with chardonnay, Riesling, pinot noir, and cabernet sauvignon.

There are five major wine-growing regions: the Wachau, which encompasses the lush Danube Valley west of Vienna; the Weinviertel (Wine Quarter), extending from the area north of Vienna to the Czech border; Burgenland, the province east of Vienna that was formerly part of Hungary; and southern Styria, bordering on Slovenia and reminiscent of Tuscany with its sweetly rolling hills. Within the city limits of Vienna itself are a number of family-owned vineyards that maintain their own Heurige.

Each wine region has its own character. Burgenland and southern Styria have warmer climates, which make for full-bodied red wines, whereas the Wachau's cool climate is tempered by the Danube River and produces more Germanic, Rhine-style whites. The Weinviertel boasts of having the least rainfall and most sunny days of all the wine-growing regions in Austria, and it has been producing wine since the Middle Ages.

Burgenland consists of two different territories: the hilly, wooded southern area and the flatlands around the vast Neusiedlersee (Lake Neusiedl), including Carnuntum, where vineyards were established as early as Celtic and Roman times. This is red wine country, famous for its Zweigelt and Blaufränkisch, and it also produces some very good dessert wines.

Though southern Styria is also blessed with a warm climate, it produces a great number of white wines as well as red. Chardonnay is rich and full-bodied here, and you will also find the spicy, fragrant Traminer and Welchriesling, the most common varietal in Styria. But Styrians swear by their Schilcher, a tart, peach-colored rosé that is unique to the region.

The Wachau produces light, fruity white wines, most notably Grüner Veltliner and Riesling, as well as some of the country's best Sekt (sparkling wine); the Kamptal, set back from the river, makes the area's best reds. The Weinviertel is also known principally for light, fresh whites, but interesting things are being done with chardonnay and Weiss Grau Burgunder (pinot gris).

Austrian wines have been steadily improving for the last decade, and the long, hot summer of 1997 produced one of the best vintages of the century. It's a perfect time to start sampling their charms.

— Bonnie and Gary Dodson

sipping a cooled Schilcher on a warm summer evening on your porch at home may be the best way of remembering a terrific trip to Austria.

FODOR'S CHOICE

No two people agree on what makes a perfect vacation, but it's fun and helpful to know what others think. Here's a compendium from the must-see lists of hundreds of Austrian travelers. For detailed information about these memories-in-the-making, refer to the appropriate chapters in this book.

Quintessential Austria

New Year's Day concert in Vienna's Musikverein. You've seen it on television, but now you're *here* in the Golden Hall—its gilt bare-breasted ladies supporting the balconies, the walls festooned with floral displays—sharing in the excitement of a Vienna Philharmonic concert seen and heard by millions around the world.

Waltzing around the clock at a Fasching ball. Whether you go to the Opera Ball or the Zuckerbäckerball (sponsored by pastry cooks), remember that gala etiquette states that a gentleman can kiss only a lady's hand.

Taking a boat through the Wachau on the Danube. The vineyards are glowing in all fall colors or the apricot and cherry trees are in bloom. Spring or fall or warm breezy summer, the setting sun always makes the villages radiate, and the great baroque monastery of Melk seems like poured gold.

The Lipizzaner stallions at the Spanish Riding School. Where else can you see horses dance to a Mozart minuet? For sheer elegance, the combination of the chestnut-colored riding habits of the trainers and the pure white of the horses' coats can't be beat.

Viewing Vienna from the Leopoldsberg. The metropolis sprawls on a plain embraced on the one side by hills, traversed on the other by the flows and canals of the Danube, its barges like toys. Every detail of the city is visible on a clear day, the great Ferris wheel of the Prater, St. Stephen's Cathedral, the refinery of Schwechat. You can see way into the distance almost all the way to Bratislava.

Driving the Wachau when the apricot trees are in blossom. In spring, the narrow Danube Valley becomes a riot of fruit trees in delicate pastel blossom sweeping up hillsides from the very riverbanks.

Great Hotels

Palais Schwarzenberg, Vienna. It's hard to believe you're in the heart of the city at this secluded hotel, set in its own vast, formal park. Built in the early 1700s, the palace is still privately owned and retains a sense of history while offering luxuriously appointed rooms. Guests are made to feel at home, whether strolling through the gardens or sipping a drink in front of a roaring fire in the drawing room on cold winter nights. *$$$$*

Schloss Dürnstein, Dürnstein. This 17th-century early baroque castle, on a rocky terrace with exquisite views over the Danube, is what memories are made of. The hotel offers classy elegance and comfort, but even if you don't stay here, be sure to stop for a coffee and pastry on the stone balcony. *$$$$*

Sacher, Vienna. One of the most famous hotels in the world, this luxurious 19th-century standby delights all with hallways and bedrooms bearing impressive original artwork, an Old-Vienna ambience, and, of course, that to-die-for Sacher cake. *$$$$*

Altstadt, Vienna. This small hotel was once a patrician home, and it's a gem. The English-style lounge has a fireplace and plump floral sofas, beckoning you to sit and read while sipping a hot toddy. Upper rooms have views out over the city roofline. *$$*

Faust Schlössl, Aschach. As you enter Aschach you're struck by the glimpse of this golden castle perched high on a hill on the opposite bank of the Danube. It's said that the Devil built this golden hilltop castle in a single night for Dr. Faustus—and haunts it still. *$$*

Memorable Restaurants and Cafés

Korso, Vienna. Don't be surprised if you see Domingo or a leading diva at the next table—this famed spot, set in the Bristol Hotel, is across from the Staatsoper, and delights with its delicious wood-paneled walls, beveled glass, tables set with fine linen, sparkling Riedel crystal, fresh flowers, massively baronial fireplace, and Salzkammergut lake trout—grilled and drizzled with a sensational shallot sauce. $$$$

Landhaus Bacher, Mautern. One of the culinary gems of the Danube Valley (on the riverbank opposite Krems), this is the domain of the consistently innovative Lisl Wagner-Bacher. Though the restaurant is famous throughout the country, it is entirely lacking in pretension. In winter, dine in the warm, inviting "Library"; in summer sit outside in the garden under chestnut trees. $$$$

Steirereck, Vienna. In Austria's top restaurant, a cheerfully blazing fire, gleaming sandstone walls, and candlelight create the perfect setting for the chef's contemporary Viennese cuisine. Extra touches include a bread trolley overflowing with freshly baked breads and, at the end of the meal, an outstanding selection of cheeses from Steirereck's own cheese cellar. $$$$

Loibnerhof, Dürnstein. It's hard to imagine a more idyllic setting for a memorable meal, especially if the weather is fine and tables are spread invitingly in the fragrant apple orchard. Across the road is the rolling Danube and high on a craggy hill are the ruins of the castle where Richard the Lion-hearted was once held captive. $$$

Artner, Vienna. Spectacular wines and goat cheese from the Artner Winery in the Carnuntum region east of Vienna are highlighted in this upscale eatery. The food is superb, offering traditional Austrian fare as well as exotic dishes, and it's fun to sample a different wine with each course. $$–$$$

Schickh, Furth bei Göttweig. Tucked away beside a brook and lovely old trees, this rambling yellow restaurant below the north side of Göttweig Abbey in the Danube Valley is worth looking for. Chef Christian Schickh creates new versions of traditional Austrian dishes, sister Eva makes sure everything runs smoothly, and Papa Schickh is proud to have guests try his own brand of schnapps. $$–$$$

Verdi Einkehr, Lichtenberg. The trendy, less pricey bistro (Austrian-style) accompaniment to Verdi, Linz's favored dinner restaurant, Verdi Einkehr shares the same

house and kitchen. The decor is rustic chic, with stone fireplaces, chintz-covered chairs, and lots of polished wood. There is also a terrace overlooking the lushly wooded hills, ideal for summer dining. $$–$$$

Café Central, Vienna. Nothing embodies the spirit of time-stained Viennese café society more than this grand, plush coffeehouse not far from the Hofburg Palace. Trotsky supposedly plotted the Russian Revolution here, using the alias Bronstein. In the late afternoon an all-woman orchestra plays Viennese waltzes. $–$$

Places to Linger

Hauptplatz, Linz. The spacious main square of the Upper Austrian capital has been handsomely restored; church spires rather than skyscrapers shape the skyline. The square is the site for local markets just as it was centuries ago, with many of the same buildings gracing the scene.

Melk Abbey, Lower Austria. Probably the most impressive of Europe's abbeys, Melk perches like a magnificent yellow-frosted wedding cake overlooking the Danube, its ornate library holding rows of priceless treasures. If you can visit only one abbey in all of Europe, Melk should be among the top contenders.

St. Florian's Abbey, Upper Austria. This abbey, where composer Anton Bruckner was organist, is impressive for its sheer size alone. Add to the symmetrical structure the glorious church and the representational rooms, and you have one of Austria's religious highlights.

St. Stephen's Cathedral, Vienna. The country's Catholic life centers on St. Stephen's, rebuilt after burning during the last days of World War II. It is one of Europe's finest Gothic structures, with two different towers, one of which can be climbed on foot; the other has an elevator and holds the *Pummerin,* Austria's largest bell. Like the exterior, the interior of the cathedral is a masterpiece, especially of stone carving.

Schönbrunn, Vienna. Was the palace an excuse for the gardens, or vice versa? The manicured trees, the symmetrical walkways, the discoveries at various intersections— all add to the pleasure of exploration here. Climb to the Gloriette, which now houses a moderately good café, for a sweeping perspective of the gardens and the city beyond.

Steyr, Upper Austria. Wonderfully colorful decorative facades address the main square, brooded over by the castle above. Tiny, half-concealed stairways lead upward to the castle area, and other stone steps take you down the opposite side to the riverbank. The setting is an ensemble worthy of Hollywood; in this case, it's all charmingly real.

2 VIENNA

Magnificent, magnetic, and magical,
Vienna beguiles one and all with its old-
world charm and courtly grace. It is a place
where headwaiters still bow as though
addressing a Habsburg prince, and
Lipizzaner stallions dance their intricate
minuets to the strains of Mozart. Here is a
city that waltzes and works in measured
three-quarter time. Like a well-bred grande
dame, Vienna doesn't rush about, and
neither should you. Saunter through its
stately streets—and rub elbows with the
spirits of Beethoven and Strauss, Metternich
and Freud—and marvel at its baroque
palaces. Then dream an afternoon away
at a cozy *Kaffeehaus*.

Updated by
Bonnie Dodson

PROPER CITIZENS OF VIENNA, it has been said, waltz only from the waist down, holding their upper bodies ramrod straight while whirling around the crowded dance floor. The movement resulting from this correct posture is breathtaking in its sweep and splendor, and its elegant coupling of freewheeling exuberance and rigid formality—of license and constraint—is quintessentially Viennese. The town palaces all over the inner city—built mostly during the 18th century—present in stone and stucco a similar artful synthesis. They make Vienna a baroque city that is, at its best, an architectural waltz.

Those who tour Vienna today might feel they're keeping step in three-quarter time. As they explore churches filled with statues of gilded saints and cheeky cherubs, wander through treasure-packed museums, or take in the delights of a mecca of mocha (the ubiquitous cafés), they may feel destined to enjoy repeated helpings of the beloved *Schlagobers,* the rich, delicious whipped cream that garnishes the most famous Viennese pastry of all, the Sachertorte. The ambience of the city is predominantly ornate: white horses dance to elegant music; snow frosts the opulent draperies of Empress Maria Theresa's monument, set in the formal patterns of "her" lovely square; a gilded Johann Strauss perpetually plays amid a grove of trees; town houses present a dignified face to the outside world while enclosing lavishly decorated interior courtyards; dark Greek legends are declawed by the voluptuous music of Richard Strauss; Klimt's paintings glitter with geometric impasto; a mechanical clock intones the hour with a stately pavane. All these will create in the visitor the sensation of a metropolis that likes to be visited and admired—and which indeed is well worth visiting and admiring.

For centuries, this has been the case. One of the great capitals of Europe, Vienna was for centuries the main stamping grounds of the Habsburg rulers of the Austro-Hungarian Empire. The empire is long gone, but many reminders of the city's imperial heyday remain, carefully preserved by the tradition-loving Viennese. When it comes to the arts, the glories of the past are particularly evergreen, thanks to the cultural legacy created by the many artistic geniuses nourished here.

From the late 18th century on, Vienna's culture—particularly its musical forte—was famous throughout Europe. Haydn, Mozart, Beethoven, Schubert, Brahms, Strauss, Mahler, and Bruckner all lived in the city, composing glorious music still played in concert halls all over the world. And at the tail end of the 19th century the city's artists and architects— Gustav Klimt, Egon Schiele, Oskar Kokoschka, Josef Hoffmann, Otto Wagner, and Adolf Loos among them—brought about an unprecedented artistic revolution, a revolution that swept away the past and set the stage for the radically experimental art of the 20th century. "Form follows function," the artists of the late-19th-century Jugendstil proclaimed. Their echo is still heard in the city's contemporary arts and crafts galleries—even in the glinting, Space Needle–like object that hovers over the north end of Vienna—actually the city's waste incinerator, designed by the late, great artist Friedensreich Hundertwasser.

At the close of World War I the Austro-Hungarian Empire was dismembered, and Vienna lost its cherished status as the seat of imperial power. Its influence was much reduced, and its population began to decline (unlike what happened in Europe's other great cities), falling from around 2 million to 1.8 million. Today, however, the city is growing again, and the future looks brighter, suggesting that Vienna has regained its traditional status as one of the hubs of Central Europe.

For many first-time visitors, the city's one major disappointment concerns the Danube River. The inner city, it turns out, lies not on the river's main course but on one of its narrow offshoots, known as the Danube Canal. As a result, the sweeping river views expected by most newcomers fail to materialize.

For this the Romans are to blame, for when Vienna was founded as a Roman military encampment around AD 100, the walled garrison was built not on the Danube's main stream but rather on the largest of the river's eastern branches, where it could be bordered by water on three sides. The wide, present-day Danube did not take shape until the late 19th century, when, to prevent flooding, its various branches were rerouted and merged.

The Romans maintained their camp for some 300 years (the emperor Marcus Aurelius is thought to have died in Vindobona, as it was called, in 180) not abandoning the site until around 400. The settlement survived the Roman withdrawal, however, and by the 13th century development was sufficient to require new city walls to the south. According to legend, the walls were financed by the English: in 1192 the local duke kidnapped King Richard I (the Lion-Hearted), en route home from the Third Crusade, and held him prisoner in Dürnstein, upriver, for several months, then turning him two years over to the Austrian king, until he was expensively ransomed by his mother, Eleanor of Aquitaine.

Vienna's third set of walls dates from 1544, when the existing walls were improved and extended. The new fortifications were built by the Habsburg dynasty, which ruled the Austro-Hungarian Empire for an astonishing 640 years, beginning with Rudolf I in 1273 and ending with Karl I in 1918. These walls stood until 1857, when Emperor Franz Josef decreed that they finally be demolished and replaced by the series of boulevards that make up the famous tree-lined Ringstrasse.

During medieval times the city's growth was relatively slow, and its heyday as a European capital did not begin until 1683, after a huge force of invading Turks laid siege to the city for a two-month period before being routed by an army of Habsburg allies. Among the supplies that the fleeing Turks left behind were sacks filled with coffee beans, and it was these beans, so the story goes, that gave a local entrepreneur the idea of opening the first public coffeehouse; they remain a Viennese institution to this day.

The passing of the Turkish threat encouraged a Viennese building boom, with the baroque style becoming the architectural choice of the day. Flamboyant, triumphant, joyous, and extravagantly ostentatious, the new art form—imported from Italy—transformed the city into a vast theater over the course of the 17th and 18th centuries. Life became a dream—the gorgeous dream of the baroque, with its gilt madonnas and cherubs; its soaring, twisted columns; its painted heavens on the ceilings; and its graceful domes. In the early 19th century a reaction began to set in—with middle-class industriousness and sober family values leading the way to a new epoch, characterized by the Biedermeier style. Then followed the Strauss era—that lighthearted period that conjures up imperial balls, "Wine, Women, and Song," heel clicking, and hand kissing. Today's visitors will find that each of these eras has left its mark on Vienna, making it a city possessed of a special grace. It is this grace that gives Vienna the cohesive architectural character that sets the city so memorably apart from its great rivals— London, Paris, and Rome.

Pleasures and Pastimes

Café Society

It has been said that there were more cafés and coffeehouses in Vienna than there were banks in Switzerland. Whether or not this can still be claimed, the true flavor of Vienna can't be savored without visiting some of its great café landmarks. Every afternoon at 4, the coffee-and-pastry ritual of *Kaffeejause* takes place from one end of the city to the other. Regulars take their *Stammtisch* (usual table), where they sit until they go home for dinner. And why not? They come to gossip, read the papers, negotiate business, play cards, meet a spouse (or someone else's), or—who knows?—perhaps just have a cup of coffee. Whatever the reason, the Viennese use cafés and coffeehouses as club, pub, bistro, and even a home away from home. (Old-timers recall the old joke: "Pardon me, would you mind watching my seat for a while so I can go out for a cup of coffee?")

In fact, to savor the atmosphere of the coffeehouse, you must allow time. There is no need to worry about outstaying one's welcome, even over a single small cup of coffee—so set aside a morning or afternoon, and take along this book. For historical overtones, head for the Café Central—Lev Bronstein, otherwise known as Leon Trotsky, at one time enjoyed playing chess here. For old-world charm, check out the opulent Café Landtmann, which was Freud's favorite meeting place, or the elegant Café Sacher (famous for its Sachertorte); for the smoky art scene, go to the Café Hawelka. Wherever you end up, never ask for a plain cup of coffee; at the very least, order a Melange *mit Schlag* (with whipped cream) from the *Herr Ober,* or any of many other delightful variations.

The Heurige

It makes for a memorable experience to sit at the edge of a vineyard on the Kahlenberg with a tankard of young white wine and listen to the *Schrammel* quartet playing sentimental Viennese songs. The wine taverns, called *Heurige* (the singular is *Heuriger*) for the new wine that they serve, are very much a part of and typical of the city (although not unique to Vienna). Heurige sprang up in 1784 when Joseph II decreed that owners of vineyards could establish their own private wine taverns; soon the Viennese discovered it was cheaper to go out to the wine than to bring it inside the city walls, where taxes were levied. The Heuriger owner is supposed to be licensed to serve only the produce of his own vineyard, a rule more honored in the breach than the observance (it would take a sensitive palate indeed to differentiate between the various vineyards).

These taverns in the wine-growing districts on the outskirts of the city (in such villages as Neustift am Walde, Sievering, Nussdorf, and Grinzing) vary from the simple front room of a vintner's house to ornate settings. The true Heuriger is open for only a few weeks a year to allow the vintner to sell a certain quantity of his production, tax-free, when consumed on his own premises. The commercial establishments keep to a somewhat more regular season but still sell only wine from their own vines.

The choice is usually between a "new" and an "old" white (or red) wine, but you can also ask for a milder or sharper wine according to your taste. Most Heurige are happy to let you sample the wines before you order. You can also order a *Gespritzter,* half wine and half soda water. The waitress brings the wine, usually in a ¼-liter mug or liter carafe, but you serve yourself from the food buffet. The wine tastes as mild as lemonade, but it packs a punch. If it isn't of good quality, you will know by a raging headache the next day.

Jugendstil Jewels

From 1897 to 1907, the Vienna Secession movement gave rise to one of the most spectacular manifestations of the pan-European style known as art nouveau. Viennese took to calling the look *Jugendstil,* or the "young style." In such dazzling edifices as Otto Wagner's Wienzeile majolica-adorned mansion and Adolf Loos's Looshaus, Jugendstil architects rebelled against the prevailing 19th-century historicism that had created so many imitation Renaissance town houses and faux Grecian temples. Josef Maria Olbrich, Josef Hoffman, and Otto Schönthal took William Morris's Arts and Crafts movement, added dashes of Charles Rennie Mackintosh and flat-surface Germanic geometry, and came up with a luxurious style that shocked turn-of-the-century Viennese traditionalists (and infuriated Emperor Franz Josef). Many artists united to form the Vienna Secession—whose most famous member was painter Gustav Klimt—and the Wiener Werkstätte, which transformed the objects of daily life with a sleek modern look. Today, Jugendstil buildings are among the most fascinating structures in Vienna. The shrine of the movement is the world-famous Secession Building—the work of Josef Maria Olbrich—the cynosure of all eyes on the Friedrichstrasse.

Museums and Marvels

You could spend months perusing the contents of Vienna's 90 museums. Subjects range, alphabetically, from art to wine, and in between are found marvels such as carriages and clocks, memorial dedicatees such as Mozart and martyrs, and oddities such as bricks and burials. If your time is short, the one museum not to be overlooked is the Kunsthistorisches Museum, Vienna's most famous art museum and one of the great museums of the world, with masterworks by Titian, Rembrandt, Vermeer, and Velásquez, and an outstanding collection of Brueghels.

Given a little more time, the Schatzkammer, or Imperial Treasury, is well worth a visit, for its opulent bounty of crown jewels, regal attire, and other trappings of court life. The sparkling new Silberkammer, a museum of court silver and tableware, is fascinating for its "behind-the-scenes" views of state banquets and other elegant representational affairs. The best-known museums tend to crowd up in late-morning and midafternoon hours; you can beat the mobs by going earlier or around the noon hour, at least to the larger museums that are open without a noontime break.

The Sound—and Sights—of Music

What closer association to Vienna is there than music? Boasting one of the world's greatest concert venues (Musikverein), two of the world's greatest symphony orchestras (Vienna Philharmonic and Vienna Symphony), and one of the top opera houses (Staatsoper), it's no wonder that music and the related politics are subjects of daily conversation. During July and August—just in time for tourists—the city hosts the Vienna Summer of Music, with numerous special events and concerts.

For the music-loving tourist who is excited by the prospect of treading in the footprints of the mighty, seeing where masterpieces were committed to paper or standing where a long-loved work was either praised or damned at its first performance, Vienna is tops: the city is saturated with musical history. There is the apartment where Mozart wrote his last three symphonies, the house where Schubert was born, and, just a tram ride away, the path that inspired Beethoven's *Pastoral* Symphony. Just below, you'll find a handy list of these musical landmarks.

Of course, there is also music to delight as well as inspire. The statue of Johann Strauss II in the Stadtpark tells all. To see him, violin tucked under his chin, is to imagine those infectious waltzes, "Wine, Women, and Song," "Voices of Spring," and best of all, the "Emperor." But quite possibly you will not need to imagine them. Chances are, somewhere in the environs, an orchestra will be playing them. Head for the Theater an der Wien to hear great operetta (*Die Fledermaus* and the *Merry Widow* both premiered here) or to the Volksoper. Although the traditional classics are the main fare for the conservative, traditional Viennese, acceptance of modern music is growing, as are the audiences for pop and jazz.

Musicians' residences abound, and many are open as museums. The most famous are Mozart's Figarohaus and Beethoven's Pasqualatihaus, which are discussed in the Exploring sections below. Vienna has many other music landmarks scattered over the city—here's a sample:

Schubert—a native of the city, unlike most of Vienna's other famous composers—was born at Nussdorferstrasse 54 (☎ 01/317–3601, U-Bahn: U2/Schottenring, then Streetcar 37 or 38 to Canisiusgasse), in the 9th District, and died in the **4th District** at Kettenbrückengasse 6 (☎ 01/581–6730, U-Bahn: U4/Kettenbrückengasse). **Joseph Haydn's house,** which includes a Brahms memorial room, is at Haydngasse 19 (☎ 01/596–1307, U-Bahn: U4/Pilgramgasse or U3/Zieglergasse) in the 6th District. **Beethoven's Heiligenstadt residence,** where at age 32 he wrote the "Heiligenstadt Testament," an anguished cry of pain and protest against his ever-increasing deafness, is at Probusgasse 6 in the 19th District (☎ 01/370–5408, U-Bahn: U4/Heiligenstadt, then Bus 38A to Wählamt). All the above houses contain commemorative museums. Admission is €1.80; a block of 10 €1.80 tickets for city museums costs €11.60. All are open Tuesday through Sunday 9–12:15 and 1–4:30. The home of the most popular composer of all, waltz king **Johann Strauss the Younger,** can be visited at Praterstrasse 54 (☎ 01/214–0121, U-Bahn: U4/Nestroyplatz), in the 2nd District; he lived here when he composed "The Blue Danube Waltz" in 1867.

Stepping Out in Three-Quarter Time

Ever since the 19th-century Congress of Vienna—when pundits laughed "*Elle danse, mais elle ne marche pas*" (the city "dances, but it never gets anything done")—Viennese extravagance and gaiety have been world famous. Fasching, the season of Prince Carnival, was given over to court balls, opera balls, masked balls, chambermaids' and bakers' balls, and a hundred other gatherings, many held within the glittering interiors of baroque theaters and palaces. Presiding over the dazzling evening gowns and gilt-encrusted uniforms, towering headdresses, flirtatious fans, *chambres séparées,* "Wine, Women, and Song," *Die Fledermaus,* "Blue Danube," hand kissing and gay abandon, was the baton of the waltz emperor, Johann Strauss. White-gloved women and men in white tie would glide over marble floors to his heavenly melodies. They still do. Now, as in the days of Franz Josef, Vienna's old three-quarter-time rhythm strikes up anew each year during Carnival, from New Year's Eve until Mardi Gras.

During January and February, as many as 40 balls may be held in a single evening, the most famous—some say too famous—being the Opernball. This event transforms the Vienna Opera House into the world's most beautiful ballroom (and transfixes all of Austria when shown live on national television). For a price, theoretically, anyone can attend, but corporate interests often buy up most of the tickets. The invitation to the Opernball reads, "*Frack mit Dekorationen,*" which means that it's time to dust off your Legion of Honor medal and women mustn't wear white (reserved for debutantes). Remember that you must dance the *Linkswalzer*—the counterclockwise, left-turning waltz that is the only correct way to dance in Vienna. After your gala evening, finish off the morning with a *Kater Frühstuck*—a hangover breakfast—of goulash soup.

EXPLORING VIENNA

To the Viennese, the most prestigious address of Vienna's 23 *Bezirke,* or districts, is the 1st District, which comprises the all-important Innere Stadt, or inner city, bounded by the Ringstrasse and the Danube Canal. The vast majority of sightseeing attractions are to be found here. Of course, what is now the 1st District used to encompass the entire city of Vienna. In 1857 Emperor Franz Josef decided to demolish the original ancient wall surrounding the city to create the more cosmopolitan Ringstrasse, the multilane avenue that still encircles the expansive heart of Vienna. At that time, several small villages bordering the inner city were given district numbers and incorporated into Vienna. Today the former villages go by their official district number, but they are still known by their old village or neighborhood name, too. In conversation, the Viennese most often say the number of the district they are referring to, though sometimes they use the neighborhood name instead.

The circular 1st District is bordered on its northeastern section by the Danube Canal and 2nd District, and clockwise from there along the Ringstrasse by the 3rd, 4th, 6th, 7th, 8th, and 9th districts. Across the Danube Canal from the 1st District, the 2nd District—Leopoldstadt—is home to the venerable Prater amusement park, with its famous *Riesenrad* (Ferris wheel), as well as a huge park used for horseback riding and jogging. Along the southeastern edge of the 1st District is the 3rd District—Landstrasse—containing a number of embassies and the famed Belvedere Palace. The southern tip, the 4th District—Wieden—is fast becoming Vienna's new hip area, with trendy restaurants, art galleries, and shops opening up every week, plus Vienna's biggest outdoor market, the Naschmarkt, which is lined with dazzling Jugendstil buildings.

The southwestern 6th District—Mariahilf—includes the biggest shopping street, Mariahilferstrasse, with small, old-fashioned shops competing with smart restaurants, movie theaters, bookstores, and department stores. Directly west of the 1st District is the 7th District—Neubau. Besides the celebrated Kunsthistorisches Museum and headline-making MuseumsQuartier, the 7th District also houses the charming Spittelberg quarter, its cobblestone streets lined with beautifully preserved 18th-century houses. Moving up the western side you come to the 8th District—Josefstadt—which is known for its theaters, good restaurants, and antiques shops. And completing the circle surrounding the Innere Stadt on its northwest side is the 9th District—Alsergrund—once Sigmund Freud's neighborhood and today a nice residential area with lots of outdoor restaurants, curio shops, and lovely early 20th-century apartment buildings.

The other districts—the 5th, and the 10th through the 23rd—form a concentric second circle around the 2nd through 9th districts. These are mainly residential suburbs, and only a few hold sights of interest for tourists. The 11th District—Simmering—contains one of Vienna's new architectural wonders, Gasometer, a former gasworks that has been remodeled into a housing and shopping complex. The 13th District—Hietzing—whose centerpiece is the fabulous Schönbrunn Palace, is also a coveted residential area, including the neighborhood Hütteldorf. The 19th District—Döbling—is Vienna's poshest residential neighborhood and also bears the nickname the "Noble District" because of all the embassy residences on its chestnut-tree-lined streets. The 19th District also incorporates several other neighborhoods within its borders, in particular, the wine villages of Grinzing, Sievering, Nussdorf, and Neustift am Walde. The 22nd District—Donaustadt—now headlines Donau City, a modern business and shopping complex that has grown around the United Nations center. The 22nd also has several grassy spots for swimming and sailboat watching along the Alte Donau (old Danube).

It may be helpful to know the neighborhood names of other residential districts. These are the 5th/Margareten; 10th/Favoriten; 12th/Meidling; 14th/Penzing; 15th/Fünfhaus; 16th/Ottakring; 17th/Hernals; 18th/Währing; 20th/Brigittenau; 21st/Floridsdorf; and 23rd/Liesing. For neighborhood site listings below, information will be given for both the district and neighborhood name, *except* the 1st District, which will not include a neighborhood name.

For hard-core sightseers who wish to supplement the key attractions that follow, the tourist office has a booklet, "Vienna from A–Z" (€3.60), that gives short descriptions of some 250 sights around the city, all numbered and keyed to a fold-out map at the back, as well as to numbered wall plaques on the buildings themselves. Note that the nearest U-Bahn (subway) stop to most city attractions described below is included at the end of the service information (also listed in this chapter's subway system map). The more important churches have coin-operated (€1–€2) tape machines that give an excellent commentary in English on the structure's history and architecture.

Vienna is a city to explore and discover on foot. The description of the city on the following pages is divided into eight areas: seven that explore the architectural riches of central Vienna and an eighth that describes Schönbrunn Palace and its gardens. Above all, *look up* as you tour Vienna: some of the most fascinating architectural and ornamental bits are on upper stories or atop the city's buildings.

Numbers in the text correspond to numbers in the margin and on the Vienna, Hofburg, and Schönbrunn Palace and Park maps.

Great Itineraries

IF YOU HAVE 1 DAY

Touring Vienna in a single day is a proposition as strenuous as it is unlikely, but those with more ambition than time should first get a quick view of the lay of the city by taking a streetcar ride around the Ringstrasse, the wide boulevard that encloses the city's heart. Then spend the time until early afternoon exploring the city center, starting at Vienna's cathedral, the **Stephansdom** ①, followed by a stroll along the Graben and Kärntnerstrasse, the two main pedestrian shopping streets in the center. About 1 PM, head for **Schönbrunn Palace** ⑧ to spend the afternoon touring the magnificent royal residence, or visit the **Kunsthistoriches Museum** ⑤, one of the great art museums of the world. After the museum closes at 6 PM, relax over coffee at a café; then spend a musical evening at a concert, opera, or operetta or a convivial evening at a Heuriger, one of the wine restaurants for which Vienna is also famous.

IF YOU HAVE 3 DAYS

Given three days, Day 1 can be a little less hectic, and in any case you'll want more time for the city center. Rather than going on the do-it-yourself streetcar ride around the Ringstrasse, take an organized sightseeing tour, which will describe the highlights. Plan to spend a full afternoon at **Schönbrunn Palace** ⑧. Reserve the second day for art, tackling the exciting **Kunsthistoriches Museum** ⑤ before lunch, and after you're refreshed, the dazzling **MuseumsQuartier** ⑯, which comprises several major modern art collections—-the Leopold Museum; the Museum moderner Kunst Stiftung Ludwig (MUMOK); the temporary shows at the Kunsthalle; plus the children's ZOOM Kinder Museum; the Architekturzentrum (Architecture Center); and the Tabak Museum, which is devoted to the subject of tobacco. If your tastes tend to the grand and royal, visit instead the magnificent collection of old oaster drawings at the **Albertina Museum** ⑫ and the impressive **Belvedere Palace** ⑧. For a contrasting step into modern art in the afternoon, don't miss Klimt's legendary *The Kiss* at the Belvedere. Do as the Viennese do, and fill in any gaps with stops at cafés, reserving evenings for relaxing over music or wine. On the third day, head for the world-famous **Spanische Reitschule** ㉞ and watch the Lipizzaners prance through morning training. While you're in the neighborhood, view the sparkling court jewels in the Imperial Treasury, the **Schatzkammer** ㊹, and the glitzy **Silberkammer** ㊵, the museum of court silver and tableware, and take in one of Vienna's most spectacular baroque settings, the glorious Grand Hall of the **Hofbibliothek** ㊲. For a total contrast, head out to the Prater amusement park in late afternoon for a ride on the giant Ferris wheel and end the day in a wine restaurant on the outskirts, perhaps in Sievering or Nussdorf.

IF YOU HAVE 7 DAYS

Spend your first three days as outlined in the itinerary above. Then begin your fourth day getting better acquainted with the 1st District—the heart of the city. Treasures here range from Roman ruins to the residences of Mozart and Beethoven, the **Figarohaus** ㊸ and the **Pasqualatihaus** ㉑; then, slightly afield, the **Freud Apartment** ㊺ (in the 9th District) or the oddball **Hundertwasserhaus** (in the 3rd). Put it all in contemporary perspective with a backstage tour of the magnificent **Staatsoper** ㊻, the State Opera. For a country break on the fifth day, take a tour of the **Vienna Woods** (☞ Chapter 3) or the Danube Valley, particularly the glorious **Wachau district** (☞ Chapter 4), where vineyards sweep down to the river's edge. On the sixth day, fill in some of the blanks with a stroll around the **Naschmarkt** ㊶ food-market district, taking in the nearby **Secession Building** ㊅ with Gustav Klimt's famous *Beethoven Frieze*. Don't overlook the superb Jugendstil buildings on the north side of the market. If you're still game for museums, head for any one of the less usual offerings, such as the Jewish Museum, the Haus der Musik, or the Ephesus Museum, in the **Hofburg,** or visit the city's historical museum, **Historisches Museum der Stadt Wien** ㊼; by now, you'll have acquired a good concept of the city and its background, so the exhibits will make more sense. Cap the day by visiting the **Kaisergruft** ㊶ in the Kapuzinerkirche to view the tombs of the Habsburgs responsible for so much of Vienna.

The Inner City: Historic Heart of Vienna

A good way to break the ice on your introduction to Vienna is to get a general picture of its layout as presented to the cruising bird or airplane pilot. There are several beautiful vantage points from which you can look down and over the city—including the terrace of the Upper Belvedere Palace—but the city's preeminent lookout point, offering fine views in all directions, is from the Stephansdom, reached by toiling up the 345 steps of der Alte Steffl (Old Stephen, its south tower) to the observation platform. The young and agile will make it up in 8 to 10 minutes; the slower-paced will make it in closer to 20. An elevator, and no exertion, will present you with much the same view from the terrace. From atop, you can see that St. Stephen's is the veritable hub of the city's wheel.

Most of Vienna lies roughly within an arc of a circle, with the straight line of the Danube Canal as its chord. Its heart, the Innere Stadt (Inner City) or 1st District—in medieval times the entire city of Vienna—is bounded by the Ringstrasse (Ring), which forms almost a circle, with a narrow arc cut off by the Danube Canal, diverted from the main river just above Vienna and flowing through the city to rejoin the parent stream just below it. The city spreads out from the Stephansdom, accented by the series of magnificent buildings erected—beginning in the 1870s, when Vienna reached the zenith of its imperial prosperity—around the Ringstrasse: the State Opera, the Art History Museum and the Museum of Natural History, the "New Wing" of the Hofburg, the House of Parliament, the Rathaus, the University, and the Votivkirche. For more than eight centuries, the enormous bulk of the cathedral has remained the nucleus around which the city has grown. The bird's-eye view can be left until the last day of your visit, when the city's landmarks will be more familiar. First day or last, the vistas are memorable, especially if you catch them as the cathedral's famous *Pummerin* (Boomer) bell is tolling.

A Good Walk

Stephansplatz, in the heart of the city, is the logical starting point from which to track down Vienna's past and present, as well as any acquaintance (natives believe that if you wait long enough at this intersection of eight streets you'll run into anyone you're searching for). Although it's now in what is mainly a pedestrian zone, **Stephansdom** ①, the mighty cathedral, marks the point from which distances to and from Vienna are measured. Visit the cathedral (it's quite impossible to view all its treasures, so just soak up its reflective Gothic spirit) and consider climbing its 345-step tower, der Alte Steffl, or descending into its Habsburg crypt. Vienna of the Middle Ages is encapsulated in the streets in back of St. Stephen's Cathedral. You could easily spend half a day or more just prowling the narrow streets and passageways—Wollzeile, Bäckerstrasse, Blutgasse—typical remnants of an early era.

Wander up the Wollzeile, cutting through the narrow Essiggasse and right into the Bäckerstrasse, to the **Universitätskirche** ② or Jesuitenkirche, a lovely Jesuit church. Note the contrasting Academy of Science diagonally opposite (Beethoven premiered his *Battle Symphony*—today more commonly known as "Wellington's Victory"—in its Ceremonial Hall). Follow the Sonnenfelsgasse, ducking through one of the tiny alleys on the right to reach the Bäckerstrasse; turn right at Gutenbergplatz into the Köllnerhofgasse, right again into tiny Grashofgasse, and go through the gate into the surprising **Heiligenkreuzerhof** ③, a peaceful oasis (unless a handicrafts market is taking place). Through the square, enter the Schönlaterngasse (Beautiful Lantern Street) to admire the house fronts—film companies at times block this street to take shots of the picturesque atmosphere—on your way to the **Dominikanerkirche** ④, the Dominican church with its marvelous baroque interior. Head east two blocks to that repository of Jugendstil treasures, the **Museum für Angewandte Kunst** ⑤, then head north along the Stubenring to enjoy the architectural contrast of the **Postsparkasse** ⑥ and former War Ministry, facing each other. Retrace your steps, following Postgasse into **Fleischmarkt** ⑦. Nearby Hoher Markt, reached by taking Rotenturmstrasse west to Lichtensteg or Bauernmarkt, was part of the early Roman encampment; witness the

Roman ruins under **Hoher Markt** ⑧. The extension of Fleischmarkt ends in a set of stairs leading up past the eccentric Kornhäusal Tower. Up the stairs to the right on Ruprechtsplatz is the **Ruprechtskirche** ⑨, St. Rupert's Church, allegedly the city's oldest. Take Sterngasse down the steps, turn left into Marc Aurel-Strasse, and turn right into Salvator-gasse to discover the lacework **Maria am Gestade** ⑩, Maria on the Banks, which once sat above a small river, now underground.

TIMING

If you're pressed for time and happy with facades rather than what's behind them, this route could take half a day, but if you love to look inside and stop to ponder and explore the myriad narrow alleys, figure at least a day for this walk. During services, wandering around the churches will be limited, but otherwise, you can tackle this walk any time, at your convenience.

Sights to See

❹ **Dominikanerkirche** (Dominican Church). The Postgasse, to the east of Schönlaterngasse, introduces an unexpected visitor from Rome: the Dominikanerkirche. Built in the 1630s, some 50 years before the Viennese baroque building boom, its facade is modeled after any number of Roman churches of the 16th century. The interior illustrates why the baroque style came to be considered the height of bad taste during the 19th century and still has many detractors today. "Sculpt 'til you drop" seems to have been the motto here, and the viewer's eye is given no respite. This sort of Roman architectural orgy never really gained a foothold in Vienna, and when the great Viennese architects did pull out all the decorative stops—Hildebrandt's interior at the Belvedere Palace, for instance—they did it in a very different style and with far greater success. ✉ *Postg. 4, 1st District,* ☎ *01/512–7460–0. U-Bahn: U3 Stubentor/Dr.-Karl-Lueger-Pl.*

❼ **Fleischmarkt.** Fleischmarkt and the picturesque tiny Griechengasse just beyond the glittering 19th-century Greek Orthodox church are part of the city's oldest core. This corner of the inner city has a medieval feel that is quite genuine; there has been a tavern at Fleischmarkt 11 for some 500 years. The wooden carving on the facade of the current Griechenbeisl restaurant commemorates Max Augustin—best known today from the song "Ach du lieber Augustin"—an itinerant musician who sang here during the plague of 1679. ✉ *1st District. U-Bahn: U1 or U4/Schwedenpl.*

❸ **Heiligenkreuzerhof.** Tiny side streets and alleys run off Sonnenfelsgasse, parallel to Bäckerstrasse. Amid the narrow streets is Heiligenkreuzerhof (Holy Cross Court), one of the city's most peaceful backwaters. This complex of buildings dates from the 17th century but got an 18th-century face-lift. Appropriately, the restraint of the architecture—with only here and there a small outburst of baroque spirit—gives the courtyard the distinct feeling of a retreat. The square is a favorite site for seasonal markets at Easter and Christmas, and for occasional outdoor art shows. ✉ *1st District. U-Bahn: U1 or U3/Stephanspl.*

❽ **Hoher Markt.** This square was badly damaged during World War II, but the famous Anker Clock at the east end survived the artillery fire. The huge mechanical timepiece took six years (1911–17) to build and still attracts crowds at noon when the full panoply of mechanical figures representing Austrian historical personages parades by. The figures are identified on a plaque to the bottom left of the clock. The graceless buildings erected around the square since 1945 are not aging well and do little to show off the square's lovely baroque centerpiece, the St. Joseph Fountain (portraying the marriage of Joseph and Mary), designed in 1729 by Joseph Emanuel Fischer von Erlach, son of the great Johann Bernhard Fischer von Erlach. The Hoher Markt does harbor one wholly unexpected attraction, however: underground Roman ruins. ✉ *1st District. U-Bahn: U1 or U4/Schwedenpl.*

OFF THE
BEATEN PATH

HUNDERTWASSERHAUS – To see one of Vienna's most amazing buildings, travel eastward from Schwendenplatz or Julius-Raab Platz along Radetzkystrasse to the junction of Kegelgasse and Löwengasse. Here you'll find the Hundertwasserhaus, a 50-apartment public-housing complex designed by the late Austrian avant-garde artist Friedensreich Hundertwasser. The structure looks as though it was decorated by a crew of mischievous circus clowns wielding giant crayons. The building caused a sensation when it was erected in 1985 and still draws crowds of sightseers. ✉ *Löweng. and Kegelg., 3rd District/Landstrasse. U-Bahn: U1 or U4/Schwedenpl., then Tram N to Hetzg.*

KUNSTHAUS WIEN – Near the Hundertwasserhaus you'll find another Hundertwasser project, an art museum, which mounts outstanding international exhibits in addition to showings of the colorful Hundertwasser works. Like the apartment complex nearby, the building itself is pure Hundertwasser, with irregular floors, windows with trees growing out of them, and sudden architectural surprises, a wholly appropriate setting for modern art. ✉ *Untere Weissgerberstr. 13, 3rd District/Landstrasse,* ☎ *01/712–0491–0,* 🎟 *€8.* 🕐 *Daily 10–7. U-Bahn: U1 or U4/Schwedenpl., then Tram N or O to Radetzkypl.*

⑩ Maria am Gestade (St. Mary on the Banks). The middle-Gothic, seven-sided tower of Maria am Gestade, crowned by a delicate cupola, is a sheer joy to the eye and dispels the idea that Gothic must necessarily be austere. Built around 1400 (but much restored in the 17th and 19th centuries), the church incorporated part of the Roman city walls into its foundation; the north wall, as a result, takes a slight but noticeable dogleg to the right halfway down the nave. Like St. Stephen's, Maria am Gestade is rough-hewn Gothic, with a simple but forceful facade. The church is especially beloved, however, because of its unusual details—the pinnacled and saint-bedecked gable that tops the front facade, the stone canopy that hovers protectively over the front door, and (most appealing of all) the intricate openwork lantern atop the south-side bell tower. Appropriately enough in a city famous for its pastry, the lantern lends its tower an engaging suggestion of a sugar caster, although some see an allusion to hands intertwined in prayer. ✉ *Passauer Pl./Salvatorg., 1st District, U-Bahn: U1 or U3/Stephanspl.*

⑤ Museum für Angewandte Kunst (MAK) (Museum of Applied Arts). This fascinating museum contains a large collection of Austrian furniture, porcelain, art objects, and priceless Oriental carpets; the Jugendstil display devoted to Josef Hoffman and his followers at the Wiener Werkstätte is particularly fine. The museum also showcases a number of changing exhibitions of contemporary works and houses an excellent restaurant, MAK Café (closed Monday), and the museum shop sells contemporary furniture and other objects (including great bar accessories) designed by young local artists. ✉ *Stubenring 5, 1st District,* ☎ *01/711–36–0.* 🎟 *Standing exhibits €2.20, more for special exhibits, Sat. free.* 🕐 *Tues. 10 AM–midnight; Wed.–Sun. 10–6. U-Bahn: U3/Stubentor.*

⑥ Postsparkasse (Post Office Savings Bank). The Post Office Savings Bank is one of modern architecture's greatest curiosities. It was designed in 1904 by Otto Wagner, whom many consider the father of 20th-century architecture. In his famous manifesto *Modern Architecture*, Wagner condemned 19th-century revivalist architecture and pleaded for a

Vienna

66

Währingerstrasse

Hörlg.

Koling.

Maria Theresienstr.

64

Roosevelt-
pl.

65

Börsepl.

Börse.

Wipplingerstr.

Alserstrasse

Universitätsstrasse

Schottenring

Hohenstaufeng.

Grillparzerstr.

63

21

Schrey.

Oppolzerg.

Mölker
Bastei

Schottenbastei

Schottenstrasse

Helferstorferstr.

Mölker
Steig

Vogelg.

20

Renng.

Landesgerichtsstrasse

19

Herrengasse

18

Freyung

17

Tiefer Graben

Teinfaltstr.

Rosengasse

Am
Hof

23

Bognerg.

Naglerg.

Josefstädter Str.

61

62

Schenkenstrasse

Bankg.

Landhausg.

Wallnerstr.

31

Stadiong.

Dr. Karl Lueger-Ring

Löwelstr.

22

32

Kohlmarkt

Auerspergstr.

60

58

Dr. K. Renner-Ring

Schauflerg.

25

Michaelerplo

Lerchen-
felderstr.

Ballhaus-
pl.

Hofburg
33 – 53
See Detail
Map

24

Josefs-
pl.

Augustinerstr.

Neustiftg.

59

Volksgartenstr.

Bellariastr.

Heldenpl.

Hanusch-

72

Museumsstrasse

54

Burgring

Maria-
Theresien-
Platz

Burggarten

Goetheg.

Burggasse

Gutenbergg.

57

56

Museumsplatz

55

Babenbergstr.

Opernring

Operng.

Siebensterng.

Spittelberg.

Eschenbach.

Elisabethstr.

Robert Stolz-
Platz

Getreidemarkt

Schillerpl.

Nibelungeng.

**Kaiserliches
Hofmobilien-
depot**

Mariahilfer Strasse

Gumpendorferstr.

74

**Theater an
der Wien**

75

Friedrichstr.

TO TECHNISCHES
MUSEUM AND
KAISERLICHES
HOFMOBILIENDEPOT

TO SCHÖNBRUNN
PALACE

Gumpendorferstr.

Naschmarkt

Linke Wienzeile

Rechte Wienzeile

76

Wiedner Hauptstr.

77

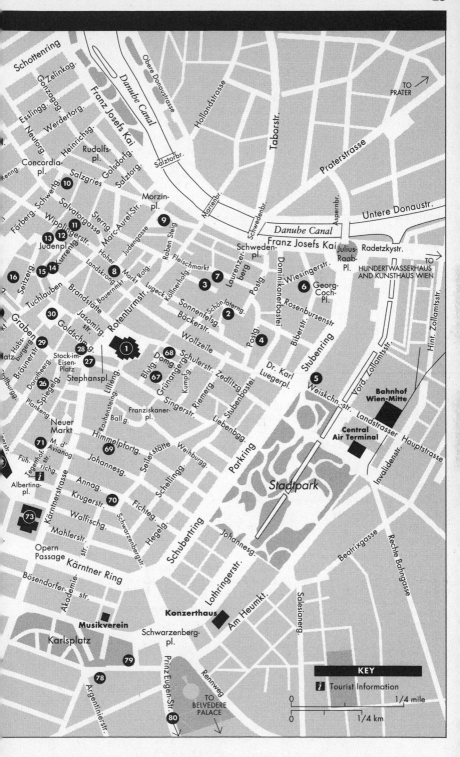

Schottenring

G. Zelinkag.
Gonzagag.
Essling g.
Werdertorg.
Neutorg.
Heinrichsg.
Rudolfs-pl.
Concordia-pl.
Salzgries
Goldsdorfg.
Salztorg.
Salzgries

Franz Josefs Kai

Danube Canal

Obere Donaustrasse

Salztorbr.

TO PRATER

Hollandstrasse

Taborstr.

Praterstrasse

Untere Donaustr.

Färberg.
Schwertg.
Salvatorgasse
Wipplingerstr.
Judenpl.
Kurrentg.
Seitzerg.
Tuchlauben
Brandstätte

Marc-Aurel-Str.
Sterng.
Hoher Markt
Landskrong.
Bauernmkt.
Rotgasse

Morzin-pl.

Judengasse

Raben Steig

Fleischmarkt

Schön latergg.
Sonnenfelsg.
Bäckerstr.
Wollzeile

Schön latergg.

Laurenzer-berg
Postg.

Schweden-pl.

Danube Canal

Franz Josefs Kai

Schwedenbr.
Marienbr.
Aspernbr.

Julius-Raab-Pl.
Radetzkystr.

Wiesingerstr.

Dominikanerbastei
Rosenbursenstr.

Biberstr.

Georg-Coch-Pl.

HUNDERTWASSERHAUS
AND KUNSTHAUS WIEN

Hint. Zollamtsstr.
Vord. Zollamtsstr.

TO

Graben
Habs-burgerg.
Bräunerstr.
Dorotheerg.
Spiegelg.
Plankeng.
Neuer Markt

Jasomirg.
Goldschm. g.
Lilieng.
Bauernmkt.

Stock-im-Eisen-Platz
Stephanspl.
Bräunerstr.
Dorotheerg.

Rotenturmstr.
Lugeck
Köllnerhofg.
Kumpfg.
Riemerg.
Grünangerg.
Domg.
Blutg.
Schulerstr. Zedlitzg.
Singerstr.
Rauhensteing.
Ball g.

Franziskaner-pl.

Stubenbastei

Stubenring

Dr. Karl Luegerpl.

Weiskchn.-str.

Landstrasser Hauptstrasse
Invalidenstr.

Bahnhof Wien-Mitte

Central Air Terminal

M. d. Avianog.
Füh.-richg.
Tegetthoffstr.
Albertina-pl.

Himmelpfortg.
Johannesg.
Seilerstätte
Schellingg.
Fichteg.
Weihburgg.
Liebenbgg.

Parking

Stadtpark

Beatrixgasse
Rechte Bahngasse

Annag.
Krugerstr.
Walfischg.
Mahlerstr.

Schwarzenbergstr.

Hegelg.
Schubertring

Johannesg.

Lothringerstr.

Salesianerg.

Opern Passage
Bösendorfer str.
Akademie-str.

Kärntner Ring

Musikverein

Karlsplatz

Schwarzenberg-pl.

Konzerthaus

Am Heumkt.

Prinz-Eugen-Str.

Rennweg

TO BELVEDERE PALACE

KEY

🛈 Tourist Information

0 ———— 1/4 mile

0 ———— 1/4 km

modern style that honestly expressed modern building methods. Accordingly, the exterior walls of the Post Office Savings Bank are mostly flat and undecorated; visual interest is supplied merely by varying the pattern of the bolts used to hold the marble slabs in place on the wall surface during construction. Later architects were to embrace Wagner's beliefs wholeheartedly, although they used different, truly modern building materials: glass and concrete rather than marble. The Post Office Savings Bank was indeed a bold leap into the future, but unfortunately the future took a different path and today the whole appears a bit dated. Go inside for a look at the restored and functioning Kassa-Saal, or central cashier's hall, to see how Wagner carried his concepts over to interior design. ☒ *Georg-Coch-Pl. 2, 1st District,* ☎ *01/51400.* ☺ *Lobby weekdays 8–3. U-Bahn: U1 or U4/Schwedenpl., then Tram 1 or 2/Julius-Raab-Pl.*

OFF THE BEATEN PATH

PRATER – Vienna's most famous park and most beloved attraction for children can be found by heading out northeast from the historic city center, across the Danube Canal along Praterstrasse: the famous Prater, the city's foremost amusement park. In 1766, to the dismay of the aristocracy, Emperor Joseph II decreed that the vast expanse of imperial parklands known as the Prater would henceforth be open to the public. East of the inner city between the Danube Canal and the Danube proper, the Prater is a public park to this day, notable for its long promenade (the Hauptallee, more than 4½ km, or 3 mi, in length); its sports facilities (a golf course, a stadium, a racetrack, and a swimming pool, for starters); the landmark giant Ferris wheel (Riesenrad); the traditional, modern amusement-park rides; a number of less-innocent indoor, sex-oriented attractions; a planetarium; and a small but interesting museum devoted to the Prater's long history. If you look carefully, you can discover a handful of children's rides dating from the 1920s and '30s that survived the fire that consumed most of the Volksprater in 1945. The best-known attraction is the 200-ft Ferris wheel that figured so prominently in the 1949 film *The Third Man.* One of three built in Europe at the end of the last century (the others were in England and France but have long since been dismantled), the wheel was badly damaged during World War II and restored shortly thereafter. Its progress is slow and stately (a revolution takes 10 minutes), the views from its cars magnificent, particularly toward dusk. Try to eat at the famous **Schweizerhaus** (☒ Strasse des 1. Mai 116, ☎ 01/728–0152; closed Nov.–Feb.), which has been serving frosty mugs of beer, roast chicken, and *Stelze* (a huge hunk of crispy roast pork on the bone) for more than 100 years. Its informal setting with wood-plank tables indoors or in the garden in summer adds to the fun. Credit cards are not accepted. ☒ *2nd District/Leopoldstadt.* ☜ *Park free, Riesenrad €7.50.* ☺ *Apr., daily 10 AM–11 PM; May–Sept., daily 9 AM–midnight; Oct., daily 10–10; Nov.–Feb., daily 10–late afternoon (check with tourist office for exact hrs). U-Bahn: U1/Praterstern.*

❾ **Ruprechtskirche** (St. Ruprecht's Church). Ruprechtsplatz, another of Vienna's time-warp backwaters, lies to the north of the Kornhäusel Tower. The church in the middle, Ruprechtskirche, is the city's oldest. According to legend it was founded in 740; the oldest part of the present structure (the lower half of the tower) dates from the 11th century. Set on the ancient ramparts overlooking the Danube Canal, it is serene and unpretentious. It is usually closed, but sometimes opens for local art shows and summer evening classical concerts. ☒ *Ruprecht-spl., 1st District, U-Bahn: U1 or U4 Schwedenpl.*

Schönlaterngasse (Beautiful Lantern Street). Once part of Vienna's medieval Latin Quarter, Schönlaterngasse is the main artery of a historic neighborhood that has reblossomed in recent years. Thanks in part to government Kultur schillings—or renovation loans—the quarter has been revamped. Streets are lined with beautiful baroque town houses (often with colorfully painted facades), now distinctive showcases for art galleries, chic shops, and coffeehouses. The most famous house of the quarter is the **Basiliskenhaus** (House of the Basilik, ⊠ Schönlaterng. 7, 1st District). According to legend, it was first built for a baker; on June 26, 1212, a foul-smelling basilisk (half rooster, half toad, with a glance that could kill) took up residence in the courtyard well, poisoning the water. An enterprising apprentice dealt with the problem by climbing down the well armed with a mirror; when the basilisk saw its own reflection, it turned to stone. The petrified creature can still be seen in a niche on the building's facade. Today, modern science accounts for the contamination with a more prosaic explanation: natural-gas seepage. Be sure to take a look in the house's miniature courtyard for a trip back to medieval Vienna (the house itself is private). The picturesque street is named for the ornate wrought-iron wall lantern at Schönlaterngasse 6. Just a few steps from the Basilikenhaus, note the baroque courtyard at Schönlaterngasse 8—one of the city's prettiest. A blacksmith's workshop, **Alte Schmiede** (Old Smithy, ⊠ Schönlaterng. 9, U-Bahn: U1 or U3/Stephanspl.), is now a museum.

★ ❶ **Stephansdom** (St. Stephen's Cathedral). Vienna's soaring centerpiece, this beloved cathedral enshrines the heart of the city—although it is curious to note that when first built in 1144–47 it actually stood outside the city walls. Vienna can thank a period of hard times for the Mother Church for the cathedral's distinctive silhouette. Originally the structure was to have had matching 445-ft-high spires, a standard design of the era, but funds ran out, and the north tower to this day remains a happy reminder of what gloriously is not. The lack of symmetry creates an imbalance that makes the cathedral instantly identifiable from its profile alone. The cathedral, like the Staatsoper and some other major buildings, was very heavily damaged in World War II. Since then, it has risen from the fires of destruction like a phoenix, and like the phoenix, it is a symbol of regeneration.

It is difficult now, sitting quietly in the shadowed peace, to tell what was original and what parts of the walls and vaults were reconstructed. No matter: its history-rich atmosphere is dear to all Viennese. That noted, St. Stephen's has a fierce presence that is blatantly un-Viennese. It is a stylistic jumble ranging from 13th-century Romanesque to 15th-century Gothic. Like the exterior, St. Stephen's interior lacks the soaring unity of Europe's greatest Gothic cathedrals, with much of its decoration dating from the later baroque era.

The wealth of decorative sculpture in St. Stephen's can be intimidating to the nonspecialist, so if you wish to explore the cathedral in detail, you may want to buy the admirably complete English-language description sold in the small room marked Dom Shop. One particularly masterly work, however, should be seen by everyone: the stone pulpit attached to the second freestanding pier on the left of the central nave, carved by Anton Pilgram around 1510. The delicacy of its decoration would in itself set the pulpit apart, but even more intriguing are its five sculpted figures. Carved around the outside of the pulpit proper are the four Latin Fathers of the Church (from left to right: St. Augustine, St. Gregory, St. Jerome, and St. Ambrose), and each is given an individual personality so sharply etched as to suggest satire, perhaps of living models. There is no satire suggested by the fifth figure, however; below the pulpit's stairs Pilgram sculpted a fine self-portrait, showing himself peering out a half-open window. Note the toads,

MOZART, MOZART, MOZART!

FOR THE MUSICAL TOURIST who is excited at the prospect of treading in the footprints of the mighty, seeing where masterpieces were committed to paper, or standing where a long-loved work was either praised or damned at its first appearance, Vienna is tops. The city is saturated with musical history. One of its leading players, of course, was Wolfgang Amadeus Mozart (1756–91), who crammed a prodigious number of compositions into the 35 short years of his life—the mere cataloging of them is the subject of a ponderous work, impressively entitled *Chronologisch-thematisches Verzeichnis sämtlicher Tonwerke Wolfgang Amadeus Mozarts*, the work of Ludwig von Köchel. Certainly, it's easy to find the places he lived in or visited, all carefully restored or marked by memorial plaques. But a knowledge of his troubled relations with his homeland makes the experience a poignant one.

From the beginning of Wolfgang's precocious career, his father, frustrated in his own musical ambitions at the archbishopric in Salzburg, looked beyond the boundaries of the Austro-Hungarian empire to promote the boy's fame. At the age of six, his son was presented to the royal courts of Europe and caused a sensation with his skills as an instrumentalist and impromptu composer. As he grew up, however, his virtuosity lost its power to amaze and he was forced to make his way as an "ordinary" musician, which then meant finding a position at court. In this he was not much more successful than his father had been, in spite of what would seem to be the decisive advantage of genius. In Salzburg he was never able to rise beyond the level of organist (allowing him, as he noted with sarcastic pride, to sit above the cooks at table), and his attempts to have his compositions performed were rebuffed.

In disgust, he severed his ties with the archbishop and tried his luck in Vienna, where despite the popularity of his operas and the admiration of his peers (Joseph Haydn early recognized him as the greatest composer of the time) he was able to obtain only an unpaid appointment as assistant kapellmeister at St. Stephen's mere months before his death. By then he had been invited by friends to come to London (where Haydn later made a fortune), and subscriptions had been taken up in Hungary and the Netherlands that would have paid him handsomely. But it was too late. Whatever the truth of the theories still swirling around his untimely death, the fact remains that not only was he not given the state funeral he deserved, but he was buried in an unmarked grave after a hasty, sparsely attended funeral.

Only a hard-boiled cynic can fail to be moved. Only the flint-hearted can stand in Vienna's Währingerstrasse and look at the windows behind which Mozart wrote those last three symphonies in the incredible short time of six weeks in the summer of 1788 and not be touched. For this was the time when the Mozart fortunes had slumped to their lowest. "If you, my best of friends, forsake me, I am unhappily and innocently lost with my poor sick wife and my child," he wrote.

If one is inclined to accuse Mozart's fellow countrymen of neglect, they would seem to have made up for it with a vengeance. The visitor to Vienna and Salzburg can hardly ignore the barrage of Mozart candies, wine, beer, coffee mugs, T-shirts, baseball caps—not to mention the gilt statues that make do for a nonexistent monumental tomb. Indeed, he has become a thriving brand-name industry and one of the centerpieces of Austrian tourism. And Mozart, always one to appreciate a joke, even at his own expense, would surely see the irony in the belated veneration.

— Gary Dodson

lizards, and other creatures climbing the spiral rail alongside the steps up to the pulpit. As you walk among the statues and aisles, remember that many notable events occurred here, including Mozart's marriage in 1782 and his funeral in December 1791.

St. Stephen's was devastated by fire in the last days of World War II, and the extent of the damage may be seen by leaving the cathedral through the south portal, where a set of prereconstruction photographs commemorates the disaster. Restoration was protracted and difficult, but today the cathedral once again dominates the center of the city. Note the "O5" carved into the stone to the right of the outer massive front door. The "O" stands for Österreich, or Austria, and the "5" is for the fifth letter of the alphabet. This translates into OE, the abbreviation for Österreich, and was a covert sign of resistance to the Nazi annexation of Austria. The bird's-eye views from the cathedral's beloved **Alte Steffl** tower will be a highlight for some. The tower is 450 ft high and was built between 1359 and 1433. The climb or elevator ride up is rewarded with vistas that extend to the rising slopes of the Wienerwald. ✉ *Stephanspl., 1st District,* ☎ *01/515–5237–67.* 🖂 *Guided tour, €3.45; catacombs, €3; elevator to Pummerin bell, €3.50.* ☉ *Daily 6 AM–10 PM. Guided tours in English daily Apr.–Oct. at 3:45; catacombs tour (minimum 5 people) Mon.–Sat. every half hr 10–11:30 and 1:30–4:30, Sun. every half hr 1:30–4:30; North Tower elevator to Pummerin bell, Apr.–Oct., daily 9–6; July–Aug., daily 9–6:30; Nov.–Mar., daily 8:30–5. U-Bahn: U1 or U3/Stephanspl.*

NEED A BREAK?	If you're in the mood for ice cream, head for **Zanoni & Zanoni** (✉ Am Lugeck 7, 1st District, ☎ 01/512–7979) near St. Stephen's, between Rotenturmstrasse and Bäckerstrasse, and open 365 days a year. Here you'll have trouble choosing from among 25 or more flavors of smooth, Italian-style gelato, including mango, caramel, and chocolate chip. There are also tables for those who want to rest their feet and enjoy a sundae.

❷ **Universitätskirche** (Jesuit Church). The east end of Bäckerstrasse is punctuated by Dr.-Ignaz-Seipel-Platz, named for the theology professor who was chancellor of Austria during the 1920s. On the north side is the Universitätskirche, or Jesuitenkirche, built around 1630. Its flamboyant baroque interior contains a fine trompe-l'oeil ceiling fresco by that master of visual trickery Andrea Pozzo, who was imported from Rome in 1702 for the job. You may hear a Mozart or Haydn mass sung here in Latin on many Sundays. ✉ *Dr.-Ignaz-Seipl-Pl., 1st District,* ☎ *01/512–5232–0. U-Bahn: U3 Stubentor/Dr.-Karl-Lueger-Pl.*

Bittersweet Vienna: Baroque Gems and Cozy Cafés

As the city developed and expanded, the core quickly outgrew its early confines. New urban centers sprang up, to be ornamented by government buildings and elegant town residences. Since Vienna was the beating heart of a vast empire, nothing was spared to make the edifices as exuberant as possible, with utility often a secondary consideration. The best architects of the day were commissioned to create impressions as well as buildings, and they did their job well. That so much has survived is a testimony to the solidity both of the designs and of the structures on which the ornamentation has been overlaid.

Those not fortunate enough to afford town palaces were relegated to housing that was often confining and less than elegant. Rather than suffer the discomfitures of a disruptive household environment, the city's literati and its philosophers and artists took refuge in cafés, which in effect became their combined salons and offices. To this day, cafés remain an important element of Viennese life. Many residents still have their *Stammtisch*, or regular table, at which they appear daily. Talk still prevails—but, increasingly, so do handy cell phones and even laptops.

A Good Walk

Start in the Wipplingerstrasse at the upper (west) end of Hoher Markt to find touches of both the imperial and the municipal Vienna. On the east side is the **Altes Rathaus** ⑪, which served as the city hall until 1885; on the west is the **Bohemian Court Chancery** ⑫, once diplomatic headquarters for Bohemia's representation to the Habsburg court. Turn south into the short Fütterergasse to reach Judenplatz, in the Middle Ages the center of Judaism in Vienna, and today site of the new **Judenplatz Museum** ⑬, landmarked by a memorial created by Rachel Whitehead, one of contemporary art's most important sculptors. A clock-watcher's delight is down at the end of Kurrentgasse in the form of the **Uhrenmuseum** (Clock Museum) ⑭; around the corner through the Parisgasse to Schulhof, a children's delight is the **Puppen und Spielzeug Museum** (Doll and Toy Museum) ⑮. Follow Schulhof into the huge **Am Hof** square, boasting the **Kirche Am Hof** ⑯ and what must be the world's most elegant fire station. The square hosts an antiques and collectibles market on Thursday and Friday most of the year, plus other ad hoc events. Take the minuscule Irisgasse from Am Hof into the Naglergasse, noting the mosaic Jugendstil facade on the pharmacy in the Bognergasse, to your left. Around a bend in the narrow Naglergasse is the **Freyung,** an irregular square bounded on the south side by two wonderfully stylish palaces: **Palais Ferstel** ⑰, now a shopping arcade, and the elegantly restored **Palais Harrach** ⑱ next door, now an outpost of the Kunsthistoriches Museum. Opposite, the privately run **Kunstforum** art museum mounts varied and outstanding exhibitions. The famous **Kinsky Palace** ⑲ at the beginning of Herrengasse is still partly a private residence. The north side of the Freyung is watched over by the **Schottenkirche** ⑳, a Scottish church that was, in fact, established by Irish monks; the complex also houses a small but worthwhile museum of the order's treasures. Follow Teinfaltstrasse from opposite the Schottenkirche, turning right into Schreyvogelgasse. Climb the ramp on your right past the socalled Dreimäderlhaus at Schreyvogelgasse 10—note the ornate facade of this pre-Biedermeier patrician house—to reach Molker Bastei, where Beethoven lived in the **Pasqualatihaus** ㉑, now housing a museum commemorating the composer. Follow the ring south to Löwelstrasse, turning left into Bankgasse; then turn right into Abraham-a-Santa Clara-Gasse (the tiny street that runs off the Bankgasse) to Minoritenplatz and the **Minoritenkirche** ㉒, the Minorite Church, with its strangely hatless tower. Inside is a kitschy mosaic of the *Last Supper*. Landhausgasse will bring you to Herrengasse, and diagonally across the street, in the back corner of the Palais Ferstel, is the **Café Central** ㉓, one of Vienna's hangouts for the famous. As you go south up Herrengasse, on the left is the odd Hochhaus, a 20th-century building once renowned as Vienna's skyscraper. Opposite are elegant baroque former town palaces, now used as museum and administration buildings by the province of Lower Austria.

TIMING

The actual distances in this walk are relatively short, and you could cover the route in 1½ hours or so. But if you take time to linger in the museums and sample a coffee with whipped cream in the Café Central, you'll develop a much better understanding of the contrasts between old and newer in the city. You could easily spend a day following this walk, if you were to take in all of the museums; note that these, like many of Vienna's museums, are closed on Monday.

Sights to See

⓫ Altes Rathaus (Old City Hall). Opposite the Bohemian Chancery stands the Altes Rathaus, dating from the 14th century but displaying 18th-century baroque motifs on its facade. The interior passageways and courtyards, which are open during the day, house a Gothic chapel (open at odd hours); a much-loved baroque wall-fountain (Georg Raphael Donner's **Andromeda Fountain** of 1741); and display cases exhibiting maps and photos illustrating the city's history. ✉ *Wipplingerstr./ Salvatorg. 7, 1st District. U-Bahn: U1 or U4/Schwedenpl.*

Am Hof. Am Hof is one of the city's oldest squares. In the Middle Ages the ruling Babenberg family built their castle on the site of No. 2; hence the name of the square, which means simply "at court." The grand residence hosted such luminaries as Barbarossa and Walter von der Vogelweide, the famous Minnesinger who stars in Wagner's *Tannhäuser*. The baroque **Column of Our Lady** in the center dates from 1667, marking the Catholic victory over the Swedish Protestants in the Thirty Years' War (1618–48). The onetime **Civic Armory** at the northwest corner has been used as a fire station since 1685 (the high-spirited facade, with its Habsburg eagle, was "baroqued" in 1731) and today houses the headquarters of Vienna's fire department. The complex includes a fire-fighting museum (open only on Sunday mornings). Presiding over the east side of the square is the noted Kirche Am Hof. In Bognergasse to the right of the Kirche Am Hof, around the corner from the imposing Bank Austria headquarters building, at No. 9, is the **Engel Apotheke** (pharmacy) with a Jugendstil mosaic depicting winged women collecting the elixir of life in outstretched chalices. At the turn of the 20th century the inner city was dotted with storefronts decorated in a similar manner; today this is the sole survivor. Around the bend from the Naglergasse is the picturesque Freyung square. ✉ *1st District. U-Bahn: U3/Herreng.*

⓬ Bohemian Court Chancery. One of the architectural jewels of the Inner City can be found at Wipplingerstrasse 7, the former Bohemian Court Chancery, built between 1708 and 1714 by Johann Bernhard Fischer von Erlach. Fischer von Erlach and his contemporary Johann Lukas von Hildebrandt were the reigning architectural geniuses of baroque-era Vienna; they designed their churches and palaces during the building boom that followed the defeat of the Turks in 1683. Both had studied architecture in Rome, and both were deeply impressed by the work of the great Italian architect Francesco Borromini, who brought to his designs a wealth and freedom of invention that were looked upon with horror by most contemporary Romans. But for Fischer von Erlach and Hildebrandt, Borromini's ideas were a source of triumphant architectural inspiration, and when they returned to Vienna they produced between them many of the city's most beautiful buildings. Alas, narrow Wipplingerstrasse allows little more than an oblique view of this florid facade. The back side of the building, on Judenplatz, is less elaborate but gives a better idea of the design concept. The building first served as diplomatic and representational offices of Bohemia (now a part of the Czech Republic) to the Vienna-based monarchy and, today, still houses government offices. ✉ *Wipplingerstr. 7, 1st District. U-Bahn: U1 or U4/Schwedenpl.*

㉓ Café Central. Part of the **Palais Ferstel** complex, the Café Central is one of Vienna's more famous cafés, its full authenticity blemished only by complete restoration in recent years. In its prime (before World War I), the café was "home" to some of the most famous literary figures of the day, who dined, socialized, worked, and even received mail here. The denizens of the Central favored political argument; indeed, their heated discussions became so well known that in October 1917, when Austria's foreign secretary was informed of the outbreak of the Russian Revolution, he dismissed the report with a facetious reference to a well-known local Marxist, the chess-loving (and presumably harmless) "Herr Bronstein from the Café Central." The remark was to become famous all over Austria, for Herr Bronstein had disappeared and was about to resurface in Russia bearing a new name: Leon Trotsky. No matter how crowded the café may become, you can linger as long as you like over a single cup of coffee and a newspaper from the huge international selection provided. Across the street at Herrengasse 17 is the **Café Central Konditorei,** an excellent pastry and confectionery shop associated with the café. ✉ *Herreng. 14, 1st District,* ☎ *01/533– 3763–26. AE, DC, MC, V. U-Bahn: U3/Herreng.*

The Freyung. Naglergasse, at its curved end, flows into Heidenschuss, which in turn leads down a slight incline from Am Hof to one of Vienna's most prominent squares, the Freyung, meaning "freeing." The square was so named because for many centuries the monks at the adjacent Schottenhof had the privilege of offering sanctuary for three days. In the center of the square stands the allegorical **Austria Fountain** (1845), notable because its Bavarian designer, one Ludwig Schwanthaler, had the statues cast in Munich and then supposedly filled them with cigars to be smuggled into Vienna for black-market sale. Around the sides of the square are some of Vienna's greatest patrician residences, including the Ferstel, Harrach, and Kinsky palaces. ✉ *At the intersection of Am Hof and Herreng, 1st District. U-Bahn: U3/Herreng.*

🔟 **Judenplatz Museum.** In what was once the old Jewish ghetto, construction workers discovered the remains of a 13th-century synagogue while digging for a new parking garage. Simon Wiesenthal (a Vienna resident) helped to turn it into a museum dedicated to the Austrian Jews who died in World War II. Marking the outside is a rectangular concrete cube resembling library shelves, signifying Jewish love of learning, designed by Rachel Whitehead. Downstairs are three exhibition rooms on medieval Jewish life and the synagogue excavations. Also in Judenplatz is a statue of the 18th-century playwright Gotthold Ephraim Lessing, erected after World War II. ✉ *Judenpl. 8, 1st District,* ☎ *01/ 535–0431.* 🎫 *€3; combination ticket with Jewish Museum €7.* ☉ *Sun.– Thurs. 10–6, Fri. 10–2. U-Bahn: U1 or U4/Schwedenpl.*

🔟 **Kinsky Palace.** Just one of the architectural treasures that make up the urban set piece of the Freyung, the Palais Kinsky is the square's best-known palace, and is one of the most sophisticated pieces of baroque architecture in the whole city. It was built between 1713 and 1716 by Hildebrandt, and its only real competition comes a few yards farther on: the Greek-temple facade of the Schottenhof, which is at right angles to the Schottenkirche, up the street from the Kinsky Palace. The palace now houses Wiener Kunst Auktionen, a public auction business offering artworks and antiques. ✉ *Freyung 4, 1st District,* ☎ *01/532– 4200,* 🏳 *01/532–42009.* ☉ *Weekdays 10–6. U-Bahn: U3/Herreng.*

🔟 **Kirche Am Hof.** On the east side of the Am Hof square, the Kirche Am Hof, or the Church of the Nine Choirs of Angels, is identified by its sprawling baroque facade, designed by Carlo Carlone in 1662. The somber interior lacks appeal, but the checkerboard marble floor may remind you of Dutch churches. ✉ *Am Hof 1, 1st District. U-Bahn: U3/Herreng.*

Kunstforum. The huge gold ball atop the doorway on the Freyung at the corner of Renngasse marks the entrance to the Kunstforum, an extensive art gallery run by Bank Austria and featuring outstanding

temporary exhibitions. ✉ *Freyung 8, 1st District,* ☎ *01/53733.* 🎟
€8.70. ⊙ *Daily 10–6 during special exhibits. U-Bahn: U3/Herreng.*

㉒ **Minoritenkirche** (Church of the Minorite Order). The Minoritenplatz
is named after its centerpiece, the Minoritenkirche, a Gothic affair with
a strange stump of a tower, built mostly in the 14th century. The front
is brutally ugly, but the back is a wonderful, if predominantly 19th-
century, surprise. The interior contains the city's most imposing piece
of kitsch: a large mosaic reproduction of Leonardo da Vinci's *Last Supper,* commissioned by Napoléon in 1806 and later purchased by Emperor Francis I. ✉ *Minoritenpl. 2A, 1st District,* ☎ *01/533–4162.
U-Bahn: U3/Herreng.*

⑰ **Palais Ferstel.** At Freyung 2 stands the recently restored Palais Ferstel,
which is not a palace at all but a commercial shop-and-office complex
designed in 1856 and named for its architect, Heinrich Ferstel. The facade is Italianate in style, harking back, in its 19th-century way, to the
Florentine palazzi of the early Renaissance. The interior is unashamedly
eclectic: vaguely Romanesque in feel and Gothic in decoration, with
here and there a bit of Renaissance or baroque sculpted detail thrown
in for good measure. Such eclecticism is sometimes dismissed as mind-
lessly derivative, but here the architectural details are so respectfully
and inventively combined that the interior becomes a pleasure to explore. The 19th-century stock-exchange rooms upstairs are now gloriously restored and used for conferences and concerts. ✉ *Freyung 2,
1st District. U-Bahn: U3/Herreng.*

⑱ **Palais Harrach.** Next door to the Palais Ferstel is the newly renovated
Palais Harrach, part of which now houses a small but worthwhile gallery
of paintings and art objects from the main Kunsthistorisches Museum
(which has far more treasures than space in which to display them)
as well as special exhibits. ✉ *Freyung 3, 1st District,* ☎ *01/52524–
404.* 🎟 *€7.20.* ⊙ *During special exhibits, daily 10–6. U-Bahn: U3/
Herreng.*

㉑ **Pasqualatihaus.** Beethoven lived in the Pasqualatihaus while he was
composing his only opera, *Fidelio,* as well as his Seventh Symphony
and Fourth Piano Concerto. Today his apartment houses a small commemorative museum (in distressingly modern style). After navigating
the narrow and twisting stairway, you might well ask how he maintained the jubilant spirit of the works he wrote there. This house is around
the corner from *The Third Man* Portal. ✉ *8 Mölker Bastei, 1st District,* ☎ *01/535–8905.* 🎟 *€1.80.* ⊙ *Tues.–Sun. 9–12:15 and 1–4:30.
U-Bahn: U2/Schottentor.*

⑮ **Puppen und Spielzeug Museum** (Doll and Toy Museum). As appealing as the clockworks of the Uhrenmuseum located just next door is
this doll and toy museum, with its collections of dolls, dollhouses, teddy
bears, and trains. ✉ *Schulhof 4, 1st District,* ☎ *01/535–6860.* 🎟 *€4.70.*
⊙ *Tues.–Sun. 10–6. U-Bahn: U1 or U3/Stephanspl.*

Schottenhof. Found on the Freyung square and designed by Joseph Kornhäusel in a very different style from his Fleischmarkt tower, the
Schottenhof is a shaded courtyard. The facade typifies the change that
came over Viennese architecture during the Biedermeier era (1815–48).
The Viennese, according to the traditional view, were at the time so
relieved to be rid of the upheavals of the Napoleonic Wars that they
accepted without protest the iron-handed repression of Prince Metternich,
chancellor of Austria, and retreated into a cozy and complacent do-
mesticity. Restraint also ruled in architecture, with baroque license re-
jected in favor of a new and historically "correct" style that was far
more controlled and reserved. Kornhäusel led the way in establishing

this trend in Vienna; his Schottenhof facade is all sober organization and frank repetition. But in its marriage of strong and delicate forces it still pulls off the great Viennese-waltz trick of successfully merging seemingly antithetical characteristics. ⊠ *1st District. U-Bahn: U2/ Schottentor.*

NEED A
BREAK?
In summer, **Wienerwald** restaurant, in the delightful tree-shaded courtyard of the Schottenhof at Freyung 6, is ideal for relaxing over lunch or dinner with a glass of wine or frosty beer. The specialty here is chicken, and you can get it just about every possible way. Especially good is the spit-roasted *Knoblauch* (garlic) chicken. It's open daily.

❷⓿ **Schottenkirche.** From 1758 to 1761, the noted Italian *vedutiste* (scene-painter), Bernardo Bellotto, did paintings of the Freyung square looking north toward the Schottenkirche; the pictures hang in the Kunsthistorisches Museum, and the similarity to the view you see about 240 years later is arresting. In fact, a church has stood on the site of the Schottenkirche since 1177; the present edifice dates from the mid-1600s, when it replaced its predecessor, which had collapsed after the architects of the time had built on weakened foundations. The interior, with its ornate ceiling and a decided surplus of cherubs and angels' faces, is in stark contrast to the plain exterior. The adjacent small **Museum im Schottenstift** holds the best of the monastery's artworks, including the celebrated late-Gothic high altar, dating from about 1470. The winged altar is fascinating for its portrayal of the Holy Family in flight into Egypt—with the city of Vienna clearly identifiable in the background. ⊠ *Freyung 6, 1st District,* ☎ *01/534–98–600.* 📠 *Church free, museum €4.* ☉ *Museum Thurs.–Sun. 10–5. U-Bahn: U2/ Schottentor.*

Third Man Portal. The doorway at Schreyvogelgasse 8 (up the incline) was made famous in 1949 by the classic film *The Third Man* (☞ Tracking Down the *Third Man* box, *below*); it was here that Orson Welles, as the malevolently knowing Harry Lime, stood hiding in the dark, only to have his smiling face illuminated by a sudden light from the upper-story windows of the house across the alley. The film enjoys a renaissance each summer in the Burg Kino and is fascinating for its portrayal of a postwar Vienna still in ruins. To get here from the nearby and noted Schottenkirche, follow Teinfaltstrasse one block west to Schreyvogel-gasse on the right. ⊠ *1st District. U-Bahn: U2/Schottentor.*

❶❹ **Uhrenmuseum** (Clock Museum). Kurrentgasse leads south from the east end of Judenplatz; the beautifully restored 18th-century houses on its east side make this one of the most unpretentiously appealing streets in the city. And at the far end of the street is one of Vienna's most appealing museums: the Uhrenmuseum, or Clock Museum (enter to the right on the Schulhof side of the building). The museum's three floors display a splendid parade of clocks and watches—more than 3,000 timepieces—dating from the 15th century to the present. The ruckus of bells and chimes pealing forth on any hour is impressive, but for the full cacophony try to be here at noon. Right next door is the Puppen und Spielzeug Museum. ⊠ *Schulhof 2, 1st District,* ☎ *01/533–2265.* 📠 *€3.60.* ☉ *Tues.–Sun. 9–4:30. U-Bahn: U1 or U3/Stephanspl.*

Vienna's Shop Window: From Michaelerplatz to the Graben

The compact area bounded roughly by the back side of the Hofburg palace complex, the Kohlmarkt, the Graben, and Kärntnerstrasse belongs to the oldest core of the city. Remains of the Roman city are just

TRACKING DOWN THE *THIRD MAN*

PROBABLY NOTHING HAS DONE MORE to create the myth of post-war Vienna than Carol Reed's classic 1949 film *The Third Man*. The bombed-out ruins of this proud, imperial city created an indelible image of devastation and corruption in the war's aftermath. Vienna was then divided into four sectors, each commanded by one of the victorious American, Russian, French, and British armies. But their attempts at rigid control could not prevent a thriving black market. Reed's film version of the great Graham Greene thriller features Vienna as a leading player, from the top of its Ferris wheel in the Prater to the depth of its lowest sewers–"which run right into the Blue Danube"—thrillingly used for the famous chase scene. It is only fitting to note that this was the first British film to be shot entirely on location.

In the film, Joseph Cotten plays Holly Martins, a pulp-fiction writer who comes to Vienna in search of his friend Harry Lime (Orson Welles). He makes the mistake of delving too deeply into Lime's affairs, even falling in love with his girlfriend, Anna Schmidt (Alida Valli), with fatal consequences.

Many of the sites where the film was shot still remain and are easily visited. Harry Lime appears for the first time nearly one hour into the film in the doorway of Anna's apartment building at No. 8 Schreyvogelgasse, around the corner from the Mölker-Bastei (a remnant of the old city wall). He then runs to Am Hof, a lovely square lined with baroque town houses and churches, which appears much closer to Anna's neighborhood than it actually is.

The famous scene between Lime and Martins on the Ferris wheel was filmed on the Riesenrad at the Prater, the huge amusement park across the Danube canal. While the two friends talk in the enclosed compartment, the wheel slowly makes a revolution, with all Vienna spread out below them.

In the memorable chase at the end of the movie, Lime is seen running through the damp, sinister sewers of Vienna, hotly pursued by the authorities. In reality, he would not have been able to use the sewer system as an escape route because the tunnels were too low and didn't connect between the different centers of the city. But a movie creates its own reality. In fact, a more feasible, if less cinematic, possibility of escape was offered by the labyrinth of cellars that still connected many buildings in the city.

Lime's funeral is held at the Zentral-friedhof (Central Cemetery), reachable by the 71 streetcar. This is the final scene of the movie, where Anna Schmidt walks down the stark, wide avenue (dividing sections 69 and 70), refusing to acknowledge the wistful presence of Holly Martins.

After touring sewers and cemeteries, a pick-me-up might be in order. You couldn't do better than to treat yourself to a stop at the Hotel Sacher, used for a scene in the beginning of the movie when Holly Martins is using the telephone in the lobby. The bar in the Sacher was a favorite hangout of director Carol Reed, and when filming finally wrapped, he left a signed note to the bartender, saying: "To the creator of the best Bloody Marys in the whole world."

— Bonnie Dodson

below the present-day surface. This was and still is the commercial heart of the city, dense with shops and markets for various commodities; today, the Kohlmarkt and Graben in particular offer the choicest luxury shops, overflowing into the Graben end of Kärntnerstrasse. The area is marvelous for its visual treats, ranging from the squares and varied architecture to shop windows. The evening view down Kohlmarkt from the Graben is an inspiring classic, with the night-lit gilded dome of Michael's Gate to the palace complex as the glittering backdrop.

A Good Walk

Start your walk through this fascinating quarter at **Michaelerplatz** ㉔, one of Vienna's most evocative squares, where the feel of the imperial city remains very strong; the buildings around the perimeter present a synopsis of the city's entire architectural history: medieval church spire, Renaissance church facade, baroque palace facade, 19th-century apartment house, and 20th-century bank. Look in the Michaelerkirche (St. Michael's Church). Opposite the church is the once-controversial **Looshaus** ㉕, considered a breakthrough in modern architecture (visitors are welcome to view the restored lobby). From Michaelerplatz, take the small passageway to the right of the church; in it on your right is a relief dating from 1480 of Christ on the Mount of Olives. Follow the Stallburggasse through to Dorotheergasse, and turn right to discover the **Dorotheum,** the government-run auction house and Viennese equivalent of Christie's or Sotheby's. On your right in the Dorotheergasse (toward the Graben) is the enlarged **Jewish Museum** ㉖, which includes a bookstore and café. On the left is the famous Café Hawelka, haunt to the contemporary art and literature crowd. Turn right in the Graben to come to **Stock-im-Eisen** ㉗; the famous nail-studded tree trunk is encased in the corner of the building with the Bank Austria offices. Opposite and impossible to overlook is the aggressive **Neues Haas-Haus** ㉘, an upmarket restaurant and shopping complex. Wander back through the **Graben** for the full effect of this harmonious street and look up to see the ornamentation on the buildings. Pass the **Pestsäule** ㉙, or Plague Column, which shoots up from the middle of the Graben like a geyser of whipped cream. Just off to the north side is the **Peterskirche** ㉚, St. Peter's Church, a baroque gem almost hidden by its surroundings. At the end of the Graben, turn left into the **Kohlmarkt** ㉛ for the classic view of the domed arch leading to the Hofburg, the imperial palace complex. Even if your feet aren't calling a sit-down strike, finish up at **Demel** ㉜, at Kohlmarkt 14, for some of the best *Gebäck* (pastries) in the world.

TIMING

Inveterate shoppers, window or otherwise, will want to take time to pause before or in many of the elegant shops during this walk, which then could easily take most of a day or even longer. If you're content with facades and general impressions, the exercise could be done in a bit over an hour, but it would be a shame to bypass the narrow side streets. In any case, look into St. Michael's and consider the fascinating Dorotheum, itself easily worth an hour or more.

Sights to See

★ ㉜ **Demel.** Vienna's best-known pastry shop, Demel's offers a dizzying selection, so if you have a sweet tooth, a visit will be worth every euro. And in a city famous for its tortes, their Senegaltorte takes the cake. Chocolate lovers will want to participate in the famous Viennese Sachertorte debate by sampling Demel's version and then comparing it with its rival at the **Café Sacher,** which is in the Hotel Sacher. ✉ *Kohlmarkt 14, 1st District,* ☎ *01/535–1717–0. U-Bahn: U1 or U3/ Stephanspl.*

Dorotheum. The narrow passageway just to the right of St. Michael's, with its large 15th-century relief depicting Christ on the Mount of Olives, leads into the Stallburggasse. The area is dotted with antiques stores, attracted by the presence of the Dorotheum, the famous Viennese auction house that began as a state-controlled pawnshop in 1707 (affectionately known as "Aunt Dorothy" to its patrons). Merchandise coming up for auction is on display at Dorotheergasse 17. The showrooms—packed with everything from carpets and pianos to cameras and jewelry and postage stamps—are well worth a visit. Some wares are not for auction but for immediate sale. ⊠ *Dorotheerg. 17, 1st District,* ☎ *01/515–60–0.* ⊙ *Weekdays 10–6, Sat. 9–5. U-Bahn: U1 or U3/Stephanspl.*

The Graben. One of Vienna's major crossroads, the Graben, leading west from Stock-im-Eisen-Platz, is a street whose unusual width gives it the presence and weight of a city square. It owes its shape to the Romans, who dug the city's southwestern moat here (Graben literally means "moat" or "ditch") adjacent to the original city walls. The Graben's centerpiece is the effulgently baroque **Pestsäule.** ⊠ *At the intersections of Kärntnerstr. and Kohlmarkt, 1st District. U-Bahn: U1 or U3/ Stephanspl.*

㉖ Jewish Museum. The former Eskeles Palace, once an elegant private residence, now houses the city's Jüdisches Museum der Stadt Wien. Permanent exhibitions tell of the momentous role that Vienna-born Jews played in realms from music to medicine, art to philosophy, both in Vienna—until abruptly halted in 1938—and in the world at large. Changing exhibits add contemporary touches. The museum complex includes a café and bookstore. ⊠ *Dorotheerg. 11, 1st District,* ☎ *01/ 535–0431.* 🎟 *€5.09.* ⊙ *Sun.–Fri. 10–6, Thurs. 10–8. U-Bahn: U1 or U3/Stephanspl.*

㉛ Kohlmarkt. The Kohlmarkt, aside from its classic view of the domed entryway to the imperial palace complex of the Hofburg, is best known as Vienna's most elegant shopping street. The shops, not the buildings, are remarkable, although there is an entertaining odd-couple pairing: No. 11 (early 18th century) and No. 9 (early 20th century). The mixture of architectural styles is similar to that of the Graben, but the general atmosphere is low-key, as if the street were consciously deferring to the showstopper dome at the west end. The composers Haydn and Chopin lived in houses on the street, and indeed, the Kohlmarkt lingers in the memory when flashier streets have faded. ⊠ *At the intersections of Hofburg Palace and Kohlmarkt, 1st District. U-Bahn: U3/Herreng.*

★ ㉕ Looshaus. In 1911, Adolf Loos, one of the founding fathers of 20th-century modern architecture, built the Looshaus on august Michaelerplatz, facing the Imperial Palace entrance. It was considered nothing less than an architectural declaration of war. After 200 years of baroque and neo-baroque exuberance, the first generation of 20th-century architects had had enough. Loos led the revolt against architectural tradition; *Ornament and Crime* was the title of his famous manifesto, in which he inveighed against the conventional architectural wisdom of the 19th century. Instead, he advocated buildings that were plain, honest, and functional. When he built the Looshaus for Goldman and Salatsch (men's clothiers) in 1911, the city was scandalized. Archduke Franz Ferdinand, heir to the throne, was so offended that he vowed never again to use the Michaelerplatz entrance to the Imperial Palace. Today the Looshaus has lost its power to shock, and the facade seems quite innocuous; argument now focuses on the postmodern Neues Haas-Haus opposite St. Stephen's Cathedral. The recently restored interior of the Looshaus remains a breathtaking surprise; the building now houses a bank, and you can go inside to see the stylish chambers and staircase. ⊠ *Michaelerpl. 3, 1st District. U-Bahn: U3/Herreng.*

㉔ Michaelerplatz. One of Vienna's most historic squares, this small plaza is now the site of an excavation revealing Roman plus 18th- and 19th-century layers of the past. The excavations are a latter-day distraction from the Michaelerplatz's most noted claim to fame—the eloquent entryway to the palace complex of the Hofburg.

In 1945 American soldiers forced open the doors of the crypt in the **Michaelerkirche** for the first time in 150 years and made a singular discovery. Found lying undisturbed, obviously for centuries, were the mummified remains of former wealthy parishioners of the church—even the finery and buckled shoes worn at their burial had been preserved by the perfect temperatures contained within the crypt. Fascinatingly ghoulish tours are offered hourly from Monday to Friday, May to October at 11 and from 1 to 4; during the winter season, November to April, the tours are given at 11 and 3 from Monday to Friday. The cost during summer is €3.20 including a church exhibit, and €2.50 in winter, and it is given first in German and then in English. Visitors are led down into the shadowy gloom and through a labyrinth of passageways, pausing at several tombs (many of which are open in order to view the remains), with a brief explanation of the cause of death given at each site. ⊠ *At the intersections of Hofburg Palace and Kohlmarkt, 1st District. U-Bahn: U3/Herreng.*

㉘ Neues Haas-Haus. Stock-im-Eisen-Platz is home to central Vienna's most controversial (for the moment, at least) piece of architecture: the Neues Haas-Haus (☞ Vienna's New Architecture box, *below*) designed by Hans Hollein, one of Austria's best-known living architects. Detractors consider its aggressively contemporary style out of place opposite St. Stephen's, seeing the cathedral's style parodied by being stood on its head; advocates consider the contrast enlivening. Whatever the ultimate verdict, the restaurant and shopping complex has not proved to be the anticipated commercial success; its restaurants may be thriving, but its boutiques are not. ⊠ *Stephanspl. 12, 1st District.* ☉ *Shops weekdays 9–6, Sat. 9–noon. U-Bahn: U1 or U3/Stephanspl.*

㉙ Pestsäule (Plague Column). Erected by Emperor Leopold I between 1687 and 1693 as thanks to God for delivering the city from a particularly virulent plague, today the representation looks more like a host of cherubs doing their best to cope with the icing of a wedding cake wilting under a hot sun. Staunch Protestants may be shocked to learn that the foul figure of the Pest stands also for the heretic plunging away from the "True Faith" into the depth of hell. But they will have to get used to the fact that the Catholic Church has triumphed over Protestantism in Austria and frequently recalls the fact in stone and on canvas. ⊠ *Graben, 1st District. U-Bahn: U1 or U3/Stephanspl.*

★ **㉚ Peterskirche** (St. Peter's Church). Considered the best example of church baroque in Vienna—certainly the most theatrical—the Peterskirche was constructed between 1702 and 1708 by Lucas von Hildebrandt. According to legend, the original church on this site was founded in 792 by Charlemagne, a tale immortalized by the relief plaque on the right side of the church. The facade has angled towers, graceful turrets (said to have been inspired by the tents of the Turks during the siege of 1683), and an unusually fine entrance portal. Inside the church, the baroque decoration is elaborate, with some fine touches (particularly the glass-crowned galleries high on the walls to either side of the altar and the amazing tableau of the martyrdom of St. John Nepomuk), but the lack of light and the years of accumulated dirt create a prevailing gloom, and the much-praised ceiling frescoes by J. M. Rottmayr are impossible to make out. Just before Christmastime each year, the basement crypt is filled with a display of nativity scenes. The church is shoehorned into tiny Petersplatz, just off the Graben. ⊠ *Peterspl., 1st District U-Bahn: U1 or U3/Stephanspl.*

㉗ **Stock-im-Eisen.** In the southwest corner of Stock-im-Eisen-Platz, set into the building on the west side of Kärntnerstrasse, is one of the city's odder relics: the Stock-im-Eisen, or the "nail-studded stump." Chronicles first mention the Stock-im-Eisen in 1533, but it is probably far older, and for hundreds of years any apprentice metalsmith who came to Vienna to learn his trade hammered a nail into the tree trunk for good luck. During World War II, when there was talk of moving the relic to a museum in Munich, it mysteriously disappeared; it reappeared, perfectly preserved, after the threat of removal had passed. ⊠ *At the intersection of the Graben and Singerstr., 1st District. U-Bahn: U1 or U3/Stephanspl.*

An Imperial City: The Hofburg

A walk through the Imperial Palace, known as the **Hofburg,** brings you back to the days when Vienna was the capital of a mighty empire. You can still find in Vienna shops vintage postcards and prints that show the revered and bewhiskered Emperor Franz Josef leaving his Hofburg palace for a drive in his carriage. Today, at the palace—which faces Kohlmarkt on the opposite side of Michaelerplatz—you can walk in his very footsteps, gaze at the old tin bath the emperor kept under his simple iron bedstead, marvel at his bejeweled christening robe, and, along the way, feast your eyes on great works of art, impressive armor, and some of the finest baroque interiors in Europe.

Until 1918 the Hofburg was the home of the Habsburgs, rulers of the Austro-Hungarian Empire. As a current tourist lure, it has become a vast smorgasbord of sightseeing attractions: the Imperial Apartments, two Imperial treasuries, six museums, the National Library, and the famous Winter Riding School all vie for attention. The entire complex takes a minimum of a full day to explore in detail; if your time is limited (or if you want to save most of the interior sightseeing for a rainy day), you should omit the Imperial Apartments and all the museums mentioned below except the new museum of court silver and tableware, the Silberkammer, and probably the Schatzkammer. An excellent multilingual, full-color booklet describing the palace in detail is for sale at most ticket counters within the complex; it gives a complete list of attractions and maps out the palace's complicated ground plan and building history wing by wing.

Vienna took its imperial role seriously, as evidenced by the sprawling Hofburg complex, which is still today, as then, the seat of government. But this is generally understated power; although the buildings cover a considerable area, the treasures lie within, not to be flamboyantly flaunted. Certainly under Franz Josef II the reign was beneficent—witness the broad Ringstrasse he ordained and the panoply of museums and public buildings it hosts. With few exceptions (Vienna City Hall and the Votive Church), rooflines are kept to an even level, creating an ensemble effect that helps integrate the palace complex and its parks into the urban landscape without making a domineering statement. Diplomats still bustle in and out of high-level international meetings along the elegant halls. Horse-drawn carriages still traverse the Ring and the roadway that cuts through the complex. Ignore the cars and tour buses and you can easily imagine yourself in a Vienna of a hundred or more years ago.

Architecturally, the Hofburg—like St. Stephen's—is far from refined. It grew up over a period of 700 years (its earliest mention in court documents is from 1279, at the very beginning of Habsburg rule), and its spasmodic, haphazard growth kept it from attaining any sort of unified identity. But many of the bits and pieces are fine, and one interior (the National Library) is a tour de force.

A Good Walk

When you begin to explore the Hofburg you realize that the palace complex is like a nest of boxes, courtyards opening off courtyards and wings (*Trakte*) spreading far and wide. First tackle **Josefsplatz** ㉝, the remarkable square that interrupts Augustinerstrasse, ornamented by the equestrian statue of Josef II—many consider this Vienna's loveliest square. Indeed, the beautifully restored imperial decor adorning the roof of the buildings forming Josefsplatz is one of the few visual demonstrations of Austria's onetime widespread power and influence. On your right to the north is the **Spanische Reitschule** ㉞, the Spanish Riding School—one emblem of Vienna known throughout the world— where the famous white horses reign. Across Reitschulgasse under the arches are the **Lipizzaner Museum** ㉟ and the Imperial Stables. To the south stands the **Augustinerkirche** ㊱, St. Augustine's Church, where the Habsburg rulers' hearts are preserved in urns. The grand main hall (Prunksaal) of the **Hofbibliothek** ㊲, the National Library, is one of the great baroque treasures of Europe, a site not to be missed (enter from the southwest corner of Josefsplatz).

Under the Michaelerplatz dome is the entrance to the **Kaiserappartements** ㊳, hardly the elegance you would normally associate with royalty, but Franz Josef II, the residing emperor from 1848 to 1916, was anything but ostentatious in his personal life. For the representational side, however, go through into the **In der Burg** ㊴ courtyard and look in at the elegant **Silberkammer** ㊵ museum of court silver and tableware. Go through the **Schweizertor** ㊶, the Swiss gate, to the south off In der Burg, to reach the small **Schweizer Hof** ㊷ courtyard with stairs leading to the **Hofburgkapelle** ㊸, the Imperial Chapel where the Vienna Boys Choir makes its regular Sunday appearances. In a back corner of the courtyard is the entrance to the **Schatzkammer** ㊹, the Imperial Treasury, overflowing with jewels, robes, and royal trappings. From In der Burg, the roadway leads under the **Leopold Wing** ㊺ of the complex into the vast park known as **Heldenplatz** ㊻, or Hero's Square. The immediately obvious heroes are the equestrian statues of Archduke Karl and Prince Eugene of Savoy. The Hofburg wing to the south with its concave facade is the **Neue Burg** ㊼, the "new" section of the complex, now housing four specialized museums. Depending on your interests, consider the **Ephesus Museum** ㊽, with Roman antiquities; the **Musical Instruments Collection** ㊾, where you also hear what you see; the impressive **Weapons Collection** ㊿, with tons of steel armor; or the **Ethnological Museum** ⑤, including Montezuma's headdress. Ahead, the **Burgtor** ② gate separates the Hofburg complex from the Ringstrasse. The quiet oasis in back of the Neue Burg is the **Burggarten** ③. Catch your breath and marvel that you've seen only a small part of the Hofburg—a large part of it still houses the offices of the Austrian government and is not open to the public.

TIMING

You could spend a day in the Hofburg complex. For most of the smaller museums, figure on anything from an hour upward.

Sights to See

㊱ **Augustinerkirche** (Augustinian Church). Across Josefsplatz from the Riding School is the entrance to the Augustinerkirche, built during the

14th century and presenting the most unified Gothic interior in the city. But the church is something of a fraud; the interior, it turns out, dates from the late 18th century, not the early 14th. A historical fraud the church may be, but a spiritual fraud it is not. The view from the entrance doorway is stunning: a soaring harmony of vertical piers, ribbed vaults, and hanging chandeliers that makes Vienna's other Gothic interiors look earthbound by comparison. The imposing baroque organ sounds as heavenly as it looks, and the Sunday morning high mass sung here—frequently by Mozart or Haydn—can be the highlight of a trip. To the right of the main altar in the small Loreto Chapel stand silver urns containing the hearts of Habsburg rulers. This rather morbid sight is viewable after early mass on Sunday, Monday, or by appointment. ⊠ *Josefspl., 1st District,* ☎ *01/533–7099–0. U-Bahn: U3/Herreng.*

53 **Burggarten.** The intimate Burggarten in back of the Neue Burg is a quiet oasis that includes a statue of a contemplative Kaiser Franz Josef and an elegant statue of Mozart, moved here from the Albertinaplatz after the war, when the city's charred ruins were being rebuilt. The former greenhouses are now the Schmetterlinghaus (Butterfly House) and the Palmenhaus restaurant. ⊠ *Access from Opernring and Hanuschg./Goetheg, 1st District. U-Bahn: U2/MuseumsQuartier; Tram: 1, 2, and D/Burgring.*

Schmetterlinghaus. The Butterfly House was recently relocated from Schönbrunn Palace to the old Hofburg Palace conservatory. The tropical indoor garden is home to hordes of live butterflies, orchids, and other floral displays. ⊠ *Entrance in Burggarten, 1st District,* ☎ *01/ 533–8570.* 🎟 *€4.72.* ☉ *Apr.–Oct., weekdays 10–4:45, weekends 10– 6:15; Nov.–Mar., daily 10–3:45. U-Bahn: U2/MuseumsQuartier; Trams: 1, 2, and D/Burgring*

52 **Burgtor.** The failure to complete the **Hofburg** building program left the old main palace gate stranded in the middle of the Heldenplatz.

48 **Ephesus Museum.** One of the museums in the Neue Burg, the Ephesus Museum contains exceptional Roman antiquities unearthed by Austrian archaeologists in Turkey at the turn of the century. ⊠ *Hofburg, 1st District.* 🎟 *Combined ticket with Musical Instruments Collection and Weapons Collection €7.50, more for special exhibits).* ☉ *Wed.– Mon. 10–6. U-Bahn: U2/MuseumsQuartier.*

51 **Ethnological Museum** (Museum für Völkerkunde). This anthropology museum is entered at the west end pavilion in the Neue Burg. Montezuma's feathered headdress is a highlight of its collections. ⊠ *Hofburg, 1st District.* 🎟 *€7.20.* ☉ *Wed.–Mon. 10–6. U-Bahn: U2/ MuseumsQuartier.*

46 **Heldenplatz.** The long wing with the concave bay on the south side of the square is the youngest section of the palace, called the Neue Burg. Although the Neue Burg building plans were not completed and the Heldenplatz was left without a discernible shape, the space is nevertheless punctuated by two superb equestrian statues depicting Archduke Karl and Prince Eugene of Savoy. The older section on the north includes the offices of the federal president. ⊠ *Hofburg, 1st District. Tram: 1, 2, and D/Burgring.*

★ **37** **Hofbibliothek** (formerly Court, now National Library). This is one of the grandest baroque libraries in the world, in every sense a cathedral of books. Its centerpiece is the spectacular Prunksaal—the Grand Hall of the National Library—which probably contains more book treasures than any comparable collection outside the Vatican. The main entrance to the ornate reading room is in the left corner of Josefsplatz.

The Hofburg (Imperial Palace)

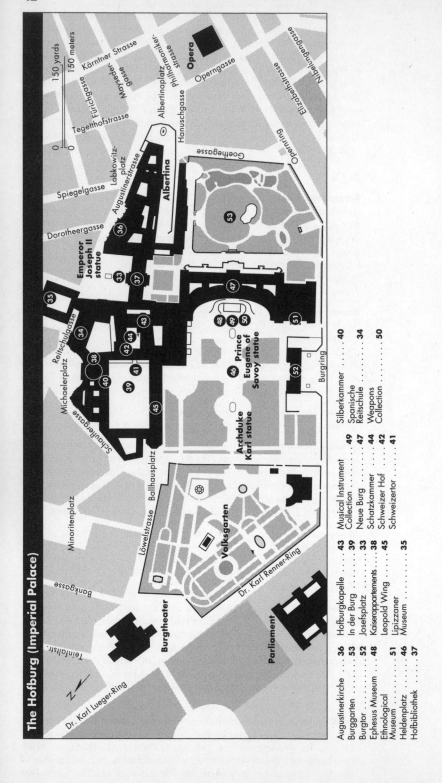

Designed by Fischer von Erlach the Elder just before his death in 1723 and completed by his son, the Grand Hall is full-blown high baroque, with trompe-l'oeil ceiling frescoes by Daniel Gran. This floridly baroque library may not be to everyone's taste, but in the end it is the books themselves that come to the rescue. They are as lovingly displayed as the gilding and the frescoes, and they give the hall a warmth that the rest of the palace decidedly lacks. On the third floor is an intriguing museum of cartographic globes that should not be overlooked. ⊠ *Josef-spl. 1, 1st District,* ☎ *01/534–100.* ☜ *€5.* ☉ *May–Oct., daily 10–4, Thurs. 10–7; Nov.–Apr., Mon.–Sat. 10–2. U-Bahn: U3/Herreng.*

43 **Hofburgkapelle** (Chapel of the Imperial Palace). The Vienna Boys Choir (Wiener Sängerknaben) sings mass at 9:15 on Sundays from mid-September to June. Alas, the arrangement is such that you *hear* the choirboys but don't see them; their soprano and alto voices peal forth from a gallery behind the seating area. ⊠ *Hofburg, Schweizer Hof, 1st District,* ☎ *01/533–9927,* ℻ *01/533–9927–75. U-Bahn: U3/Herreng.*

39 **In der Burg.** This prominent courtyard of the Hofburg complex is centered around a statue of Francis II and the noted **Schweizertor** gateway. Note the **clock** on the far upper wall at the north end of the courtyard: it tells time by the sundial, also gives the time mechanically, and even, above the clock face, indicates the phase of the moon. ⊠ *Hofburg, 1st District. U-Bahn: U3/Herreng.*

33 **Josefsplatz.** Josefsplatz is the most imposing of the Hofburg courtyards, with an equestrian **statue of Emperor Joseph II** (1807) in the center. ⊠ *Herreng., 1st District. U-Bahn: U3/Herreng.*

38 **Kaiserappartements** (Imperial Apartments). The long, repetitive suite of conventionally luxurious rooms has a sad and poignant feel. The decoration (19th-century imitation of 18th-century rococo) tries to look regal, but much like the empire itself in its latter days it is only going through the motions and ends up looking merely official. Among the few signs of genuine life are Emperor Franz Josef's spartan, iron field bed, on which he slept every night, and Empress Elisabeth's wooden gymnastics equipment (obsessed with her looks, she suffered from anorexia and was fanatically devoted to exercise). Amid all the tired splendor these artifacts look decidedly forlorn. ⊠ *Hofburg, Schweizer Hof, 1st District,* ☎ *01/533–7570.* ☜ *€6.90, with guided tour €9.40.* ☉ *Daily 9–4:30. U-Bahn: U3/Herreng.*

45 **Leopold Wing.** A long tract of offices known as the Leopold Wing separates the In der Burg courtyard from the vast Heldenplatz. ⊠ *Hofburg, 1st District. U-Bahn: U3/Herreng.*

35 **Lipizzaner Museum.** If you're interested in learning more about the Lipizzaners, visit this museum, located in what used to be the old imperial pharmacy. Exhibitions document the history of the Lipizzans, including paintings, photographs, and videos giving an overview from the 16th century to the present. A highlight is a visit to the stables, where you can see the horses up close, through a glass window. ⊠ *Reitschulg. 2, 1st District,* ☎ *01/533–8659–0,* ℻ *01/533–38–53.* ☜ *€5; combined ticket with morning training session €14.50.* ☉ *Daily 9–6. U-Bahn: U3/Herreng.*

49 **Musical Instruments Collection.** This Neue Burg museum houses pianos that belonged to Brahms, Schumann, and Mahler. An acoustic guided tour allows you actually to hear the various instruments on headphones as you move from room to room. ⊠ *Hofburg, 1st District.* ☜ *Combined ticket with Ephesus Museum and Weapons Collection*

€7.50, *more for special exhibits.* ⊙ *Wed.–Mon. 10–6. U-Bahn: U2/
MuseumsQuartier.*

47 **Neue Burg.** The Neue Burg stands today as a symbol of architectural
overconfidence. Designed for Emperor Franz Josef in 1869, this "new
château" was part of a much larger scheme that was meant to make
the Hofburg rival the Louvre, if not Versailles. The German architect
Gottfried Semper planned a twin of the present Neue Burg on the opposite side of the Heldenplatz, with arches connecting the Neue Burg
and its twin with the other pair of twins on the Ringstrasse, the Kunsthistorisches Museum (Museum of Art History), and the Naturhistorisches Museum (Museum of Natural History). But World War I
intervened, and with the empire's collapse the Neue Burg became
merely the last in a long series of failed attempts to bring architectural
order to the Hofburg. (From its main balcony, in April 1938, Adolf
Hitler, telling a huge cheering crowd below of his plan for the new German empire, declared that Vienna "is a pearl! I am going to put it into
a setting of which it is worthy!") Today crowds flock to the Neue Burg
because it houses no fewer than four specialty museums: the **Ephesus
Museum, Musical Instruments Collection, Ethnological Museum,** and
Weapons Collection. For details on these museums, see separate listings. ⊠ *Heldenpl., 1st District,* ☎ *01/525240. U-Bahn: U2/Museums-
Quartier.*

44 **Schatzkammer** (Imperial Treasury). The entrance to the Schatzkammer, with its 1,000 years of treasures, is tucked away at ground level
behind the staircase to the Hofburgkapelle. The elegant display is a welcome antidote to the monotony of the Imperial Apartments, for the
entire Treasury was completely renovated in 1983–87, and the crowns
and relics and vestments fairly glow in their new surroundings. Here
you'll find such marvels as the Holy Lance—reputedly the lance that
pierced Jesus' side—the Imperial Crown (a sacred symbol of sovereignty
once stolen on Hitler's orders), and the Saber of Charlemagne. Don't
miss the Burgundian Treasure, connected with that most romantic of
medieval orders of chivalry, the Order of the Golden Fleece. ⊠ *Schweizer
Hof, 1st District,* ☎ *01/525240.* ▧ *€7.* ⊙ *Wed.–Mon. 10–6. U-Bahn:
U3/Herreng.*

42 **Schweizer Hof.** This courtyard was named after the Swiss guards who
were once stationed here. In the southeast corner (at the top of the steps)
is the entrance to the Hofburgkapelle. ⊠ *Hofburg, 1st District. U-Bahn:
U3/Herreng.*

41 **Schweizertor** (Swiss Gate). Dating from 1552 and decorated with
some of the earliest classical motifs in the city, the Schweizertor leads
from In der Burg through to the oldest section of the palace, a small
courtyard known as the Schweizer Hof. The gateway is painted ma-
roon, black, and gold; it gives a fine Renaissance flourish to its building facade. ⊠ *Hofburg, Schweizertor, 1st District. U-Bahn: U3/Herreng.*

40 **Silberkammer** (Museum of Court Silver and Tableware). The large
courtyard on the far side of the Michaelertor rotunda is known as In
der Burg; here on the west side is the entrance to the sparkling new Silberkammer. There's far more than forks and finger bowls here; stunning decorative pieces vie with glittering silver and gold for attention.
Highlights include Franz Josef's vermeil banqueting service, the jardinière
given to Empress Elisabeth by Queen Victoria, and gifts from Marie-
Antoinette to her brother Josef II. The presentation of full table settings
gives an idea of court life both as lived daily and on festive occasions.
⊠ *Hofburg, Michaelertrakt, 1st District,* ☎ *01/533–7570.* ▧ *€6.90,
including Kaiserappartements.* ⊙ *Daily 9–4:30. U-Bahn: U3/Herreng.*

★ ㉞ **Spanische Reitschule** (Spanish Riding School). Between Augustinerstrasse and the Josefsplatz is the world-famous Spanish Riding School, a favorite for centuries, and no wonder: who can resist the sight of the stark-white Lipizzan horses going through their masterful paces? For the last 300 years they have been perfecting their *haute école* riding demonstrations to the sound of baroque music in a ballroom that seems to be a crystal-chandeliered stable. The breed was started in 1580, and the horses proved themselves in battle as well as in the complicated "dances" for which they are famous. The interior of the riding school, the 1735 work of Fischer von Erlach the Younger, is itself an attraction—surely Europe's most elegant sports arena—and if the prancing horses begin to pall, move up to the top balcony and examine the ceiling. The school's popularity is hardly surprising, and tickets to some performances must be ordered in writing many weeks in advance, or through their Web site (www.srs.at). Information offices have a brochure with the detailed schedule (performances are usually March through December, with the school on vacation in July and August). Generally the full, 80-minute show takes place Sunday at 11 AM plus selected Fridays at 6 PM. There are two yearly classical dressage final rehearsals with music, at the end of August and the end of December. Check the Web site for details.

Morning training sessions with music are held Tuesday through Saturday from 10 to noon. Tickets can be bought *only* at the door for these morning training sessions, at the Josefsplatz entrance between 9:40 and 12:30. It's best to get there early to get a place in line. Note that if you purchase your tickets through a ticket agency for an actual performance, they can legally add a commission of 22%–25% to the face price of the ticket. For performance ticket orders, write to **Spanische Reitschule** (✉ Hofburg, A–1010 Vienna). Pick up reserved tickets at the office under the Michaelerplatz rotunda dome. ✉ *Michaelerpl. 1, Hofburg, A–1010, 1st District,* ☎ *01/533–9031–0,* FAX *01/535–0186,* WEB *www.srs.at.* 💶 *€33–€145; standing room €22–€25, morning training sessions €11.60; Sat. classical dressage final rehearsal, €20.* ☉ *Mar.–June and late Aug.–mid-Dec. Closed tour wks. U-Bahn: U3/Herreng.*

㊿ **Weapons Collection.** Rivaling the armory in Graz as one of the most extensive arms and armor collections in the world is this Neue Burg museum. Enter at the triumphal arch set into the middle of the curved portion of the facade. ✉ *Heldenpl., 1st District.* 💶 *Combined ticket with Ephesus Museum and Musical Instruments Collection €7.50, more for special exhibits.* ☉ *Wed.–Mon. 10–6. U-Bahn: U2/Museums-Quartier.*

The Ringstrasse and Its Environs

Along with the Hofburg, the Ringstrasse makes up Vienna's major urban set piece. This grand series of thoroughfares circles the heart of Vienna, the Innere Stadt (Inner City), or 1st District. It follows the lines of what were, until an imperial decree ordered them leveled in 1857, the city's defenses. By the 1870s Vienna had reached the zenith of her imperial prosperity, and this found ultimate expression in the series of magnificent buildings erected around the Ringstrasse—the Opera House, the Kunsthistoriches Museum, the Naturhistorisches Museum, and the Rathaus, the University, and the Votivkirche.

A Good Walk

Is there a best way to explore the Ring? You can walk it from one end to the other—from where it begins at the Danube Canal to where it returns to the canal after its curving flight. Or, you can explore it whenever you happen to cross it on other missions. Although it is a pleasant sequence of boulevards, seeing its succession of rather pompous buildings all in one walk can be overpowering. Or, you can obtain the best of both options by following this suggested itinerary, which leavens the bombast of the Ring with some of Vienna's most fascinating sights.

Immediately across the Ringstrasse from the Hofburg are twin buildings, both museums. To the west is the **Naturhistorisches Museum** ㉔; to the east, the **Kunsthistorisches Museum** ㉕, the art museum packed with world-famous treasures. Allow ample time for exploration here. Not far away is the new, headline-making **MuseumsQuartier** ㉖, a museum complex that includes several highly important modern art collections, including the Leopold Collection of Austrian Art and the Museum Moderner Kunst. Farther west of the museum square is the compact and hip **Spittelberg Quarter** ㉗ of tiny streets between Burggasse and Sibensterngasse, often the site of handicraft and seasonal fairs. For more, and superspectacular, evidence of handicraft of an earlier era, detour south to Mariahilferstrasse and the **Kaiserliches Hofmobiliendepot,** the repository of much of the sumptuous furnishings of the old Habsburg palaces.

Heading back to the Ring, the **Volksgarten** ㉘ on the inside of the Ringstrasse to the north of the museum square includes a café and rose garden among its attractions; look also for the small memorial to Franz Josef's wife, Empress Elisabeth, in the rear corner. Tackle the Ringstrasse buildings by starting with the **Justizpalast** ㉙ (Central Law Courts), moving along to **Parliament** ㉐, the **Rathaus** ㉑ (City Hall), the **Burgtheater** ㉒ opposite on the inside of the Ring, then the **Universität** ㉓ (the main building of Vienna's university) beyond, again on the outside of the Ring. Next to the university stands the neo-Gothic **Votivkirche** ㉔. If you still have time and energy, walk farther along the Ring to discover the **Börse** ㉕ (Stock Exchange) at the corner of the Ring and Wipplingerstrasse. The outside end of Hohenstaufengasse leads into Liechtensteinstrasse, which will bring you to Berggasse. Turn right to reach No. 19, the **Freud Apartment** ㉖, now a museum and research facility.

TIMING

If you can, plan to visit Vienna's Louvre—the Kunsthistorisches Museum—early in the day before the crowds arrive, although the size of crowds depends greatly on whatever special shows the museum may be exhibiting. As for the main sights off the Ringstrasse, you could easily lump together visits to the Freud Apartment and the Museum of Modern Art, figuring on about a half day for the two combined.

Sights to See

㉕ **Börse** (Vienna Stock Exchange). This imposing rose-brick building with a pillared portico was constructed in 1874–77 and was designed by Theophil Hansen, who also designed the Academy of Fine Arts. In addition to the stock exchange, the building houses a couple of shops and the unusual flower-shop restaurant Hansen. The stock exchange is not open to the public. ⊠ *Strauchg. 1–3, 1st District. Tram: 2 and D/Börse.*

㉒ **Burgtheater** (National Theater). One of the most important theaters in the German-speaking world, the Burgtheater was built between 1874 and 1888 in the Italian Renaissance style, replacing the old court theater at Michaelerplatz. Emperor Franz Josef's mistress, Katherina Schratt, was once a star performer here, and famous Austrian and German actors still stride across this stage. The opulent interior, with its 60-ft relief *Worshippers of Bacchus* by Rudolf Wyer and foyer ceiling frescoes by Ernst and Gustav Klimt make it well worth a visit. ⊠ *Dr. Karl-Lueger-Ring 2, 1st District,* ☎ *01/51444.* ⌨ *€4.50.* ⊘ *Guided tours Mon.–Sat. at 3; Sun. at 11 and 3. Tram: 1, 2, and D/Burgtheater, Rathaus.*

66 **Freud Apartment.** Not far from the historic Hofburg district, beyond the Votivkirche at the Schottenring along the Ringstrasse, you can skip over several centuries and visit that outstanding symbol of 20th-century Vienna: Sigmund Freud's apartment at Berggasse 19 (Apartment 6, one flight up; ring the bell and push the door simultaneously); this was his residence from 1891 to 1938. The five-room collection of memorabilia is mostly a photographic record of Freud's life, with some documents, publications, and a portion of his collection of antiquities also on display. The waiting-room furniture is authentic, but the consulting room and study furniture (including the famous couch) can be seen only in photographs. ⊠ *Bergg. 19, 9th District/Alsergrund,* ☎ *01/319–1596.* ⌨ *€5.* ⊘ *Jan.–June and Oct.–Dec. daily 9–5; July–Sept., daily 9–6. U-Bahn: U2/Schottentor.*

59 **Justizpalast** (Central Law Courts). Alexander Wielemans designed this monumental building in the Italian Renaissance style. It was built between 1875 and 1881. The main hall is nearly 70 ft high, and is topped by a glass ceiling. At the end of World War II this area was the center of the Austrian resistance movement, known as the "O5." The "O" stands for Österreich, or Austria, and the "5" is for the fifth letter of the alphabet, which translates into Ö, or OE, the abbreviation for Österreich. Between 1945 and 1955 it served as the headquarters for the Allied military leadership. The Justizpalast is not open to the public. ⊠ *Schmerlingpl. 10–11, 1st District. Tram: 1, 2, or D/Stadiong., Parliament.*

★ 55 **Kunsthistorisches Museum** (Museum of Fine Art). However short your stay in Vienna, you will surely want to pay a visit to one of the greatest art collections in the world, that of the Kunsthistorisches Museum. For this is no dry-as-dust museum illustrating the history of art, as its name implies. Rather its collections of old master paintings reveal the royal taste and style of many members of the mighty House of Habsburg, who during the 16th and 17th centuries ruled over the greater part of the Western world. Today you can enjoy what this great ruling house assiduously (and in most cases, selectively) brought together through the centuries. The collection stands in the same class with those of the Louvre, the Prado, and the Vatican. It is most famous for the largest collection of paintings under one roof by the Netherlandish 16th-century master Pieter Brueghel the Elder—just seeing his sublime *Hunters in the Snow* is worth a trip to Vienna, many art historians will tell you. Brueghel's depictions of peasant scenes, often set in magnificent landscapes, distill the poetry and magic of the 16th century as few other paintings do. Room RX is the Brueghel shrine—on its walls, in addition to *Hunters in the Snow,* hang *Children's Games,* the *Tower of Babel,* the *Peasant Wedding,* the *Nest-Robber,* and eight other priceless canvases. But there are also hundreds of other celebrated old master paintings here, most assembled by the Habsburgs over many centuries. Even a cursory description would run on for pages, but a brief selection of the museum's most important works will give you an idea of the riches to be enjoyed. The large-scale works concentrated in the main galleries shouldn't distract you from the equal share of masterworks in the more intimate side wings.

The Flemish wing includes Rogier van der Weyden's *Triptych Crucifixion,* Holbein's *Portrait of Jane Seymour, Queen of England,* a fine series of Rembrandt portraits, and Vermeer's peerless *Allegory of the*

Art of Painting. The grand style of the 17th century is represented by Rubens's towering altarpieces and his *Nude of Hélène Fourment.* In the Italian wing are works by Titian, including his *Portrait of Isabella d'Este,* whose fiercely intelligent eyes make you realize why she was the first lady of the Renaissance, and Giorgione's *The Three Philosophers,* an enigmatic composition in uniquely radiant Venetian coloring. A short list of other highlights include Raphael's *Madonna in the Meadow,* Correggio's *Jupiter Embracing Io,* Parmigianino's *Cupid Cutting a Bow,* Guercino's *Return of the Prodigal Son,* and Caravaggio's *Madonna of the Rosary.* One level down is the remarkable, less-visited *Kunstkammer,* displaying priceless objects created for the Habsburg emperors. These include curiosities made of gold, silver, and crystal (including Cellini's famous salt cellar), and more exotic materials, such as ivory, horn, and gemstones. In addition, there are rooms devoted to Egyptian antiquities, Greek and Roman art, sculpture (ranging from masterworks by Tilmann Riemenschneider to Italian Mannerist bronzes, which the Habsburgs collected by the roomful) and the decorative arts, and numerous other collections.

When your feet are ready to call a sit-down strike, repair to the wonderful café on the museum's second floor. Set under a grand dome, adorned with paintings, sculpture, and framed by gilt-tipped black marble columns, this spot is run by Gerstner, the famed pastry shop. The fruit tortes and comfy armchairs here add up to a refined time-out. ⊠ *Maria-Theresien-Pl., 7th District/Neubau,* ☏ *01/525240.* ⌑ €8.70. ☉ *Tues.–Sun. 10–6; extended hrs for picture galleries, Thurs. until 9* PM. *U-Bahn: U2/MuseumsQuartier, U2, or U3/Volkstheater.*

★ ☕ ❺❻ **MuseumsQuartier** (Museum Quarter). New and old, past and present, baroque and modernism dazzlingly collide in this headline-making, vast culture center, newly opened in 2001. Claiming to be the largest of its kind in the world, the MuseumsQuartier is housed in what was once the Imperial Court Stables, the 250-year-old baroque complex designed by Fischer von Erlach and ideally situated in the heart of the city, near the Hofburg and set, appropriately between the great old master treasures of the Kunsthistorisches Museum and the Spittelberg neighborhood, today one of Vienna's hippest enclaves. Where once 900 Lipizzaner horses were housed, now thousands of artistic masterworks of the 20th century and beyond are exhibited, all in a complex that is architecturally an expert and subtle blending of historic and cutting-edge—the original structure (fetchingly adorned with pastry-white stuccoed ceilings and rococo flourishes) was retained, and ultramodern wings were added to house five museums, most of which showcase modern art at its best. Once ensconced in the Palais Liechtenstein, the **Leopold Museum** comprises the holdings amassed by Rudolf and Elizabeth Leopold and famously contains one of the greatest collections of Egon Schiele in the world, as well as impressive works by Gustav Klimt and Oskar Kokoschka. Other artists worth noting are Josef Dobrowsky, Anton Faistauer, and Richard Gerstl. Emil Jakob Schindler's landscapes are well represented, as are those by Biedermeier artist Ferdinand Georg Waldmüller. Center stage is held by Schiele (1890–1918), who died young, along with his wife and young baby, in one of Vienna's worst Spanish flu epidemics. His colorful, appealing landscapes are here, but all eyes are invariably drawn to the artist's tortured and racked depictions of nude mistresses, orgiastic self-portraits, and provocatively sexual couples, all elbows and organs.

Adjacent, in a broodingly modernistic, dark stone edifice, is the **Museum moderner Kunst Stiftung Ludwig (MUMOK),** or Museum of Modern Art, which houses the national collection of 20th-century art

on eight floors, mainly a bequest of Herr Ludwig, a billionaire indus-
trialist who collected the cream of the crop of 20th-century art. Top
works here are of the American pop art school, but all the trends of
the last century—nouveau réalisme, radical realism, and hyperrealism
of the sixties and seventies, Fluxus, Viennese actionism, conceptual art
and minimal art, land art and arte povera, as well as installation art
vie for your attention. Names run from René Magritte and Max Ernst
to Andy Warhol, Jackson Pollock, Cy Twombly, Nam June Paik, and
the very latest superstars of contemporary art, such as Chris Burden
(whose installation was of $1 million worth of gold ingots) and Kara
Walker's daringly revisionist silhouettes. Kids will make a beeline for
Claes Oldenburg's walk-in sculpture in the shape of Mickey Mouse.

Nearby, the **Kunsthalle** is used for temporary exhibitions—gigantic halls
used for the installation of avant-avant-garde art. The emphasis is on
the ethos of "temporariness," so these halls are used to show off myriad works of contemporary art in an ever-changing schedule of in-
stallations and happenings—one recent exposition was called "Scandal
and Myth," so you can take it from there. A definite change of pace
is offered by the **ZOOM Kinder Museum**, which caters to children. In
the ZOOM lab, kids age 7 and up can experience the fine line between
the real and virtual world, making their imagined screenplays come to
life by becoming directors, sound technicians, authors, and actors. For
the little ones there's the ZOOM Ozean (ocean), where with their parents they can enter a play area inhabited by magical creatures from the
underwater world, featuring a ship with a captain's quarters and light-
house. It's probably a good idea to reserve tickets in advance for this
museum (☎ 01/524–7908, ፲AX 01/524–7908–1818). The **Architekturzentrum** (Architecture Center) displays new architecture models, with
computers showing the latest techniques used in restoring old buildings. And the often overlooked **Tabak Museum** (Tobacco Museum) has
a fascinating collection of elaborate snuffboxes and pipes.

The **Quartier21,** which opened in late 2002, showcases artists and musicians in the huge Fischer von Erlach wing facing the Museumsplatz.
Artists will have their own studios, open to the public for free, and at
the end of two years their output will be judged by a panel of visiting
museum curators who will decide if they should be invited to remain
another two years. In addition to all this, the annual Wiener Festwochen
(theater-arts festival) and the International Tanzwochen (dance festival) are held every year in the former Winter Riding Hall, and a theater for the annual Viennale Film Festival is planned. All in all,
modern-art lovers will find it very easy to spend the entire day at MuseumsQuartier (even that may not be enough), and with several cafés,
restaurants, gift shops and bookstores, they won't need to venture outside. ⊠ *Museumspl. 1–5, 7th District/Neubau,* ☎ *01/523–5881,* ⓌⒺⒷ
www.mqw.at ✉ *Leopold Museum €5.50; Kunst Stiftung Ludwig
€6.50; Kunsthalle €6.50; Architekturzentrum €5; ZOOM Kinder-
museum €4.50; Tabak Museum €3.60; combination ticket to all museums €25.* ⊘ *Open daily 10–7. U-Bahn: U2 MuseumsQuartier/U2
or U3/Volkstheater.*

⑤④ **Naturhistorisches Museum** (Natural History Museum). The formal museum complex just outside the Ring has two elements—to the east is
the celebrated Kunsthistorisches Museum, to the west is the Naturhistorisches Museum, or Natural History Museum. This is the home of,
among other artifacts, the famous Venus of Willendorf, a tiny statuette
(actually, a replica—the original is in a vault) thought to be some 20,000
years old; this symbol of the Stone Age was originally unearthed in the
Wachau Valley, not far from Melk. The reconstructed dinosaur skele-

VIENNA'S NEW ARCHITECTURE

ONE MORNING IN 1911 the revered and bewhiskered Emperor Franz Josef, starting out on a morning drive in his carriage from the Hofburg, opened his eyes in amazement as he beheld the defiantly plain Looshaus, constructed just opposite the Michaelerplatz entrance to the imperial palace. Never again, it was said, did the royal carriage ever use the route, so offensive was this modernist building to His Imperial Highness. One can, then, only imagine the Josefian reaction to the Neues Haas-Haus, built in 1985 on Vienna's Stephansplatz. Here, across from the Gothic cathedral of St. Stephen's, famed architect Hans Hollein has designed a shopping and restaurant complex whose elegant curved surfaces and reflecting glass interact beautifully—critics now unanimously agree—with its environment. It proves an intelligent alternative to the demands of historicism on one hand and aggressive modernism on the other.

This balancing act has always been a particular challenge in Vienna. For a few critics, the Gaudiesque eccentricities of the late Friedensreich Hundertwasser (besides the Kunsthaus museum by the Danube canal he is also responsible for the multicolored, golden globe–topped central heating tower that has become almost as much a part of the skyline as St. Stephen's spire) did the trick. But for all their charm, they have been overshadowed by the Viennese modernism of today. Indeed, the current architectural scene is the most creative since the heyday of the Jugendstil master Otto Wagner. A generation of Austrian architects who tried out their ideas in small private and commercial commissions in the 1960s and '70s have now made their mark in a very public way, in part spurred on by the city's expansion following the fall of the Iron Curtain in 1989. Vienna's unique history as a former imperial capital that produced both grand official buildings imitating a variety of historical styles and a vibrant modernist reaction has proved fertile ground for innovation.

If a single building can stand as the manifesto of the present revival, it would have to be the Neues Haas-Haus. The controversy that surrounded its construction opposite the city's medieval cathedral echoed exactly the uproar caused by the building of the Loos Haus facing the baroque opulence of the Hofburg 80 years earlier. In fact, the building codes had to be changed to allow Hollein's design; it was finally conceded that the requirement to imitate the surrounding architecture made no sense in an area that included a veritable catalog of historical styles.

If the Haas-Haus is the most prominent example of Vienna's new architecture, the vast MuseumsQuartier is by necessity the most discreet. Hidden behind the baroque facade of the former imperial stables, the design by Laurids and Manfred Ortner uses its enclosed space to set up a counterpoint between Fischer von Erlach's riding school and the imposing new structures built to house the Leopold Museum and the Modern Art Museum. From the first, old and new collide: to enter the complex's Halle E + G, you pass below the Emperor's Loge, whose double-headed Imperial eagles now form a striking contrast to a silver-hued steel double staircase. Again, the modern buildings manage to complement the historical surroundings dynamically, breathing new life into a construction whose original purpose had long ago become obsolete.

Other important projects—notably the new underground museum devoted to Jewish history on the Judenplatz (landmarked by a stark cube memorial by award-winning English sculptor Rachel Whitehead); the Gasometer complex, an entire planned community recycled from the immense brick drums of the 19th-century gasworks to the east of the city; and ecologically responsible Donau City—are among the architectural landmarks on tours now organized by the Architecture Center (AZW) of the MuseumsQuartier; their maps and brochures can be used for self-guided tours.

— Gary Dodson

tons understandably draw the greatest attention. ✉ *Maria-Theresien-Pl., 7th District/Neubau,* ☎ *01/521–77–0.* 🎫 *€3.60.* 🕐 *Wed. 9–9, Thurs.–Mon. 9–6:30. U-Bahn: U2 or U3/Volkstheater.*

⑥⓪ **Parliament.** This sprawling building reminiscent of an ancient Greek temple is the seat of Austria's elected representative assembly. An embracing, heroic ramp on either side of the main structure is lined with carved marble figures of ancient Greek and Roman historians. Its centerpiece is the **Pallas-Athene-Brunnen** (fountain), designed by Theophil Hansen, which is crowned by the goddess of wisdom and surrounded by water nymphs symbolizing the executive and legislative powers governing the country. ✉ *Dr. Karl-Renner-Ring 1, 1st District,* ☎ *01/401–100.* 🎫 *€3.* 🕐 *Tours mid-Sept.–June, Mon.–Thurs. 11 and 3 (except on days when Parliament is in session); Fri. 11, 1, 2, and 3; July–mid-Sept. weekdays 9, 10, 11, 1, 2, and 3. Tram: 1, 2, or D/Stadiong., Parliament.*

⑥① **Rathaus** (City Hall). Designed by Friedrich Schmidt and resembling a Gothic fantasy castle with its many spires and turrets, the Rathaus was actually built between 1872 and 1883. The facade holds a lavish display of standard-bearers brandishing the coats of arms of the city of Vienna and the monarchy. Guided tours include the banqueting hall and various committee rooms. A regally landscaped park graces the front of the building and it is usually brimming with activity. In winter it is the scene of the *Christkindlmarkt,* the most famous Christmas market in Vienna; in summer, concerts are performed here. ✉ *Rathauspl. 1, 1st District,* ☎ *01/4000–0.* 🎫 *Free.* 🕐 *Guided tours (5-person minimum) Mon., Wed., Fri., at 1. Tram: 1, 2, or D/Rathaus.*

Ringstrasse. Late in 1857, Emperor Franz Josef issued a decree announcing the most ambitious piece of urban redevelopment Vienna had ever seen. The inner city's centuries-old walls were to be torn down, and the *glacis*—the wide expanse of open field that acted as a protective buffer between inner city and outer suburbs—was to be filled in. In their place was to rise a wide, tree-lined boulevard, upon which would stand an imposing collection of new buildings that would reflect Vienna's special status as the political, economic, and cultural heart of the Austro-Hungarian Empire. During the 50 years of building that followed, many factors combined to produce the Ringstrasse as it now stands, but the most important was the gradual rise of liberalism after the failed Revolution of 1848. By the latter half of the Ringstrasse era, support for constitutional government, democracy, and equality—all the concepts that liberalism traditionally equates with progress—was steadily increasing. As the Ringstrasse went up, it became the definitive symbol of this liberal progress; as Carl E. Schorske put it in his *Fin-de-Siècle Vienna,* it celebrated "the triumph of constitutional *Recht* (right) over imperial *Macht* (might), of secular culture over religious faith. Not palaces, garrisons, and churches, but centers of constitutional government and higher culture dominated the Ring."

The highest concentration of public buildings is found in the area around the Volksgarten, where are clustered (moving from south to north, from Burgring to Schottenring) the **Kunsthistorisches Museum,** the **Naturhistorisches Museum,** the **Justizpalast** (Central Law Courts), the **Parliament,** the **Rathaus** (City Hall), the **Burgtheater** (National Theater), the **Universität** (University of Vienna), the **Votivkirche** (Votive Church), and slightly farther along, the **Börse** (Stock Exchange) on Schottenring. As an ensemble, the collection is astonishing in its architectural presumption: it is nothing less than an attempt to assimilate and summarize the entire architectural history of Europe. As critics were quick to notice, however, the complex suffers from a serious organizational flaw: most of the buildings lack effective context. Rather than being the focal points of an organized overall plan, they are plunked haphazardly down on an avenue that is itself too wide to present a unified, visually comprehensible character.

To some the monumentality of the Ringstrasse is overbearing; others find the architectural panorama exhilarating, and growth of the trees over 100 years has served to put the buildings into a different perspective. There is no question but that the tree-lined boulevard with its broad sidewalks gives the city a unique ribbon of green and certainly the distinction that the emperor sought. ⊠ *1st, 7th Districts. U-Bahn: U2 or U3/Volkstheater, U2/MuseumsQuartier, U3/Volkstheater, U2/Schottentor; Tram: 1, 2, and D/Burgtheater, Rathaus.*

★ ⑤⑦ **Spittelberg Quarter.** People like to come to the Spittelberg because it's a slice of Old Vienna, a perfectly preserved little enclave that allows you to experience the 18th century by strolling along cobblestone pedestrian streets lined with pretty baroque town houses. As such, the quarter—situated one block northwest of Maria-Theresien-Platz off the Burggasse—offers a fair visual idea of the Vienna that existed outside of the city walls a century ago. Most buildings have been replaced, but the engaging 18th-century survivors at Burggasse 11 and 13 are adorned with religious and secular decorative sculpture, the latter with a niche statue of St. Joseph, the former with cherubic work-and-play bas-reliefs. For several blocks around—walk down Gutenberggasse and back up Spittelberggasse—the 18th-century houses have been beautifully restored. The sequence from Spittelberggasse 5 to 19 is an especially fine array of Viennese plain and fancy. Around holiday times, particularly Easter and Christmas, the Spittelberg quarter, known for arts and handicrafts, hosts seasonal markets offering unusual and interesting wares. Promenaders will be able to also enjoy some art galleries and loads of restaurants. ⊠ *Off Burgg., 7th District/Spittelberg. U-Bahn: U2 or U3/Volkstheater.*

OFF THE BEATEN PATH
KAISERLICHES HOFMOBILIENDEPOT (IMPERIAL FURNITURE MUSEUM) – In the days of the Habsburg empire, palaces remained practically empty if the ruling family was not in residence. Cavalcades laden with enough furniture to fill a palace would set out in anticipation of a change of scene, while another caravan accompanied the royal party, carrying everything from traveling thrones to velvet-lined portable toilets. Much of this furniture is now on display here, allowing you a fascinating glimpse into everyday court life. The upper floors contain re-created rooms from the Biedermeier to the Jugendstil periods, and document the tradition of furniture making in Vienna. Explanations are in German and English. ⊠ *Mariahilferstr. 88/entrance on Andreasg., 7th District/Neubau,* ☎ *01/ 524–3357–0.* 🎟 *€6.90.* ☉ *Tues.–Sun. 9–5. U-Bahn: U3 Zieglerg./follow signs to Otto-Bauer-G./exit Andreasg.*

⑥③ **Universität** (University of Vienna). After the one in Prague, Vienna's is the oldest university in the German-speaking world. It was founded in 1365 by Duke Rudolf IV and reorganized during the reign of Maria Theresa. The main section of the university is a massive block in Italian Renaissance style designed by Heinrich Ferstel and built between 1873 and 1884. Thirty-eight statues representing important men of letters decorate the front of the building, whereas the rear, which encompasses the library (with nearly 2 million volumes), is adorned with sgraffito. In the courtyard is the *Kastaliabrunnen*, the fountain for the guardians of spring, designed by Edmund Hellmer in 1904. ⊠ *Dr. Karl-Lueger-Ring/Universitätstr, 1st District. U-Bahn: U2/Schottentor.*

⑤⑧ **Volksgarten.** Just opposite the Hofburg is a green oasis with a beautifully planted rose garden, a 19th-century Greek temple, and a rather wistful white marble monument to Empress Elisabeth—Franz Josef's Bavarian wife, who died of a dagger wound inflicted by an Italian anarchist in Geneva in 1898. If not overrun with latter-day hippies, these can offer appropriate spots to sit for a few minutes while contemplating Vienna's most ambitious piece of 19th-century city planning: the famous Ringstrasse. ⊠ *Volksgarten, 1st District. Tram: 1, 2 or D/Rathauspl., Burgtheater.*

⑥④ **Votivkirche** (Votive Church). When Emperor Franz Josef was a young man, he was strolling along the Mölker Bastei, now one of the few remaining portions of the old wall that once surrounded the city, when he was taken unawares and stabbed in the neck by an Italian tailor. The assassination attempt was unsuccessful, and in gratitude for his survival Franz Josef ordered that a church be built exactly at the spot he was gazing at when he was struck down. The neo-Gothic church was built of gray limestone with two openwork turrets between 1856 and 1879. ⊠ *Rooseveltpl., 9th District/Alsergrund,* ☎ *01/406–1192.* ⊙ *Tours by prior arrangement. U-Bahn: U2/Schottentor.*

Monarchs and Mozart: From St. Stephen's to the Opera House

The cramped, ancient quarter behind St. Stephen's Cathedral offers a fascinating contrast to the luxurious expanses of the Ringstrasse and more recent parts of Vienna. This was—and still is—concentrated residential territory in the heart of the city. Mozart lived here; later, Prince Eugene and others built elegant town palaces as the smaller buildings were replaced. Streets—now mostly reserved for pedestrians—are narrow, and tiny alleyways abound. Facades open into courtyards that once housed carriages and horses. The magnificent State Opera shares with St. Stephen's the honor of being one of the city's most familiar and beloved landmarks.

A Good Walk

To pass through these streets is to take a short journey through history and art. In the process—as you visit former haunts of Mozart, kings, and emperors—you can be easily impressed with a clear sense of how Vienna's glittering Habsburg centuries unfolded. Start from St. Stephen's Cathedral by walking down Singerstrasse to Blutgasse and turn left into the **Blutgasse District** ⑥⑦—a neighborhood redolent of the 18th century. At the north end, in Domgasse, is the so-called **Figarohaus** ⑥⑧, now a memorial museum, the house in which Wolfgang Amadeus Mozart lived when he wrote the opera *The Marriage of Figaro*. Follow Domgasse east to Grünangergasse, which will bring you to Franziskanerplatz and the Gothic-Renaissance Franziskanerkirche (Franciscan Church). Follow the ancient Ballgasse to Rauhensteingasse, turning left onto **Himmelpfortgasse**—Gates of Heaven Street. Prince Eugene of Savoy had his town palace here at No. 8, now the **Finanzministerium** ⑥⑨, living here when he wasn't enjoying his other residence, the Belvedere Palace. Continue down Himmelpfortgasse to Seilerstätte to visit a museum devoted to the wonders of music, the **Haus der Musik** ⑦⓪. Then turn into Annagasse with its beautiful houses, which brings you back to the main shopping street, **Kärntnerstrasse,** where you can find everything from Austrian jade to the latest Jill Sander fashion turnouts. Turn left, walking north two blocks, and take the short Donnergasse to reach **Neuer Markt** square and the Providence Fountain. At the southwest corner of the square is the **Kaisergruft** ⑦① in the Kapuzinerkirche (Capuchin Church), the burial vault for rows of Habsburgs. Tegetthofstrasse south will bring you to Albertinaplatz, the square noted for the obvious war memorial and even more for the **Albertina Museum** ⑫, one of the world's great collections of old master drawings and prints. The southeast side of the square is bounded by the famous **Staatsoper** ⑬, the State Opera House; check for tour possibilities or, better, book tickets for a great *Rosenkavalier.*

TIMING

A simple walk of this route could take you a full half day, assuming you stop occasionally to survey the scene and take it all in. The restyled Figarohaus is worth a visit, and the Kaisergruft in the Kapuzinerkirche is impressive for its shadows of past glories, but there are crowds, and you may have to wait to get in; the best times are early morning and around lunchtime. Tours of the State Opera House take place in the afternoons; check the schedule posted outside one of the doors on the arcaded Kärntnerstrasse side. Figure about an hour each for the various visits and tours.

Sights to See

⑫ **Albertina Museum.** Some of the greatest old master drawings—including Dürer's legendary *Praying Hands*—are housed in this unassuming building, home to the world's largest collection of drawings, sketches, engravings, and etchings. Dürer leads the list, but there are many other highlights, including works by Rembrandt, Michelangelo, and Correggio. In fact, the holdings are so vast that only a limited number can be shown at one time, and some drawings are so delicate that they can be shown only in facsimile. The building is undergoing restoration and is scheduled to reopen sometime in spring 2003. For the past several years the collection was housed in the Akademiehof near the Secession, but that is now closed as well while everything is being reassembled. ✉ *Augustinerstr. 1, 1st District,* ☎ *01/534–830. Closed for renovation, scheduled to reopen Mar. 2003; check with tourist office for opening hrs. U-Bahn: U3/Herreng.*

⑰ **Blutgasse District.** The small block bounded by Singerstrasse, Grünangergasse, and Blutgasse is known as the Blutgasse District. Nobody knows for certain how the gruesome name—*Blut* is German for "blood"—originated, although one legend has it that Knights Templar were slaughtered here when their order was abolished in 1312, although in later years the narrow street was known in those unpaved days as Mud Lane. Today the block is a splendid example of city renovation and restoration, with cafés, small shops, and galleries tucked into the corners. You can look inside the courtyards to see the open galleries that connect various apartments on the upper floors, the finest example being at Blutgasse 3. At the corner of Singerstrasse sits the 18th-century **Neupauer-Breuner Palace,** with its monumental entranceway and inventively delicate windows. Opposite at Singerstrasse 17 is the **Rottal Palace,** attributed to Hildebrandt, with its wealth of classical wall motifs. For contrast, turn up the narrow Blutgasse, with its simple 18th-century facades. ✉ *1st District. U-Bahn: U1 or U3/Stephanspl.*

Café Sacher. Popular with prominent Viennese and tourists alike since the Sacher Hotel opened in 1876, the Sacher Cafe is steeped in tradition, and though it's elegant and dignified, you don't need to wear a suit and tie to be admitted. Choose a table in either the formal café with its sparkling chandeliers and plush wine-red banquettes, the more modern Wintergarten, or the small outdoor café with its glimpse of the Opera and try to decide among an abundance of tempting pastries—though here, and only here, can you sample the original Sachertorte. After decades of court battles with their rival, Demel, the Sacher was finally granted the distinction of possessing the secret, original recipe for the densely rich chocolate cake. Order it with a generous dollop of *Schlag* (barely sweetened whipped cream) on the side, and a *Melange*, for a truly Viennese experience. There is live piano music every day from 4:30 'til 7 PM. ⊠ *Philharmonikerstr. 4, 1st District,* ☎ *01/514560. AE, DC, MC.* ☉ *Open daily 8 AM–11:30 PM. U-Bahn: U1, U2, or U4/ Karlspl.*

68 **Figarohaus.** One of Mozart's 11 rented Viennese residences, the Figarohaus has its entrance at Domgasse 5, on the tiny alley behind St. Stephen's (although the facade on Schulerstrasse is far more imposing). It was in this house that Mozart wrote *The Marriage of Figaro* and the six quartets dedicated to Joseph Haydn (who once called on Mozart here, saying to Leopold, Mozart's father, "Your son is the greatest composer that I know in person or by name"). The apartment he occupied now contains a small commemorative museum—"created," alas, by an architect more interested in graphic blandishment than a sense of history; you'll have to use your imagination to picture how Mozart lived and worked here. ⊠ *Domg. 5, 1st District,* ☎ *01/513–6294.* 🎫 €*1.80.* ☉ *Tues.–Sun. 9–6. U-Bahn: U1 or U3/Stephanspl.*

69 **Finanzministerium** (Ministry of Finance). The architectural jewel of Himmelpfortgasse, this imposing abode—designed by Fischer von Erlach in 1697 and later expanded by Hildebrandt—was originally the town palace of Prince Eugene of Savoy. As you study the Finanzministerium, you'll realize its baroque details are among the most inventively conceived and beautifully executed in the city; all the decorative motifs are so softly carved that they appear to have been freshly squeezed from a pastry tube. The Viennese are lovers of the baroque in both their architecture and their pastry, and here the two passions seem visibly merged. Such baroque elegance may seem inappropriate for a finance ministry, but the contrast between place and purpose could hardly be more Viennese. ⊠ *Himmelpfortg. 8, 1st District. U-Bahn: U1 or U3/Stephanspl.*

☁ **70** **Haus der Musik** (House of Music). It would be easy to spend an entire day at this ultra-high-tech museum housed on several floors of an early 19th-century palace near Schwarzenbergplatz. Pride of place goes to the special rooms dedicated to each of the great Viennese composers—Haydn, Mozart, Beethoven, Strauss, and Mahler—complete with music samples and manuscripts. Other exhibits trace the evolution of sound (from primitive noises to the music of the masters) and illustrate the mechanics of the human ear (measure your own frequency threshold). There are also dozens of interactive computer games. You can even take a turn as conductor of the Vienna Philharmonic—the conductor's baton is hooked to a computer, which allows you to have full control of the computer-simulated orchestra. ⊠ *Seilerstätte 30, 1st District,* ☎ *01/51648–51.* 🎫 €*8.50.* ☉ *Daily 10–10. Restaurant, café. U-Bahn: U1, U2, or U4/Karlspl., then Tram D/Schwarzenbergpl.*

NEED A BREAK? Take a break at a landmark café in one of the most charming squares in Vienna, between Himmelpfortgasse and Singerstrasse. The **Kleines Cafe** (⊠ Franziskanerpl. 3, 1st District), open daily, is more for coffee, cocktails, and light snacks than for pastries, and few places are more delightful to sit in and relax on a warm afternoon or evening. In summer, tables are set outside on the intimate cobblestone square where the only sounds are the tinkling fountain and the occasional chiming of bells from the ancient Franciscan monastery next door. Before heading on, be sure to take a short stroll up Ballgasse, the tiny 18th-century street opposite the café.

Himmelpfortgasse. The maze of tiny streets including Ballgasse, Rauhen-steingasse, and Himmelpfortgasse (literally, "Gates of Heaven Street") masterfully conjures up the Vienna of the 19th century. The most impressive house on the street is the Ministry of Finance. The back side of the Steffl department store on Rauhensteingasse now marks the site of the house in which Mozart died in 1791. There's a commemorative plaque that once identified the streetside site together with a small memorial corner devoted to Mozart memorabilia that can be found on the fifth floor of the store. ⊠ *1st District. U-Bahn: U1 or U3/Stephanspl.*

␶ Kaisergruft (Imperial Burial Vault). In the basement of the Kapuzin-erkirche, or Capuchin Church (on the southwest corner of the Neuer Markt), is one of the more intriguing sights in Vienna: the Kaisergruft, or Imperial Burial Vault. The crypts contain the partial remains of some 140 Habsburgs (the hearts are in the Augustinerkirche and the entrails in St. Stephen's) plus one non-Habsburg governess ("She was always with us in life," said Maria Theresa, "why not in death?"). Perhaps starting with their tombs is the wrong way to approach the Habsburgs in Vienna, but it does give you a chance to get their names in sequence as they lie in rows, their coffins ranging from the simplest explosions of funerary conceit—with decorations of skulls and other morbid symbols—to the lovely and distinguished tomb of Maria Theresa and her husband. Designed while the couple still lived, their monument shows the empress in bed with her husband—awaking to the Last Judgment as if it were just another weekday morning—whereas the remains of her son (the ascetic Josef II) lie in a simple casket at the foot of the bed as if he were the family dog. ⊠ *Neuer Markt/Tegetthoffstr. 2, 1st District,* ☎ *01/512–6853–12.* 🎫 *€3.60.* ☉ *Daily 9:30–4. U-Bahn: U1, U3/Stephanspl. or U1, U4/Karlspl.*

Kärntnerstrasse. The Kärntnerstrasse remains Vienna's leading central shopping street. These days Kärntnerstrasse is much maligned. Too commercial, too crowded, too many tasteless signs, too much gaudy neon—the complaints go on and on. Nevertheless, when the daytime tourist crowds dissolve, the Viennese arrive regularly for their evening promenade, and it is easy to see why. Vulgar the street may be, but it is also alive and vital, with an energy that the more tasteful Graben and the impeccable Kohlmarkt lack. For the sightseer beginning to suffer from an excess of art history, classic buildings, and museums, a Kärntner-strasse window-shopping respite will be welcome. ⊠ *1st District. U-Bahn: U1, U4/Karlspl., or U1, U3/Stephanspl.*

␸ Staatsoper (State Opera House). The famous Vienna Staatsoper on the Ring vies with the cathedral for the honor of marking the emotional heart of the city—it is a focus for Viennese life and one of the chief symbols of resurgence after the cataclysm of World War II. Its directorship is one of the top jobs in Austria, almost as important as that of president, and one that comes in for even more public attention. Everyone thinks he or she could do it just as well, and since the huge salary comes out of taxes, they feel they have every right to criticize, often and loudly. The first of the Ringstrasse projects to be completed (in 1869), the opera house suffered disastrous bomb damage in the last days of World War II (only the outer walls, the front facade, and the main staircase area behind it survived). The auditorium is plain when compared with the red and gold eruptions of London's Covent Garden or some of the Italian opera houses, but it has an elegant individuality that shows to best advantage when the stage and auditorium are turned into a ballroom for the great Opera Ball.

The construction of the Opera House is the stuff of legend. When the foundation was laid, the plans for the Opernring were not yet complete, and in the end the avenue turned out to be several feet higher than originally planned. As a result, the Opera House lacked the commanding prospect that its architects, Eduard van der Nüll and August Sicard von Sicardsburg, had intended, and even Emperor Franz Josef pronounced the building a bit low to the ground. For the sensitive van der Nüll (and here the story becomes a bit suspect), failing his beloved emperor was the last straw. In disgrace and despair, he committed suicide. Sicardsburg died of grief shortly thereafter. And the emperor, horrified at the deaths his innocuous remark had caused, limited all his future artistic pronouncements to a single immutable formula: *"Es war sehr schön, es hat mich sehr gefreut"* ("It was very nice, it pleased me very much").

Renovation could not avoid a postwar look, for the cost of fully restoring the 19th-century interior was prohibitive. The original basic design was followed in the 1945–55 reconstruction, meaning that sight lines from some of the front boxes are poor at best. These disappointments hardly detract from the fact that this is one of the world's half-dozen greatest opera houses, and experiencing a performance here can be the highlight of a trip to Vienna. Tours of the Opera House are given regularly, but starting times vary according to opera rehearsals; the current schedule is posted at the east-side entrance under the arcade on the Kärntnerstrasse marked GUIDED TOURS, where the tours begin. Alongside under the arcade is an information office that also sells tickets to the main opera and the Volksoper. ⊠ *Opernring 2, 1st District,* ☎ *01/514–44–2613.* ⊡ *€4.* ☉ *Tours year-round when there are no rehearsals, but call for times. U-Bahn: U1, U2 or U4 Karlspl.*

Pomp and Circumstance: South of the Ring to the Belvedere

City planning in the late 1800s and early 1900s clearly was essential to manage the growth of the burgeoning imperial capital. The elegant Ringstrasse alone was not a sufficient showcase, and anyway, it focused on public rather than private buildings. The city fathers as well as private individuals commissioned the architect Otto Wagner to plan and undertake a series of projects. The area around Karlsplatz and the fascinating open food market remains a classic example of unified design. Not all of Wagner's concept for Karlsplatz was realized, but enough remains to be convincing and to convey the impression of what might have been. The unity concept predates Wagner's time in the former garden of Belvedere Palace, one of Europe's greatest architectural triumphs.

A Good Walk

The often overlooked **Akademie der bildenen Künste** ㉔, or Academy of Fine Arts, is an appropriate starting point for this walk, as it puts into perspective the artistic arguments taking place around the turn of the century. Whereas the Academy represented the conservative viewpoint, a group of modernist revolutionaries broke away and founded the Secessionist movement, with its culmination in the gold-crowned **Secession Building** ㉕. Now housing changing exhibits and Gustav Klimt's provocative *Beethoven Frieze*, the museum stands appropriately close to the Academy; from the Academy, take Makartgasse south one block. The famous **Naschmarkt** ㉖ open food market starts diagonally south from the Secession; follow the rows of stalls southwest. Pay attention to the northwest side of the Linke Wienzeile, to the Theater an der Wien at the intersection with Millöckergasse (Mozart and Beethoven personally premiered some of their finest works at this opera house–theater) and to the **Otto Wagner Houses** ㉗. Head back north through the Naschmarkt; at the top end, cross Wiedner Haupt-strasse to your right into the park complex that forms Karlsplatz, creating a frame for the classic **Karlskirche** ⑦. Around **Karlsplatz,** note the Technical University on the south side, and the Otto Wagner subway station buildings on the north. Across Lothringer Strasse on the north side are the Künstlerhaus art exhibit hall and the Musikverein. The out-of-place and rather undistinguished modern building to the left of Karlskirche houses the worthwhile **Historisches Museum der Stadt Wien** ⑦. Cut through Symphonikerstrasse (a passageway through the modern complex) and take Brucknerstrasse to **Schwarzenbergplatz.** The Jugendstil edifice on your left is the French Embassy; ahead is the Russian War Memorial. On a rise behind the memorial sits Palais Schwarzenberg, a jewel of a onetime summer palace and now a luxury hotel. Follow Prinz Eugen-Strasse up to the entrance of the **Belvedere Palace** ⑧ complex on your left. Besides the palace itself are other structures and, off to the east side, a remarkable botanical garden. After viewing the palace and the grounds, you can exit the complex from the lower building, Untere Belvedere, into Rennweg, which will steer you back to Schwarzenbergplatz.

TIMING

The first part of this walk, taking in the Academy of Fine Arts and the Secession, plus the Naschmarkt and Karlsplatz, can be accomplished in an easy half day. The Museum of the City of Vienna is good for a couple of hours, more if you understand some German. Give the Belvedere Palace and grounds as much time as you can. Organized tours breeze in and out—without so much as a glance at the outstanding modern art museum—in a half hour or so, not even scratching the surface of this fascinating complex. If you can, budget up to a half day here, but plan to arrive fairly early in the morning or afternoon before the busloads descend. Bus tourists aren't taken to the Lower Belvedere, so you'll have that and the formal gardens to yourself.

Sights to See

⑦ **Akademie der bildenen Künste** (Academy of Fine Arts). An outsize statue of the German author Schiller announces the Academy of Fine Arts on Schillerplatz. (Turn around and note his more famous contemporary, Goethe, pompously seated in an overstuffed chair, facing him from across the Ring.) The Academy was founded in 1692, but the present Renaissance revival building dates from the late 19th century. The idea was conservatism and traditional values, even in the face of a growing movement that scorned formal rules. It was here in 1907 and 1908 that aspiring artist Adolf Hitler was refused acceptance on grounds of insufficient talent. The Academy includes a museum focusing on old masters. The collection is mainly of interest to specialists, but Hieronymus Bosch's famous *Last Judgment* triptych hangs here—an imaginative, if gruesome, speculation on the hereafter. ⊠ *Schillerpl. 3, 1st District,* ☎ *01/588–16–225.* ⊡ *€3.63.* ⊙ *Tues.–Sun. 10–4. U-Bahn: U1, U2, or U4 Karlspl.*

OFF THE BEATEN PATH | **AM STEINHOF CHURCH –** Otto Wagner's most exalted piece of Jugendstil architecture is not in the inner city but in the suburbs to the west: the Am Steinhof Church, designed in 1904 during his Secessionist phase. You can reach the church by taking the U4 subway line, which is adjacent to the Otto Wagner Houses. On the grounds of the Vienna City Psychiatric Hospital, Wagner's design unites mundane functional details (rounded edges on the pews to prevent injury to the patients and a slightly sloped tile floor to facilitate cleaning) with a soaring, airy dome and glittering Jugendstil decoration (stained glass by Koloman Moser). The church is open Saturdays at 3 for a guided tour (in German) for €4. English tours can be arranged in advance at €4 per person *if* it's a group of 10 people. If there are only 2 of you, then you still must pay the total price for 10. You may come during the week to walk around the church on your own, but you must call first for an appointment. In 2003 the exterior of the church will be renovated, but it won't affect the guided tours of the interior. Renovations are planned for the interior in 2004, so check first to see if it's open before going. ✉ *Baumgartner Höhe 1, 13th District/ Hütteldorf,* ☎ *01/91060–11-204.* 🎫 *Free.* ☉ *Sat. 3–4. U-Bahn: U4/ Unter-St.-Veit, then Bus 47A to Psychiatrisches Krankenhaus; or U2/ Volkstheater, then Bus 48A.*

★ ⑳ **Belvedere Palace.** Baroque architect Lucas von Hildebrandt's most important Viennese work—the Belvedere Palace—is wedged between Rennweg (entry at No. 6A) and Prinz Eugen-Strasse (entry at No. 27). In fact the Belvedere is two palaces with extensive gardens between. Built outside the city fortifications between 1714 and 1722, the complex originally served as the summer palace of Prince Eugene of Savoy; much later it became the home of Archduke Franz Ferdinand, whose assassination in 1914 precipitated World War I. Though the lower palace is impressive in its own right, it is the much larger upper palace, used for state receptions, banquets, and balls, that is acknowledged as Hildebrandt's masterpiece. The usual tourist entrance for the Upper Belvedere is the gate on Prinz-Eugen-Strasse; for the Lower Belvedere, use the Rennweg gate—but for the most impressive view of the upper palace, approach it from the south garden closest to the South Rail Station. The upper palace displays a remarkable wealth of architectural invention in its facade, avoiding the main design problem common to all palaces because of their excessive size: monotony on the one hand and pomposity on the other. Hildebrandt's decorative manner here approaches the rococo, that final style of the baroque era when traditional classical motifs all but disappeared in a whirlwind of seductive asymmetric fancy. The main interiors of the palace go even further: columns are transformed into muscle-bound giants, pilasters grow torsos, capitals sprout great piles of symbolic imperial paraphernalia, and the ceilings are set aswirl with ornately molded stucco. The result is the finest rococo interior in the city.

Today both the upper and lower palaces of the Belvedere are noted museums devoted to Austrian painting. The **Österreichisches Barockmuseum** (Austrian Museum of Baroque Art) in the lower palace at Rennweg 6A displays Austrian art of the 18th century (including the original figures from Georg Raphael Donner's Providence Fountain in the Neuer Markt)—and what better building to house it? Next to the Baroque Museum (outside the west end) is the converted Orangerie, devoted to works of the medieval period.

The main attraction in the upper palace's **Österreichische Galerie** (Austrian Gallery) is the legendary collection of 19th- and 20th-century Austrian paintings, centering on the work of Vienna's three preeminent early 20th-century artists: Gustav Klimt, Egon Schiele, and Oskar Kokoschka. Klimt was the oldest, and by the time he helped found the Secession movement he had forged a highly idiosyncratic painting style that combined realistic and decorative elements in a way that was completely revolutionary. *The Kiss*—his greatest painting and one of the icons of modern art—is here on display. Schiele and Kokoschka went even further, rejecting the decorative appeal of Klimt's glittering abstract designs and producing works that completely ignored conventional ideas of beauty. Today they are considered the fathers of modern art in Vienna. Modern music, too, has roots in the Belvedere complex: the composer Anton Bruckner lived and died here in 1896 in a small garden house now marked by a commemorative plaque. ⊠ *Prinz-Eugen-Str. 27, 3rd District/Landstrasse,* ☎ *01/795–57–134.* ⊠ *€7.50.* ☉ *Tues.–Sun. 10–5, Apr.–Oct. daily 10–6. U-Bahn: U1, U2, or U4 Karlspl., then Tram D/Belvedereg.*

㊴ Historisches Museum der Stadt Wien (Museum of Viennese History). Housed in an incongruously modern building at the east end of the regal Karlsplatz, this museum possesses a dazzlement of Viennese historical artifacts and treasures: models, maps, documents, photographs, antiquities, stained glass, paintings, sculpture, crafts, and reconstructed rooms. Paintings include works by Klimt and Schiele, and there's a life-size portrait of the composer Alban Berg painted by his contemporary Arnold Schönberg. Display information and designations in the museum are in German and English. ⊠ *Karlspl., 4th District/Wieden,* ☎ *01/505–8747.* ⊠ *€3.60.* ☉ *Tues.–Sun. 9–6. U-Bahn: U1, U2, or U4 Karlspl.*

★ **㊲ Karlskirche.** Dominating the Karlsplatz is one of Vienna's greatest buildings, the Karlskirche, dedicated to St. Charles Borromeo. At first glance, the church seems like a fantastic vision—one blink and you half expect the building to vanish. For before you is a giant baroque church framed by enormous freestanding columns, mates to Rome's famous Trajan's Column. These columns may be out of keeping with the building as a whole, but were conceived with at least two functions in mind: one was to portray scenes from the life of the patron saint, carved in imitation of Trajan's triumphs, and thus help to emphasize the imperial nature of the building; and the other was to symbolize the Pillars of Hercules, suggesting the right of the Habsburgs to their Spanish dominions, which the emperor had been forced to renounce. Whatever the reason, the result is an architectural tour de force.

The Karlskirche was built in the early 18th century on what was then the bank of the River Wien and is now the southeast corner of the park complex. The church had its beginnings in a disaster. In 1713 Vienna was hit by a brutal plague outbreak, and Emperor Charles VI made a vow: if the plague abated, he would build a church dedicated to his namesake, St. Charles Borromeo, the 16th-century Italian bishop who was famous for his ministrations to Milanese plague victims. In 1715 construction began, using an ambitious design by Johann Bernhard Fischer von Erlach that combined architectural elements from ancient Greece (the columned entrance porch), ancient Rome (the Trajanesque columns), contemporary Rome (the baroque dome), and contemporary Vienna (the baroque towers at either end). When it was finished, the church received a decidedly mixed press. History, incidentally, delivered a negative verdict: in its day the Karlskirche spawned no imitations, and it went on to become one of European architecture's most famous curiosities. Notwithstanding, seen lit at night, the building is magical in its setting.

The main interior of the church utilizes only the area under the dome and is surprisingly conventional given the unorthodox facade. The space and architectural detailing are typical high baroque; the fine vault frescoes, by J. M. Rottmayr, depict St. Charles Borromeo imploring the Holy Trinity to end the plague. ⊠ *Karlspl., 4th District/Wieden,* ☎ *01/504–61–87.* ☉ *Daily 8–6. U-Bahn: U1, U2, or U4 Karlspl.*

Karlsplatz. Like the space now occupied by the Naschmarkt, Karlsplatz was formed when the River Wien was covered over at the turn of the century. At the time, Wagner expressed his frustration with the result—too large a space for a formal square and too small a space for an informal park—and the awkwardness is felt to this day. The buildings surrounding the Karlsplatz, however, are quite sure of themselves: the area is dominated by the classic **Karlskirche,** made less dramatic by the unfortunate reflecting pool with its Henry Moore sculpture, wholly out of place, in front. On the south side of the Resselpark, that part of Karlsplatz named for the inventor of the screw propeller for ships, stands the **Technical University** (1816–18). In a house that occupied the space closest to the church, Italian composer Antonio Vivaldi died in 1741; a plaque marks the spot. On the north side, across the heavily traveled roadway, are the **Künstlerhaus** (the exhibition hall in which the Secessionists refused to exhibit, built in 1881 and still in use) and the famed **Musikverein.** The latter, finished in 1869, is now home to the Vienna Philharmonic. The downstairs lobby and the two halls upstairs have been gloriously restored and glow with fresh gilding. The main hall has what may be the world's finest acoustics; this is the site of the annual, globally televised New Year's Day concert.

Some of Otto Wagner's finest Secessionist work can be seen two blocks east on the northern edge of Karlsplatz. In 1893 Wagner was appointed architectural supervisor of the new Vienna City Railway, and the matched pair of small pavilions he designed for the Karlsplatz **train station** in 1898 are among the city's most ingratiating buildings. Their structural framework is frankly exposed (in keeping with Wagner's belief in architectural honesty), but they are also lovingly decorated (in keeping with the Viennese fondness for architectural finery). The result is Jugendstil at its very best, melding plain and fancy with grace and insouciance. The pavilion to the southwest is utilized as a small, specialized museum. In the course of redesigning Karlsplatz, it was Wagner, incidentally, who proposed moving the fruit and vegetable market to what is now the Naschmarkt. ⊠ *4th District/Wieden. U-Bahn: U1, U2, or U4/Karlspl.*

76 **Naschmarkt.** The area between Linke and Rechte Wienzeile has for 80 years been address to the Naschmarkt, Vienna's main outdoor produce market, certainly one of Europe's—if not the world's—great open-air markets, where packed rows of polished and stacked fruits and vegetables compete for visual appeal with braces of fresh pheasant in season; the nostrils, meanwhile, are accosted by spice fragrances redolent of Asia or the Middle East. It's open Monday to Saturday 6:30–6:30 (many stalls close two hours earlier in winter months). When making a purchase, be sure you get the correct change. ⊠ *Between the Linke and Rechte Wienzeile, 4th District/Wieden. U-Bahn: U1, U2, or U4 Karlspl. (follow signs to Secession).*

NEED A BREAK? Who can explore the Naschmarkt without picking up a snack? A host of Turkish stands offer tantalizing *Döner* sandwiches—thinly sliced lamb with onions and a yogurt sauce in a freshly baked roll. If you're in the mood for Italian *tramezzini*—crustless sandwiches filled with tuna and olives or buffalo mozzarella and tomato—there are a couple of huts to choose from on the Linke Wienzeile side about midway through the market. You can also have sushi and other fish snacks at the glass-enclosed seafood huts at the Karlsplatz end.

77 **Otto Wagner Houses.** The Ringstrasse-style apartment houses that line the Wienzeile are an attractive, if generally somewhat standard, lot, but two stand out: **Linke Wienzeile 38 and 40**—the latter better known as the "Majolica House"—designed (1898–99) by the grand old man of Viennese fin-de-siècle architecture, Otto Wagner, during his Secessionist phase. A good example of what Wagner was rebelling against can be seen next door, at **Linke Wienzeile 42,** where decorative enthusiasm has blossomed into baroque revival hysteria. Wagner had come to believe that this sort of display was nothing but empty pretense and sham; modern apartment houses, he wrote in his pioneering text *Modern Architecture,* are entirely different from 18th-century town palaces, and architects should not pretend otherwise. Accordingly, he banished classical decoration and introduced a new architectural simplicity, with flat exterior walls and plain, regular window treatments meant to reflect the orderly layout of the apartments behind them. There the simplicity ended. For exterior decoration, he turned to his younger Secessionist cohorts Joseph Olbrich and Koloman Moser, who designed the ornate Jugendstil patterns of red majolica-tile roses (No. 40) and gold stucco medallions (No. 38) that gloriously brighten the facades of the adjacent houses—so much so that their baroque-period neighbor is ignored. The houses are privately owned. ⊠ *4th District/Wieden. U-Bahn: U1, U2, or U4/Karlspl.*

Schwarzenbergplatz. A remarkable urban ensemble, the Schwarzenbergplatz comprises some notable sights. The center of the lower square off the Ring is marked by an oversize equestrian sculpture of Prince Schwarzenberg—he was a 19th-century field marshal for the imperial forces. Admire the overall effect of the square and see if you can guess which building is the newest; it's the one on the northeast corner (No. 3) at Lothringer Strasse, an exacting reproduction of a building destroyed by war damage in 1945 and dating only from the 1980s. The military monument occupying the south end of the square behind the fountain is the **Russian War Memorial,** set up at the end of World War II by the Soviets; the Viennese, remembering the Soviet occupation, call its unknown soldier the "unknown plunderer." South of the memorial is the stately **Schwarzenberg Palace,** designed as a summer residence by Johann Lukas von Hildebrandt in 1697, completed by Fischer von Erlach father and son, and now (in part) a luxury hotel. The delightful formal gardens wedged between Prinz Eugen-Strasse and the Belvedere gardens can be enjoyed from the hotel restaurant's veranda. ⊠ *Schwarzenbergpl., 3rd District/Landstrasse. Tram: Schwarzenbergpl.*

★ ⑦⑤ **Secession Building.** If the Academy of Fine Arts represents the conservative attitude toward the arts in the late 1800s, then its antithesis can be found in the building immediately behind it to the southeast: the Secession Pavilion. Restored in the mid-1980s after years of neglect, the Secession building is one of Vienna's preeminent symbols of artistic rebellion. Rather than looking to the architecture of the past, like the revivalist Ringstrasse, it looked to a new antihistoricist future. It was, in its day, a riveting trumpet-blast of a building and is today considered by many to be Europe's first example of full-blown 20th-century architecture.

The Secession began in 1897, when 20 dissatisfied Viennese artists, headed by Gustav Klimt, "seceded" from the Künstlerhausgenossenschaft, the conservative artists' society associated with the Academy of Fine Arts. The movement promoted the radically new kind of art known as Jugendstil, which found its inspiration in both the organic, fluid designs of art nouveau and the related but more geometric designs of the English arts-and-crafts movement. (The Secessionists founded an arts-and-crafts workshop of their own, the famous Wiener Werkstätte, in an effort to embrace the applied arts.) The Secession building, designed by the architect Joseph Olbrich and completed in 1898, was the movement's exhibition hall. The lower story, crowned by the entrance motto *Der Zeit Ihre Kunst, Der Kunst Ihre Freiheit* ("To the age its art, to art its freedom"), is classic Jugendstil: the restrained but assured decoration (by Koloman Moser) beautifully complements the facade's pristine flat expanses of cream-color wall. Above the entrance motto sits the building's most famous feature, the gilded openwork dome that the Viennese were quick to christen "the golden cabbage" (Olbrich wanted it to be seen as a dome of laurel, a subtle classical reference meant to celebrate the triumph of art). The plain white interior—"shining and chaste," in Olbrich's words—was also revolutionary; its most unusual feature was movable walls, allowing the galleries to be reshaped and redesigned for every show. One early show, in 1902, was an exhibition devoted to art celebrating the genius of Beethoven; Gustav Klimt's *Beethoven Frieze*, painted for the occasion, has now been restored and is permanently installed in the building's basement. ⊠ *Friedrichstr. 12, 4th District/Wieden,* ☎ *01/587–5307–0.* 🎫 *€5.09.* ◷ *Tues.–Sun. 10–6, Thurs. 10–8. U-Bahn: U1, U2, or U4 Karlspl.*

OFF THE BEATEN PATH
ZENTRALFRIEDHOF – Taking a streetcar out of Schwarzenbergplatz, music lovers will want to make a pilgrimage to the **Zentralfriedhof** (Central Cemetery), which contains the graves of most of Vienna's great composers: Ludwig van Beethoven, Franz Schubert, Johannes Brahms, the Johann Strausses (father and son), and Arnold Schönberg, among others. The monument to Wolfgang Amadeus Mozart is a memorial only; the approximate location of his unmarked grave can be seen at the now deconsecrated St. Marx-Friedhof at Leberstrasse 6–8. ⊠ *Simmeringer Hauptstr., 11th District/Simmering. Tram: 71 to St. Marxer Friedhof, or on to Zentralfriedhof Haupttor/2.*

Splendors of the Habsburgs: A Visit to Schönbrunn Palace

The glories of imperial Austria are nowhere brought together more convincingly than in the Schönbrunn Palace (Schloss Schönbrunn) complex. Brilliant "Maria Theresa yellow"—she, in fact, caused Schöbrunn to be built—is everywhere in evidence. An impression of imperial elegance, interrupted only by tourist traffic, flows unbroken throughout the grounds. This is one of Austria's primary tourist sites, although sadly, few stay long enough to discover the real Schönbrunn (including the little maiden with the water jar, after whom the complex is named). Although the assorted outbuildings might seem eclectic, they served as centers of entertainment when the court moved to Schönbrunn in the summer, accounting for the zoo, the priceless theater, the fake Roman ruins, the greenhouses, and the walkways. In Schönbrunn you step back 300 years into the heart of a powerful and growing empire and follow it through to defeat and demise in 1917.

A Good Walk

The usual start for exploring the Schönbrunn complex is the main palace. There's nothing wrong with that approach, but as a variation, consider first climbing to the **Gloriette** ⑧ on the hill overlooking the site, for a bird's-eye view to put the rest in perspective (take the stairs to the Gloriette roof for the ultimate experience). While at the Gloriette, take a few steps west to discover the **Tiroler House** ⑧ and follow the zigzag path downhill to the palace; note the picture-book views of the main building through the woods. Try to take the full tour of **Schönbrunn Palace** ⑧ rather than the shorter, truncated version. Check whether the ground-floor back rooms (*Berglzimmer*) are open to viewing. After the palace guided tour, take your own walk around the grounds. The Schöner Brunnen, the namesake fountain, is hidden in the woods to the southeast; continue along to discover the convincing (but fake) Roman ruins. At the other side of the complex to the west are the excellent **Tiergarten** ⑧ (zoo), and the **Palmenhaus** ⑧ (tropical greenhouse). Closer to the main entrance, both the **Wagenburg** ⑧ (carriage museum) and Schlosstheater (palace theater) are frequently overlooked treasures. Before heading back to the city center, visit the **Hofpavillon** ⑧⑦, the private subway station built for Emperor Franz Josef, located to the west across Schönbrunner Schlossstrasse.

TIMING

If you're really pressed for time, the shorter guided tour will give you a fleeting impression of the palace itself, but try to allot at least half a day to take the full tour and include the extra rooms and grounds as well. The 20-minute hike up to the Gloriette is a bit strenuous but worthwhile, and there's now a café as reward at the top. The zoo is worth as much time as you can spare, and figure on at least a half hour to an hour each for the other museums. Tour buses begin to unload for the main building about midmorning; start early or utilize the noon lull to avoid the worst crowds. The other museums and buildings in the complex are far less crowded.

Sights to See

⑧① **Gloriette.** At the crest of the hill, topping off the Schönbrunn Schlosspark, sits a baroque masterstroke: Johann Ferdinand von Hohenberg's incomparable Gloriette, now restored to its original splendor. Perfectly scaled, the Gloriette—a palatial pavilion that once offered royal guests a place to rest and relax on their tours of the palace grounds and that now houses an equally welcome café—holds the whole vast garden composition together and at the same time crowns the ensemble with a brilliant architectural tiara. This was a favorite spot of Maria Theresa's, though in later years she grew so obese it took six men to carry her in her palanquin to the summit. ⊠ *13th District. U-Bahn: U4Schönbrunn.*

⑧⑦ **Hofpavillon.** The most unusual interior of the Schöbrunn Palace complex, the restored imperial subway station known as the Hofpavillon is just outside the palace grounds (at the northwest corner, a few yards east of the Hietzing subway station). Designed by Otto Wagner in conjunction with Joseph Olbrich and Leopold Bauer, the Hofpavillon was built in 1899 for the exclusive use of Emperor Franz Josef and his entourage. Exclusive it was: the emperor used the station only once. The exterior, with its proud architectural crown, is Wagner at his best, and the lustrous interior is one of the finest examples of Jugendstil decoration in the city. ⊠ *Schönbrunner Schloss-Str., next to Hietzing subway station, 13th District/Hietzing,* ☎ *01/877–1571.* ⊡ *€1.80.* ☉ *Tues.–Sun. 1:30–4:30. U-Bahn: U4 Hietzing.*

⑧⑤ **Palmenhaus.** On the grounds to the west of Schönbrunn Palace is a huge greenhouse filled with exotic trees and plants. ⊠ *Nearest entrance Hietzing, 13th District/Hietzing,* ☎ *01/877–5087–406.* ⊡ *€3.30.* ☉ *May–Sept., daily 9:30–5:30; Oct.–Apr., daily 9:30–4:30.*

★ ⑧③ **Schönbrunn Palace.** Designed by Johann Bernhard Fischer von Erlach in 1696, Schönbrunn Palace, the huge Habsburg summer residence, lies well within the city limits, just a few subway stops west of Karlsplatz on line U4. The vast and elegantly planted gardens are open daily from dawn until dusk, and multilingual guided tours of the palace interior are offered daily. A visit inside the palace is not included in most general city sightseeing tours, which offer either a mercilessly tempting drive past or else an impossibly short half hour or so to explore. The four-hour commercial sightseeing-bus tours of Schönbrunn offered by tour operators cost several times what you'd pay if you tackled the easy excursion yourself; their advantage is that they get you there and back with less effort. Go on your own if you want time to wander through the magnificent grounds.

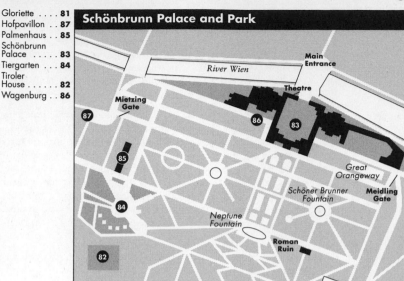

Schönbrunn Palace and Park

The most impressive approach to the palace and its gardens is through the front gate, set on Schönbrunner Schloss-Strasse halfway between the Schönbrunn and Hietzing subway stations. The vast main courtyard is ruled by a formal design of impeccable order and rigorous symmetry: wing nods at wing, facade mirrors facade, and every part stylistically complements every other. The courtyard, however, turns out to be a mere appetizer; the feast lies beyond. The breathtaking view that unfolds on the other side of the palace is one of the finest set pieces in all Europe and one of the supreme achievements of baroque planning. Formal *allées* (garden promenades) shoot off diagonally, the one on the right toward the zoo, the one on the left toward a rock-mounted obelisk and a fine false Roman ruin. But these, and the woods beyond, are merely a frame for the astonishing composition in the center: the sculpted fountain; the carefully planted screen of trees behind; the sudden, almost vertical rise of the grass-covered hill beyond, with the **Gloriette** a fitting crown.

Within the palace, the magisterial state salons are quite up to the splendor of the gardens, but note the contrast between these chambers and the far more modest rooms in which the rulers—particularly Franz Josef—lived and spent most of their time. Of the 1,400 rooms, 40 are open to the public on the regular tour, of which two are of special note: the Hall of Mirrors, where the six-year-old Mozart performed for Empress Maria Theresa in 1762 (and where he met six-year-old Marie-Antoinette for the first time, developing a little crush on her), and the Grand Gallery, where the Congress of Vienna (1815) danced at night after carving up Napoléon's collapsed empire during the day. Ask about viewing the ground-floor living quarters (*Berglzimmer*), where the walls are fascinatingly painted with palm trees, exotic animals, and tropical views. As you go through the palace, glance occasionally out the windows; you'll be rewarded by a better impression of the beautiful

patterns of the formal gardens, punctuated by hedgerows and foun-
tains. These window vistas were enjoyed by rulers from Maria Theresa
and Napoléon to Franz Josef. ⊠ *Schönbrunner Schloss-Str., 13th Dis-
trict/Hietzing,* ☎ *01/81113–239.* ⊠ *Guided grand tour of palace interior (40 rooms) €12.30, self-guided tour €9.80.* ☉ *Apr.–June and
Sept.–Oct., daily 8:30–5; July–Aug., daily 8:30–7; Nov.–Mar., daily 8:30–
4:30. U-Bahn: U4/Schönbrunn.*

Schönbrunn Schlosspark (Palace Park). The palace grounds entice with
a bevy of splendid divertissements, including a grand zoo (the Tiergarten)
and a carriage museum (the Wagenburg). Climb to the Gloriette for a
panoramic view out over the city as well as of the palace complex. If
you're exploring on your own, seek out the intriguing Roman ruin, now
used as a backdrop for outdoor summer opera. The marble *schöner
Brunnen* ("beautiful fountain"), with the young girl pouring water from
an urn, is nearby. The fountain gave its name to the palace complex.
⊠ *Schönbrunner Schlosspark, 13th District/Hietzing.* ☉ *Daily 9–
dusk. U-Bahn: U4/Schönbrunn.*

👆 ⑧④ **Tiergarten.** Claimed to be the world's oldest, the Tiergarten zoo has
retained its original baroque decor and today has acquired world-
class recognition under director Helmut Pechlaner. New settings have
been created for both animals and public; in one case, the public looks
out into a new, natural display area from one of the baroque former
animal houses. The zoo is constantly adding new attractions and undergoing renovations, so there's plenty to see. ⊠ *Schönbrunner Schlosspark, 13th District/Hietzing,* ☎ *01/877–9294–0.* ⊠ *€9; combination
ticket with Palmenhaus €10.* ☉ *Nov.–Jan., daily 9–4:30; Feb., daily
9–5; Mar. and Oct., daily 9–5:30; Apr., daily 9–6; May–Sept., daily 9–
6:30. U-Bahn: U4/Schönbrunn.*

⑧② **Tiroler House.** This charming building to the west of the Gloriette was
a favorite retreat of Empress Elisabeth; it now includes a small restaurant (open according to season and weather). ⊠ *Schönbrunner Schlosspark, 13th District/Hietzing. U-Bahn: U4/Schönbrunn.*

👆 ⑧⑥ **Wagenburg** (Carriage Museum). Most of the carriages are still road-
worthy and, indeed, Schönbrunn dusted off the gilt-and-black royal
funeral carriage that you see here for the burial ceremony of Empress
Zita in 1989. ⊠ *Schönbrunner Schlosspark, 13th District/Hietzing,* ☎
01/877–3244. ⊠ *€4.50.* ☉ *Apr.–Oct. daily 9–6; Nov.–Mar., Tues.–
Sun. 10–4. U-Bahn: U4 Schönbrunn.*

DINING

Ever since joining the European Union in 1995, Austria has undergone
a gastronomic revolution, and nowhere is this more evident than in
the capital city of Vienna. It has emerged from its provincial stagna-
tion with flying colors and now offers its share of world-class restaurants, and they're not only limited to the luxury establishments.

In a first-class restaurant in Vienna you will pay as much as in most other
major Western European capitals. But you can still find good food at re-
freshingly low prices in the simpler restaurants, particularly at neighborhood *Gasthäuser* in the suburbs. If you eat your main meal at noon
(as the Viennese do), you can take advantage of the luncheon specials.
Be aware that the basket of bread put on your table is not free. Most of
the older-style Viennese restaurants charge €0.80–€1.50 for each roll
that is eaten, but more and more establishments are beginning to charge
a per person cover charge—anywhere from €1.50 to €4—which includes
all the bread you want, plus usually an herb spread and butter.

Vienna's restaurant fare ranges from Arabic to Yugoslav, with strong doses of Chinese, Italian, and Japanese. Assuming you've come for what makes Vienna unique, our listings focus not on exotic spots but on places where you'll meet the Viennese and experience Vienna.

Many restaurants are closed one or two days a week (often weekends), and most serve meals only 11:30–2 and 6–10. An increasing number now serve after-theater dinners, but reserve in advance. The paperback book *Wien wie es isst* ("Vienna, How It Eats" in German; available at almost any bookstore) gives up-to-date information on the restaurant, café, and bar scene. Note that neighborhoods and U-Bahn stations are listed *only* for restaurants located outside the 1st District.

CATEGORY	COST*
$$$$	over €25
$$$	€20–€25
$$	€15–€20
$	under €15

*per person for a main course at dinner

Restaurants

$$$$ ✕ **Imperial.** This exquisite restaurant in the Imperial Hotel ranks among the top eateries in the city. The setting is elegant—dark polished wood, private alcoves, candlelight, with a pianist playing softly in the background. Lobster bisque is intensified with a dash of Armagnac, and the unusual baby lamb and lettuce soup is deliciously rich. Main courses include Styrian beef in Barolo with spinach gnocchi and spring vegetables, or chicken with green and white lasagna, asparagus tips, and balsamic shallots. Service is friendly and attentive without being intrusive. ✉ *Kärntner Ring 16,* ☎ *01/501–10–356,* FAX *01/50110–410. AE, DC, MC, V. Closed 3 wks in July or Aug. No lunch.*

$$$$ ✕ **Julius Meinl am Graben.** Just a few doors down from the Hofburg
★ Palace, Julius Meinl opened as caterer to the Habsburgs in 1862, and has remained Vienna's poshest grocery store ever since. An upscale restaurant now inhabits part of the second floor, with deep orange banquettes, dark wood, and stunning views of the Graben. Start with lobster terrine and a side of lobster bisque, served adorably in an espresso cup, then go on to grilled *Rochenflügel* (skate) with gnocchi and wild mushrooms, or sizzling duck, carved tableside and served with roasted chestnuts and apple-studded *Rotkraut* (red cabbage). If you can't get a table reservation, full meals are served at the bar. ✉ *Graben 19 (entrance after 7 PM from outdoor elevator on Naglerg.),* ☎ *01/532–3334–99,* FAX *01/532–3334–615. Reservations essential. Jacket and tie. AE, DC, MC, V. Closed Sun.*

$$$$ ✕ **Korso.** Set in the Bristol Hotel, just across from the Staatsoper
★ (don't be surprised if you see Domingo or a leading diva at the next table), the Korso bei Der Oper has long been regarded as Vienna's top restaurant. Chef Reinhard Gerer is known throughout Austria for his creative touch—and the salons for such gastronomic excellence are appropriately delicious, with gleaming wood-paneled walls, beveled glass, tables set with fine linen, sparkling Riedel crystal, fresh flowers, and a massively baronial fireplace, complete with period columns. Fish is Gerer's specialty, and he prepares it in ways like no other chef in Vienna. Delicately fried *Rotbarsch* (rosefish) is paired with tiny, crispy fried parsley and the smoothest of pureed polenta, Salzkammergut lake trout is grilled and drizzled with a sensational shallot sauce, and *Saibling* (char) caviar is enhanced by organic olive oil. The taste sensations continue with such delights as *Felchen,* a delicate whitefish served with glass noodles, and fresh lobster, which comes with white beans,

Vienna Dining

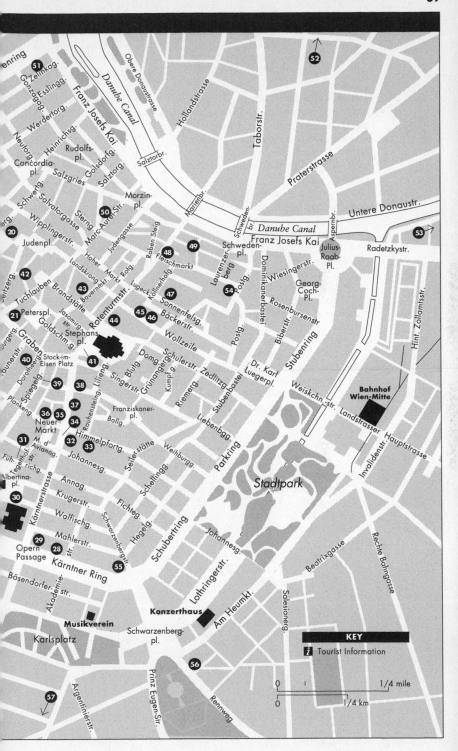

KEY

i Tourist Information

0   1   1/4 mile

0   1/4 km

arugula, and seppia polenta. Meat and game dishes are also available, and be sure to save room for the fresh-out-of-the-oven rhubarb strudel. Service can be a little stiff and formal, but it goes with the surroundings. ⊠ *Mahlerstr. 2,* ☎ *01/515–16–546,* FAX *01/515–16–550. Reservations essential. Jacket and tie. AE, DC, MC, V. Closed 3 wks in Aug. No lunch Sat.*

$$$$ ✕ **Steirereck.** This "Corner of Styria" (as the name translates) is gen-
 ★   erally conceded to be the most famous restaurant in Austria. The big news at press time is that it will be moving from its rather out-of-the-way location to a new address in the center of the Stadtpark, the main city park on the Ringstrasse, in late spring 2003. Longtime chef Helmut Österreicher has been voted chef of the year twice, and his outstanding fusion of different cultural cuisines and flavors never fails to amaze. Start with a warm artichoke cocktail, accompanied by caviar and artichoke cream, followed by crayfish with basil bread and sweet organic cherry tomatoes, or Styrian venison with sauteed *Eierschwammerl* (chanterelle) mushrooms. Fish choices may include delicate smoked catfish, turbot in an avocado crust, or char with mashed potatoes on a bed of white garlic sauce. You can choose from three elegant settings: the intimate Kaminstüberl (ask for Tables 30–33), with its Renaissance-style fireplace, sandstone walls, and decorative columns; the sunny, plant-filled Winter Garden; or modern, light, spacious rooms with French impressionist reproductions on the walls. Extra touches include a bread trolley overflowing with freshly baked breads and, at the end of the meal, an outstanding selection of cheeses from Steirereck's own cheese cellar. Steiereck offers the best special coffees in Austria, and you can be advised which one to choose to accompany your palette of homemade ice cream or brandy by a coffee sommelier, who went to school for the purpose. For a restaurant that is fully booked every night, the wait staff handles itself with a Benedictine calm, and service is friendly and even playful. ⊠ *Rasumofskyg. 2 (moving to new Stadtpark location in late spring 2003), 3rd District/Landstrasse,* ☎ *01/713–3168,* FAX *01/713–5168–2. Reservations essential. Jacket and tie. AE, DC, MC, V. Closed weekends.*

$$$$ ✕ **Zu den Drei Husaren.** Vienna's oldest luxury restaurant, from 1933, the "Three Hussars" gets its name from three soldierly noblemen who served together in World War I, and decided to open a restaurant together. The maître d' stands at attention at the end of a long, decorous corridor made for showy entrances, ready to lead you to your table through a series of sedate rooms done in yellow and dark green. The cuisine here is classic Viennese, with *Wienerschnitzel* (veal scallop, breaded, deep-fried in fresh oil) and *Tafelspitz* (boiled beef) cooked the old-fashioned (and some may say uninspired) way, though there are sometimes a few surprises, such as the veal cutlet with pesto fettuccine or lamb medallions in Serrano ham, stuffed with wild garlic, eggplant, and tomatoes. Even if dessert is not your thing, you shouldn't pass up such exquisite delights as *Husarenpfannkuchen,* the house crepes. Service is dignified, if rather lugubrious, with most of the waiters looking as if they've been there for decades. Still, the staff is eager to please and put you at ease, and the live but discreet piano music provides plenty of show tunes. The only caveat is that the enticing but unpriced evening hors d'oeuvre trolley can send your bill soaring. ⊠ *Weihburgg. 4,* ☎ *01/512–1092–0,* FAX *01/512–1092–18. Reservations essential. AE, DC, MC, V.*

$$$–$$$$ ✕ **Kochwerkstatt.** On one of the prettiest baroque streets in Vienna, in the Spittelberg district near the MuseumsQuartier, Kochwerkstatt has created a buzz about town because of its young, creative chef. The room is intimate, with close-set tables, plum walls, and slender granite columns. The changing menu may offer jumbo shrimp and tuna with mango or *Lachsforellen* (salmon trout) with sticky red rice. Be sure to end your meal with the warm chocolate-mousse pudding. The limited wine list is good, but priced at the high end. The place gets a bit smoky in winter. ⊠ *Spittelbergg. 8, 7th District/Spittelberg,* ☎ ℻ *01/523–3291. Reservations essential. No credit cards. No lunch. U-Bahn: U2, U3/Volkstheater.*

$$$ ✕ **Griechenbeisl.** An inn has been on this site since 1457, next to the glittering gold Greek Orthodox church, in one of the prettiest areas in the city. Now housed within the half-timbered walls is an old-fashioned kitchen that serves traditional, delicious Viennese dishes, such as thick and hearty goulash soup, Wienerschnitzel, and Apfelstrudel. In summer, tables are set up in the charming small square in front of the restaurant. ⊠ *Fleischmarkt 11,* ☎ *01/533–1941. AE, DC, MC, V.*

$$$ ✕ **Schnattl.** If you're not outdoors in the idyllic courtyard, the setting could be described as cool postmodern: the main room has now acquired a warmer patina but is relatively unadorned, letting you concentrate instead on the attractively set tables and excellent cuisine (which offers occasional surprises such as medallions of mountain ram). Traditional dishes like roast pork are transformed with such touches as a light mustard sauce, and lamb with a trace of rosemary, with offerings dependent on season and availability of fresh ingredients. The real bargain here is the daily €5.80 lunch special. ⊠ *Langeg. 40, 8th District/Josefstadt,* ☎ *01/405–3400. AE, DC. Closed weekends, 2 wks around Easter, and last 2 wks of Aug. U-Bahn: U2/Rathaus.*

$$$ ✕ **Vestibül.** Even if you're not attending a play at the Burgtheater, it's fun to dine in this thoroughly theatrical setting, located in what was once the vestibule of the emperor's court theater. Marble columns, secluded corners, and lots of candlelight add romance and drama to the scene. The menu changes frequently, and may include such Viennese classics as veal goulash and Wienerschnitzel, as well as pasta, Caesar salad, and grilled fish dishes. Service is impeccable. It's open late to accommodate theatergoers. ⊠ *Burgtheater/Dr. Karl-Lueger-Ring 2,* ☎ *01/532–4999,* ℻ *01/532–4999–10. AE, DC, MC, V. Closed Sun. No lunch Sat.*

$$$ ✕ **Zu ebener Erde und erster Stock.** This mint-green historic cottage
★ near the Volkstheater was named after a play by Nestroy and means "the ground level and first floor." Upstairs is the cozy Biedermeier room with crocheted pillows and old family photos on the walls, and downstairs is an informal room that appeals to diners who want a light, pretheater meal. Every month a new seasonal menu is offered, and choices may include mouthwatering chestnut soup, crispy goose breast with a polenta terrine, or delicate truffle cheese in a puff pastry. For dessert try the light *Topfenknödel* with plums. ⊠ *Burgg. 13, 7th District/Spittelberg,* ☎ *01/523–6254. Reservations essential. AE, V. Closed Sat. lunch, Sun.–Mon., and 1st 3 wks of Aug. U-Bahn: U2, U3/Volkstheater.*

$$$ ✕ **Zum Kuckuck.** Once you step inside this intimate, vaulted-ceiling restaurant, you enter Old Vienna and leave the modern world behind. Tables are set with pink linen, pewter candlesticks, and fresh flowers, and old prints from Emperor Franz Josef's time adorn the walls. Sip a glass of *Sekt* (sparkling wine) with blood-orange juice while perusing the extensive menu. The kitchen offers good, honest cooking, from beef rouladen marinated in red wine to duck in a honey and green peppercorn sauce. ⊠ *Himmelpfortg. 15,* ☎ *01/512–8470,* ℻ *01/774–1855. AE, DC, MC, V. Closed Sun.*

$$–$$$ ✕ **Artner.** This sleek, modern restaurant with discreet lighting has one
★ of the most innovative menus in the city and showcases, in addition, exceptional wines from its own 350-year-old winery in the Carnuntum region east of Vienna. Delicious appetizers include a salad of field

greens and grilled goat cheese (another house specialty), and recommended main courses are crispy pike perch with black olive risotto or wild boar schnitzel with a potato-and-greens salad. Lamb and veal dishes are also tempting. You can choose to sit at the bar and have a glass of wine and the Artner sandwich—crusty grilled bread stuffed with melted goat cheese and grilled steak strips. Arnter is located just around the corner from Taubstummengasse, one subway stop from Karlsplatz on the U1. ⊠ *Florag. 6 (entrance on Neumanng.), 4th District/Wieden,* ☎ *01/503–5033,* ℻ *01/503–5034. AE, DC, MC, V. No lunch weekends.*

\$\$–\$\$\$ ✕ Palmenhaus. Twenty-foot-high palm trees and exotic plants decorate this large, contemporary restaurant in the historic Hofburg Palace conservatory, at the back of the Burggarten and next to the Schmetterlinghaus (Butterfly House). Seafood is the focus here, and it's temptingly featured in soups and risottos or simply grilled with lemon. There's a blackboard that lists daily fish specials, and several vegetarian dishes are also offered, such as pumpkin gnocchi. The Palmenhaus is also worth a stop for coffee and pastry. In fine weather tables are set outside on the terrace overlooking the park. Service can be slow. ⊠ *Burggarten (entrance through Goetheg. gate after 8 PM),* ☎ *01/533–1033. Reservations essential. DC, MC, V. Closed Sun.–Mon. Nov.–Mar.*

\$\$ ✕ Boheme. This charming restaurant in the 18th-century Spittelberg area is a favorite hangout of opera singers, and autographed pictures of some of the opera-loving owner's more famous patrons line the walls. Opera arias play in the background, and the ambience is casual and relaxed. Start with a tasty salad of field greens and fried zucchini in a yogurt dressing or the simple sliced tomatoes with olives and fresh mozzarella; then go on to pork medallions with potato cakes in a mushroom cream sauce or the more traditional roast duck with dumplings and *Rotkraut* (red cabbage). ⊠ *Spittelbergg. 19, 7th District/Spittelberg,* ☎ *01/523–3173. AE, DC, MC, V. Closed Sun. No lunch. U-Bahn: U2, U3/Volkstheater.*

\$\$ ✕ Figlmüller. Known for its gargantuan Wienerschnitzel, which is so large it overflows the plate, Figlmüller is always packed. Guests share the benches, the long tables, and the experience. Food choices are limited, and everything is à la carte. There are two entrances; one is off the passageway from the Stephansdom. Try to get a table in the small, enclosed "greenhouse" in the passageway entry. ⊠ *Wollzeile 5,* ☎ *01/512–6177. V. Closed Aug.*

\$\$ ✕ Gösser Bierklinik. A cobblestone street leads to this engaging old-world house, which dates back four centuries and has several dining rooms, including a no-smoking one. The Wienerschnitzel here is first class and almost as large as the plate it's served on. Other good choices include *Kas'nocken,* little pasta dumplings with melted Tyrolean mountain cheese, topped with crispy fried onions, or the bountiful *Bauernsalat* (farmer's salad) with sheep's cheese. They also have a salad bar. The beer, of course, is Austrian, from the Gösser brewery in Styria. There's a menu in English, but it lists only about half of what's offered on the German one. ⊠ *Steindlg. 4,* ☎ *01/535–6897. DC, MC, V. Closed Sun.*

\$\$ ✕ Hansen. Housed downstairs in the Börse (Vienna Stock Exchange) and named for the building's 19th-century architect, Theophil Hansen, this unique restaurant is also an exotic, upscale flower market. The decor is modern and elegant, with close-set tables covered in white linen. The restaurant is at one end of the flower shop, so diners can see shoppers browsing for everything from a single rose to a \$2,000 lemon tree. The menu highlights Mediterranean-inspired dishes such as scampi risotto or spaghettini with oven-dried tomatoes in a black-olive cream sauce. There are also Austrian dishes done with a fresh slant. Lunch is the main event here, though you can also come for breakfast or a pre-theater dinner. ⊠ *Wipplingerstr. 34,* ☎ *01/532–0542. Reservations essential. AE, DC, MC, V. Closed Sun. and after 9 PM weekdays. No dinner Sat.*

$$ ✕ **Lale.** Vienna has a substantial Turkish population, and this modern, inviting restaurant in the heart of the Schwedenplatz area serves some of the best Turkish cuisine in the city. Specialties include *Huhnerspiess,* chunks of grilled chicken breast on a skewer, or the *Iskender kebab,* slivers of tender lamb served with yogurt and tomato sauce. Don't miss the tasty selection of *meze* (appetizers) temptingly arrayed in the front counter. A perfect choice for a takeout lunch is the vegetarian sandwich—a mouthwatering combination of grilled eggplant, feta, spinach, and hummus in a soft, freshly baked bun. ⊠ *Franz-Josef-Kai 29,* ☎ *01/535–2736. No credit cards.*

$$ ✕ **Lebenbauer.** Set within the shadow of the Freyung, this long-standing vegetarian restaurant even has a no-smoking room, rare in this part of Europe. The menu offers vegetarian and whole-grain items, and there's a lot to choose from. Specialties include *Hirsegröstl,* a millet hash with pumpkin seeds in an oyster mushroom sauce, and gluten-free pasta with smoked salmon and shrimp in a dill cream sauce. There are also several free-range chicken and fish entrées, all lightly prepared. ⊠ *Teinfaltstr. 3,* ☎ *01/533–5556–0. AE, DC, MC, V. Closed weekends and 3 wks in July–Aug.*

$$ ✕ **Livingstone.** If you're homesick for a hamburger, this is the place to go. Buns are homemade, the Austrian beef is of the finest quality, and crisp fries and a creditable slaw come on the side. But if the tropical-colonial setting straight out of a 1940s Bogart movie inspires you to try something more adventurous, you won't be disappointed. The open kitchen allows you to glimpse some of the exotic food being prepared, such as scallops, tiger shrimp, and mango in a puff pastry, a selection of wok dishes (including chicken, lemongrass, and coconut milk), as well as salads and pasta. Wines by the glass are unfortunately overpriced. ⊠ *Zelinkag. 4,* ☎ *01/533–3393–12. AE, DC, V. No lunch.*

$$ ✕ **Ostaria Venexiana da Pablo.** Casual and cozy, with just a handful of tables, this popular Italian restaurant is close to the Belvedere Palace. Smoked hams and sausages hang from the rafters, above an enticing selection of antipasti. Daily specials are listed on a blackboard, with several kinds of fresh pasta, roasted meats, and grilled fish to choose from, or you can order from the regular menu. Especially delicious are risotto with truffles, penne in a robust ragu sauce, and *Branzino* (sea bass) on a bed of lentils, eggplant, and sun-dried tomatoes. A nice selection of Austrian and Italian wines (look for delicious whites from the Friuli region) are offered by the glass. ⊠ *Rennweg 11, 3rd District/Landstrasse,* ☎ *01/714–6003. Reservations essential. DC, MC, V. Closed Sun. No lunch Sat. Tram: 71/Unteres Belvedere.*

$$ ✕ **Schlossgasse 21.** There are four different settings in this popular restaurant in the old Margareten area. The cavernous main room is for casual diners; the Hofstöckl offers a more elegant, intimate ambience; the designer cafe, Caudro, is where the *Schickimicki* (yuppie) crowd meets; and the lovely garden courtyard entices everyone in fine weather. The food is varied and delicious. You can make a meal of the Bauernsalat—farmer's salad with field greens, Styrian sheep's cheese, and white beans in a Kürbiskernöl (pumpkin seed oil) dressing—and main courses offer everything from tandoori burgers to Tex-Mex to exotic Asian dishes. ⊠ *Schlossg. 21, 5th District/Margareten,* ☎ *01/544–0767. V. No lunch. U-Bahn: U4/Pilgrimg.*

$$ ✕ **Strandcafé.** If you want to have a good meal along the banks of the Alte Donau, or Old Danube, this is the place to go. Tables are set on a wooden pier directly on the water, affording prime views of passing sailboats. The specialty of the house is the huge portion of meaty spareribs served on a butcher's block, but you can also choose from tempting Viennese dishes, including the delicious *Huhnerschnitzel* (fried chicken breast) and crispy french fries. This café is in the 22nd District, a suburban residential area across the river from the modern city center, so you'll want to use the U-Bahn to get here. ✉ *Florian-Berndl-G. 20, 22nd District/Donaustadt,* ☎ *01/203–6747. Reservations essential. No credit cards. U-Bahn: U1/Alte Donau.*

$$ ✕ Tancredi. Ever since this upscale Beisl with a Sicilian name opened, it's been the talk of the town because of the kitchen's fresh approach to Austrian cooking. *Beisls* (a cross between a pub and a café) are traditionally known for their solid, old-fashioned renditions of Austrian standards like Wienerschnitzel and Tafelspitz, but Tancredi has set out to revamp the Beisl image. No plain, dark wood tables, lace curtains and smoke-stained walls here—instead the decor is elegantly light and modern, dominated by a huge bar along one wall and clean-lined tables fronting the window opposite. The menu changes seasonally and may include crispy fried chicken and chunky potato salad (using homemade mayonnaise), tender, succulent steak topped with matchstick fried onions and light, grilled dumplings, or *Wels G'röstl,* hunks of catfish, vegetables, potatoes, and spätzle cooked in a blackened skillet. For dessert, try the sliced strawberries in sweet cream. ✉ *Grosse Neug. 5, 4th District/Wieden,* ☎ *01/941–0048. Reservations essential. No credit cards. Closed Sun. No lunch Sat. U1, U2 or U4/Karlspl., then Tram 62 or 65/Mayerhofg.*

$$ ✕ Wrenkh. The menu here is vegetarian and eclectic, and dishes are made from the freshest ingredients. Start with the miso soup and then go on to wild-rice risotto with mushrooms or Greek fried rice with vegetables, sheep's cheese, and olives. The minimalist-style café section offers lunch specials at a great value, and the more elegant adjacent room is perfect for a nice, relaxed lunch or dinner. There is also a no-smoking room. ✉ *Bauernmarkt 10,* ☎ *01/533–1526. AE, DC, MC, V.*

$ ✕ Beim Czaak. Pronounced "bime chalk," this simple spot with friendly service is a favorite with locals. It's long and narrow, with forest-green wainscoting, framed caricatures of a few well-known Viennese on the walls, and limited seating outdoors. Choose a glass of excellent Austrian wine to go along with Waldviertler pork stuffed with bacon, onions, and mushrooms, spinach dumplings drizzled with Parmesan and browned butter, or a big Wienerschnitzel. ✉ *Postg. 15/corner of Fleischmarkt,* ☎ *01/513–7215. No credit cards. Closed Sun.*

$ ✕ Brezl Gwölb. Housed in a medieval pretzel factory between Am Hof and Judenplatz, this snug restaurant fills up fast at night. Try the scrumptious *Tyroler G'röstl,* home-fried potatoes, ham, onions, and cheese served in a blackened skillet, or the *Kasnockerl,* spätzle in a pungent cheese sauce. Try to get a table downstairs in the real medieval cellar, which looks like a stage set from *Phantom of the Opera.* ✉ *Ledererhof 9 (near Am Hof),* ☎ *01/533–8811. AE, DC, MC, V.*

$ ✕ Fischer Bräu. This is known as Vienna's number one brewery restaurant, and though it's located in the 19th District, it's worth the effort
★ to get here. Several varieties of their own fresh beer are featured, and the menu, though extensive, is nothing fancy. You can choose from stuffed baked potatoes, salads, or Wienerschnitzel—huge and served with a side order of potato salad. Especially scrumptious is the golden-fried *Hühnerschnitzel* (chicken breast). The beer garden with its twinkling lights strung through the trees is packed on summer evenings, so come early to get a table. Every Sunday there is a popular jazz brunch, with live music. ✉ *Billrothstr. 17, 19th District/Döbling,* ☎ *01/369–5949. Reservations essential. No credit cards. No lunch, except Sun. brunch. U-Bahn: U2/Schottentor; Tram: 37 or 38/Döblinger Hauptstr.*

$ ✕ **Salzgries.** A typical old Viennese *Beisl,* which is somewhere between a cafe and a pub, the Salzgries has an unpretentious, rather worn atmosphere. It's known for having good schnitzels, and you can get either pork, milk-fed veal, or chicken breast (*Gebackenes Hühnerfilet*), all fried to a golden crispness, with potato salad on the side. The *Vanillerostbraten* (garlicky rump steak) is also worth trying, and the *Moor im Hemd,* warm chocolate cake with whipped cream, is scrumptious. ✉ *Marc-Aurel-Str. 6,* ☎ *01/968–9645. No credit cards.*

$ ✕ **Spatzennest.** This is simple, hearty Viennese cooking at its best, located on a quaint, cobblestone pedestrian street straight out of a 1930s Hollywood movie set in Old Vienna. Tasty dishes include Wienerschnitzel, roast chicken, and pillowy fried spätzle with slivers of ham and melted cheese. It's especially delightful in summer, when tables are set outside. It can be smoky indoors. ✉ *Ulrichspl. 1, 7th District/Spittelberg,* ☎ *01/526–1659. MC, V. Closed Fri.–Sat. U-Bahn: U2, U3/ Volkstheater.*

Munch on the Run

If you don't have time for a leisurely lunch, or you'd rather save your money for a splurge at dinner, here's a sampling of the best places in the city center to grab a quick, inexpensive, and tasty bite to eat. In the lower level of the Ringstrasse Galerie shopping mall, the gourmet supermarket **Billa Corso** (✉ Kärntner Ring 9–13 1st District, ☎ 01/ 512–6625; closed Sun.) has a good salad bar, and will prepare the sandwich of your choice at the deli counter. (The Ringstrasse Galerie is in two similar buildings, so make sure you're in the one on the Kärntner Ring.) The best pizza by-the-slice can be found near St. Stephen's at **Bizi Pizza** (✉ Rotenturmstr. 4, 1st District, ☎ 01/513–3705). Next to the produce section on the ground floor of Vienna's premier gourmet grocery store, **Meinl am Graben** (✉ Graben 19, 1st District, ☎ 01/532– 3334; closed Sun.) is a smart stand-up café where you can choose from a selection of soups, sandwiches, or antipasti (don't confuse it with the full-service restaurant upstairs).Near the Freyung, the epicurean deli **Radatz** (✉ Schotteng. 3a, 1st District, ☎ 01/533–8163; closed Sun.) offers made-to-order sandwiches from a vast selection of mouthwatering meats and cheeses. Around the corner from Am Hof, **Zum Schwarzen Kameel** (✉ Bognerg. 5, 1st District, ☎ 01/533–8967; closed Sun.) serves elegant little open-faced sandwiches and baby quiches in their stand-up section.

A sure way to spike a lively discussion among the Viennese is to ask which *Würstelstand* serves the most delicious grilled sausages. Here are three that are generally acknowledged to be the best: **Ehrenreich's** (✉ Naschmarkt, on the Linke Wienzeile side across from Piccini, under the clock, 1st District; closed Sun.) serves scrumptious *Käsekrainer,* beef sausages oozing with melted cheese, alongside a *Semmel* (soft roll) and mild, sweet mustard. Behind the Opera House, **Oper** (✉ Corner of Philharmonikerstr./Hanuschg., 1st District) entices passersby with its plump, sizzling *Bratwurst.* **Würstelstand am Hoher Markt** (✉ Hoher Markt, corner of Marc-Aurel Str., 1st District), serves American-style hot dogs and is open daily from 7 AM to 5 AM.

Wine Taverns

In-town wine restaurants cannot properly be called *Heurige,* since they are not run by the vintner, so the term is *Weinkeller* (wine restaurant, or cellar). Many of them extend a number of levels underground, particularly in the older part of the city. Mainly open in the evening, they are intended primarily for drinking, though you can always get something to eat from a buffet, and increasingly, full dinners are available. As at their country cousins, wine is served by the mug. Some of the better wine restaurants follow; credit cards are not accepted except where noted.

$$ ✕ **Augustinerkeller.** This ground-floor Keller is open at noontime as well as in the evening. The spit-roasted chicken is excellent, as is the filling *Stelze* (roast knuckle of pork). For dessert, try the *Apfelstrudel*, moist and warm from the oven. There's kitschy live music at night. ⊠ *Augustinerstr. 1/Albertinapl., 1st District,* ☎ *01/533–1026. AE, DC, MC, V.*

$$ ✕ **Esterházykeller.** This maze of rooms offers some of the best Keller wines in town plus a typical Vienna menu noontime and evenings, as well as a hot and cold buffet, but this cellar may be too smoky for some. ⊠ *Haarhof 1, 1st District,* ☎ *01/533–3482. No lunch weekends. Closed weekends in summer.*

$$ ✕ **Melker Stiftskeller.** Down and down you go, into one of the friendli-
★ est Keller in town, where Stelze is a popular feature, along with outstanding wines by the glass or, rather, mug. ⊠ *Schotteng. 3, 1st District,* ☎ *01/533–5530. AE, DC, MC, V. Closed Sun.–Mon. No lunch.*

$ ✕ **Zwölf Apostel-Keller.** You pass a huge wood statue of St. Peter on the way downstairs to the two underground floors in this deep-down cellar in the oldest part of Vienna. The young crowd comes for the good wines and the atmosphere, and there's buffet food as well. ⊠ *Sonnenfelsg. 3, 1st District,* ☎ *01/512–6777. AE, DC, MC, V. No lunch.*

Heurige

Few cities the size of Vienna boast wine produced within their city limits, and even fewer offer wines ranging from good to outstanding. But in various suburban villages—once well outside the center but now parts of the urban complex—the fringes of the city have spawned characteristic wine taverns and restaurants, sometimes in the vineyards themselves. Summer and fall are the seasons for visiting the Heurige, though often the more elegant and expensive establishments, called *Noble-Heurige*, stay open year-round. Heurige are concentrated in several outskirts of Vienna: Stammersdorf, Grinzing, Sievering, Nussdorf, Neustift, and a corner of Ottakring. Perchtoldsdorf, just outside Vienna, is also well known for its wine taverns.

$$ ✕ **Haslinger.** In Sievering, Haslinger offers good wines and a small but tasty buffet. The rooms are plain but honest; opt for the small, typical vine-covered garden in summer. ⊠ *Agnesg. 3, 19th District/Sievering,* ☎ *01/440–1347. No credit cards. Closed Mon. U-bahn: U4/ Heiligenstadt; Bus 39A/Sievering.*

$$ ✕ **Mayer am Pfarrplatz.** Heiligenstadt is home to this legendary Heuriger in Beethoven's former abode. The atmosphere in the collection of rooms is genuine, the à la carte offerings and buffet more than abundant, and the house wines excellent. You'll even find some Viennese among the tourists. ⊠ *Heiligenstädter Pfarrpl. 2, 19th District/Nussdorf* ☎ *01/370–1287. DC, MC, V. No lunch weekdays or Sat. Tram: D/Nussdorf from the Ring.*

$$ ✕ **Passauerhof.** If you want live folk music (offered nightly) to accompany your meal, this is the place to go. But you may have to share the experience with the tour groups that descend on Grinzing. The food from the menu, such as roast chicken and Wienerschnitzcl, is tasty, whereas the buffet offers a limited selection. It's a five-minute walk up the hill from the town center. ⊠ *Cobenzlg. 9, 19th District/Grinzing,* ☎ *01/320–6345. AE, DC, MC, V. No lunch. Closed Jan.–Feb. U-Bahn: U2/Schottentor; Tram: 38/Grinzing.*

$$ ✕ **Schreiberhaus.** In Neustift am Walde, the Schreiberhaus has one of
★ the prettiest terraced gardens in the city, with picnic tables stretching
straight up into the vineyards. The buffet offers delicious treats such
as spit-roasted chicken, salmon pasta, and a huge selection of tempt-
ing grilled vegetables and salads. The golden Traminer wine is excel-
lent. ✉ *Rathstr. 54, 19th District/Neustift am Walde,* ☎ *01/440–
3844. AE, DC, MC, V. U-Bahn: U4, U6/Spittelau; Bus 35A/Neustift
am Walde.*

$$ ✕ **Schübel-Auer.** In Nussdorf seek out the Schübel-Auer for its series
★ of atmospheric rooms and good wines. Known for its home-style cook-
ing, it also offers vegetarian dishes and has several varieties of Austrian cheese. ✉ *Kahlenbergerstr. 22, 19th District/Nussdorf,* ☎ *01/370–
2222. No credit cards. Closed Sun. No lunch. Tram: D/Nussdorf from
the Ring.*

$$ ✕ **Wieninger.** Wine and food are both top-notch here, and the charm-
ing, tree-shaded inner courtyard and series of typical vintner's rooms
are perfect for whiling away an evening. Wieninger's bottled wines are
ranked among the country's best. It's located across the Danube in Stam-
mersdorf, one of Vienna's oldest Heurige areas. ✉ *Stammersdorfer Str.
78, 21st District/Floridsdorf,* ☎ *01/292–4106. V. Closed late Dec.–
Feb. No lunch except Sun. U-Bahn: U2, U4/Schottenring; Tram: 31/
Stammersdorf.*

$$ ✕ **Zimmermann.** East of the Grinzing village center, Zimmermann has
excellent wines, an enchanting tree-shaded garden, and an endless se-
ries of small paneled rooms and vaulted cellars. You can order from
the menu or choose from the tempting buffet. This well-known Heuriger
attracts the occasional celebrity, including fashion model Claudia Schif-
fer. ✉ *Armbrusterg. 5/Grinzinger Str., 19th District/Grinzing,* ☎ *01/
370–2211. AE, DC, MC, V. No lunch. U-Bahn: U2/Schottentor; Tram:
38/Grinzing.*

$$ ✕ **Zum Martin Sepp.** The Grinzing district today suffers from mass
tourism, with very few exceptions, but at Martin Sepp at least the wine,
food, service, and ambience are all good. ✉ *Cobenzlg. 34, 19th Dis-
trict/Grinzing,* ☎ *01/328–9061. MC, V. U-Bahn: U2/Schottentor;
Tram: 38/Grinzing.*

Cafés

One of the quintessential Viennese institutions, the coffeehouse, or café,
is club, pub, and bistro rolled into one. For decades, a substantial part
of Austrian social life has revolved around them (though now less than
in the past), as Austrians by and large are rather reluctant to invite
strangers to their homes and prefer to meet them in the friendly, but
noncommittal, atmosphere of a café.

To savor these coffeehouses, allow some time; set aside an afternoon,
a morning, or at least a couple of hours, and settle down in one of your
choice. Read or catch up on your letter writing: there is no need to worry
about overstaying one's welcome, even over a single small cup of cof-
fee, though don't expect refills. (Of course, in some of the more opu-
lent coffeehouses, this cup of coffee can cost as much as a meal.)

Coffee is not just coffee in Austria. It comes in many forms and under
many names. Morning coffee is generally *Melange* (a mild roast with
steamed milk) or a stronger blend espresso, either straight, a *Schwarzer,*
or with a little cream on the side, a *Brauner.* The usual after-dinner
drink is espresso. Most delightful are the coffee-and-whipped-cream
concoctions, universally cherished as *Kaffee mit Schlag,* a taste that is
easily acquired and a menace to all but the very thin. A customer who
wants more whipped cream than coffee asks for a *Doppelschlag.* Hot

black coffee in a glass with one knob of whipped cream is an *Einspänner* (literally, "one-horse coach"). Then you can go to town on a *Mazagran,* black coffee with ice and a tot of rum, or *Eiskaffee,* cold coffee with ice cream, whipped cream, and cookies. Or you can simply order a *Portion Kaffee* and have an honest pot of coffee and jug of hot milk.

The typical Viennese café, with polished brass or marble-topped tables, bentwood chairs, supplies of newspapers, and tables outside in good weather, is a fixed institution, of which there are literally hundreds. All cafés serve pastries and light snacks in addition to beverages. Many offer a menu or fixed lunch at noon, but be aware that some can get rather expensive. Credit cards are not accepted unless noted.

Of course, when tourists think of Viennese cafés, Demel and Café Sacher leap to mind, but they are hardly typical. When you want a quick (but excellent) coffee and dessert, look for an **Aida** café; they are scattered throughout the city. **Eduscho** is a coffee chain with several locations, offering a selection of coffee for a fraction of what you'd pay in a cafe, though there's no place to sit. Sign of the times: **Starbucks** has recently opened a number of outlets in Vienna. Newspaper editorials have already decreed that to patronize these generic establishments may only serve to shutter some of the historic and wonderfully atmospheric coffeehouses that give Vienna its unique flavor.

Here's a sampling of the best of the traditional cafés: **Alte Backstube** (✉ Langeg. 34, 8th District/Josefstadt, ☎ 01/406–1101), in a gorgeous baroque house—with a café in front and restaurant in back—was once a bakery and is now a museum as well. **Bräunerhof** (✉ Stallburgg. 2, 1st District, ☎ 01/512–3893) has music on some afternoons. **Café Central** (✉ Herreng. 14/in Palais Ferstel, 1st District, ☎ 01/533–3763–26) is where Trotsky played chess. **Frauenhuber** (✉ Himmelpfortg. 6, 1st District, ☎ 01/512–4323) has its original turn-of-the-20th-century interior and a good choice of desserts. **Landtmann** (✉ Dr.-Karl-Lueger-Ring 4, 1st District, ☎ 01/532–0621) is an elegant turn-of-the-20th-century café, reputed to have been a favorite of Freud's. In fine weather you can sit outside on the front terrace, to take in glorious views of the city. **Museum** (✉ Friedrichstr. 6, 1st District, ☎ 01/586–5202), with its original interior by the architect Adolf Loos, draws a mixed crowd and has lots of newspapers. **Schwarzenberg** (✉ Kärntner Ring 17, ☎ 01/512–8998–13), with piano music in the evenings on Wednesday and Friday, and in the late afternoon on Saturday and Sunday, is highly popular, particularly its sidewalk tables in summer. **Tirolerhof** (✉ Tegetthoffstr. 8/Albertinapl., ☎ 01/512–7833), with ample papers and excellent desserts, is popular with students.

Two cafés deserve special mention, of course—whole books have been written about them. **Café Hawelka** (✉ Dorotheerg. 12, 1st District, ☎ 01/512–8230) at first glance looks just like a shabby gathering place, but its international clientele has ranged from artists to politicians since it opened shortly after World War II. Hawelka is jammed any time of day, so you share a table (and the very smoky atmosphere). In a city noted for fine coffee, Hawelka's is superb, even more so when accompanied by a freshly baked *Buchterln* (sweet roll, evenings only). **Café Sacher** (✉ Philharmonikerstr. 4, 1st District, ☎ 01/514560) began life as a delicatessen opened by Sacher, court confectioner to Metternich, the most powerful prime minister in early 19th-century Europe and fervent chocoholic. Back then, cookbooks of the day devoted more space to desserts than to main courses and Sacher's creations were practically ranked on the order of painting and sculpture. When the populace at large was allowed to enjoy the prime minister's favorite chocolate cake—a sublime mixture of flour, eggs, butter, chocolate, and apricot preserves—the fashion for Sachertorte was created. War-weary Metternich must have been amused to see a battle break out between Sacher and Demel's—a competing confectioner—as to who served the real Sachertorte, but the jury has now awarded the prize to Sacher. Red flocks the drapes, walls, and floors here, mirrors and chandeliers add glitter, and there is live piano music every day from 4:30 'til 7 PM.

Pastry Shops

Viennese pastries are said to be the best in the world. In all shops you can buy them to enjoy on the premises, usually with coffee, as well as to take out. A 200-year-old institution is **Demel** (⊠ Kohlmarkt 14, 1st District, ☎ 01/535–1717–0), Vienna's most beloved konditorei. Beyond the shop proper are stairs that lead to dining salons where the decor is almost as sweet as the chocolates, marzipan, and sugar-coated almonds on sale (☞ **Vienna's Shop Window: From Michaelerplatz to the Graben** *in* Exploring Vienna). **Gerstner** (⊠ Kärntnerstr. 11–15, ☎ 01/512–4963–77) is in the heart of the bustling Kärntnerstrasse and is one of the more modern Viennese cafés, though it has been going strong since the mid-18th century. **Heiner** (⊠ Kärntnerstr. 21–23, ☎ 01/512–6863–0; ⊠ Wollzeile 9, ☎ 01/512–2343) is dazzling for its crystal chandeliers as well as for its pastries. **Oberlaa** (⊠ Neuer Markt 16, ☎ 01/513–2936) has irresistible confections, cakes, and bonbons, as well as light lunches and salad plates, served outdoors in summer. **Sperl** (⊠ Gumpendorferstr. 11, 6th District/Mariahilf ☎ 01/586–4158), founded in 1880, has an all-around Old Viennese ambience.

LODGING

In Vienna's best hotels the staff seems to anticipate your wishes almost before you express them. Such service, of course, has its price, and if you wish, you can stay in Vienna in profound luxury. For those with more modest requirements, ample rooms are available in less expensive but entirely adequate hotels. Pensions, mainly bed-and-breakfast establishments often managed by the owner, generally represent good value. A number of student dormitories are run as hotels in summer, offering about the most reasonable quarters of all. And several apartment-hotels accommodate those who want longer stays.

When you have only a short time to spend in Vienna, you will probably choose to stay in the inner city (the 1st District, or 1010 postal code) or fairly close to it, to be within walking distance of the most important sights, restaurants, and shops. Although most of the hotels there are in the more expensive categories, excellent and reasonable accommodations can be found in the 6th, 7th, and 8th districts and put you close to the major museums. You'll also find a group of moderate ($$) and inexpensive ($) hotels in the Mariahilferstrasse–Westbahnhof area, within easy reach of the city center by subway.

For the high season, Easter–September, and around the Christmas–New Year holidays, make reservations a month or more in advance. Vienna is continually the site of some international convention or other, and the city fills up quickly.

Hotel categories correspond more or less to the official Austrian rating system, with five stars the equivalent of the very expensive ($$$$) category. Air-conditioning is customary in the top category only (and sometimes in the $$$ and $$–$$$ categories), but since Vienna has very few extremely hot days, with temperatures cooling off at night, it's usually not necessary. Breakfast is included with all *except* the highest category.

Note that neighborhoods are listed *only* for those hotels and pensions that are outside the 1st District.

Assume that all guest rooms have air-conditioning, room phones, and room TVs unless noted otherwise.

CATEGORY	COST*
$$$$	over €300
$$$	€200–€300
$$	€100–€200
$	under €100

All prices are for a standard double room in high season, including taxes and service charge.

$$$$ 🏨 **Bristol.** A Boesendorfer grand of a hotel, this venerable landmark, dating from 1892, has one of the finest locations in the city, on the Ring next to the Opera House. The accent here is on tradition, and guest rooms are sumptuously furnished in Biedermeier style with decorative fireplaces, thick carpets, wing-back chairs, crystal chandeliers, and lace curtains. Penthouse rooms have terraces with staggering views of the Opera. Sometimes the hotel offers special rates at great value. The Bristol also houses the acclaimed Korso restaurant, the convivial Café Sirk, and a music salon complete with a pianist lulling the after-theater crowd with tunes on a time-burnished Boesendorfer. ⊠ *Kärntner Ring 1, A–1010,* ☎ *01/515–16–0,* ℻ *01/515–16–550,* WEB *www. westin.com/bristol. 141 rooms. 2 restaurants, minibars, health club, bar, Internet, business services. AE, DC, MC, V.*

$$$$ 🏨 **Grand.** Vienna's first luxury hotel, dating from 1870, the Grand Hotel
★ Wien is still one of the best hotels in the city. It can best be described as palatial, and its location on the Ringstrasse next to the city's premier shopping mall makes it a top choice. The truly sumptuous guest rooms have chandeliers, tasseled drapes, brocade wallpaper, and elegant antique-style furniture, yet are also high-tech. A simple touch of a button will do everything from close your drapes to lighting the DO NOT DISTURB sign outside your door. Baths are Italian marble, and Frette terry-cloth robes are provided for lounging. Each of the eight suites is fit for a king. The hotel also houses the excellent Le Ciel restaurant on the top floor, with an innovative Continental menu, and Vienna's only authentic Japanese restaurant, Unkai. ⊠ *Kärntner Ring 9, A–1010,* ☎ *01/515–800,* ℻ *01/515–1313,* WEB *www.grandhotelwien. com. 197 rooms, 8 suites. 2 restaurants, 2 cafés, kitchenettes, minibars, gym, 2 bars, Internet, meeting rooms. AE, DC, MC, V.*

$$$$ 🏨 **Imperial.** Exemplifying the grandeur of imperial Vienna, this hotel
★ is as much a palace today as when it was formally opened in 1873 by Emperor Franz Josef as the Wurttemberg-Palais. Adjacent to the famed Musikverein concert hall and two blocks from the Staatsoper, the emphasis here is on Old Vienna elegance and privacy, which accounts for the royalty, heads of state, and celebrities staying here. Michael Jackson checks in when he's in town, and other guests have included Bruce Springsteen and Elizabeth Taylor. The beautiful rooms are furnished in antique style, with sparkling chandeliers, gorgeous fabrics, and original 19th-century paintings. Guest rooms on the top floor (the former attic) are done in Biedermeier style, and several have small terraces offering amazing views of the city. Suites come with your own personal butler. Don't overlook, as if you could, the grand marble staircase and ornate reception rooms. The hotel also houses the Imperial restaurant and the Imperial Café, which headlines the famed, handmade Imperial torte. All in all, this hotel remains one of the great landmarks of the Ringstrasse. ⊠ *Kärntner Ring 16, A–1010,* ☎ *01/501–10–0,* ℻ *01/501–10–410,* WEB *www.luxurycollection.com/imperial. 138 rooms.*

Restaurant, café, minibars, gym, piano bar, Internet, no-smoking rooms. AE, DC, MC, V.

$$$$
★ 🏨 **Sacher.** One of Europe's legends, originally founded by Eduard Sacher, chef to Prince Metternich—for whom the famous chocolate cake was invented—the Sacher dates from 1876. It has retained its sense of history over the years while providing luxurious, modern-day comfort. More important, in our experience, the staff has proved unfailingly helpful and gracious. Sacher's widow, Anna, turned the hotel into the phenomenon that it still is. In an age when every moment had to be lived in public, her *separé* dining rooms offered privacy and comfort to archdukes and their mistresses, to dancers and their hussars. It was an empire that she watched over, supreme and always with a cigar in her mouth. Today, the corridors serve as a veritable art gallery, and the exquisitely furnished bedrooms also contain original artwork. The location directly behind the Opera House could hardly be more central, and the ratio of staff to guests is more than two to one. Meals in the Red Room or Anna Sacher Room are first-rate, with both a Continental and Viennese menu. The Café Sacher, of course, is legendary. British director Carol Reed filmed some of his classic 1949 film *The Third Man* in the reception area. ⊠ *Philharmonikerstr. 4, A–1010,* ☎ *01/514–56–0,* FAX *01/514–56–810,* WEB *www.sacher.com. 113 rooms. 2 restaurants, café, minibars, bar, Internet, no-smoking rooms. AE, DC, MC, V.*

$$$–$$$$
★ 🏨 **Palais Schwarzenberg.** It's not every day you get to call a palace designed by Lukas von Hildebrandt (architect of the nearby Belvedere Palace) and Fischer von Erlach (whose Karlskirche crowns the nearby skyline) your home-away-from-home. But this enchanting residence allows you to feel like a prince—Prince Adam Franz zu Schwarzenberg, to be exact, who completed the mansion in 1716—or his princess. Complete with five historic salons, including the Marmorsaal—one of Vienna's most glittering ballrooms—and set against a vast formal park, this hotel has everything, including a 16-acre private park. Though it's just a few minutes' walk from the heart of the city, the hotel feels like a country estate—the loudest sounds you'll often hear are the thwack of croquet balls on the lawn. Guest rooms are individually and luxuriously appointed, with the family's original artwork adorning the walls; only those with ultramodern tastes will want to book the suites by Italian designer Paolo Piva, set in a separate wing in the park. All bathrooms are sleekly done, with heated towel racks and long, deep bathtubs. Happily, you don't have to be a guest here to come for a drink, coffee, or light lunch, served outside on the terrace in summer—overlooking the formal gardens studded with marble statues, this is one of Vienna's most gorgeous settings—or beside a roaring fireplace in the main sitting room in winter. ⊠ *Schwarzenbergpl. 9, 3rd District/Landstrasse,* ☎ *01/798–4515,* FAX *01/798–4714,* WEB *www.palais-schwarzenberg.com. 44 rooms. Restaurant, portable a/c units on request, minibars, tennis, bar, Internet, free parking. AE, DC, MC, V.*

$$$
🏨 **Ambassador.** Franz Lehár, Marlene Dietrich, and Mick Jagger are just a few of the celebrities who have stayed at this old dowager (from 1866), given a face-lift overhaul in 2001. The lobby is small but grand, and the high-ceilinged guest rooms, differing only in size, are uniformly decorated with pale yellow-striped wallpaper, deep blue carpets, and faux Empire furniture. Unless you want the excitement of a direct view onto the lively pedestrian Kärntnerstrasse, ask for one of the quieter rooms on the Neuer Markt side. Don't expect warmth from the staff—the trade-off is the great location. The Ambassador also houses the top-flight restaurant Mörwald, offering stunning views of the square. ⊠ *Kärntnerstr. 22/Neuer Markt 5, A–1010,* ☎ *01/961610,* FAX *01/5132–999,* WEB *www.ambassador.at. 86 rooms. Restaurant, minibars, bar, Internet. AE, DC, MC, V.*

82

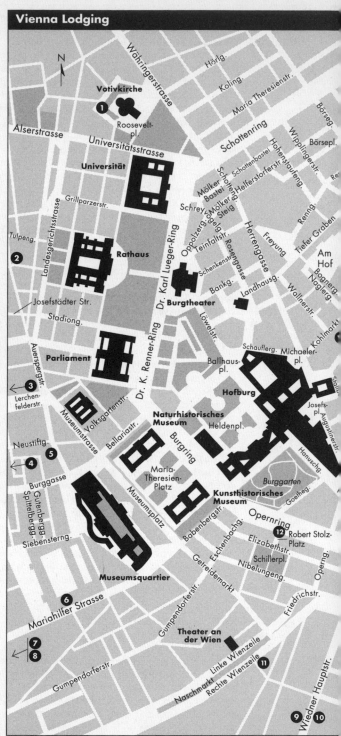

Vienna Lodging

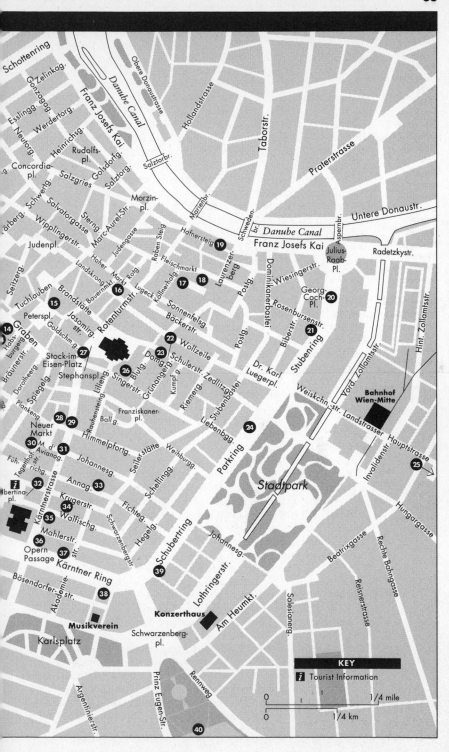

$$$ 🏨 **Arenberg.** Near Schwedenplatz and the Danube Canal, the Arenberg is an old-fashioned pension with lots of character. Despite its corner location on the Ringstrasse, serenity reigns, because the pension is set on the upper floors of the building. Rooms have a charming appearance, with plump beds, overstuffed chairs and patterned carpets. The No. 1 streetcar is virtually outside the front door, allowing easy access to the city center, or you can walk about 10 minutes up the Ring. ✉ *Stubenring 2, A–1010,* ☎ *01/512–5291,* ☒ *01/513–9356,* WEB *www.arenberg.at. 22 rooms. Internet; no a/c. AE, DC, MC, V.*

$$$ 🏨 **Biedermeier im Sünnhof.** This jewel of a hotel is tucked into a renovated 1820s house that even with all modern facilities still conveys a feeling of Old Vienna. The rooms are compact but efficient, the public areas tastefully done in the Biedermeier style, and the service is friendly. The courtyard passageway around which the hotel is built has attracted a number of interesting boutiques and handicrafts shops, but at times there is an excess of coming and going as tour groups are accommodated. It's about a 20-minute walk or a 6-minute subway ride from the center of the city. ✉ *Landstrasser Hauptstr. 28, 3rd District/ Landstrasse,* ☎ *01/716–71–0,* ☒ *01/716–71–503,* WEB *www.dorint.de. 203 rooms. Restaurant, minibars, bar, Internet in some rooms, parking (fee). AE, DC, MC, V.*

$$$ 🏨 **Das Triest.** This is a little off the beaten track but still within easy walking distance of the city center. Totally redone by Sir Terence Conran, it's now Vienna's suavest hotel, giving one the feeling you are on board an ultrasleek ocean liner—a bit surprising, considering this was once the stable of the old Vienna-Trieste posthouse. The extra little touches in the rooms here are plentiful; even the doorknobs feel nice to the touch. Decor is delightful—linen-fresh, with accents of blue carpeting and honey-hued woods, and high-style as only a Conran hotel can be. The hotel also allures with an excellent Austro-Italian restaurant, Collio, and breakfast is included in the room rate. ✉ *Wiedner Hauptstr. 12, A–1040, 4th District/Wieden,* ☎ *01/589–180,* ☒ *01/589– 1818,* WEB *www.dastriest.at. 73 rooms. Restaurant, café, minibars, health club, bar, Internet; no a/c in some rooms. AE, DC, MC, V.*

$$$ 🏨 **Kummer.** In the heart of the shopping district and with an imposing, Georgian-style exterior, this old hotel has an equally noble lobby with a grand, sweeping staircase, and a distinguished history dating back to 1872 (the Strauss family once resided in a hotel on the site; Friedrich Schlögl, one of the founding fathers of the Viennese literature tradition, began a literary and art salon in this hotel's reception rooms). Each comfortably furnished room is different, and the ones facing the busy Mariahilferstrasse have soundproof windows. Some rooms have an alcove sitting area. The hotel is also close to the Westbahnhof and major museums. ✉ *Mariahilferstr. 71a, 6th District/Mariahilf,* ☎ *01/58895,* ☒ *01/587–8133,* WEB *www.hotelkummer.at. 100 rooms. Restaurant, minibars, bar, Internet, parking (fee); no a/c. AE, DC, MC, V.*

$$$ 🏨 **Radisson.** Two former fin-de-siècle Ringstrassen palaces—the Palais Leitenberger and Palais Henckel von Donnersmarck, no less, both built in 1872 as detached family homes—have been joined together to form this stylish hotel directly across from the Stadtpark, Vienna's main city park, a truly superb location on the Ringstrasse. The rooms are quiet and comfortable, with tasteful, understated furnishings; some have pretty floral drapes and matching bedspreads. The staff is ready to help with anything. Ask for a room facing the park. The Le Siecle restaurant offers food as stylish as its decor. ✉ *Parkring 16, A–1010,* ☎ *01/ 515170,* ☒ *01/512–2216,* WEB *www.radissonsas.com. 246 rooms. 2 restaurants, café, minibars, gym, bar, Internet. AE, DC, MC, V.*

$$–$$$ ⊞ **Am Stephansplatz.** You can't get a better location than this, directly across from the magnificent front entrance of St. Stephen's Cathedral. Despite this modern hotel's gray, lackluster facade, it offers surprisingly nice, spacious rooms furnished with Turkish carpets, lovely prints and paintings, and elegant furniture. Some rooms are a bit over the top with red wallpaper, but others have more subtle shades of pale yellow and beige. If the bells from the cathedral pose a problem, ask for a room facing the inner courtyard. ⊠ *Stephanspl. 9, A–1010* ☎ *01/53405–0,* FAX *01/53405–710,* WEB *www.nethotels.com/am_stephansplatz. 57 rooms. Café, minibars, Internet; no a/c. AE, DC, MC, V.*

$$–$$$ ⊞ **Europa.** Renovated from top to bottom, this 1957-vintage hotel offers modern, rather charmless rooms with all the amenities. The selling point here is the great location. Rooms on the Neuer Markt side are quieter than those on Kärntnerstrasse. ⊠ *Neuer Markt 3, A–1010,* ☎ *01/515–94–0,* FAX *01/515–9438,* WEB *www.austria-trend.at. 113 rooms. Restaurant, café, minibars, bar, Internet. AE, DC, MC, V.*

$$–$$$ ⊞ **König von Ungarn.** In a dormered, 16th-century house in the shadow
★ of St. Stephen's Cathedral, this hotel began catering to court nobility in 1815—many Hungarian aristos rented rooms here back when. (Mozart lived in the house next door when he wrote the *Marriage of Figaro.*) A superb redesign turned it into a modern hotel, and you could hardly hope for a happier result. The hotel radiates charm—rooms (some with Styrian wood-paneled walls) are furnished with country antiques and have walk-in closets and double sinks in the sparkling bathrooms. The eight suites are two-storied, and two have balconies with rooftop views of Old Vienna. The inviting atrium bar, bedecked with marble columns, ferns, and hunting trophies, beckons you in to sit and have a drink. Insist on written confirmation of bookings. ⊠ *Schulerstr. 10, A–1010,* ☎ *01/515–840,* FAX *01/515–848,* WEB *www.kvu.at. 33 rooms. Restaurant, minibars, bar, Internet. DC, MC, V.*

$$–$$$ ⊞ **Mailberger Hof.** A former baroque town palace (of the Knights of Malta) with an atmospheric carriage entrance and a cobblestone and captivating courtyard, the Mailbergerhof has a wonderful location just off the Kärntnerstrasse. A recent renovation has given some of its formerly rather dour rooms some charm, with lovely golden and crimson bedspreads, reproduction furniture, and soft carpets. The rooms on the first floor are the most attractive; try to get one facing the pretty baroque street. In summer, the inner courtyard is set with tables for dining. ⊠ *Annag. 7, A–1010* ☎ *01/512–0641,* FAX *01/512–0641–10,* WEB *www.mailbergerhof.at. 40 rooms, 5 apartments with kitchenettes (available by the month). Restaurant, minibars, Internet; no a/c in some rooms. AE, DC, MC, V.*

$$–$$$ ⊞ **Regina.** This dignified old hotel with grand reception rooms sits regally on the edge of the Altstadt, commanding a view of Sigmund Freud Park. It's near the Votivkirche, and about a 10-minute walk from the center. The high-ceilinged rooms are quiet, spacious, and attractively decorated with contemporary furniture, and most have charming sitting areas. Freud, who lived nearby, used to eat breakfast in the hotel's café every morning. Buffet breakfast is included. ⊠ *Rooseveltpl. 15, 9th District/Alsergrund,* ☎ *01/404–460,* FAX *01/408–8392,* WEB *www. hotelregina.at. 125 rooms. Restaurant, minibars, Internet; no a/c. AE, DC, MC, V.*

$$–$$$ ⊞ **Royal.** Just around the corner from St. Stephen's and Kärntnerstrasse, this modern hotel is on the site of a former pilgrim hostel from the early 16th century. It was destroyed in World War II and rebuilt in dreary 1960s fashion. However, all the guest rooms are delightfully decorated, in art nouveau and Biedermeier styles; despite the prime location, none has a view. The hotel's Italian restaurant, Firenze Enoteca, is favored by opera singers, including Pavarotti (note that Richard Wagner's piano is on display in the lobby). In summer the restaurant also operates Settimo Cielo (Seventh Heaven), set on the rooftop terrace, complete with glass roof and a spectacular view of the Graben and St. Stephen's. ✉ *Singerstr. 3, A–1010,* ☎ *01/51568–0,* FAX *01/513–9698,* WEB *www.kremslehnerhotels.at. 81 rooms. 2 restaurants, minibars; no a/c. AE, DC, MC, V.*

$$ 🏨 **Altstadt.** A cognoscenti favorite, this small hotel was once a patri-
★ cian home and is set in one of Vienna's most pampered neighborhoods. Close to the shops of Spittelberg, this place is known for its personable and helpful management. Palm trees, a Secession-style, wrought-iron staircase, modernist fabrics, and halogen lighting make for a very design-y interior. Guest rooms are large with all the modern comforts, though they retain an antique feel. The English-style lounge has a fireplace and plump floral sofas. Upper rooms have views out over the city roofline. Last but not least, you are one streetcar stop or a pleasant walk from the main museums. ✉ *Kircheng. 41, 7th District/Neubau,* ☎ *01/526–3399–0,* FAX *01/523–4901,* WEB *www.altstadt.at. 25 rooms. Minibars, bar; no a/c. AE, DC, MC, V.*

$$ 🏨 **Austria.** This older house, tucked away on a tiny cul-de-sac, offers the ultimate in quiet and is only five minutes' walk from the heart of the city. The high-ceiling rooms are pleasing in their combination of dark wood and lighter walls; the decor is mixed, with Oriental carpets on many floors. Rooms without full bath are a bit cheaper. There is a nice courtyard terrace that is perfect for sipping coffee after a day of sightseeing. You'll feel at home here, and the staff will help you find your way around town or get opera or concert tickets. ✉ *Wolfeng. 3 (Fleischmarkt), A–1010,* ☎ *01/515–23–0,* FAX *01/515–23–506,* WEB *www. hotelaustria-wien.at. 46 rooms, 42 with bath. Minibars, Internet; no a/c. AE, DC, MC, V.*

$$ 🏨 **Erzherzog Rainer.** On a fountained square in a good location near the Naschmarkt and within walking distance of Karlsplatz and the city center, the lovely pale green Archduke Rainer opened in 1913 as a grand hotel, with its restaurant a meeting place for prominent Viennese society. Guest rooms are extremely pleasant, with a mixture of modern and antique reproduction furniture providing a regal touch, and baths are well designed. Breakfast is ample. The hotel is part of the Best Western group. ✉ *Wiedner Hauptstr. 27–29, 4th District/Wieden,* ☎ *01/ 501110,* FAX *01/50111–350,* WEB *www.schick-hotels.com. 84 rooms. Restaurant, minibars, Internet; no a/c. AE, DC, MC, V.*

$$ 🏨 **Kärntnerhof.** Behind the "Maria Theresa yellow" facade of this elegant 100-year-old house on a quiet cul-de-sac lies one of the friendliest small hotels in the center of the city. Take the gorgeously restored Biedermeier elevator to the guest rooms upstairs, which contain reproduction antiques and modern baths. The staff is adept at getting theater and concert tickets for "sold-out" performances and happily puts together special outing programs for guests. ✉ *Grashofg. 4, A–1010,* ☎ *01/512–1923–0,* FAX *01/513–1923–39,* WEB *www.karntnerhof.com. 43 rooms. Internet, some pets allowed; no a/c. AE, DC, MC, V.*

$$ 🏨 **Museum.** Set in a beautiful belle epoque mansion just a five-minute
★ walk from the Kunsthistorisches Museum, Naturhistorisches Museum, and the new MuseumsQuartier, this elegant pension offers good-size rooms with large, comfortably modern bathrooms. There is also a pretty, sunny sitting room with deep, overstuffed sofas and wing-back chairs, perfect for curling up with a good book. This is a popular place, so book ahead. ✉ *Museumstr. 3, 7th District/Neubau,* ☎ *01/523–44–260,* FAX *01/523–44–2630. 15 rooms. No a/c. AE, DC, MC, V.*

$$ 🏨 **Neuer Markt.** You're in the heart of the city at this attractive pastel-yellow pension, situated in a lofty position at the head of the pretty square bearing the same name. Rooms are modern and comfortable, and the staff is very friendly and helpful, making you feel right at home. ✉ *Seilerg. 9, A–1010,* ☎ *01/512–2316,* ☒ *01/513–9105. 37 rooms. No a/c. AE, DC, MC, V.*

$$ ⊡ **Opernring.** With an ideal location on the Ringstrasse and catercorner from the Opera House, the Opernring has rooms that are nicer than you would imagine, considering the rather unprepossessing entrance and lobby. Guest rooms are spacious with good carpets, subdued contemporary furniture, and sitting areas, and about half have small terraces. Discounts can be arranged for longer stays. ✉ *Opernring 11, A–1010,* ☎ *01/587–5518,* ☒ *01/587–5518–29,* ☒ *www.opernring. at. 35 rooms. Minibars, Internet; no a/c. AE, DC, MC, V.*

$$ ⊡ **Pension Aviano.** Tucked away in a corner of the Neuer Markt, this small pension is close to the Opera House. Rooms are cheerful and quiet, and the two junior suites have a charming turret where you can sit and gaze out over the rooftops of Vienna. In summer, breakfast tables are set outside on the balcony overlooking the inner courtyard. ✉ *Marco d'Avianog. 1, A–1010,* ☎ *01/512–8330,* ☒ *01/512–8330– 6. 17 rooms. Minibars, Internet; no a/c. DC, MC, V.*

$$ ⊡ **Pension Domizil.** Around the corner from the house where Mozart wrote *The Marriage of Figaro,* the Domizil offers quiet, well-equipped rooms furnished with rather bland contemporary furniture. The staff is pleasant, and you're right in the middle of a series of charming old-world cobblestone streets near St. Stephen's. ✉ *Schulerstr. 14,* ☎ *01/ 513–3199–0,* ☒ *01/512–3484. 40 rooms. Internet; no a/c. AE, DC, MC, V.*

$$ ⊡ **Pension Pertschy.** Housed in a former town palace just off the Graben, this pension is as central as you can get. A massive arched portal leads to a yellow courtyard, around which the house is built. A few rooms contain lovely old ceramic stoves (just for show). Most rooms are spacious, and each one is comfortable, though overall the furniture is a bit kitschy. Baths are satisfactory. Use the elevator, but don't overlook the palatial grand staircase. ✉ *Habsburgerg. 5, A–1010,* ☎ *01/534–49–0,* ☒ *01/534–49–49. 43 rooms. Minibars; no a/c. AE, DC, MC, V.*

$$ ⊡ **Schubertring.** The fantastic location on the Ringstrasse—with the Opera House down the street and the Musikverein and Konzerthaus a few steps away—make this small hotel a popular choice for music lovers. Guest rooms are cozily furnished with a fetching mix of modern pieces and reproduction antiques. Windows are on the small side since all rooms are on the top floor of the building, but this also ensures the utmost quiet. A nice plus at this price: all rooms have air-conditioning. ✉ *Schubertring 11, A–1010,* ☎ *01/717020,* ☒ *01/713– 9366,* ☒ *www.schubertring.at. 35 rooms. Some kitchenettes, minibars, bar, Internet. AE, DC, MC, V.*

$$ ⊡ **Wandl.** The restored facade identifies a 300-year-old house that has been in family hands as a hotel since 1854. You couldn't find a better location, tucked behind St. Peter's Church, just off the Graben. The hallways are punctuated by cheerful, bright openings along the glassed-in inner court. The rooms are modern, but some are a bit plain and charmless, despite parquet flooring and red accents. Ask for one of the rooms done in period furniture, with decorated ceilings and gilt mirrors; they're palatial, if slightly overdone. ✉ *Peterspl. 9, A–1010,* ☎ *01/534–55–0,* ☒ *01/534–55–77,* ☒ *www.hotel-wandl.com. 138 rooms. Bar, Internet; no a/c. AE, DC, MC, V.*

$$ ⊡ **Zur Wiener Staatsoper.** A great deal of loving care has gone into this family-owned hotel near the State Opera, reputed to be one of the Viennese settings in John Irving's *The Hotel New Hampshire.* The florid facade, with oversize torsos supporting its upper bays, is pure 19th-century Ringstrasse style. Rooms are small but have high ceilings and

are charmingly decorated with pretty fabrics and wallpaper. ⊠ *Kruger-str. 11, A–1010,* ☎ *01/513–1274–0,* FAX *01/513–1274–15,* WEB *www. zurwienerstaatsoper.at. 22 rooms. No a/c. AE, DC, MC, V.*

$–$$ 🖬 **Drei Kronen.** This nice, pastel peach hotel is across the street from the colorful Naschmarkt, Vienna's largest and most famous outdoor market. Rooms are modern and a bit dull, but perfectly adequate, and have cable TV. You'll be within walking distance of the city center. ⊠ *Schleifmühlg. 25, 4th District/Wieden,* ☎ *01/587–3289,* FAX *01/587–3289–11,* WEB *www.hoteldreikronen.at. 41 rooms. Internet in some rooms; no a/c. AE, DC, MC, V.*

$–$$ 🖬 **Fürstenhof.** This 1912 building directly across from the Westbahn-hof describes its large rooms as "old-fashioned comfortable," and you reach them via a marvelous hydraulic elevator. Furnishings are a mixed bag, but all rooms are scrupulously clean and agreeable. The side rooms are quieter than those in front, and the best deals are for three to four people. Rooms without bath are in the $ category. A very nice breakfast is included in the price. ⊠ *Neubaugürtel 4, A–1070, 7th District/Neubau,* ☎ *01/523–3267,* FAX *01/523–3267–26,* WEB *www.hotel-fuerstenhof.com. 58 rooms, 28 with bath. Minibars, Internet; no a/c. AE, DC, MC, V.*

$–$$ 🖬 **Pension Christina.** Just steps from Schwedenplatz and the Danube Canal, this quiet pension offers mainly smallish modern rooms, warmly decorated with attractive dark-wood furniture set off against beige walls. ⊠ *Hafnersteig 7, A–1010,* ☎ *01/533–2961–0,* FAX *01/533–2961–11. 33 rooms. Minibars; no a/c. MC, V.*

$–$$ 🖬 **Pension Zipser.** With an ornate facade and gilt-trimmed coat of arms, this 1904 house is one of the city's better values. It's in the picturesque Josefstadt neighborhood of small cafés, shops, bars, and good restaurants, yet within steps of the J streetcar line to the city center. The rooms are in browns and beiges, with modern furniture, and baths are well equipped. The balconies of some of the back rooms overlook tree-filled neighborhood courtyards. The accommodating staff will help get theater and concert tickets. ⊠ *Langeg. 49, A–1080, 8th District/ Josefstadt,* ☎ *01/404–540,* FAX *01/404–5413,* WEB *www.zipser.at. 47 rooms. Bar, Internet; no a/c. AE, DC, MC, V.*

$ 🖬 **Pension City.** You'll be on historic ground here: in 1791 the play-wright Franz Grillparzer was born in the house that then stood here; a bust and plaques in the entryway commemorate him. On the second floor of the present 100-year-old house, about three minutes away from St. Stephen's Cathedral, the rooms are outfitted in a successful mix of modern and 19th-century antique furniture against white walls. The baths are small but complete. ⊠ *Bauernmarkt 10, A–1010,* ☎ *01/533–9521,* FAX *01/535–5216. 19 rooms. Minibars; no a/c. AE, DC, MC, V.*

$ 🖬 **Pension Nossek.** A family-run establishment on the upper floors of
★   a 19th-century office and apartment building, the Nossek lies at the heart of the pedestrian and shopping area. The rooms have high ceil-ings and are eclectically but comfortably furnished; those on the front have a magnificent view of the Graben. Do as the many regular guests do: book early. ⊠ *Graben 17, A–1010,* ☎ *01/533–7041–0,* FAX *01/535–3646. 27 rooms, 25 with bath. Some in-room TVs, Internet; no a/c. No credit cards.*

$ 🖬 **Pension Reimer.** Friendly and comfortable, this hotel is in a prime location just off Mariahilferstrasse. The modern rooms have high ceil-ings and large windows, and the atmosphere throughout is cheerful. Breakfast is included. Note, however, that this place is located on the fourth floor and access is via an elevator that can be operated only with a key, leaving you and your arriving luggage at a bit of a loss. ⊠ *Kircheng. 18, A–1070, 7th District/Neubau,* ☎ *01/523–6162,* FAX *01/524–3782. 14 rooms. No a/c, no room phones, no room TVs. MC, V.*

$ ⚏ **Pension Riedl.** Across the square from the Postsparkasse, the 19th-century postal savings bank designed by Otto Wagner, this small establishment offers modern, pleasant rooms with cable TV. As an added touch, breakfast is delivered to your room. Cheerful owner Maria Felser is happy to arrange concert tickets and tours. ✉ *Georg–Coch–Pl. 3/4/10, A–1010,* ☎ *01/512–7919,* ℻ *01/512–79198. 8 rooms. No a/c. DC, MC, V. Closed first 2 wks of Feb.*

$ ⚏ **Pension Suzanne.** The Opera House is a stone's throw from this 1950s building on a small side street off the Ring. The rooms are not spacious but are charmingly and comfortably furnished in 19th-century Viennese style; baths are modern, although short on shelf space. ✉ *Walfischg. 4, A–1010,* ☎ *01/513–2507–0,* ℻ *01/513–2500,* WEB *www.pension-suzanne.at. 26 rooms with bath. Internet in some rooms; no a/c. AE, MC, V.*

$ ⚏ **Pension Wild.** This friendly, family-run pension on several floors of
★ an older apartment house draws a relaxed, younger crowd to one of the best values in town. Rooms are simple, modern and welcoming, with light-wood furniture, and there is a public kitchenette. An ample breakfast is included in the room rate. The close proximity to the major museums makes this a top choice. This is a gay-friendly pension. ✉ *Langeg. 1, A–1080, 8th District/Josefstadt,* ☎ *01/406–5174,* ℻ *01/402–2168,* WEB *www.pension-wild.com. 19 rooms with bath. Minibars; no a/c. AE, DC, MC, V.*

Seasonal Hotels

Student residences, which operate as hotels July–September, can provide excellent bargains in the inexpensive ($) category. They have single or double rooms, all (unless noted) with bath. The student residence hotels have central booking contacts. **Rosenhotels** (☎ 01/911–4910, ℻ 01/911–4910–69, WEB www.rosenhotel.at). **Albertina group** (☎ 01/512–7493, ℻ 01/412–1968, WEB www.albertina-hotels.at).

⚏ **Academia.** Among this group, this is a fairly luxurious choice. ✉ *Pfeilg. 3a, 8th District/Josefstadt,* ☎ *01/40176,* ℻ *01/40176–20. 300 rooms. Restaurant, bar. AE, MC, V*

⚏ **Accordia.** Belonging to the Albertina group, this is the newest of the seasonal hotels and is fairly close to the center. ✉ *Grosse Schiffg. 12, 2nd District/Leopoldstadt,* ☎ *01/212–1668,* ℻ *01/212–1668–697. 70 rooms. No credit cards.*

⚏ **Aramis.** Another one belonging to the Albertina, the Aramis has a nice garden and good buffet breakfast. It's close to transportation to the center. ✉ *Döblinger Haupstr. 55, 19th District/Döbling,* ☎ *01/369–8673,* ℻ *01/369–2480. 70 rooms. AE, D, MC, V.*

⚏ **Avis.** The Avis shares the restaurant and bar with its partner, the Academia. ✉ *Pfeilg. 4, 8th District/Josefstadt,* ☎ *01/40174,* ℻ *01/40176–20. 72 rooms. AE, MC, V.*

⚏ **Rosenhotel Burgenland 3.** For weary travelers, a decent restaurant is a three-minute walk from the hotel. ✉ *Bürgerspitalg. 19, 6th District/Mariahilf,* ☎ *01/597–9475,* ℻ *01/597–9475–9. 120 rooms. AE, DC, MC, V.*

NIGHTLIFE AND THE ARTS

The Arts

Dance

The **ballet evenings** on the Staatsoper and Volksoper seasonal schedule (☎ 01/514–44–0) measure up to international standards. Vienna

also has **Szene Wien** (✉ Hauffg. 26, 11th District/Simmering, ☎ 01/
749–3341, FAX 01/749–2206), a theater offering contemporary dance,
representing Austria's up-and-coming choreographers. **dietheater Wien**
(✉ Karlspl. 5, 1st District, ☎ 01/587–0504–0, FAX 01/587–8774–31)
is a popular venue for cutting-edge dance arts.

Film

Vienna has a thriving film culture, with viewers seeking original rather
than German-dubbed versions. There are several theaters offering
films in English. The **Artis** (✉ Corner of Shulterg./Jordang., 1st District, ☎ 01/535–6570) is near the Hoher Markt. The **Burg** (✉ Opernring 19, 1st District, ☎ 01/587–8406) features Carol Reed's
Vienna-based classic *The Third Man,* with Orson Welles in summer-
time, as well as current films. The **Haydn** (✉ Mariahilferstr. 57, 6th
District/Mariahilf, ☎ 01/587–2262) is a multiplex theater. The arty
Votiv-Kino (✉ Währinger Str. 12, 9th District/Alsergrund, ☎ 01/317–
3571) sometimes has English films or foreign films with English subtitles.

The film schedule in the daily newspaper *Der Standard* lists foreign-
language films (*Fremdsprachige Filme*) separately. In film listings,
OmU means original language with German subtitles.

The **Filmmuseum** in the Albertina shows original-version classics with
a heavy focus on English-language films and organizes retrospectives
of the work of artists, directors, and producers. The monthly program
is posted outside. If you aren't a member, you must purchase a guest
membership (€4 per day). The theater is closed July, August, and
September. ✉ *Augustinerstr. 1, 1st District,* ☎ *01/533–7054.* ⬜ *€9
(incl. €4 guest membership), €5 with €10.90 yearly membership.*

Galleries

A host of smaller galleries centers on the Singerstrasse and Grünangergasse, although there are many more scattered about the city.

Music

Vienna is one of the main music centers of the world. Contemporary
music gets its hearing, but it's the hometown standards—the works of
Beethoven, Brahms, Haydn, Mozart, and Schubert—that draw the Viennese public. A monthly program, put out by the city tourist board
and available at any travel agency or hotel, gives a general overview
of what's going on in opera, concerts, jazz, theater, and galleries, and
similar information is posted on billboards and fat advertising columns
around the city.

Vienna is home to four full symphony orchestras: the great Wiener Philharmoniker (Vienna Philharmonic), the outstanding Wiener Sym-
phoniker (Vienna Symphony), the broadcasting service's ORF Symphony
Orchestra, and the Niederösterreichische Tonkünstler. There are also
hundreds of smaller groups, from world-renowned trios to chamber
orchestras.

The most important concert halls are in the buildings of the Gesellschaft
der Musikfreunde, called the **Musikverein** (✉ Dumbastr. 3; ticket office at Karlspl. 6, ☎ 01/505–8190, FAX 01/505–8190–94, WEB www.
musikverein.at), which contains the Grosser Musikvereinssaal and the
Brahmssaal. The Musikverein, in addition to being the main venue for
such troupes as the Wiener Philharmoniker and the Wiener Sym-
phoniker, also hosts many of the world's finest orchestras—recent visitors have included the Concertgebouworchester Amsterdam and the
London Symphony Orchestra. Smaller groups such as I Solisti Veneti
also appear here. The **Konzerthaus** (✉ Lothringerstr. 20, ☎ 01/242002,

FAX 01/242–0011–0, WEB www.konzerthaus.at) houses the Grosser Konzerthaussaal, Mozartsaal, and Schubertsaal halls.

Concerts are also given in the small **Figarosaal** of Palais Palffy (✉ Josefspl. 6, ☎ 01/512–5681–0). There are a couple of other good choices. **Radio Kulturhaus** (✉ Argentinierstr. 30A, ☎ 01/501–70–377). **Bösendorfersaal** (✉ Graf Starhemberg-G. 14, ☎ 01/504–6651, FAX 01/504–6651–39). Students of the **Universität für Musik und Darstellende Kunst** (University of Music and Performing Arts) regularly give class recitals in the school's concert halls during the academic year; look for announcements posted outside for dates and times (✉ Seilerstätte 26 and Johannesg. 8, ☎ 01/711550).

Although the **Vienna Festival** (☎ 01/589–22–11), held mid-May to mid-June, wraps up the primary season, the summer musical scene is bright, with something scheduled every day. Outdoor symphony concerts are performed weekly in the vast arcaded courtyard of the Rathaus (entrance on Friedrich Schmidt-Pl.). You can catch musical events in the Volksgarten and in the St. Augustine, St. Michael's, Minorite, and University churches; at Schönbrunn Palace they're outside in the courtyard as well as part of an evening guided tour.

Mozart concerts are performed in 18th-century costume and powdered wigs in the large hall, or Mozartsaal, of the Konzerthaus; operetta concerts are held in the Musikverein, and the Hofburg and Palais Ferstel. There are no set dates, so inquire through hotels and travel and ticket agencies for availabilities. Note, however, that some of these concerts, including intermission lasting possibly an hour, are rather expensive affairs put on for tourists and are occasionally of disappointing quality.

Church music, the mass sung in Latin, can be heard Sunday mornings during the main season at St. Stephen's; in the Franciscan church, St. Michael's; the Universitätskirche; and, above all, in the Augustinerkirche. The Friday and Saturday newspapers carry details. St. Stephen's also has organ concerts most Wednesday evenings from early May to late November.

The **Vienna Boys Choir** (Wiener Sängerknaben) sings mass at 9:15 AM Sundays in the Hofburgkapelle (✉ Hofburg, Schweizer Hof, 1st District, ☎ 01/533–9927, FAX 01/533–9927–75) from mid-September to late June. Written requests for seats should be made at least eight weeks in advance (✉ Hofmusikkapelle Hofburg, A–1010 Vienna). You will be sent a reservation card, which you exchange at the box office (in the Hofburg courtyard) for your tickets. Tickets are also sold at ticket agencies and at the box office (open daily 11:00–1 and 3–5). General seating costs €5, prime seats in the front of the church €29. It's important to note that only the 10 side balcony seats allow a view of the choir; those who purchase floor seats, standing room, or center balcony will not be able to see the boys. On Sunday at 8:45 AM all unclaimed pre-ordered tickets are sold. If you've missed the Vienna Boys Choir at the Sunday mass, you may be able to hear them in a more popular program in the Konzerthaus.

TICKETS

Most theaters now reserve tickets by telephone against a credit card; you pick up your ticket at the box office with no surcharge. The same applies to concert tickets. Ticket agencies (*see* Contacts and Resources *in* Vienna A to Z) charge a minimum 22% markup and generally deal in the more expensive seats. Expect to pay (or tip) a hotel porter or concierge at least as much as a ticket-agency markup for hard-to-get tickets. Tickets to musicals and some events, including the Vienna

Festival, are available at the **"Salettl" gazebo** kiosk alongside the Opera House on Kärntnerstrasse. Tickets to that night's musicals are reduced by half after 2 PM.

Opera and Operetta

The **Staatsoper** (State Opera House, ⊠ Opernring 2, 1st District, ☎ 01/514–440, WEB www.wiener-staatsoper.at), one of the world's great opera houses, has been the scene of countless musical triumphs and a center of unending controversies over how it should be run and by whom. (When Lorin Maazel was unceremoniously dumped as head of the Opera not many years ago, he pointed out that the house had done the same thing to Gustav Mahler half a century earlier.) A performance takes place virtually every night September–June, drawing on the vast repertoire of the house, with emphasis on Mozart and Verdi works. (Opera here is nearly always performed in the original language, even Russian.) Guided tours of the Opera House are held year-round. The opera in Vienna is a dress-up event, and even designer jeans are not acceptable. Evening dress and black tie, though not compulsory, are recommended for first-night performances and in the better seats.

Opera and operetta are also performed at the **Volksoper** (⊠ Währingerstr. 78, ☎ 01/514–440, WEB www.volksoper.at), outside the city center at Währingerstrasse and Währinger Gürtel (third stop on Streetcar 41, 42, or 43, which run from "downstairs" at Schottentor, U2, on the Ring). Prices here are significantly lower than in the Staatsoper, and performances can be every bit as rewarding. This theater has a fully packed calendar, with offerings ranging from the grandest opera, such as Mozart's *Don Giovanni,* to an array of famous Viennese operettas, such as Johann Strauss's *Wiener Blut* and *Die Fledermaus,* to modern Broadway musicals (during February and March 2003, for instance, Leonard Bernstein's *West Side Story* will be presented). Most operas are sung here in German.

You'll also find musicals and operetta at several theaters. The **Raimundtheater** (⊠ Wallg. 18, ☎ 01/599–77–0, WEB www.musicalvienna.at) mostly offers musicals by local composers. For cabaret and traveling music groups, try the **Ronacher** (⊠ Seilerstätte/Himmelpfortg., ☎ 01/514–110, WEB www.musicalvienna.at). **Theater an der Wien** (⊠ Linke Wienzeile 6, ☎ 01/588–30–0, WEB www.musicalvienna.at) has glitzy musicals, such as *Mozart!* and *Jekyll and Hyde.* Opera and operetta are performed on an irregular schedule at the **Kammeroper** (⊠ Fleischmarkt 24, ☎ 01/512–01–000, WEB www.wienerkammeroper.at).

In summer, light opera or operetta performances by the Kammeroper ensemble are given in the exquisite **Schlosstheater** at Schönbrunn. Send a fax to 01/51201–00–30 for details.

TICKETS

Tickets to the **state theaters** (Staatsoper, Volksoper, Burgtheater, and Akademietheater) can be charged against your credit card. You can order them by phoning up to a month before the performance (☎ 01/513–1513) or buy them in person up to a month in advance at the Theaterkassen, the **central box office.** ⊠ *Theaterkassen, back of Opera, Hanuschg. 3, in courtyard.* ☉ *Weekdays 8–6, Sat. 9–2, Sun. and holidays 9–noon.*

You can write ahead for tickets as well. The nearest **Austrian National Tourist Office** can give you a schedule of performances and a ticket order form. Send the form (no payment is required) to the ticket office (⊠ Kartenvorverkauf Bundestheaterverband, Goetheg. 1, A–1010 Vienna), which will mail you a reservation card; when you get to Vienna, take the card to the main box office to pick up and pay for your tickets.

Theater

Vienna's **Burgtheater** (✉ Dr.-Karl-Lueger-Ring 2, 1st District, Vienna) is one of the leading German-language theaters of the world. The repertoire has recently begun mixing German classics with more modern and controversial pieces. The Burg's smaller house, the **Akademietheater** (✉ Lisztstr. 1), draws on much the same group of actors for classical and modern plays. Both houses are closed during July and August.

The **Kammerspiele** (✉ Rotenturmstr. 20, ☎ 01/42700–304) does modern plays. The **Theater in der Josefstadt** (✉ Josefstädterstr. 26, 8th District/Josefstadt, ☎ 01/42700–306) stages classical and modern works year-round in the house once run by the great producer and teacher Max Reinhardt. The **Volkstheater** (✉ Neustiftg. 1, 7th District/Neubau, ☎ 01/523–3501–0) presents dramas, comedies, and folk plays.

For theater in English (mainly standard plays), head for **Vienna's English Theater** (✉ Josefsg. 12, 8th District/Josefstadt, ☎ 01/402–1260). Another option is the equally good **International Theater** (✉ Porzellang. 8, 9th District/Alsergrund, ☎ 01/319–6272).

Nightlife

Balls

The gala Vienna evening you've always dreamed about can become a reality: among the many **balls** given during the Carnival season, several welcome the public—at a wide range of prices, from about €65 to €350 and up per person. Dates change every year, but most balls are held in January and February. Some of the more popular balls are the Blumen Ball (Florists' Ball), Kaffeesieder Ball (Coffee Brewers' Ball), Bonbon Ball (Confection Ball), and the most famous and expensive of them all, the Opernball (Opera Ball). You can book tickets through hotel concierges (for more information call ☎ 01/211140, ℻ 01/216–8492).

Bars and Lounges

Vienna has blossomed in recent years with delightful and sophisticated bars. Happy hour is popular, but note that here it means two drinks per person for the price of one—not half-price drinks. Here's a sampling of the best bars in the 1st District. In the "Bermuda Triangle" area near St. Ruprecht's you'll find **First Floor** (✉ Corner of Seitenstetteng./Rabensteig., ☎ 01/533–7866), which is actually up one floor from ground level. The **Kruger Bar** (✉ Krugerstr. 5, ☎ 01/512–2455), off Kärntnerstrasse near the Opera, has an English gentlemen's club atmosphere in a former 1950s cinema. Near the Börse (Vienna Stock Exchange) is the **Planter's Club** (✉ Zelinkag. 4, ☎ 01/533–3393–16), offering a nice selection of rums in an exotic, tropical colonial setting. Let the outdoor glass elevator at the Steffl department store whisk you up to the **Skybar** (✉ Kärntnerstr. 19, ☎ 01/513–1712) for soft piano music to go along with the stunning view. The best place to sample wines from all over Austria is the intimate **Eulennest Vinothek** (✉ Himmelpfortg. 13, ☎ 01/513–5311) located off Kärntnerstrasse. The "Owl's Nest" also has cheese, olives, and other snacks to have with your wine. The owners speak English.

Cabaret

Cabaret has a long tradition in Vienna. To get much from any of it, you'll need good German with a smattering of Viennese vernacular as well, plus some knowledge of local affairs. **Simpl** (✉ Wollzeile 36, 1st District, ☎ 01/512–4742) continues earning its reputation for barbed political wit. Another choice is **Kabarett Niedermair** (✉ Lenaug. 1A, 8th District, ☎ 01/408–4492).

Casinos

Try your luck at the casino **Cercle Wien** (⊠ Kärntnerstr. 41, 1st District, ☎ 01/512–4836), in a former town palace redone in dark-wood paneling and millions of twinkling lights. Games include roulette and blackjack. You'll need your passport for entry identification.

Disco

The disco scene is big in Vienna, and the crowd seems to follow the leader from one "in" spot to the next. A few continually draw full houses.

Atrium (⊠ Schwarzenbergpl. 10, 4th District/Wieden, ☎ 01/505–3594) offers everything from hip-hop to rap to pop rock. **Queen Anne** is still very much "in" (⊠ Johannesg. 12, 1st District, ☎ 01/512–0203). **U–4** has a different theme every night, including a gay night on Thursday (⊠ Schönbrunnerstr. 222, 12th District/Meidling, ☎ 01/815–8307).

Irish Pubs

After Austria joined the European Union several years ago, Irish pubs started popping up all over the place, and most are open all day. Along with British and Irish expatriates, you can find a substantial Viennese crowd. Here are the best in the 1st District. Live Irish music is offered some nights at **Bockshorn** (⊠ Naglerg. 7 [entrance on Körblerg.], ☎ 01/532–9438). Offering light dishes to go along with Guinness on tap is **Flanagan's** (⊠ Schwarzenbergstr. 1–3, ☎ 01/513–7378). You can eat fish-and-chips in a book-lined "library" at the popular **Molly Darcy's** (⊠ Teinfaltstr. 6, ☎ 01/533–2311).

Jazz Clubs

Vienna has good jazz, though places where it can be heard tend to come and go. Nothing gets going before 9 PM. Live groups appear almost nightly at **Jazzland** (⊠ Franz-Josefs-Kai 29, 1st District, ☎ 01/533–2575). **Der Neue Engel** (⊠ Rabensteig 5, 1st District, ☎ 01/535–4105), in the Bermuda Triangle, offers live jazz some evenings.

Nightclubs

Vienna has no real nightclub tradition, although there are a number of clubs in town. Most of the ones with floor shows are horribly expensive and not very good; some are outright tourist traps. One where you run the least risk is the upscale **Moulin Rouge** (⊠ Walfischg. 11, ☎ 01/512–2130). A leading spot for dancing is the **Eden Bar,** which always has a live band and is for the well-heeled, mature crowd (⊠ Lilieng. 2, ☎ 01/512–7450). **Havana** has lively salsa and a younger crowd (⊠ Mahlerstr. 11, ☎ 01/513–2075). The **Volksgarten** (⊠ Volksgarten, Burgring 2, ☎ 01/532–0907), is where a mixed younger set comes, particularly in summer for outdoor dancing. All of the above are in the 1st District.

OUTDOOR ACTIVITIES AND SPORTS

Participant Sports

Bicycling

Look for the special pathways either in red brick or marked with a stylized cyclist image in yellow. Note and observe the special traffic signals at some intersections. You can take a bike on the subway (except during rush hours) for an additional half fare, but only in cars with a blue shield on the door, and only on stairs or elevators with the "bike" shield, not on escalators. The city tourist office has a brochure in German with useful cycling maps, plus a leaflet, "See Vienna by Bike," with tips in English. At most bookstores you can purchase a cycling map of Vienna put out by a local cycling organization known as ARGUS.

It's possible to rent a bike in the Prater. **Radverleih Hochschaubahn** (☎ 12/729–5888) is open mid-March–October and is located in the Prater amusement park by the Hochschaubahn, slightly right after the Ferris wheel. **Radverleih Praterstern** is open April–October and can be found at street level under the Praterstern North rail station.

Pedal Power (✉ Ausstellungsstr. 3, 2nd District, Leopoldstadt, ☎ 01/ 729–7234, FAX 01/729–7235) offers guided bike tours of Vienna and the surrounding vicinity in English from April to October, including the main sights of the city, or tours to the outlying vineyards for a glass of wine. It's also possible to rent a bike and do your own exploring. Rentals cost €5 per hour; a three-hour guided tour costs €23 (€19 for students); a four-hour bike rental on your own is €17; for a full day, €27. Pedal Power will also deliver a bike to your hotel for an additional fee.

Boating
Both the Alte Donau (Old Danube)—a series of lakes to the north of the main stream—and the Neue Donau, on the north side of the Donauinsel (the artificial island in the river), offer good waters for paddleboats, rowboats, kayaks, sailboats, and Windsurfers. The Danube itself is somewhat too fast-moving for anything but kayaks.

There are several places to rent boats along the Alte Donau (Old Danube). **Fritz Eppel** (✉ Wagramerstr. 48a, 22nd District, ☎ 01/263– 3530). **Wolfgang Irzl** (✉ Florian-Berndl-G. 34, 22nd District, ☎ 01/ 203–6743). **Peter Kukla** (✉ Wagramerstr. 48d, 22nd District, ☎ 01/ 263–3393). For details about sailing and sailing events, check with **Haus des Sports** (✉ Prinz-Eugen-Str. 12, 22nd District, ☎ 01/505–3742–0).

Golf
The top in-town golf course is at **Freudenau** in the Prater (☎ 01/728– 9564–0, FAX 01/728–9564–20). This 18-hole, par-70 course is popular year-round and has a €60 greens fee. It is closed Saturday and Sunday. You can also try **Süssenbrunn** (✉ Weingartenallee, ☎ 01/256– 8282), located 15 minutes from the city center in the 22nd District. Süssenbrun is an 18-hole, par-72 course open to the public.

There are other alternatives, but these, too, are generally overbooked. Weekdays, of course, will be best for any of the courses, particularly those farthest from Vienna. **Golf and Country Club Brunn** is an 18-hole, par-72 course about 10 km (6 mi) to the southwest (✉ Rennweg 50, Brunn am Gebirge, ☎ 02236/33711, FAX 02236/33863). **Colony Club Gutenhof** is 10 km (6 mi) to the southeast, with two courses of 18 holes, par 73 each, at Himberg (✉ Gutenhof, ☎ 02235/87055–0). **Golfclub Am Wienerberg** is a 9-hole, par-35 course on the south side of Vienna, open March–November (✉ Gutheil Schoder-G. 9, ☎ 01/66123–0). **Golfclub Hainburg** is 50 km (31 mi) east of Vienna, with 18 holes and par 72 (✉ Auf der Heide 762, Hainburg, ☎ 02165/62628, FAX 02165/ 65331).

Health and Fitness Clubs
One of the more popular clubs is **Fitness Center Harris** (✉ Niebelungeng. 7, 1st District, ☎ 01/587–3710). **Femme Fitness** (✉ Ringstrasse Galerie/Kärntner Ring, 1st District, ☎ 01/512–1020) is for women only.

Ice-Skating
The **Wiener Eislaufverein** (✉ Lothringer Str. 22, behind InterContinental Hotel, 3rd District, ☎ 01/713–6353–0) has outdoor skating with skate rentals, October–mid-March. Weekends are crowded. For indoor

skating, check the **Wiener Stadthalle** (✉ Vogelweidpl. 14, 15th District, ☎ 01/981–00–0).

Jogging

Jogging paths run alongside the Danube Canal, and runners also frequent the Stadtpark and the tree-lined route along the Ring, particularly the Parkring stretch. Farther afield, in the 2nd District, the Prater Hauptallee, 4 km (2½ mi) from Praterstern to the Lusthaus, is a favorite.

Riding

Splendid bridle paths crisscross the Prater park. There are a couple of places in the area to hire a mount. **Reitclub Donau** (✉ Hafenzufahrtstr. 63, 2nd District, ☎ 01/728–9716). **An der Praterau-Reitstall/ Gerlinde Reinagl** (✉ Dammhaufen 62, ☎ 0676/478–7920).

Skiing

A nearby slope, **Hohe Wand,** west of the city in the 14th District, offers limited skiing, with a ski lift and man-made snow when the heavens refuse. Take Bus 49B from the Hütteldorf stop of the U4 subway. Serious Viennese skiers (that includes nearly everybody) will take a train or bus out to nearby Niederösterreich (Lower Austria), with the area around the **Semmering,** about an hour from the city, one of the favorite locations for a quick outing.

Swimming

Vienna has at least one pool for each of its 23 districts; most are indoor pools, but some locations have an outdoor pool as well. An indoor favorite is **Rogner's** (✉ Strohbachg. 7–9, 5th District, Margareten, ☎ 01/587–0844–0), complete with water slide.

For a less formal environment, head for the swimming areas of the Alte Donau or the Donauinsel. The pools and the Alte Donau (paid admission) will be filled on hot summer weekends, so the Donauinsel can be a surer bet. Some beach areas are shallow and suitable for children, but the Donauinsel has no lifeguards, though there are rescue stations for emergencies. Changing areas are few and lockers nonexistent, so don't take valuables. And don't be tempted to jump into the Danube Canal; the water is definitely not for swimming, nor is the Danube itself, because of heavy undertows and a powerful current.

The city has information on all places to swim; contact the **Magistratesabteilung 44** (✉ ☎ 01/601120). Ask for someone who speaks English to give directions to reach the following:

Donauinsel Nord is a huge, free recreation area with a children's section and nude bathing. **Donauinsel Süd** is free and offers good swimming and boating and a nude bathing area. It's harder to get to and less crowded than other areas, and food facilities are limited. **Gänsehäufel** is a bathing island in the Alte Donau with paid admission, lockers, changing rooms, children's wading pools, topless and nude areas, and restaurants; on sunny weekends it's likely to be full by 11 AM or earlier. **Krapfenwaldbad** is an outdoor park-pool tucked among the trees on the edge of the Vienna Woods, full of Vienna's beautiful people and singles. Get there early on a sunny Sunday or you won't get in. **Stadionbad** is an enormous sports complex popular with the younger crowd; go early. For the fun of it, ride the miniature railway (*Liliputbahn*) from behind the Ferris wheel in the Prater amusement park to the Stadion station and walk the rest of the way.

Tennis

Though Vienna has plenty of courts, they'll be booked solid. Try anyway; your hotel may have good connections. **Sportcenter Donau City** (✉ Arbeiterstrandbadstr. 128, 22nd District, ☎ 01/269–9630) has 21 sand courts. Top business people and political leaders head to **Tennis Point Vienna** (✉ Nottendorferg./Baumg, 3rd District, Landstrasse, ☎ 01/799–9997) for the 10 indoor courts, squash, sauna, and an outstanding fitness studio; a bar and an excellent and remarkably reasonable restaurant are here as well. **Tennisplätze Arsenal** (✉ Arsenalstr. 3, by the Südbahnhof, 3rd District, ☎ 01/799–0101; ✉ Gudrunstr. 31, 10th District, ☎ 01/602–1521) has 57 sand courts. In the Josefstadt area is **Vereinigte Tennisanlagen** (✉ Lerchenfelderstr. 66–68, 8th District, ☎ 01/407–6690). Behind the Inter-Continental hotel is **Wiener Eislaufverein** (✉ Lothringer Str. 22, 3rd District, ☎ 01/713–6353–0).

Spectator Sports

Football (Soccer)
Matches are played mainly in the **Ernst–Happel–Stadion** (stadium) in the Prater (✉ Meiereistr. 7, 2nd District, ☎ 01/728–0854). Indoor soccer takes place in the **Stadthalle** (✉ Vogelweidpl. 14, 15th District, ☎ 01/981–00–01). Tickets can usually be bought at the gate, but the better seats are available through ticket agencies (*see* Contacts and Resources *in* Vienna A to Z).

Horse Racing
Two **racetracks** (flat and sulky racing) are in the Prater. **Galopprennen:** (✉ Freudenau, ☎ 01/728–9517, FAX 01/728–9517–4). **Trabrennen:** (✉ Krieau, ☎ 01/728–0046, FAX 01/728–0046–20). The season runs April–November. The highlight is the Derby, which usually takes place in June.

Tennis
Professional matches are played in the Prater or in the ☞ Stadthalle. Ticket agencies will have details.

SHOPPING

Shopping Districts
The Kärntnerstrasse, Graben, and Kohlmarkt pedestrian areas in the 1st District, **Inner City,** claim to have the best shops in Vienna, and for some items, such as jewelry, some of the best anywhere, although you must expect high prices. The side streets within this area have developed their own character, with shops offering antiques, art, clocks, jewelry, and period furniture. **Ringstrasse Galerie,** the indoor shopping plaza at Kärntner Ring 5–7, brings a number of shops together in a modern complex, although many of these stores have other, larger outlets elsewhere in the city. Outside the center, concentrations of stores are on **Mariahilferstrasse,** straddling the 6th and 7th districts; **Landstrasser Hauptstrasse** in the 3rd District; and, still farther out, **Favoritenstrasse** in the 10th District.

A collection of attractive small boutiques can be found in the **Palais Ferstel** passage at Freyung 2 in the 1st District. A modest group of smaller shops has sprung up in the **Sonnhof** passage between Landstrasser Hauptstrasse 28 and Ungargasse 13 in the 3rd District. The **Spittelberg** market, on the Spittelberggasse between Burggasse and Siebensterngasse in the 7th District, has drawn small galleries and handicrafts shops and is particularly popular in the weeks before Christmas and Easter. Christmas is the time also for the tinselly **Christkindlmarkt** on Rathausplatz in front of City Hall; in protest over its commercialization, smaller markets specializing in handicrafts have sprung up on such traditional spots as Am Hof and the Freyung (1st District), also the venue for other seasonal markets.

98

Vienna Shopping

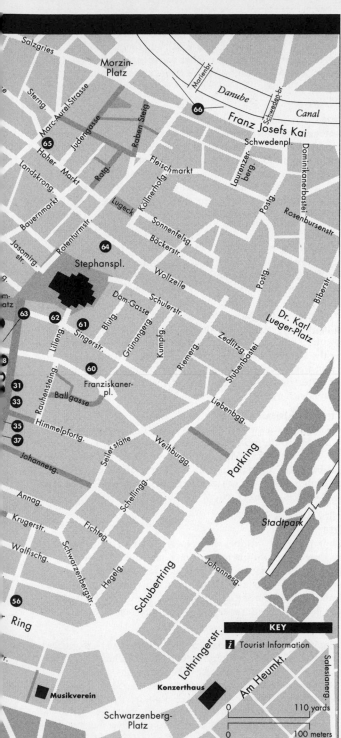

KEY

i Tourist Information

0   110 yards

0   100 meters

Vienna's **Naschmarkt** (between Linke and Rechte Wienzeile, starting at Getreidemarkt) is one of Europe's great and most colorful food and produce markets. Stalls open at 5 or 6 AM, and the pace is lively until 5 or 6 PM. Saturday is the big day, when farmers come into the city to sell at the back end of the market, but shops close around 3 PM. Also Saturday there's a huge flea market at Kettenbrückengasse end. It is closed Sunday.

Auctions

The **Dorotheum** (✉ Dorotheerg. 17, ☎ 01/515–60–0) is a state institution dating from 1707, when Emperor Josef I determined not to allow his people's exploitation by pawnbrokers. The place is intriguing, with goods ranging from furs to antique jewelry to paintings and furniture auctioned almost daily. Information on how to bid is available in English. Some items are for immediate cash sale. Also check out **Palais Kinsky** (✉ Freyung 4, ☎ 01/532–42009) for paintings and antiques.

Flea Markets

Every Saturday (except holidays), rain or shine, from about 7:30 AM to 4 or 5, the **Flohmarkt** in back of the Naschmarkt, stretching along the Linke Wienzeile from the Kettenbrückengasse U4 subway station, offers a staggering collection of stuff ranging from serious antiques to plain junk. Haggle over prices. On Thursdays and Fridays from late spring to midfall, an outdoor combination arts-and-crafts, collectibles, and flea market takes place on **Am Hof.** On Saturday and Sunday in summer from about 10 to 6, an outdoor **art and antiques market** springs up along the Danube Canal, stretching from the Schwedenbrücke to beyond the Salztorbrücke. Lots of books are sold, some in English, plus generally better goods and collectibles than at the Saturday flea market. Bargain over prices.

Department Stores

The **Steffl** department store (✉ Kärntnerstr. 19, 1st District) is moderately upscale without being overly expensive. The larger department stores are concentrated in Mariahilferstrasse. By far the best is **Peek & Cloppenburg** (✉ Mariahilferstr. 26–30, 6th District). Farther up the street you will find slightly cheaper goods at **Gerngross** (✉ Mariahilferstr. and Kircheng., 6th District).

Specialty Stores

ANTIQUES

You will find the best antiques shops located in the 1st District, many clustered close to the Dorotheum auction house, in the Dorotheergasse, Stallburggasse, Plankengasse, and Spiegelgasse. You'll also find interesting shops in the Josefstadt (8th) district, where prices are considerably lower than those in the center of town. Wander up Florianigasse and back down Josefstädterstrasse, being sure not to overlook the narrow side streets.

D&S Antiquitäten (✉ Dorotheerg. 13, ☎ 01/512–1011) specializes in old Viennese clocks. For military memorabilia, including uniforms, medals, and weapons from the Austrian monarchy through World War I, go to **Doppeladler** (✉ Opernring 9, ☎ 01/581–6232). For art deco, look to **Galerie bei der Albertina** (✉ Lobkowitzpl. 1, ☎ 01/513–1416). **Galerie im Palais Harrach** (✉ Freyung 3, ☎ 01/535–4590) has lovely 19th- and 20th-century paintings from all over Europe. Look in at **Glasgalerie Kovacek** (✉ Spiegelg. 12, ☎ 01/512–9954) to see a remarkable collection of glass paperweights and other glass objects. You'll find sculptures and 19th- and 20th-century Austrian paintings at **Kunst Salon Kovacek** (✉ Stallburgg. 2, ☎ 01/512–8358).

BOOKS

Several good stores whose stock includes books in English are on the Graben and Kärntnerstrasse in the 1st District. The perfect place for maps and books on art and architecture (some in English) is **Georg Prachner** (⊠ Kärntnerstr. 30, 1st District, ☎ 01/512–8549). Prachner also has another shop in the MuseumsQuartier. For more bookstores specializing in English-language books, *see* Contacts and Resources *in* Vienna A to Z.

CERAMICS AND PORCELAIN

Berger (⊠ Weihburgg. 17, 1st District, ☎ 01/512–1434) has a nice selection of ceramics. Gmunden primitive country ceramics are downstairs at **Pawlata** (⊠ Kärntnerstr. 14, 1st District, ☎ 01/512–1764). More country ceramics can be found at **Plessgott** (⊠ Kärntner Durchgang, 1st District, ☎ 01/512–5824). The place to find beautiful hand-painted Viennese porcelain is at **Augarten** (⊠ Graben/Stock-im-Eisen-Pl. 3, 1st District, ☎ 01/512–1494–0). **Albin Denk** (⊠ Graben 13, 1st District, ☎ 01/512–4439) sells exquisite Wedgwood and Augarten porcelain. Another shop for browsing for Wedgwood patterns is **Rosenthal** (⊠ Kärntnerstr. 16, 1st District, ☎ 01/512–3994).

CRYSTAL AND GLASS

Select famous Vienna glassware at **Bakalowits** (⊠ Spiegelg. 3, ☎ 01/512–6351–0). **Lobmeyr** (⊠ Kärntnerstr. 26, ☎ 01/512–0508–0), another glassware vendor, also has a small museum of its creations upstairs; the firm supplied the crystal chandeliers for the Metropolitan Opera in New York City, which were a gift from the Austrian government.

There are a few places to buy exquisite Riedl crystal in the city center. **Albin Denk** (⊠ Graben 13, ☎ 01/512–4439) is one. **Berndorf** (⊠ Wollzeile 12, ☎ 01/512–2944) is a great favorite. **Rasper & Söhne** (⊠ Graben 15, ☎ 01/534–33–0) has long been a popular option. For fun kitchen items go to **Rasper Loft** (⊠ Habsburgerg. 10, ☎ 01/534–33–39).

GIFT ITEMS

Giesswein (⊠ Kärntnerstr. 5–7, ☎ 01/512–4597) has beautiful traditional Austrian clothes for women as well as children's clothing. **Österreichische Werkstätten** (⊠ Kärntnerstr. 6, ☎ 01/512–2418) offers outstanding and unusual handmade handicrafts, gifts, and quality souvenirs ranging from jewelry to textiles. **Souvenir in der Hofburg** (⊠ Hofburgpassage 1 and 7, ☎ 01/533–5053) is another source of more traditional gift items. **Wiener Geschenke** (⊠ Reitschulg. 4/Michaelerpl., ☎ 01/533–7078) has a nice selection of quality gift and traditional souvenir items and is open Sunday during part of the year.

JADE

Discover interesting pieces of Austrian jade at **Burgenland** (⊠ Opernpassage, ☎ 01/587–6266).

JEWELRY

Haban (⊠ Kärntnerstr. 2, ☎ 01/512–6730–0; ⊠ Kärntnerstr. 17, ☎ 01/512–6750) has a fine selection of watches and jewelry. **A. Heldwein** (⊠ Graben 13, ☎ 01/512–5781) sells elegant jewelry, silverware, and watches. **A. E. Köchert** (⊠ Neuer Markt 15, ☎ 01/512–5828–0) has outstanding original creations. **Eleonora Kunz** (⊠ Neuer Markt 13, ☎ 01/512–7112) sells stunning modern pieces for men and women. **Schullin** (⊠ Kohlmarkt 7, ☎ 01/533–9007–0) has some of the most original work found anywhere.

MEN'S CLOTHING

Clothing in Vienna is far from cheap but is of good quality. The best shops are in the 1st District.

Sir Anthony (⌧ Kärntnerstr. 21–23, 1st District, ☎ 01/512–6835) is the place to go for the classic look. For designer labels for all ages, go to **E. Braun** (⌧ Graben 8, ☎ 01/512–5505–0). **House of Gentlemen** (⌧ Kohlmarkt 12, 1st District, ☎ 01/533–3258) has beautiful cashmere sweaters and jackets. Another place for that special classic look is **Malowan** (⌧ Opernring 23, 1st District, ☎ 01/587–6296). **Venturini** (⌧ Spiegelg. 9, 1st District, ☎ 01/512–8845) has custom-made shirts.

For men's *Trachten,* or typical Austrian clothing, including lederhosen, try **Loden-Plankl** (⌧ Michaelerpl. 6, 1st District, ☎ 01/533–8032). For the appropriate hat, go to **Collins Hüte** (⌧ Opernpassage, 1st District, ☎ 01/587–1305).

MUSIC

Look for CDs at the **Virgin Megastore** (⌧ Mariahilferstr. 37–39, 6th District, ☎ 01/588370), if you haven't got the same thing at home. Opera buffs can find CDs at **Arcardia** (⌧ Opera House, ☎ 01/513–9568-0). **EMI** (⌧ Kärntnerstr. 30, ☎ 01/512–3675) has a wide selection of pops, plus classics upstairs.

Havlicek (⌧ Herreng. 5, ☎ 01/533–1964) features classics and is particularly knowledgeable and helpful. **Da Caruso** (⌧ Operng. 4, ☎ 01/513–1326) specializes in classics, with an emphasis on opera.

NEEDLEWORK

There are a couple of shops where you can go for Vienna's famous petit point. **Petit Point Kovacec** (⌧ Kärntnerstr. 16, ☎ 01/512–4886). **Stransky** (⌧ Hofburgpassage 2, ☎ 01/533–6098).

SHOES AND LEATHER GOODS

R. Horn (⌧ Bräunerstr. 7, ☎ 01/513–8294) sells gorgeous leather purses and briefcases. **Humanic** (⌧ Kärntnerstr. 51, ☎ 01/512–5892; ⌧ Singerstr. 2, ☎ 01/512–9101) is the place to go for hip shoes. **Popp & Kretschmer** (⌧ Kärntnerstr. 51, ☎ 01/512–6421–0) offers leather clothing and handbags. **Zak** (⌧ Kärntnerstr. 36, ☎ 01/512–7257) has a great selection of leather boots, handbags, and belts.

WOMEN'S CLOTHING

Top designer fashions can be found at **Donna** (⌧ Tuchlauben 7a, ☎ 01/535–6050). For conservative, high-quality clothing, go to the **Geiger Boutique** (⌧ Kärntnerstr. 19, ☎ 01/513–1398) in the Steffl department store. Austrian designer **Schella Kann** (⌧ Singerstr. 14/2, ☎ 01/513–2287) has a studio on the second floor where you can choose from her latest, midpriced collection. You'll find modern clothing for women over 30 at **Maldone** (⌧ Kärntnerstr. 27, ☎ 01/512–6828; ⌧ Mariahilferstr. 65, ☎ 01/587–9278). For a big selection of fashion stockings go to **Wolford** (⌧ Kärntnerstr. 29, ☎ 01/535–9900).

There are a few places to shop for a selection of dirndls and women's *Trachten,* the typical Austrian costume with white blouse, print skirt, and apron. **Giesswein** (⌧ Kärntnerstr. 5–7, ☎ 01/512–4597) has some children's clothes. **Lanz** (⌧ Kärntnerstr. 10, ☎ 01/512–2456) offers traditional clothing for all ages. **Loden-Plankl** (⌧ Michaelerpl. 6, ☎ 01/533–8032) has gorgeous hand-embroidered jackets. **Resi Hammerer** (⌧ Kärntnerstr. 29–31, ☎ 01/512–6952) has conservative traditional blouses and skirts. **Tostmann** (⌧ Schotteng. 3a, ☎ 01/533–5331) offers made-to-order dirndls.

VIENNA A TO Z

To research prices, get advice from other travelers, and book travel arrangements, visit www.fodors.com.

ADDRESSES

Vienna is divided into 23 numbered districts; for a complete rundown on the various districts, or *Bezirke,* see the introductory text to the Exploring Vienna section near the top of this chapter. Taxi drivers may need to know which district you seek, as well as the street address. The district number is coded into the postal code with the second and third digits; thus A–1010 (the "01") is the 1st District, A–1030 is the 3rd, A–1110 is the 11th, and so on. Some sources and maps still give the district numbers, either in Roman or Arabic numerals, as Vienna X or Vienna 10.

AIR TRAVEL

Austrian Airlines flies into Schwechat from North America.
➤ AIRLINES AND CONTACTS: **Austrian Airlines** (☎ 05/1789).

AIRPORTS AND TRANSFERS

Vienna's airport is at Schwechat, about 19 km (12 mi) southeast of the city.
➤ AIRPORT INFORMATION: **Vienna International Airport** (☎ 01/7007–0 for flight information).

AIRPORT TRANSFERS

Beginning in mid-December 2003, a new super-fast airport link double-decker train will begin running from Vienna's Schwechat Airport to Wien-Mitte (the center of the city). The ride will take only 15 minutes and will operate every 30 minutes between 5:30 AM and midnight. The cost is estimated at around €8. During the construction period for the new rail lines, the Schnellbahn train may be closed at times.

If you are landing in Vienna, the cheapest way to get to the city is the S7 train, called the *Schnellbahn*), which shuttles twice an hour between the airport basement and the Landstrasse/Wien–Mitte (city center) and Wien–Nord (north Vienna) stations; the fare is €3 and it takes about 35 minutes. Your ticket is also good for an immediate transfer to your destination within the city on the streetcar, bus, or U-Bahn. Another cheap option is the bus, which has two separate lines. One line goes to the City Air Terminal at the Hilton Hotel (near the city's 1st District) every 20 minutes between 6:30 AM and 11 PM, and every 30 minutes after that; traveling time is 20 minutes. The other line goes to the South and West train stations (Südbahnhof and Westbahnhof) in 20 and 35 minutes respectively. Departure times are every 30 minutes from 8:10 AM to 7:10 PM, hourly thereafter, and not at all 12:10 to 3:30 AM. Fare is €5.81 one-way, €10.90 for a round-trip.
➤ TAXIS AND SHUTTLES: C+K Airport Service (☎ 01/44444, FAX 01/689-6969). **City Air Terminal** (✉ Am Stadtpark, ☎ 01/5800–33369 or 01/2300).

BOAT AND FERRY TRAVEL

If you arrive in Vienna via the Danube, the Blue Danube Steamship Company/DDSG will leave you at Praterlände near Mexikoplatz. The Praterlände stop is a two-block taxi ride or hike from the Vorgartenstrasse U1/subway station, or you can take a taxi directly into town.
➤ BOAT AND FERRY INFORMATION: **Blue Danube Steamship Company/DDSG** (✉ Friedrichstr. 7, ☎ 01/588–800).

BUS TRAVEL TO AND FROM VIENNA

International long-distance bus service (Bratislava, Brno) and most postal and railroad buses arrive at the Wien Mitte central bus station, across from the Hilton Hotel on the Stadtpark.

➤ BUS INFORMATION: **Wien Mitte** (✉ Landstrasser Hauptstr. 1b, ☎ 01/711–01).

BUS AND TRAM TRAVEL WITHIN VIENNA

Within the heart of the city, bus lines 1A, 2A, and 3A are useful crosstown routes. Should you miss the last streetcar tram or bus, special night buses with an *N* designation operate at half-hour intervals over several key routes; the starting (and transfer) points are the Opera House and Schwedenplatz. The night-owl buses now accept all normal tickets. There is no additional fare.

CAR RENTAL

Rental cars can be arranged at the airport or in town. Major firms include the following. Buchbinder is a local firm with particularly favorable rates and clean cars.

➤ MAJOR AGENCIES: **Avis** (✉ Airport, ☎ 01/7007–32700; ✉ Opernring 5, ☎ 01/587–6241). **Buchbinder** (✉ Schlachthausg. 38, ☎ 01/71750–0). **Budget** (✉ Airport, ☎ 01/7007–32711; ✉ Hilton Hotel, Am Stadtpark, ☎ 01/714–6565). **Europcar** (✉ Airport, ☎ 01/7007–33316; ✉ Erdberg Park & Ride, ☎ 01/799–6176). **Hertz** (✉ Kärntner Ring 17, ☎ 01/512–8677).

CAR TRAVEL

Vienna is 300 km (187 mi) east of Salzburg, 200 km (125 mi) north of Graz. Main routes leading into the city are the A1 Westautobahn from Germany, Salzburg, and Linz and the A2 Südautobahn from Graz and points south.

PARKING

The entire 1st and 6th through 9th districts are limited-parking zones and require that a *Parkschein,* a paid-parking chit available at most newsstands and tobacconists, be displayed on the dash during the day. Parkscheine cost €0.40 for 30 minutes, €0.80 for 1 hour, and €1.20 for 90 minutes. You can park 10 minutes free of charge, but you must get a violet "gratis" sticker to put in your windshield. You can also park free in the First District on Saturday and Sunday, but not overnight. Overnight street parking in the 1st and 6th through 9th districts is restricted to residents with special permits; all other cars are subject to expensive ticketing or even towing, so in these districts be sure you have off-street garage parking.

RULES OF THE ROAD

On highways from points south or west or from the airport, ZENTRUM signs clearly mark the route to the center of Vienna. From there, however, finding your way to your hotel can be no mean trick, for traffic planners have installed a devious scheme prohibiting through traffic in the city core (the 1st District), scooting cars out again via a network of exasperating one-way streets. In the city itself a car is a burden, though very useful for trips outside town.

Traffic congestion within Vienna has gotten out of hand, and driving to in-town destinations generally takes longer than public transportation. City planners' solutions have been to make driving as difficult as possible, with one-way streets and other tricks, and a car in town is far more of a burden than a pleasure. Drivers not familiar with the city literally need a navigator.

EMBASSIES AND CONSULATES

➤ CANADA: (✉ Laurenzerberg 2, on the 3rd floor of Hauptpost building complex, 1st District, ☎ 01/53138–3000).

➤ UNITED KINGDOM: (✉ Jauresg. 12 Landstrasse, 3rd District/Landstrasse, ☎ 01/71613–5151).

➤ UNITED STATES: (U.S. Embassy, ✉ Boltzmanng. 16, 9th District/Alsergrund, ☎ 01/313–39; United States Consulate, ✉ Gartenbaupromenade, Parkring 12A, Marriott building, 1st District, ☎ 01/313–39).

EMERGENCIES

If you need a doctor and speak no German, ask your hotel, or in an emergency, phone your consulate. In each area of the city one pharmacy stays open 24 hours; if a pharmacy is closed, a sign on the door will tell you the address of the nearest one that is open. Call the number listed below for names and addresses (in German) of the pharmacies open that night.

➤ EMERGENCY SERVICES: **Ambulance** (☎ 144). **Fire** (☎ 122). **Police** (☎ 133).

➤ LATE-NIGHT PHARMACIES: **Pharmacy information** (☎ 01/1550).

ENGLISH-LANGUAGE MEDIA

BOOKS

➤ BOOKSTORES: **British Bookstore** (✉ Weihburgg. 24–26, 1st District, ☎ 01/512–1945–0; ✉ 7th District/Neubau, Mariahilferstr. 4, ☎ 01/522–6730). **Shakespeare & Co.** (✉ Sterng. 2, 1st District, ☎ 01/535–5053).

VIDEOS

Alphaville has the best selection in the city of English-language DVDs and videotapes to rent.

➤ VIDEOSTORES: **Alphaville** (✉ Schleifmühlg. 5, 4th District/Wieden, ☎ 01/585–1966).

LODGING

RESERVING A ROOM

If you need a room upon arrival and have not made previous reservations, go to Information-Zimmernachweis, operated by the Verkehrsbüro in the Westbahnhof and in the Südbahnhof. At the airport, the information and room-reservation office in the arrivals hall is open daily 8:30 AM–9 PM.

If you're driving into Vienna, get information or book rooms through the Vienna Tourist Board's hotel assistance hot line. It's open daily from 9 to 7.

➤ CONTACTS: **Information-Zimmernachweis** (☎ 01/892–3392 in Westbahnhof; 01/505–3132 in Südbahnhof). **Vienna Tourist Board's hotel assistance hot line** (☎ 01/24555, FAX 01/24–555–666, WEB www.info.wien.at).

SUBWAY TRAVEL

Five subway (*U-Bahn*) lines, whose stations are prominently marked with blue *U* signs, crisscross the city. Karlsplatz and Stephansplatz are the main transfer points between lines. The last subway (U4) runs at about 12:30 AM.

TAXIS

Taxis in Vienna are relatively reasonable. The initial charge is €2 for as many as four people daytime, and about 5% more from 11 PM until 6 AM. Radio cabs ordered by phone have an initial charge of €4. They also may charge for each piece of luggage that must go into the trunk, and a charge is added for waiting beyond a reasonable limit. It's

Vienna Subways

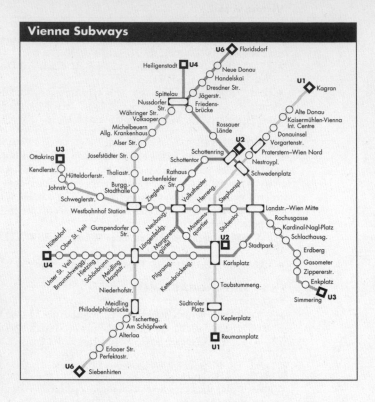

customary to round up the fare to cover the tip. Service is usually prompt, but when you hit rush hour, the weather is bad, or you need to keep to an exact schedule, call ahead and order a taxi for a specific time. If your destination is the airport, ask for a reduced-rate taxi. For the cheapest taxi to the airport, *see* Transfers.

There are several companies that offer chauffeured limousines, which are listed below.

➤ TAXI COMPANIES: **Göth** (☎ 01/713–7196). **Mazur** (☎ 01/604–2530). **Peter Urban** (☎ 01/713–5255).

TOURS

BUS TOURS

When you're pressed for time, a good way to see the highlights of Vienna is via a sightseeing bus tour, which gives you a once-over-lightly of the heart of the city and allows a closer look at Schönbrunn and Belvedere palaces. You can cover almost the same territory on your own by taking either Streetcar 1 or 2 around the Ring and then walking through the heart of the city. For tours, there are a couple of reputable firms: Vienna Sightseeing Tours and Cityrama Sightseeing.

Vienna Sightseeing Tours and Cityrama Sightseeing run daily "get acquainted" tours lasting about three hours (€32), including visits to the Schönbrunn and Belvedere palace grounds. The entrance fee and guided tour of Schönbrunn is included in the price, but not a guided tour of Belvedere, just the grounds. Both firms offer a number of other tours as well (your hotel will have detailed programs) and provide hotel pickup for most tours.

All three bus tour operators offer short trips outside the city. Check their offerings and compare packages and prices to be sure you get what you want. Your hotel will have brochures.

➤ FEES AND SCHEDULES: **Cityrama Sightseeing** (✉ Börseg. 1, ☎ 01/534–130, 𝔽𝔸𝕏 01/534–13–28). **Vienna Sightseeing Tours** (✉ Stelzhammerg. 4/11, ☎ 01/712–4683-0, 𝔽𝔸𝕏 01/714–1141).

STREETCAR TOURS

From early May to early October, a 1929 vintage streetcar leaves each Saturday at 11:30 AM and 1:30 PM and Sundays and holidays at 9:30, 11:30 AM, and 1:30 PM from the Otto Wagner Pavilion at Karlsplatz for a guided tour. For €15 (€13.50 if you have the Vienna-Card), you'll go around the Ring, out past the big Ferris wheel in the Prater, and past Schönbrunn and Belvedere palaces in the course of the two-hour trip. Prices may go up in 2003, and departure times may change; be sure to check ahead. The old-timer trips are popular, so make your reservation at the transport-information office underground at Karlsplatz, weekdays 7 AM–6 PM, weekends and holidays 8:30–4. You must buy your ticket on the streetcar.
➤ FEES AND SCHEDULES: **Transport-information office** (☎ 01/7909–43426).

PRIVATE GUIDES

Guided walking tours (in English) are a great way to see the city highlights. Tour topics range from "Unknown Underground Vienna" to "1,000 Years of Jewish Tradition" and "Vienna Around Sigmund Freud." Tours take about 1½ hours, are held in any weather provided at least three people turn up, and cost €11, plus any entry fees. No reservations are needed. Get a list of the guided-tour possibilities at the city information office. Ask for the monthly brochure "Walks in Vienna," which details the tours, days, times, and starting points. You can also arrange to have your own privately guided tour for €102 for a half day.
➤ CONTACTS: **City information office** (✉ Am Albertinapl. 1).

WALKING TOURS

For a wide range of interesting guided tours, including informative walks through the old Jewish Quarter and a *Third Man* tour from the classic film starring Orson Welles, contact Vienna Walks and Talks.

Get a copy of "Vienna Downtown Walking Tours" by Henriette Mandl from any bookshop. The six tours take you through the highlights of central Vienna with excellent commentary and some entertaining anecdotes that most of your Viennese acquaintances won't know. The booklet "Vienna from A–Z" (in English, €3.60; available at bookshops and city information offices) explains the numbered plaques attached to all major buildings.
➤ CONTACTS: **Vienna Walks and Talks** (✉ Werdertorg. 9/2, 1st District, ☎ 01/774–8901, 𝔽𝔸𝕏 01/774–8933).

TRAIN TRAVEL

Trains from Germany, Switzerland, and western Austria arrive at the Westbahnhof (West Station), on Europaplatz, where Mariahilferstrasse crosses the Gürtel. If you're coming from Italy or Hungary, you'll generally arrive at the Südbahnhof (South Station). There are two current stations for trains to and from Prague and Warsaw: Wien Nord (North Station) and Franz-Josef Bahnhof. Central train information will have details about schedule information for train departures all over Austria. However, it's hard to find somebody who can speak English, so it's best to ask your hotel for help in calling.
➤ TRAIN INFORMATION: **Central train information** (☎ 05/1717). **Westbahnhof** (✉ Westbahnhof, 15th District/Fünfhaus). **Franz-Josef Bahnhof** (✉ Julius-Tandler-Pl., 9th District/Alsergrund). **Südbahnhof** (✉ Wiedner Gürtel 1, 4th District/Wieden). **Wien Nord** (✉ Praterstern, 2nd District/Leopoldstadt).

TRANSPORTATION AROUND VIENNA

Vienna is a city to tackle on foot. With the exception of the Schönbrunn and Belvedere palaces and the Prater amusement park, most sights
are concentrated in the center, the 1st District (A–1010), much of
which is a pedestrian zone anyway.

Vienna's public transportation system is fast, clean, safe, and easy to
use. Get public transport maps at a tourist office or at the transport-
information offices (*Wiener Verkehrsbetriebe*), underground at Karlsplatz, Stephansplatz, and Praterstern. You can transfer on the same
ticket between subway, streetcar, bus, and long stretches of the fast suburban railway, *Schnellbahn* (*S-Bahn*).

Buy single tickets for €1.50 from dispensers on the streetcar tram or
bus; you'll need exact change. The ticket machines at subway stations
(*VOR-Fahrkarten*) give change and dispense 24-hour, 72-hour, and eight-
day tickets, as well as single tickets separately and in blocks of two
and five. At *Tabak-Trafik* (cigarette shops/newsstands) or the underground *Wiener Verkehrsbetriebe* offices you can get a block of five tickets for €7.50, each ticket good for one uninterrupted trip in more or
less the same general direction with unlimited transfers. Or you can
get a three-day ticket for €12, good on all lines for 72 hours from the
time you validate the ticket; there's also a 24-hour ticket for €5. If you're
staying longer, get an eight-day ticket (€24), which can be used on eight
separate days or by any number of people (up to eight) at any one time.
Prices may go up in 2003. Children under 6 travel free on Vienna's
public transport system; children under 15 travel free on Sundays, public holidays, and during Vienna school holidays.

Public transportation is on the honor system, but if you're caught
without a punched ticket, the fine is €60, payable within three days,
or €120 afterward. Tabak-Trafik Almassy is open every day from 8
AM to 7 PM and has tickets as well as film and other items.

The first streetcars run from about 5:15 AM. From then on, service (bar-
ring gridlock on the streets) is regular and reliable, and most lines operate until about midnight. Where streetcars don't run, buses do; route
maps and schedules are posted at each bus or subway stop.

A *Fiaker*, or horse cab, will trot you around to whatever destination
you specify, but this is an expensive way to see the city. A short tour
of the inner city takes about 20 minutes and costs €40; a longer one
including the Old Town and part of the Ringstrasse lasts about 40 minutes and costs €65, and an hour-long tour of the inner city and the
whole Ringstrasse costs €95. The carriages accommodate four (five if
someone sits next to the coachman). Starting points are Heldenplatz
in front of the Hofburg, Stephansplatz beside the cathedral, and across
from the Albertina, all in the 1st District. For longer trips, or any variation of the regular route, agree on the price first.
➤ CONTACTS: **Tabak-Trafik Almassy** (✉ Stephanspl. 4, to the right behind cathedral, ☎ 01/512–5909).

TRAVEL AGENCIES

American Express, Kuoni Cosmos, Carlson/Wagons-Lit, and Österreichisches Verkehrsbüro serve as general travel agencies. American Express, Kuoni Cosmos, and Vienna Ticket Service/Cityrama are agencies
that offer tickets to various sights and events in Vienna.
➤ LOCAL AGENT REFERRALS: **American Express** (✉ Kärntnerstr. 21–23,
1st District, ☎ 01/515–40–0, FAX 01/515–40–777). **Carlson/Wagons-
Lit** (✉ Millennium Tower 94/Handelskai, 20th District, ☎ 01/240600,
FAX 01/24060–65). **Kuoni Cosmos** (✉ Kärntner Ring 15, 1st District,

☎ 01/515–33–0, ℻ 01/513–4147). Österreichisches Verkehrsbüro (✉ Friedrichstr. 7, 4th District, opposite the Secession Building, ☎ 01/588–00–0, ℻ 01/588–000–280). **Vienna Ticket Service/Cityrama** (✉ Börseg. 1, 1st District, ☎ 01/534130, ℻ 01/534–1328).

VISITOR INFORMATION

The main center for information (walk-ins only) is the Vienna City Tourist Office, open daily 9–9 and centrally located between the Hofburg and Kärntnerstrasse.

Ask at tourist offices or your hotel about a Vienna-Card; costing €15.25, the card combines 72 hours' use of public transportation and discounts at certain museums and shops.

If you've lost something valuable, check with the police at the Fundangelegenheiten (Lost and Found). If your loss occurred on a train in Austria, call the central number and ask for Reisegepäck. Losses on the subway system or streetcars can be checked by calling the Fundstelle U-Bahn.

➤ TOURIST INFORMATION: **Fundangelegenheiten** (✉ Wiedner Gürtel 1, ☎ 01/580–0356–56). **Fundstelle U-Bahn** (☎ 01/7909–43500). **Reisegepäck (Central Train Information)** (☎ 05/1717). **Vienna City Tourist Office** (✉ Am Albertinapl. 1, 1st District, ☎ 01/24555, ℻ 01/216–84–92).

3 SIDE TRIPS FROM VIENNA

FROM THE VIENNA WOODS
TO THE WEINVIERTEL

Is it the sun or the soil? Or the dreamy, castle-capped peaks? Whatever the lure, the idyllic regions outside Vienna have always offered irresistible pastoral escapes for the Viennese. Rich in scenic splendor, this countryside is also saturated with musical history: here Beethoven was inspired to write his *Pastoral* Symphony, Johann Strauss set the Vienna Woods to music, and a glass of intoxicating Retzer Wein moved Richard Strauss to compose the "Rosenkavalier Waltz." From the elegant spa of Baden to mysterious Mayerling, the region offers a multitude of delights to the day-tripper.

THE VIENNESE ARE UNDENIABLY LUCKY. Few populaces enjoy such glorious—and easily accessible—options for day-tripping. Droves of stressed-out city residents tie their bicycles to the roof racks of their Mercedes on Saturdays and Sundays; vacationers in Vienna can share in the natives' obvious pleasure in the city's outer environs any day of the week. For many the first destination is, of course, the Wienerwald, the deservedly fabled Vienna Woods—a rolling range of densely wooded hills extending from Vienna's doorstep to the outposts of the Alps in the south (and not a natural park or forest, as you might think from listening to Strauss or the tourist blurbs). This region is criss-crossed by country roads and hiking paths, dotted with forest lodges and inns, and solidifies every now and then into quaint little villages and market towns.

Updated by Bonnie Dodson

In addition to such natural pleasures, the regions outside of Vienna offer attractions for every interest. History and mystery? Turning south to Mayerling leads you to the site where in 1889 the successor to the Austrian throne presumably took his own life after shooting his secret love—a mystery still unresolved. Prefer scenic beauty? Head northeast, into wonderfully encompassing woods and sweetly rolling hills sprinkled with elegant summer palaces. To the north, you can have one long, liquid, adventure by exploring the Weinstrasse (Wine Road), along which vast expanses of vineyards produce excellent, mainly white, wines. Here, you'll find Gumpoldskirchen, one of Austria's most famous wine-producing villages and the source of one of Europe's most pleasant white wines. Vintners' houses line its main street, their gates leading into vine-covered courtyard-gardens where the *Heuriger* (wine of the last vintage) is served at wooden tables, sometimes to the tune of merry or not-so-merry melodies played on an accordion. Another choice is to follow the trail of the defensive castles that protected the land from invaders from the north; or you can even trace the early days of Masonic lore in Austria—both Haydn and Mozart were members of what was then a secret and forbidden brotherhood. For a contrast, head to the elegant spa town of Baden, where Beethoven passed 15 summers and composed large sections of the Ninth Symphony.

These subregions of Lower Austria (which derives its name from the fact that for centuries it was the "lower"—in the sense of the Danube's course—part of the archduchy of Austria) are simple, mainly agricultural, country areas. People live close to the earth, and on any sunny weekend from March through October you'll find whole families out working the fields. This isn't to suggest that pleasure is neglected; just as often, you'll stumble across a dressy parade with the local brass band decked out in lederhosen and feathered hats. Sunday here is still generally a day of rest, with many families venturing to morning mass, then retiring to the local *Gasthaus* to discuss weather and politics. Whatever destination you choose in this area, however, the lakes are waiting, the biking paths are open, and the lovely countryside cafés beckon.

Pleasures and Pastimes

Bicycling

The Carnuntum region and the southeast corner of the Weinviertel, a region known as the Marchfeld, offer outstanding cycling, with a number of marked routes. Cycle paths follow the southern bank of the Danube past Carnuntum (Petronell) through Bad Deutsch–Altenburg to Hainburg, and other parts of the region are flat enough to offer fine cycling without exertion. In the Marchfeld, another marked route close to the March River includes the baroque castles at Marchegg and Schlosshof.

Castles

Taking advantage of the natural line of defense formed by the course of the Danube, barons and bailiffs decided centuries ago to fortify bluffs along the river. Castles were the best answer, and a wonderful string of these more or less follows the course of the Thaya River, starting in Weitra and Heidenreichstein close to the Czech border, then eastward to Raabs, Riegersburg, and Hardegg. The 17th- and 18th-century structures range from turreted hilltop fortresses to more elegant moated bastions, but all were part of a chain against invaders. Several are basically intact, others are restored, and all are impressive relics worth visiting. Castle concerts have become popular during summer months, when the buildings are open for tours as well.

Dining

With very few exceptions, food in this region, although influenced by Viennese cuisine, is on the simple side. The basics are available in abundance: roast meats, customary schnitzel variations, game in season, fresh vegetables, and standard desserts such as *Palatschinken* (crepes filled with jam or with nuts topped with chocolate sauce). Imaginative cooking is rare; this is not tourist territory, and the local population demands little beyond reasonable quality and quantity.

Wines are equally taken for granted, although four of the areas included here are designated as separate wine regions—the Weinviertel, or wine quarter to the north of Vienna; the Kamptal, which divides the Weinviertel from the Waldviertel to the west; the Carnuntum–Petronell region, just below the Danube to the southeast of Vienna; and the Thermen region, south and southwest of the capital. The specialties are mainly white wines, with the standard types, Grüner Veltliner and Rieslings and increasingly Weissburgunder, predominating. Reds are coming more into favor, with lighter reds such as Zweigelt and even rosés to be found in the northern areas, the heavier reds such as Blaufränkisch and St. Laurent and the spicier Gewürztraminer and Müller–Thurgau whites in the south. Most vintners work small holdings, so output is limited. The wine market in Poysdorf, center of one of Austria's largest wine regions, offers an opportunity to sample a wide choice of area vintages.

CATEGORY	COST*
$$$$	over €20
$$$	€15–€20
$$	€10–€15
$	under €10

per person for a main course at dinner

Hiking and Walking

The celebrated Vienna Woods to the west and southwest of Vienna are crisscrossed by hundreds of easy hiking paths, numbered, color-coded, and marked for destinations. Excellent hiking maps available from most bookstores will give ideas and routes. Paths will take you through woods, past meadows and vineyards, and alongside streams and rivers, with an occasional tavern hidden away deep in the woods where you can stop for refreshment or a cold snack. Deer, wild boar, and a host of small animals inhabit these preserves. The area is protected, and development is highly restricted, making it ideal for pleasurable hiking.

Lodging

Accommodations in the countryside around Vienna are pretty basic. This is underdeveloped tourist territory, prime turf for the more adventuresome, with rooms frequently to be found as an adjunct to the local Gasthaus. Nearly all are family-run; the younger members will speak at least some school English. You'll probably have to carry your own bags, and elevators to upper floors are scarce. Booking ahead is a good idea, as most places have relatively few rooms, particularly rooms with full bath. Window screens are almost unknown in Austria, as bugs are few, but in farming areas both flies and occasionally mosquitoes can be a nuisance in the warmer seasons. Since you'll want windows open at night, take along a can of bug spray and you'll sleep more soundly. The standard country bed covering is a down-filled feather bed, so if you're allergic to feathers or want more warmth, ask for blankets.

Some hotels offer half-board, with dinner in addition to buffet breakfast. The half-board room rate is usually an extra €15–€30 per person. Occasionally quoted room rates for hotels already include half-board accommodations, though a "discounted" rate is usually offered if you prefer not to take the evening meal. Inquire when booking. Room rates include taxes and service, and usually breakfast—although you should always ask about the latter.

CATEGORY	COST*
$$$$	over €135
$$$	€100–€135
$$	€65–€100
$	under €65

All prices are for a standard double room in high season and include breakfast and dinner if half-board plan is offered.

Exploring Vienna's Environs

The region surrounding Vienna divides itself logically into four areas. The Vienna Woods, that huge, unspoiled belt of forest green stretching westward south of the Danube, was celebrated by composers Beethoven, Schubert, and Strauss and remains beloved by the Viennese today. The towns to the south—Mödling, Baden, and Bad Vöslau—mark the east end of the rolling, wooded hills. There the fertile Vienna Basin begins, sweeping east to the low, wooded Leitha Mountains, which shelter the Puszta plain extending on into Hungary. The northern part of the basin widens into the Danube Valley, forming the Carnuntum agricultural and wine region, with Slovakia to the east.

North of the Danube, two great regions are divided by the Kamp River, with the wooded Waldviertel (or Forest District) to the northwest adjoining the Czech Republic, and the undulating hills of the agricultural Weinviertel (or Wine District) to the northeast, bordering on the Czech Republic and on Slovakia, where the March River flows into the Danube.

Great Itineraries

The four districts surrounding Vienna are compact, and each can be explored in a day or two. To pursue the lives of the famous composers Schubert and Beethoven, take the route to the south, to Mödling and Baden; for Haydn's birthplace, go to the east to Rohrau, then possibly on to Eisenstadt. To tour a chain of defensive castles, head for the forested Waldviertel. To enjoy rolling hills and vast expanses of vineyards and to sample their output, seek out the Weinviertel to the north.

Numbers in the text correspond to numbers in the margin and on the Baden and Environs and the Waldviertel and Weinviertel maps.

South of the Danube

IF YOU HAVE 1 DAY

To get a taste of the fringes of the Vienna Woods to the capital's south and west, head for **Mödling** ② and **Baden** ⑦. Both are smaller com-

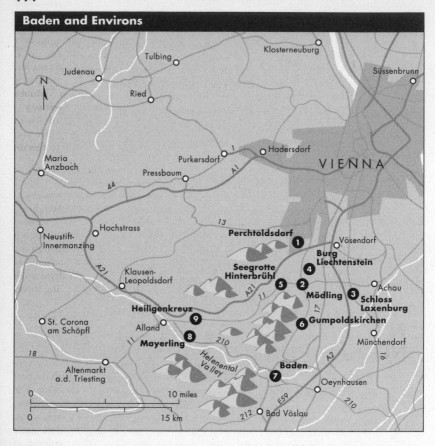

munities with unspoiled 17th-century town centers on a scale easy to assimilate. The route to Baden runs through the band of rolling wooded hills that mark the eastern edge of the Vienna Woods. The hills are skirted by vineyards forming a "wine belt," which also follows the valleys south of Vienna.

IF YOU HAVE 3 DAYS

With more time, you might spend two days in the Vienna Woods area, starting off with two particularly picturesque towns, **Perchtoldsdorf** ① and **Mödling** ②—with perhaps a look at the grand garden of **Schloss Laxenburg** ③—then following the scenic Weinstrasse (Wine Road) through the lush vineyard country to the noted wine-producing village of **Gumpoldskirchen** ⑥. Overnight in 🏨 **Baden** ⑦; then spend your second day taking in the sights of the fashionable spa town, including its grand Kurpark and Casino. Set out in the afternoon for mysterious 🏨 **Mayerling** ⑧. After an evocative dawn and morning there, head for the great abbey at **Heiligenkreuz** ⑨, continuing on to Vienna.

North of the Danube

IF YOU HAVE 1 DAY

The decision will be woods or wine, if you're tight on time. If woods, then head for **Waidhofen an der Thaya** ⑳, returning via picturesque **Raabs an der Thaya** ㉑, **Geras** ㉔, and **Horn** ⑪. If wine, start at the bustling shipbuilding city of Korneuburg, then head northward to the border town of **Laa an der Thaya** ㉘ and return via **Poysdorf** ㉙, famous as a wine center.

IF YOU HAVE 3 DAYS

Spend a leisurely two days tracking the castles of the Waldviertel, starting at **Ottenstein** ⑬; moving on to **Zwettl** ⑭, with its magnificent abbey; overnighting at the noted castle-hotel–Masonic museum in ⊞ **Rosenau** ⑮; and continuing on to **Weitra** ⑯, with its painted facades, for the start of the defensive castles route. The next mighty castle is at **Heidenreichstein** ⑲; follow the castle route with an overnight in ⊞ **Raabs an der Thaya** ㉑ and proceed onward to **Barockschloss Riegersburg** ㉒ and **Burg Hardegg** ㉓, overlooking the river forming the border with the Czech Republic. A stop in the ancient city of **Retz** ㉗ will give you a taste of the wine country; to end your excursion, head on to **Laa an der Thaya** ㉘ and **Poysdorf** ㉙.

When to Tour Vienna's Environs

Most of the regions around Vienna are best seen in the temperate seasons between mid-March and mid-November. The Waldviertel, however, with its vast stands of great forest, offers picture-book scenery throughout the year. The combination of oaks and evergreens offers a color spectrum ranging from intense early spring green, through the deep green of summer, and into traces of autumn foliage, particularly in the Kamp River valley; in winter, occasional spectacular displays of hoarfrost and snowswept vistas turn the region into a glittering three-dimensional Christmas card.

ON THE ROAD TO BADEN AND MAYERLING

This short, though history-rich tour takes you to Baden through the part of the legendary Vienna Woods that borders Vienna on the west. The hills are skirted by vineyards forming a "wine belt," which also follows the valleys south of Vienna. You can visit this area easily in a day's outing, either by car or by public transportation, or you can spend the night in Baden, Mödling, or Alland to allow for a more leisurely exploration of Mayerling, Heiligenkreuz, and a few other sights in the area.

Perchtoldsdorf

❶ *12 km (7½ mi) southwest of Vienna center.*

Just over the Vienna city line to the southwest lies Perchtoldsdorf, a charmingly picturesque market town with many wine taverns, a 13th-century Gothic parish church, and the symbol of the town—an imposing stone tower completed in 1511, once forming a piece of the town's defense wall. Familiarly known as Pedersdorf, the town is a favorite excursion spot for the Viennese, who come mainly for the good local wines. Wander around the compact town square to admire the Renaissance houses, some with arcaded courtyards. The Pestsäule (Plague Column) in the center of the square, which gives thanks for rescue from the dreaded 16th-century plague, was created by the famous baroque architect Fischer von Erlach and is similar to the Plague Column that adorns the Graben in Vienna. The most recent version of *The Three Musketeers*, starring Chris O'Donnell and Charlie Sheen, was partly filmed here within the old defense walls. Without a car, you can reach Perchtoldsdorf from Vienna by taking the S-Bahn, or train, from the Westbahnhof, to Liesing, and then a short cab ride to the town.

Dining

$–$$ ✕ **Sonnberghaus.** A former 19th-century carriage house, the Sonnberghaus offers country casual dining with a friendly welcome. You can order from the menu or choose from the plentiful hot and cold buffet. Tasty standards include *Käsespätzle* (little pasta dumplings baked with cheese) and a salad, or *Wienerschnitzel* (veal scallop, breaded, deep-fried in fresh oil). The wine list is good and reasonably priced. Dining at a picnic table in the inviting courtyard is a delightful way to spend a summer evening. ⊠ *Sonnbergstr. 22,* ☎ *01/869–8181. AE, DC, MC, V. Closed Sun.–Mon. No lunch.*

Mödling

② *20 km (12½ mi) southwest of Vienna.*

Founded in the 10th century, Mödling has a delightful town center, now a pedestrian zone. Here you can admire centuries-old buildings, most one- or two-story, which give the town an intimate feeling. Composers Beethoven and Schubert appreciated this in the early 1800s; Mödling was one of Beethoven's favored residences outside of Vienna. Note the domineering **St. Othmar Gothic parish church** on a hill overlooking the town proper, a Romanesque 12th-century charnel house (where the bones of the dead were kept), and the town hall, which has a Renaissance loggia. Later eras added art nouveau, which mixes happily with the several 16th- and 17th-century buildings.

③ A couple of miles southeast of Mödling is **Schloss Laxenburg,** a complex consisting of a large baroque Neues Schloss (New Castle), a small 14th-century Altes Schloss (Old Castle), and an early 19th-century neo-Gothic castle set into the sizable lake. The large park is full of birds and small game, such as roe deer and hare, and is decorated with statues, cascades, imitation temples, and other follies. The park and grounds are a favorite with the Viennese for Sunday outings. The Altes Schloss was built in 1381 by Duke Albrecht III as his summer residence, and several Habsburg emperors spent summers in the Neues Schloss, which now houses the International Institute of Applied Systems Analysis. Opposite is the large baroque convent of the Charitable Sisters. The castle is currently occupied by a research institute and is generally not open to the public, but the gardens are open daily. ⊠ *Schlosspl. 1,* ☎ *02236/712–26–0,* WEB *www.schloss-laxenburg.at.* 🎫 *Garden €1.24, boat to castle €0.44, tour €3.63.* ☉ *Gardens daily 24 hrs, tours at 11, 2, and 3.*

④ **Burg Liechtenstein,** an imposing medieval castle perched formidably on a crag, overlooks the Vienna Woods a couple miles northeast of Mödling. The pale stone walls and turrets have withstood marauding armies and the elements for more than 800 years, but the interior has been largely restored and includes a squires' hall, kitchen, bedchambers, a chapel, and even a medieval toilet. Not to be missed is the Tower Room, with its 13th-century red Italian marble fireplace and carved wooden spiral staircase. The Tower Room was the last refuge in case of an attack, and you can see where boiling water and refuse were poured onto the attackers. In summer, concerts are held in the courtyard. ⊠ *Maria Enzersdorf,* ☎ *02236/44294.* 🎫 *€4.36.* ☉ *Apr.–Oct., daily 9:30–5.*

⑤ West of Mödling on Route 11 is the **Seegrotte Hinterbrühl,** a fascinating but now somewhat commercialized underground sea, created years ago when a mine filled up with water. You can take a 45-minute motorboat trip and look at the reflections through the arched caverns of the mine. Some of the recent film *The Three Musketeers,* starring Charlie Sheen and Chris O'Donnell, was filmed here. ⊠ *Grutschg. 2, Hinterbrühl,* ☎ *02236/26364.* 🎫 *€4.72.* ☉ *Apr.–Oct., daily 9–noon and 1–5; Nov.–Mar., daily 9–noon and 1–3.*

Dining

$$–$$$ ✕ **Hotel-Restaurant Höldrichsmühle.** Höldrichsmühle, where a mill has turned since the 12th century, is now a famed 200-year-old country inn. Legend holds that the linden tree and the well found here inspired composer Franz Schubert to one of his better-known songs. Stop at this traditional restaurant for fish, game, or various wild mushroom dishes in season. ✉ *Gaadnerstr. 34,* ☎ *02236/26274–0,* FAX *02236/ 48729,* WEB *www.hoeldrichsmuehle.at. AE, DC, MC, V.*

Gumpoldskirchen

⑥ *4 km (2½ mi) west of Mödling.*

From Mödling, follow the scenic Weinstrasse (an unnumbered road to the west of the rail line) through the lush vineyard country to the famous wine-producing village of Gumpoldskirchen. This tiny village on the eastern slopes of the last Alpine rocks has lived for wine for 2,000 years, and its white wines enjoy a fame that is widespread. At one stage, there was more Gumpoldskirchner on the world markets than the village could ever have produced—a situation reminiscent of the medieval glut of pieces of the True Cross. **Vintners' houses** line the main street, many of them with the typical large wooden gates that lead to vine-covered courtyards where the Heuriger (wine of the latest vintage) is served by the owner and his family at simple wooden tables with benches. Gumpoldskirchen also has an arcaded Renaissance town hall, a market fountain made from a Roman sarcophagus, and the (private) castle of the Teutonic Knights, whose descendants still own some of the best vineyard sites in the area.

Dining

$$ ✕ **Altes Zechhaus.** Perched at the top of the Old Town, this centuries-old drinking tavern is still going strong. Choose from the tempting panoply of salads downstairs and then order a hearty schnitzel, spit-roasted chicken, or duck, which will be brought to your table piping hot. Try to get a table upstairs in the wood-beamed Gothic Room, where plank tables are set against ancient stone walls and mullioned windows. Be sure to check out their house wine with its bawdy label, on display in the foyer. ✉ *Kirchenpl. 1,* ☎ *02252/62247,* FAX *02252/63541. AE, DC, MC, V.*

Baden

★ **⑦** *7 km (4½ mi) south of Gumpoldskirchen, 32 km (20 mi) southwest of Vienna.*

The Weinstrasse brings you to the serenely elegant spa town of Baden. Since antiquity, Baden's sulfuric thermal baths have attracted the ailing and the fashionable from all over the world. When the Romans came across the springs, they dubbed the town Aquae; the Babenbergs revived it in the 10th century; and when the Russian czar Peter the Great visited in 1698, Baden's golden age began. Austria's emperor Franz II spent 31 successive summers here. Every year for 12 years before his death in 1835, the royal entourage moved from Vienna for the season. Later in the century, Emperor Franz Josef II was a regular visitor, becoming the inspiration for much of the regal trappings the city still displays. In Baden, Mozart composed his "Ave Verum"; Beethoven spent 15 summers here and wrote large sections of his Ninth Symphony and *Missa Solemnis* when he lived at Frauengasse 10; Franz Grillparzer wrote his historical dramas here; and Josef Lanner, both Johann Strausses (father and son), Carl Michael Ziehrer, and Karl Millöcker composed and directed many of their waltzes, marches, and operettas.

For many people the primary reason for a visit to Baden is the lovely, sloping **Kurpark** in the center of town, where occasional outdoor public concerts still take place. Operetta is performed under the skies in the

Summer Arena (its roof closes if it rains); in winter, it is performed in the Stadttheater. People sit quietly under the old trees or walk through the upper sections of the Kurpark for a view of the town from above. The old Kurhaus, now enlarged and renovated, incorporates a convention hall. ✉ *Kaiser Franz-Ring.*

The ornate **Casino**—with a bar, restaurant, and gambling rooms—still includes traces of its original 19th-century decor but has been enlarged and, in the process, overlaid with glitz rivaling that of Las Vegas. ✉ *Kaiser Franz-Ring 1–3, Kurpark,* ☎ *02252/44496–0.* ⏱ *Casino daily from 1* PM, *gambling daily from 3* PM.

Music lovers will want to visit the **Beethoven Haus** (✉ Rathausg. 10, ☎ 02252/86800–231). This is just one of several addresses Beethoven called his own hereabouts—the great man was always on the run from his creditors and moved frequently. Admission is €2.50, and hours are Tuesday–Friday 4–6, weekends 9–11 and 4–6. Children of all ages will enjoy the enchanting **Badener Puppen und Spielzeug Museum** (Doll and Toy Museum) (✉ Erzherzog Rainer-Ring 23, ☎ 02252/41020). Admission is €2.50, and the museum is open Tuesday–Friday 4–6, weekends 9–11 and 4–6.

One of the pleasures associated with Baden is getting there. You can reach the city directly from Vienna by bus or, far more fun, by interurban streetcar, in about 50 minutes—the bus departs from the Ring directly opposite the Opera; the blue streetcar departs from the Ring across from the Bristol Hotel. Both drop you in the center of Baden. By car from Vienna, travel south on Route A2, turning west at the junction of Route 305. It is possible, with advance planning, to go on to Mayerling and Heiligenstadt on post office buses (☎ 02252/22600–0).

Dining and Lodging

$$$$ ✕🏨 **Grand Hotel Sauerhof.** "Maria Theresa yellow" marks this ap-
★ pealing country house, which has elegant rooms in the Old Vienna style. The hotel caters heavily to seminars and group activities, but individual guests are not ignored, and accommodations are very comfortable. It is also possible to go for a day's outing to their Beauty Farm and pamper yourself with the full body treatment. The hotel's Rauhenstein restaurant is famous in Baden (try the veal with a red-wine mushroom sauce, and for dessert, the famous house crepes). ✉ *Weilburgstr. 11–13, A–2500,* ☎ *02252/41251,* 🅵🅰🆇 *02252/48047,* 🆆🅴🅱 *www.sauerhof. at. 88 rooms. Restaurant, minibars, tennis court, indoor pool, gym, sauna, bar, Internet, meeting rooms; no a/c. AE, DC, MC, V.*

$$$–$$$$ ✕🏨 **Schloss Weikersdorf.** A restored Renaissance castle whose earli-
★ est foundations go back to 1233, the Weikersdorf is just minutes away from the center of Baden. Set on the edge of a vast public park, the hotel estate offers bonuses of a rose garden featuring 600 varieties and boating on the lake. Rooms and baths are luxuriously outfitted. The restaurant is excellent—make a beeline for the anglerfish in a saffron sauce with morel risotto, or pork ribs in a tomato-olive crust. In fine weather, tables are set outside on the Renaissance loggia overlooking the rose garden. ✉ *Schlossg. 9–11, A–2500,* ☎ *02252/48301,* 🅵🅰🆇 *02252/48301–150. 107 rooms. Restaurant, minibars, tennis courts, indoor pool, sauna, bowling, bar, Internet, meeting rooms; no a/c. AE, DC, MC, V.*

$$$ ✕🏨 **Krainerhütte.** Located 5 km (3¹⁄₁₀ mi) from Baden, this friendly house, in typical Alpine style with balconies and lots of natural wood, has been family-run since 1876. The site on the outskirts of town is ideal for relaxing or exploring the surrounding woods. Facilities are up to date, and the restaurant offers a choice of cozy rooms or an outdoor terrace along with international and Austrian cuisine, with fish and game from the hotel's own reserves. ⊠ *Helenental, A–2500,* ☎ *02252/ 44511–0,* 🗷 *02252/44514. 60 rooms. Restaurant, tennis court, indoor pool, sauna; no a/c. AE, DC, MC, V.*

Mayerling

❽ *11 km (7 mi) northwest of Baden, 29 km (18 mi) west of Vienna.*

Scenic Route 210 takes you through the quiet Helenental valley west of Baden to Mayerling, scene of a tragedy that is still passionately discussed and disputed by the Austrian public, press, and historians at the slightest provocation, and still provides a torrid subject for moviemakers and novelists in many other parts of the world. On the snowy evening of January 29, 1889, the 30-year-old Habsburg heir, Crown Prince Rudolf, Emperor Franz Josef's only son, and his 17-year-old mistress, Baroness Marie Vetsera, met a violent and untimely end at the emperor's hunting lodge at Mayerling. Most historians believe it was a suicide pact between two desperate lovers (the Pope had refused an annulment to Rudolf's unhappy marriage to Princess Stephanie of Belgium). There are those, however, who feel Rudolf's pro-Hungarian political leanings might be a key to the tragedy. Given information gleaned from private letters that have recently come to light, it is also possible Rudolf was hopelessly in love with a married woman and killed himself in despair, taking Marie Vetsera with him. In an attempt to suppress the scandal—the full details are not known to this day—the baroness's body, propped up between two uncles, was smuggled back into the city by carriage (she was buried hastily in nearby Heiligenkreuz). The bereaved emperor had the hunting lodge where the suicide took place torn down and replaced with a rather nondescript Carmelite convent. Mayerling remains beautiful, haunted—and remote: the village is infrequently signposted.

Heiligenkreuz

❾ *4 km (2½ mi) west of Mayerling, 14 km (8¾ mi) west of Mödling.*

Heiligenkreuz, in the heart of the southern section of the Vienna Woods, is a magnificent Cistercian abbey with a famous Romanesque and Gothic church, founded in 1135 by Leopold III. The church itself is lofty and serene, with beautifully carved choir stalls (the Cistercians are a singing order) surmounted by busts of Cistercian saints. The great treasure here is the relic of the cross that Leopold V is said to have brought back from his crusade in 1188. The cloisters are interesting for the Chapel of the Dead, where the brothers lie in state guarded by four gesticulating skeletons holding a candelabra. The chapter house contains the tombs of Babenberg rulers. In a corner of the abbey grounds, you can follow the baroque stations of the cross along paths lined with chestnut and linden trees. ⊠ *Heiligenkreuz 1,* ☎ *02258/8703,* 🕸 *www.heiligenkreuz. at.* 🖃 *Abbey free, tour €5.20.* ⊙ *Tours Mon.–Sat. at 10, 11, 2, 3, and 4, Sun. at 11, 2, 3, and 4 (additional tour at 5 daily in summer).*

From Vienna, reach Heiligenkreuz by taking Route A21 southwest or via bus from Südtirolerplatz.

Dining and Lodging

$$ ✕🏠 **Landgasthof Zur Linde.** In the heart of the Vienna Woods, some 24 km (15 mi) northwest of Mayerling, lies the small town of Laaben bei Neulengbach—equidistant (about 22½ km/14 mi northwest of Mayerling) from Mayerling and Heiligenkreuz, in the shadow of the 2,900-ft Schöpfl Mountain. This family-run country inn offers an excellent base from which to explore the countryside. Rooms are modest but complete and comfortable, with rustic trimmings. The rambling restaurant, with its several wood-beamed rooms, serves standard tasty

Austrian fare, with seasonal specialties such as lamb, asparagus, and game. ⊠ *Hauptpl. 28, A–3053 Laaben bei Neulengbach,* ☎ *02774/8378–0,* FAX *02774/8378–20. 10 rooms. Restaurant; no a/c. DC, MC, V. Closed Tues., Wed., 1 wk in Mar.*

THE WALDVIERTEL

The "Forest Quarter" north of the Danube and to the northwest of Vienna was long dormant, cut off from neighboring Czechoslovakia until 1990 by a sealed border. Today, with the reopening of many crossing points, the Waldviertel has reawakened. Here gentle hills bearing stands of tall pine and oak are interspersed with small farms and friendly country villages. The region can be seen in a couple of days, longer if you pause to explore the museums, castles, and other attractions. Zwettl and Raabs an der Thaya, where facilities are more modest and much less expensive than those of the major tourism routes, make good bases for discovering this area.

The main rail line from Vienna to Prague passes through the Waldviertel, making the region accessible by train. In addition, post office buses cover the area fairly well and with reasonable frequency. Bus hubs are Horn, Waidhofen, and Zwettl. An express bus service runs between Vienna and Heidenreichstein via Waidhofen an der Thaya.

Kleinwetzdorf

⑩ *52 km (32½ mi) northwest of Vienna.*

The celebrated Austrian field marshal Joseph Wenzel Graf von Radetsky (1766–1858) is buried at **Heldenberg,** near the tiny village of Kleinwetzdorf, in elegant but lugubrious surroundings. The great field marshal was instrumental in defeating Napoléon in 1814, thus saving the Habsburg crown for the young Franz Josef II. Radetzky's tomb, arranged for by a wealthy uniform supplier, is marked by an obelisk set in a park studded with dozens of larger-than-life-size busts of Austrian royalty and nobility. Follow the marked path to the west back of the park past the memorial to young emperor Franz Josef II to reach the lion-guarded memorial to Radetzky's military campaigns in Italy and Hungary. The whole complex is a slightly eerie phantasmagoria—but historically fascinating. ⊠ *Heldenberg 50,* ☎ *02956/2372.* ☒ *Free.* ☉ *Mid-Mar.–Apr. and mid-Sept.–mid-Nov., Tues.–Sun. 10–17, May–mid-Sept., daily 10–6.*

The small, 17th-century **Schloss Wetzdorf** (at press time, closed for renovation—so call to confirm for reopening) has a **Radetzky museum,** although of all the memorials to the field marshal, probably Johann Strauss Sr.'s "Radetzky March" is the best known. Half hidden to the south of the castle is a freestanding arched gate surmounted with wonderful reclining lions. The castle's **Schlosstaverne** (open only on weekends and holidays) offers light snacks and basics such as Wienerschnitzel, coffee, and cooling drinks. The courtyard makes a delightful option in good weather. ⊠ *Kleinwetzdorf 1,* ☎ *02956/2372.* ☒ *Unknown at press time.* ☉ *Tour May–Oct. 26, weekends 10–6.*

Dining and Lodging

$$–$$$ ✕☰ **Restaurant Naderer.** A fine "food-with-a-view" spot, the Naderer is at the top of the hill above Maissau, 14 km (9 mi) northwest of Kleinwetzdorf on Route 4. The cuisine is of a standard that draws diners from as far away as Vienna. The menu spotlights innovative twists on old Austrian favorites, such as the delicious *Wallergröstl,* chunks of mild, local white lake fish mixed with home-fried potatoes and slivers

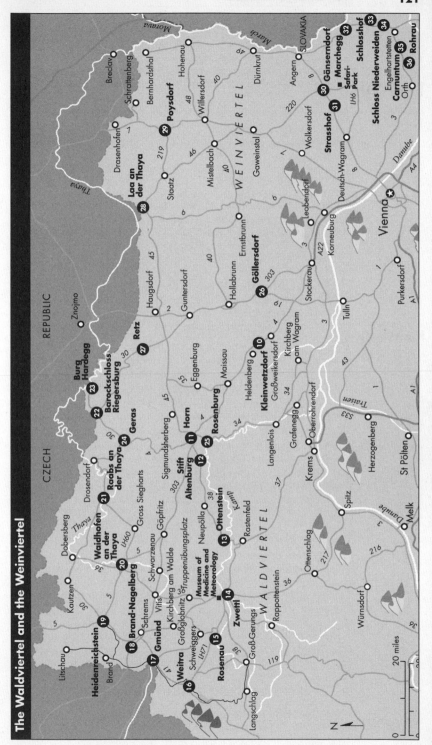

The Waldviertel and the Weinviertel

of red and yellow peppers. The cakes from the house kitchens are particularly good. Most of the excellent wines come from the surrounding vineyards. In summer, lunching on the terrace overlooking the valley can be a particularly pleasurable experience. Eight hotel rooms are available for overnights. ✉ *Am Berg 44, A–3712 Maissau,* ☎ *02958/ 82334. 8 rooms. AE, DC. Closed July, Nov., Thurs. in winter, and 1 wk in Feb.*

Horn

⑪ *32 km (20 mi) northwest of Kleinwetzdorf, 81 km (50½ mi) northwest of Vienna.*

Horn lies at the eastern edge of the Waldviertel. Remnants of the impressive fortification walls, with its watchtowers built in 1532 to defend against invading Turks, are still obvious. Wander through the core of the Old City, which dates from the 15th century. Note the painted Renaissance facade on the house (1583) at Kirchenplatz 3. **St. Stephen's parish church** on the edge of the cemetery out of the center allures with its Gothic choir and a late-Gothic stone chancel. The baroque **Piarist church,** built in 1660, is noted for its 1777 altar painting by the renowned regional artist Kremser Schmidt. The castle, started in the 1500s and completely rebuilt in the 18th century, sits at the edge of the large, attractive Schlosspark. Horn is host to an international chamber music festival in summer.

⑫ About 5 km (3 mi) west of Horn, at Altenburg on Route 38, **Stift Altenburg** was built in 1144 and rebuilt in 1645–1740 after its destruction by the Swedes. The library and the frescoed ceilings by the master artist Paul Troger are glorious. ✉ *Altenburg 1,* ☎ *02982/3451–14,* FAX *02982/3451–13,* WEB *www.stift-altenburg.at.* 🎟 *€7.* ☼ *Easter–Oct. daily 10–5.*

⑬ Almost 35 km (21 mi) west of Altenburg, on Route 38 in Rastenfeld, the castle (✉ Ottenstein 1, ☎ 02826/254) at **Ottenstein** has a number of impressive reception rooms and parts dating to 1178. Ottenstein defied the invading Swedes in 1645 only to be devastated by the Russians in 1945. The nearby Lichtenfels castle ruins can also be explored.

Zwettl

⑭ *49 km (31 mi) west of Horn, 125 km (78 mi) northwest of Vienna.*

Zwettl lies in the heartland of the Forest District. The town center, squeezed within a river bend, is attractive for its gabled houses and colorful pastel facades. The city wall, dating from the Middle Ages, still includes eight defensive towers. But Zwettl is best known for the vast **Stift Zwettl,** a Cistercian abbey dating from 1138, about 2¼ km (1½ mi) west of the town. The Zwettl abbey, perched above the Kamp River, was established as an outpost of the abbey at Heiligenkreuz in the Vienna Woods. The imposing south gate in the cloisters remains from the original edifice; the church, with its massive Gothic choir, was completed in 1348. Later renovations added the glorious baroque touches, including the 292-ft tower that crowns the west wall. An international organ festival is held here annually from the end of June to the end of July. ☎ *02822/550–57,* WEB *www.stift-zwettl.co.at.* 🎟 *€4.70.* ☼ *Tours May– June and Oct., Mon.–Sat. at 10, 11, 2, and 3, Sun. at 11, 2, and 3; July– Sept., additional tour daily at 4. Closed Nov.–Apr.*

Dining and Lodging

$ ✕ **Stiftstaverne-Restaurant.** Set just outside the Zwettl abbey, this spacious tavern complex serves good Austrian country fare such as roast pork with bread dumplings as well as salad with sesame-coated turkey strips, vegetable strudel, or smoked fish. The outstanding beer, fresh from the nearby brewery, is alone worth a stop, as are the wines, which come from the abbey's own cellars. ✉ *Stift Zwettl,* ☎ *02822/550–36. No credit cards. Closed Tues. from Nov. to Easter.*

$ 🏨 **Gasthof Hamerlingsaal.** The cream-color plain facade set somewhat to the east of the town center gives way to a relatively simple but modernized family-run hotel. Rooms are comfortable enough, and the buffet breakfast is ample. ✉ *Galgenbergstr. 3, A–3910,* ☎ *02822/52344– 0,* 𝖥𝖠𝖷 *02822/52344–85. 24 rooms. AE, DC, MC, V.*

Rosenau

⑮ *9 km (5 mi) west of Zwettl.*

Schloss Rosenau, with its prominent central tower, is an impressive Renaissance structure built in 1590 with later baroque additions. The castle was ravaged by the Soviets in 1945, then rebuilt as a hotel and museum complex housing the unique **Freimaurer-Museum** (Freemasonry Museum). A secret room once used for lodge ceremonies was discovered during the renovations and is now part of the museum. Displays show the ties of Haydn and Mozart to freemasonry, and many exhibits reflect the origins of the brotherhood. ☎ *02822/58221.* 🎫 *€4.* ⊙ *Mid-Apr.–Oct., daily 9–5; call for tour times.*

Dining and Lodging

$$$ ✕🏨 **Schloss Rosenau.** Mozart supposedly stayed in this elegant baroque
★ castle, which today offers country quiet to the stressed-out. A few of the rooms are furnished with Biedermeier antiques, though most have a modern air. The theme of the hotel is "the rose," and roses are everywhere, even strewn throughout the rooms, making it a very romantic retreat. The wood-paneled restaurant is one of the best in the area, featuring Waldviertler potato cream soup and turkey medallions with Spätzle, little pasta dumplings. In summer, food seems to taste even better on the outdoor terrace, which is surrounded by hedges of miniature yellow roses and overlooks the wooded hills. ☎ *02822/58221–0,* 𝖥𝖠𝖷 *02822/58221–8,* 𝖶𝖤𝖡 *www.tiscover.com/schloss.rosenau. 18 rooms. Restaurant, minibars, tennis court, sauna, fishing, horseback riding; no a/c. AE, DC, MC, V.*

Weitra

★ ⑯ *16 km (11 mi) northwest of Rosenau.*

The small town of Weitra, set along the main road LH71, is renowned for its stunning, ornate painted house facades (*sgraffiti*) dating from the 17th and 18th centuries. A charming small brewery has been in business here since 1321. And the tradition is well founded: as early as 1645, 33 of Weitra's citizens held the right to operate breweries. The 15th-century fortress **Schloss Weitra,** with its Renaissance features, is privately owned, though some rooms are open to the public; the rococo theater, the ceremonial hall, the tower, and the extensive Schlosskeller (with an exhibition on beer brewing) are particularly worthwhile. This is the westernmost of the line of castles built to defend against possible invaders from the north. ☎ *02856/3311.* 🎫 *€6.90.* ⊙ *May–Oct., Wed.–Mon. 10–5.*

Dining and Lodging

$ ✕🏨 **Gasthof Waschka.** This cheery yellow Gasthaus in the center of town is typically Austrian, with green and yellow banquettes in the casual Bierstube. Order the Waschka family's home-brewed beer, Libellen Bräu, to go along with the tasty Waldviertler *Knödelgröstl,* a hefty portion of fried dumplings mixed with crispy onions and fried egg, or Bohemian *Rindsbraten* (roast beef). The front terrace, perfect for dining in summer, overlooks the medieval square. There are modern, pleasant rooms upstairs for overnighters. ✉ *Rathauspl. 8, A–3970,* ☎ *02856/2296. 12 rooms. Restaurant, sauna, bar; no a/c. AE, DC, MC, V. Closed Wed. and 1st 2 wks of Mar.*

Gmünd

🅱 *16 km (10 mi) north of Weitra, 55 km (34½ mi) northwest of Horn.*

The town of Gmünd was curiously divided in 1918 when the border with Czechoslovakia was established. The actual line passes through a few houses and backyards, but, with the barbed-wire defenses now removed, the border is a harmless affair. The core of the Old Town remains in Austria and is worth viewing for the painted facades (sgraffiti) around the main square. Adjacent to the square is the once-moated (private) castle, which dates from the 16th century.

Railroad fans have a field day in Gmünd; the Czechs still use some steam locomotives for switching, and on the Austrian side Gmünd is one of ⓒ the main points on the delightful narrow-gauge **Waldviertler Schmalspurbahn** (☎ 02852/52588–0), which runs occasional steam excursions plus some regular services. The excursion runs generally include a club car with refreshments.

Northwest of Schrems, a detour west from Route 30, on Route 303, 🅱 leads to **Brand–Nagelberg,** pressed against the Czech border and a center of glassmaking since 1740. Among the operating glassworks that you can visit to see how glass is made and blown is **Glasstudio Zalto** (✉ Neu–Nagelberg 58, ☎ 02859/7217). Another, **Stölzle Kristall** (✉ Hauptstr. 45, Alt–Nagelberg, ☎ 02859/7531–0), has a showroom and factory outlet.

Heidenreichstein

🅱 *9 km (5½ mi) southwest of Gmünd, 51 km (32 mi) northwest of Horn.*

★ ⓒ The scenic route north from Schrems parallels the narrow-gauge railway to Heidenreichstein, noted for the massive moated **Burg Heidenreichstein,** with its corner towers, which has never been captured by enemy forces since it was built in the 15th century; some of the walls, 10 ft thick, went up in the 13th century. This is one of the most remarkable "water" castles in Austria. Water—or moated—castles were surrounded by a body of water (natural or artificial) for defense purposes, whereas "hill" castles exploited steep, often rocky and inaccessible slopes for protection. The building is in remarkable condition, the best-preserved of all moated castles in Austria, and some of the rooms are furnished with pieces dating from the 15th and 16th centuries. It is open for tours only. ✉ *Schremserstr. 1,* ☎ *02862/52268.* 🎫 *Tour €5.* ☉ *Tours mid-Apr.–mid-Oct., Tues.–Sun. at 9, 10, 11, 2, 3, and 4.*

Waidhofen an der Thaya

🅱 *14 km (9 mi) east of Heidenreichstein, 32 km (20 mi) north of Zwettl, 37 km (23 mi) northwest of Horn.*

Route 5 between Heidenreichstein and Waidhofen an der Thaya is particularly scenic. Waidhofen itself is a three-sided, walled defense city typical of those of the 13th century. Fires destroyed much of the early character of the town, but the town square, rebuilt at the end of the 19th century, has a pleasing unity. The town is dominated by its baroque **parish church,** locally known as the Cathedral of the Thaya

Valley; the rococo Mary chapel includes a Madonna of 1440 and distinguished portraits marking the stations of the cross. Outside the city walls, the **Bürgerspitalkapelle** has a side altar with a Gothic carved-wood relief of the Madonna and child and 13 attendants dating from about 1500.

Raabs an der Thaya

㉑ *21 km (13 mi) northeast of Waidhofen an der Thaya, 42 km (26 mi) northwest of Horn.*

The Thaya River wanders leisurely through Raabs an der Thaya, an unusually attractive village watched over by 11th-century **Burg Raabs,** perched dramatically on a rock outcropping and reflected in the river below. This was one of the chain of defensive castles through the Waldviertel region. The river is popular for fishing and swimming. The castle is now privately owned.

Dining and Lodging

$ ✕☲ **Hotel Thaya.** A friendly, family-run hotel directly on the river, the Thaya offers comfortable, modern, if slightly spartan rooms in the annex. Rooms directly overlooking the river are the favorites. The restaurant prepares such solid local specialties as roast pork and veal. ✉ *Hauptstr. 14, A–3820,* ☎ *02846/202–0,* ☏ *02846/8202–20. 25 rooms. Restaurant, gym, sauna, bar, beer garden, dance club; no a/c. V. Closed Feb. and possibly other winter months.*

OFF THE BEATEN PATH **DROSENDORF –** Northeast of Raabs along Route 30 is the border town of Drosendorf, with a castle built in 1100 and a historic center typical of a small walled community. The encircling wall is virtually intact and complete with watchtowers.

Riegersburg

28 km (17½ mi) east of Raabs an der Thaya, 33 km (20½ mi) north of Horn, 18½ km (11½ mi) northwest of Retz.

㉒ The impressive **Barockschloss Riegersburg** was originally moated before the substantial edifice was given a baroque makeover in 1731 and again virtually rebuilt after the Russians inflicted heavy damage in 1945. Thankfully, you can now see the elegant public rooms and period furnishings fully restored. Note the window variations and the classical figures that ornament the roofline. ☎ *02916/400,* WEB *www.members.eunet.at/pilati.* ▨ *€8, combination ticket with Burg Hardegg €12.50.* ☉ *Easter–mid-Nov., daily 9–5; July–Aug., daily 9–6.*

Hardegg, about 6 km (4 mi) east of Riegersburg on an unnumbered road, is the smallest village in Austria. It is landmarked by the wonderfully eclectic **Burg Hardegg,** which stands mightily on a rock promontory high above the Thaya River, watching over the Czech Republic. (The river midstream marks the boundary; as recently as 1990 the pedestrian bridge was impassable, the border sealed, and Czech border defenses were concealed in the woods opposite.) The earliest parts of the castle date from 1140. The armory and armament collection, chapel, and the museum's exhibits on the emperor Maximilian in Mexico alone are worth a visit. In addition, the kitchen and other working rooms of the castle give a real feeling for the daily life of an earlier era. An English-speaking guide is available for small group tours. ✉ *Hardegg,* ☎ *02916/400,* WEB *www.members.eunet.at/pilati.* ▨ *Castle €5.30, tour €2.50.* ☉ *Easter–mid-Nov., daily 9–5; July–Aug., daily 9–6.*

Geras

㉔   *14 km (8½ mi) southwest of Riegersburg, 22 km (14 mi) north of Horn, 23 km (14½ mi) southeast of Raabs an der Thaya.*

Another of the Waldviertel's great abbeys, **Stift Geras,** is situated here. Established in 1120, the impressive complex has had from its beginnings close ties to its agricultural surroundings. The abbey was given a glorious full-blown baroque treatment in the course of rebuilding following a fire in 1730, including a transcendently spiritual fresco by the noted Paul Troger in the 18th-century Marble Hall, now often used for concerts. Although the abbey still functions as a religious center, the complex is also a noted school for arts and crafts. ✉ *Hauptstr. 1,* ☎ *02912/345,* WEB *www.stiftgeras.at.* 🎫 *€5.* ☉ *Tours Easter–Oct., Tues.–Sat. at 10, 11, 2, 3, Sun. at 11, 2, and 3.*

Dining and Lodging

$$ ✕🏨 **Stiftsrestaurant und Hotel "Alter Schüttkasten."** A former granary outbuilding of the abbey has been turned into a modern hotel with all the amenities. Rooms are comfortable; those on the front look out over the fields toward the abbey. The restaurant offers seasonal specialties such as fish and game in addition to pork, beef, and other regional standards. ✉ *Vorstadt 11, A–2093,* ☎ *02912/3320,* FAX *02912/332–33,* WEB *www. kloesterreich.at. 26 rooms. Restaurant, sauna; no a/c. DC, MC, V.*

Kamptal

Rosenburg is 23 km (14½ mi) south of Geras, 80 km (50 mi) northwest of Vienna.

㉕   The gloriously scenic Kamp River valley (Kamptal), running from **Rosenburg** in the north some 30 km (19 mi) south roughly to Hadersdorf am Kamp, technically belongs to the Waldviertel, though for the amount of wine produced here, it might as well be a part of the Weinviertel, the Wine District to the east. The river, road, and railroad share the frequently narrow and twisting route that meanders some 25 km (15½ mi) through the valley from Rosenburg south to Langenlois. The villages along the route—Gars am Kamp, Schönberg am Kamp, Zöbing, Strass, and Langenlois—are all known for excellent wines, mainly varietal whites. Strass in particular has become an active center of viticulture, and many vintners offer wine tastings. Castle ruins dot the hilltops above the woods and vineyards; the area has been populated since well before 900 BC. Route 34 takes you through more vineyards to Kollersdorf, where Route 3 east will return you to Vienna.

🎫   The massive fortress **Rosenburg Forstverwaltung Hoyos** dates from 1200 and dominates the north entrance to the Kamptal valley. Note the original jousting field (now the forecourt) and impressive reception rooms inside, where armor and other relics of the period are on display. Curious Renaissance balconies and small courtyards are incorporated into the design, although the variety in the 13 towers added in the 15th century is the touch that immediately catches the eye. The first Sunday of the month, falconry demonstrations are performed in medieval costume. ✉ *Rosenburg am Kamp,* ☎ *02982/2911,* WEB *www.rosenburg. at.* 🎫 *€8 for both guided tour and falconry demonstration.* ☉ *Apr.– Nov. 1, daily 9–5; falconry demonstration Apr.–Nov., daily at 11 and 3; tour begins 1 hr before demonstration.*

Dining

$–$$ ✕ **Bründlmayer.** This country Heuriger in the center of Langenlois offers outstanding wines from one of Austria's top vintners, as well as a tasty hot-and-cold buffet, all in an indoor stone-vaulted hall with a cheery fireplace or outdoors in the Renaissance courtyard. Four different warm dishes are offered every week, and the simple but delicious fare might include *Krautfleckerl,* a cabbage and noodle dish with cheese and lightly smoked ham. Take the opportunity to taste some of their excellent wines, including the crisp and fruity Grüner Veltliner Alte Reben, made with grapes from old vines. ⊠ *Walterstr. 14, Langenlois,* ☎ *02734/21720. DC, MC, V.* ⊘ *Thurs.–Fri. 3–11, weekends 11:30– 11 PM. Closed mid-Dec.–Jan.*

THE WEINVIERTEL

Luckily, Austria's Weinviertel (Wine District) has been largely neglected by the "experts," and its deliciously fresh wines reward those who enjoy drinking wine but dislike the all-too-frequent nonsense that goes with it. This region takes its name from the rustic and delightful rolling countryside north of Vienna. The Weinviertel is bounded by the Danube on the south, the Thaya River and the reopened Czech border on the north, the March River and Slovakia to the east. No well-defined line separates the Weinviertel from the Waldviertel to the west; the Kamp River valley, officially part of the Waldviertel, is an important wine region. Whether wine, crops, or dairies, this is farming country, its broad expanses of vineyards and farmlands broken by patches of forest and neat villages. A tour by car, just for the scenery, can be made in a day; you may want two or three days to savor the region and its wines— these are generally on the medium-dry side. Don't expect to find here the elegant facilities found elsewhere in Austria; prices are low by any standard, and village restaurants and accommodations are mainly *Gasthäuser* that meet local needs. This means that you'll be rubbing shoulders with the country folk over your glass of wine or beer.

Göllersdorf

㉖ *10 km (6 mi) north of Stockerau West interchange on Rte. 303/E59.*

The verdant hills and agricultural lands of the southwest Weinviertel around Hollabrunn offer little excitement other than panoramas and scenic pleasures, but one exception is **Schloss Schönborn,** about 2 km (1 mi) south of Göllersdorf on Route 303. The castle was laid out in 1712 by that master of baroque architecture Johann Lukas von Hildebrandt. Today the castle is in private hands, but the harmony of design can be appreciated from the outside. The parish church in Göllersdorf is also a baroque Hildebrandt design from 1740 imposed on a Gothic structure dating from the mid-1400s.

Retz

★ ㉗ *43 km (27 mi) north of Göllersdorf, 70 km (44 mi) north of Vienna.*

Retz, at the northwest corner of the Weinviertel, is a charming town with an impressive rectangular central square formed by buildings dating mainly from the 15th century. Take time to explore Retz's tiny streets leading from the town square; the oldest buildings and the wall and gate-tower defenses survived destruction by Swedish armies in 1645, during the Thirty Years' War. The Dominican church (1295) at the southwest corner of the square also survived, and it is interesting for its long, narrow design. The pastel Biedermeier facades along with the sgraffiti add appeal to the square, which is further marked by the impressive city hall with its massive Gothic tower in the center. The landmark of the town is the pretty **Windmühle,** a Dutch windmill set incongruously in the middle of vineyards on the edge of town. Follow the markers leading up to the summit, where you can sit and rest on benches offering a stunning view of the surrounding countryside.

Retz is best known for its red wines. Here you can tour the **Retzer Erlebniskeller,** Austria's largest wine cellar, tunneled 65 ft under the town, and at the same time taste wines of the area. Some of the tunnels go back to the 13th century, and at the end of the 15th century each citizen was permitted to deal in wines and was entitled to storage space in the town cellars. Efforts to use the cellars for armaments production during World War II failed because of the 88% humidity. The temperature remains constant at 8°C–10°C (47°F–50°F). Entrance to the cellars is at the Rathauskeller, in the center of town. ⊠ *Hauptpl.,* ☎ *02942/2700.* ⊡ *Tour €6.50.* ☉ *Tour daily, May–Oct., 10:30, 2, and 4; Mar.–Apr., Nov.–Dec., daily at 2; Jan.–Feb. by appointment.*

Dining and Lodging

$$$ ✕⊡ **Althof Retz/Hotel Burghof.** Two hotels are tucked into an ancient estate building just off the town square. Take your choice between the upscale Hotel Burghof or the slightly less expensive Althof, which also serves as a training hotel. Both are done in whites and light wood. Rooms are modern, comfortable, and have all facilities. The restaurant has been less successful, but the standards and regional specialties are fine. The excellent wines naturally come mainly from the area. ⊠ *Althofg. 14, A–2070,* ☎ *02942/3711–0,* ⩍ *02942/3711–55. 65 rooms. Restaurant, Internet; no a/c. AE, DC, MC, V.*

Laa an der Thaya

❷❽   *39 km (24 mi) east of Retz, 65 km (41 mi) north of Vienna.*

From 1948 until about 1990, Laa an der Thaya was a town isolated by the cold war, directly bordering what was then Czechoslovakia. Laa is considerably livelier now that the border is open. (As long as you have your passport with you, you can cross into the Czech Republic and return without complication.) The town's huge central square is adorned with a massive neo-Gothic city hall, in stark contrast to the low, colorful buildings that form the square. A good time to visit is mid-September, during the Onion Festival, when all varieties of onions are prepared in every imaginable way in food stalls set up throughout the village. If you're traveling from Retz to Laa an der Thaya, retrace your way south on Route 30 to Route 45.

Laa is noted for its **Bier Museum,** located in the town fortress, that traces the history of beer (the nearby Hubertus brewery has been in business since 1454) and displays an imposing collection of beer bottles. ☎ *02522/ 2501–29.* ⊡ *€1.50.* ☉ *May–Sept., weekends 2–4.*

Dining

$ ✕ **Restaurant Weiler.** Light woods and country accessories set the tone
★   in this family-run restaurant; in summer, dinner is served in the outdoor garden. Try the delicate cream of garlic soup or the house specialty, game in season. For dessert, the delicious cakes of the house are temptingly displayed in a showcase. ⊠ *Staatsbahnstr. 60,* ☎ *02522/ 2379. No credit cards. Closed Mon., 2 wks in Feb., and July.*

Poysdorf

❷❾   *22 km (13 mi) southeast of Laa an der Thaya, 61 km (38 mi) north of Vienna.*

Poysdorf is considered by many the capital of the Weinviertel. Wine making here goes back to the 14th century. Poysdorf vintages, mainly whites, rank with the best Austria has to offer. Narrow paths known as *Kellergassen* (cellar streets) on the northern outskirts are lined with wine cellars set into and under the hills. A festival in early September marks the annual harvest. At the **wine market** (⊠ Singerstr. 2) in the center of town, you can taste as well as buy; the market is open Monday–Thursday 8–5, Friday 8–6, and weekends 10–noon and 1–6.

The town **Museum** includes a section on viticulture and wine making. ⊠ *Brünnerstr. 9,* ☎ *02552/3209.* ☞ *€3.* ☉ *Easter–Oct., Wed.–Mon. 9–noon and 1–5; call to confirm.*

Dining and Lodging

$ ✕ **Gasthaus Schreiber.** Choose the shaded garden under huge trees or the country-rustic decor indoors. The typical Austrian fare—roast pork, stuffed breast of veal, boiled beef, fillet steak with garlic—is commendable, as is the house-made ice cream. The wine card lists more than 60 area labels. ⊠ *Bahnstr. 2,* ☎ *02552/2348. No credit cards. Closed Tues. and late Jan.–Feb. No dinner Mon.*

$$–$$$ ✕☲ **Zur Linde.** This friendly family-run restaurant with rustic decor
★   16 km (10 mi) south of Poysdorf is setting higher standards for such traditional fare as roast pork, stuffed breast of veal, flank steak, and fresh game in season. Desserts are excellent; try the extraordinary *Apfelstrudel.* A major attraction here is the remarkable parade of wines from the neighborhood at altogether reasonable prices. The Zur Linde also has several well-equipped, modern rooms for overnighters. ⊠ *Bahnhofstr. 49, Mistelbach,* ☎ *02572/2409,* 𝗪𝗘𝗕 *www.zur-linde. at/fam.polak. 19 rooms. Restaurant, minibars, Internet; no a/c. AE, DC, MC, V. Closed Mon., late Jan.–mid-Feb., and late July–mid-Aug. No dinner Sun.*

Gänserndorf

③⓪   *41 km (26 mi) south of Poysdorf, 30 km (19 mi) northeast of Vienna.*

☺   Three kilometers (2 miles) south of Gänserndorf, the **Safari-Park und Abenteuerpark** (Safari Park and Adventure Park) allows you to drive through re-created natural habitats of live wild animals, many of which (lions and tigers) are hardly indigenous to Austria. The adventure takes five to six hours, allowing time for the petting zoo and the extra animal shows, which start every half hour. For those without a car, a safari bus leaves for the circuit every hour. ⊠ *Siebenbrunner Str.,* ☎ *02282/70261–0,* 𝗙𝗔𝗫 *02282/70261–27,* 𝗪𝗘𝗕 *www.safaripark.at.* ☞ *€14.* ☉ *Early Apr.–Oct., daily 9:30–4.*

Strasshof

③①   *3 km (2 mi) southwest of Gänserndorf.*

☺   The **Eisenbahnmuseum Das Heizhaus,** north of Strasshof, is a fascinating private collection of dozens of steam locomotives and railroad cars stored in a vast engine house. Enthusiasts have painstakingly rebuilt and restored many of the engines; steam locomotives are up and running on the first Sunday of each month. The complex includes a transfer table, water towers, and a coaling station, and few can resist climbing around among many of the locomotives awaiting restoration. ⊠ *Sillerstr. 123,* ☎ *01/603–5301,* 𝗙𝗔𝗫 *01/602–2196–22,* 𝗪𝗘𝗕 *www.heizhaus.com.* ☞ *€5.50, steam days €7, including tour.* ☉ *Apr.–Oct. 26, Tues.–Sun. 10–4.*

Dining

$$$$ ✕ **Marchfelderhof.** In nearby Deutsch Wagram, this sprawling complex, with its eclectic series of rooms bounteously decorated with everything from antiques to hunting trophies, has a reputation for ex-

cess in the food department as well. The menu's standards—Wiener-schnitzel, roast pork, lamb—are more successful than the more expensive efforts at innovation. Deutsch Wagram is 9 km (5½ mi) southwest of Strasshof on Route 8, 17 km (11 mi) northeast of Vienna on Route 8. ✉ *Bockfliesser Str. 31, Deutsch Wagram,* ☎ *02247/2243–0,* FAX *02247/ 2236–13. AE, DC, MC, V.*

Marchegg

③② *16 km (10 mi) southeast of Gänserndorf, 43 km (27 mi) east of Vi-enna.*

The tiny corner of the lower Weinviertel to the southeast of Gänsern-dorf is known as the Marchfeld, for the fields stretching east to the March River, forming the border with Slovakia. In this region—known as the granary of Austria—a trio of elegant baroque castles are worth a visit; they have been totally renovated in recent years and given over to changing annual exhibits, concerts, and other public activities. These country estates have lost none of their gracious charm over the centuries.

The northernmost of the trio is the **Jagdschloss Marchegg,** its oldest parts dating from 1268. What you see today is the baroque overlay added in 1733 to the basic building from the Middle Ages. The castle now houses a hunting and African art museum. To reach Marchegg from Gänserndorf, take Route 8a 6 km (4 mi) east to Route 49, then Route 49 10 km (6 mi) south. Jagdschloss Marchegg will be closed for renovation until possibly late 2003. ☎ *02285/8224.* 🎫 *Admission un-known at press time.* ⊙ *Mid-Mar.–Nov., Tues.–Sun. 9–noon and 1–5.*

③③ The castle at **Schlosshof** is a true baroque gem, a product of that mas-ter designer and architect Johann Lukas von Hildebrandt, who in 1732 reconstructed the four-sided castle into an elegant U-shape build-ing, opening up the eastern side to a marvelous baroque formal gar-den that gives way toward the river. The famed landscape painter Bernardo Bellotto, noted for his Canaletto-like vistas of scenic land-marks, captured the view before the reconstruction (now that the gar-dens are being restored to their baroque state, Bellotto's three paintings of the hof are proving the most important sources for this work). The castle—once owned by Empress Maria Theresa—is now used for changing annual exhibits, but you can walk the grounds without pay-ing admission. The castle is about 8 km (5 mi) south of Marchegg. ✉ *Schlosshof,* ☎ *02285/6580,* WEB *www.schlosshof.at.* 🎫 *€6.* ⊙ *Late Mar.– early Nov., Tues.–Sun. 10–5.*

About 4 km (2½ mi) southwest of Schlosshof and north of Engelhart-
③④ stetten, **Schloss Niederweiden** was designed as a hunting lodge and built in 1694 by that other master of the baroque, Fischer von Erlach. This jewel was subsequently owned in turn by Prince Eugene and Empress Maria Theresa, who added a second floor and the mansard roof. An-nual exhibits now take place here, and in a *vinothek* (winery) you can sample the wines of the surrounding area. ☎ *02285/6580.* 🎫 *€2.50.* ⊙ *Early May–early Nov., Thurs.–Sun. 10–5.*

Carnuntum

③⑤ *32 km (20 mi) east of Vienna.*

The remains of the important Roman legionary fortress Carnuntum, which once numbered 55,000 inhabitants, is in the tiny village of Petronell, reachable by the S7, a local train that departs from Wien Mitte/Landstrasse or Wien-Nord. Though by no means as impressive as Roman ruins in Italy and Spain, Carnuntum still merits a visit, with three amphitheaters (the first one seating 8,000) and the foundations of former residences, baths, and trading centers, some with mosaic floors. The ruins are quite spread out, with the impressive remains of a Roman arch, the **Heidentor** (Pagans' Gate), a good 15 minutes' walk from the main excavations. A pleasant path along the north end of the ruins leads past a dilapidated 17th-century palace once belonging to the counts of Traun, to the remains of a Roman bath. In summer Greek plays are sometimes performed in English at the **main amphitheater** (☎ 02163/ 3400). ✉ *Petronell,* ☎ *02163/33770,* WEB *www.carnuntum.co.at.* ✆ *€2.50.* ☉ *Late Mar.–early Nov., Mon.–Sat. 9–5, Sun. 10–6; July– Aug., daily 10–6.*

Many of the finds from excavations at Carnuntum are housed 4 km (2½ mi) northeast of Petronell in the village of Bad Deutsch–Altenburg, in the Museum **Carnuntium.** The pride of the collection is a carving of Mithras killing a bull. ✉ *Badg. 40–46, Petronell,* ☎ *02163/33770,* WEB *www.carnuntum.co.at.* ✆ *€4.50, combination ticket with Carnuntum €8.* ☉ *Late Mar.–early Nov., Tues.–Fri. 10–5, weekends 11–5.*

36 Just 5 km (3 mi) south of Petronell, in the tiny village of **Rohrau,** is the birthplace of Joseph Haydn. The quaint reed-thatched cottage where the composer, son of the local blacksmith, was born in 1732, is now a small museum, with a pianoforte he is supposed to have played, as well as letters and other memorabilia. After Haydn had gained world-wide renown, he is said to have returned to his native Rohrau and knelt to kiss the steps of his humble home. ✉ *Hauptstr. 60, Rohrau,* ☎ *02164/ 2268.* ✆ *€2.* ☉ *Tues.–Sun. 10–5.*

Also in Rohrau is the cream-and-beige palace **Schloss Rohrau,** where Haydn's mother worked as a cook for Count Harrach. The palace has one of the best private art collections in Austria, with emphasis on 17th- and 18th-century Spanish and Italian painting. ✉ ☎ *02164/2252.* ✆ *€5.* ☉ *Open Apr.–Oct., Tues.–Sun. 10–5.*

OFF THE   **ARTNER WEINBAU –** Some of the best wines and freshly made
BEATEN PATH   *Ziegenkäse* (goat cheese) in the region can be found in the tiny village of Höflein, 12 km (7½ mi) southwest of Petronell. Artner has been a family business since 1650, and owner Hannes Artner is proud to offer tastings of his wines, including Chardonnay Barrique, cabernet sauvignon, and Blauer Zweigelt Kirchtal. Check for the opening times of the outdoor Heuriger during selected weeks from May to August, when the new wine is available for tasting. ✉ *Heuriger, Dorfstr. 43; winery, Dorfstr. 93, Höflein,* ☎ *02162/63142,* WEB *www.artner.co.at.*

SIDE TRIPS FROM VIENNA A TO Z

To research prices, get advice from other travelers, and book travel arrangements, visit www.fodors.com.

BUS TRAVEL

Buses are a good possibility for getting around, although if you're not driving, a combination of bus and train is probably a better plan in many cases. Frequent scheduled bus service runs between Vienna and Baden, departing across from the Opera House in Vienna to the center of Baden. Connections are available to other towns in the area. Bus service runs between Vienna and Carnuntum–Petronell, and on to Hainburg. Service to the Waldviertel is less frequent but is available between Vienna and Horn, Zwettl, Waidhofen, and Raabs an der Thaya. From these points you can get buses to other parts of the Waldviertel. An express bus service runs between Vienna and Heidenreich-stein via Waidhofen an der Thaya. In the Weinviertel, bus service is fairly good between Vienna and Laa an der Thaya and Poysdorf.

CAR RENTAL

Cars can be rented from all leading companies at the Vienna airport. In Baden, try Autoverleih Buchbinder. Also good is Autoverleih Schmidt. ➤ LOCAL AGENCIES: **Autoverleih Buchbinder** (☎ 02252/48693). **Autoverleih Schmidt** (☎ 0663/803289).

CAR TRAVEL

The autobahn A1 traverses the Vienna Woods in the west; the A2 autobahn runs through the edge of the Vienna Woods to the south. The A4 autobahn is a quick way to reach the Carnuntum region. The Waldviertel and Weinviertel are accessed by major highways but not autobahns.

Driving through these regions is by far the best way to see them, since you can wander the byways and stop whenever and wherever you like. To get to the Weinviertel and the Waldviertel, follow signs to Prague, taking Route E461 toward Mistelbach and Poysdorf if you want to go northeast. Or take the A22 toward Stockerau, changing to Route 303 or the E49 in the northwesterly direction of Horn and Retz. If you're going east to Carnuntum, follow signs to the A23 and the airport (Schwechat). And if you're going to Baden and the surrounding villages, take the A2 south in the direction of Graz, getting off in Baden and taking Route 210 west.

EMERGENCIES

For any medical emergency, dial 144.
➤ EMERGENCY SERVICES: **Ambulance** (☎ 144). **Fire** (☎ 122). **Police** (☎ 133).

TOURS

The Vienna Woods is one of the standard routes offered by the sight-seeing-bus tour operators in Vienna, and it usually includes a boat ride through the "underground sea" grotto near Mödling. These short tours give only a quick taste of the region; if you have more time, you'll want to investigate further. For details, check with your hotel or with Cityrama Sightseeing. Another good option is Vienna Sightseeing Tours.
➤ FEES AND SCHEDULES: **Cityrama Sightseeing** (☎ 01/534–130). **Vienna Sightseeing Tours** (☎ 01/712–4683–0).

TRAIN TRAVEL

The main east–west train line cuts through the Vienna Woods; the main north–south line out of Vienna traverses the eastern edge of the Vienna Woods. The main line to Prague and onward runs through the Waldviertel. Train service in the Weinviertel is regular to Mistelbach, irregular after that. The rail line east out of Vienna to the border town of Wolfstal cuts through the Carnuntum region. The line to the north of the Danube to Bratislava runs through the middle of the Marchfeld.

You can get to the Weinviertel from Vienna's Franz Josef Bahnhof, with buses running between the small villages. The main rail line from Vienna to Prague passes through the Waldviertel, making the region accessible by train, but you'll need a bus connection to reach the smaller towns.

The Schnellbahn No. 7 (suburban train) running from Wien-Mitte (Landstrasser Hauptstrasse) stops at Petronell, with service about once an hour. Carnuntum is about a 10-minute walk from the Petronell station. Trains go on to Hainburg, stopping at Bad Deutsch–Altenburg.

➤ Train Information: ÖBB—Österreichisches Bundesbahn (☎ 05/ 1717).

VISITOR INFORMATION
For information on Lower Austria, call the Niederösterreich Tourismus in Vienna. Local tourist offices in the Vienna Woods, which include ones in Baden, Gumpoldskirchen, Mödling, and Perchtoldsdorf, are generally open weekdays. The Waldviertel district has numerous tourist offices, including Gars am Kamp, Gmünd, Waidhofen an der Thaya, and Zwettl. The Weinviertel region also has several tourist centers: Gänserndorf, Laa an der Thaya, Poysdorf, and Retz.
➤ Tourist Information: **Baden** (✉ Brusattipl. 3, ☎ 02252/22600–600, FAX 02252/22600–622). **Gars am Kamp** (✉ Hauptpl. 83, ☎ 02985/2276, FAX 02985/3181). **Gänserndorf** (✉ Rathauspl. 1, ☎ 02282/2651–16, FAX 02282/2651–587, WEB www.gaenserndorf.at). **Gmünd** (✉ Weitraerstr. 44, ☎ 02852/53212, FAX 02852/54713). **Gumpoldskirchen** (✉ Kajetan Schellmanng. 27, ☎ 02252/63536, FAX 02252/63495). **Laa an der Thaya** (✉ Rathaus, ☎ 02522/2501–29, FAX 02522/2501–99). **March–Donauland** (✉ Hauptpl. 296, A–2404 Petronell/Carnuntum, ☎ 02163/3555, FAX 02163/3556). **Mödling** (✉ Elisabethstr. 2, ☎ 02236/26727, FAX 02236/26727–10, WEB www. moedling.at). **Niederösterreich Tourismus** (✉ ☎ 01/53610–6200, FAX 01/53610–6060). **Perchtoldsdorf** (✉ Marktpl. 11, ☎ 01/86683–34). **Poysdorf** (✉ Kolpingstr. 7, ☎ 02552/3515, FAX 02552/3715). **Retz** (✉ Hauptpl. 30, ☎ 02942/2700, WEB www.retz.at). **Waidhofen an der Thaya** (✉ Hauptstr. 25, ☎ 02842/51500, FAX 02842/51547). **Waldviertel** (✉ Hamerlingstr. 2, A–3910 Zwettl, ☎ 02822/54109–0, FAX 02822/ 54109–36). **Weinviertel** (✉ Kolpingstr. 7, A–2170 Poysdorf, ☎ 02552/ 3515, FAX 02552/3715). **Wienerwald** (✉ Hauptpl. 11, A–3002 Purkersdorf, ☎ 02231/62176, FAX 02231/65510). **Zwettl** (✉ Hauptpl. 4, ☎ 02822/503–129, FAX 02822/54100–36, WEB www.zwettl.gv.at).

4 THE DANUBE VALLEY

A tonic in any season, a trip up the Austrian Danube unveils a parade of storybook-worthy sights: fairy-tale castles-in-air, medieval villages, and baroque abbeys crowned with "candlesnuffer" cupolas. The Danube River itself is a marvel—on a summer day it even takes on the authentic shade of Johann Strauss blue. Along its banks you'll discover the beautiful Wachau Valley and the cheery town of Linz, whose pastry shops are said to produce the best Linzertortes around.

T O THE SIGHTSEER, a trip along the Austrian Danube unfolds rather like a treasured picture book. Roman ruins (some built by Emperor Claudius), remains of medieval castles-in-air, and baroque monasteries crowned with "candlesnuffer" cupolas perch precariously above the river, stimulating the imagination with their historic legends and myths. This is where Isa—cousin of the Lorelei—lured sailors to the shoals; where Richard the Lion-Hearted was locked in a dungeon for a spell; and where the Nibelungs—immortalized by Wagner— caroused operatically in battlemented forts. Once, Roman sailors used to throw coins into the perilous whirlpools around Grein in hopes of placating Danubius, the river's tutelary god. Today, thanks to the technology of modern dams, travelers have the luxury of seeing this part of Austria from the tame deck of a comfortable river steamer. In clement weather, the nine-hour trip upriver to Linz is highly rewarding. If you have more time to spare, the voyage onward to Passau may be less dramatic but gives more time to take in the picturesque vineyards and the castles perched like so many eagles' aeries on crags above bends in the river.

Updated by Bonnie Dodson

Even more of the region's attractions can be discovered if you travel by car or bus. You can explore plunging Gothic streets, climb Romanesque towers, and then linger over a glass of wine in a vaulted *Weinkeller* (wine restaurant, or cellar). River and countryside form an inspired unity here, with fortress-topped outcroppings giving way to broad pastures that swoop down to the very riverbanks. Many visitors classify this as one of Europe's great trips: you feel you can almost reach out and touch the passing towns and soak up the intimacy unique to this stretch of the valley. This chapter follows the course of the Danube upstream from Vienna as it winds through Lower Austria (Niederösterreich) and a bit of Upper Austria (Oberösterreich) to Linz, past monasteries and industrial towns, the riverside vineyards of the lower Weinviertel, and fragrant expanses of apricot and apple orchards.

Linz, Austria's third-largest city (and its most underrated), is a key industrial center. It's also a fine town for shopping; the stores are numerous and carry quality merchandise, often at more reasonable prices than in Vienna or the larger resorts. Concerts and operas performed at Linz's modern Brucknerhaus offer every bit as good listening as those staged in Vienna or Salzburg.

It is, however, the Danube itself, originating in Germany's Black Forest and emptying into the Black Sea, that is this chapter's focal point: the route that brought the Romans to the area and contributed to its development remains one of Europe's important waterways, with four national capitals on its banks—Vienna, Bratislava, Budapest, and Belgrade. It was not only the Romans who posited "Whoever controls the Danube controls all Europe." The Kuenringer (robber knights who built many of the hilltop castles) thrived by sacking the baggage caravans of the early Crusaders; later on, castles were financed through somewhat more commercial means—Frederick Barbarossa, leading his army downstream, had to pay a crossing toll at Mauthausen. Subsequently, cities sprang up to serve as ports for the salt, wood, ores, and other cargo transported on the river. Today, modern railroads and highways parallel most of the blue Danube's course.

This is a wonderful trip to take in early spring or in the fall after the grape harvest, when the vineyards turn reddish blue and a bracing chill settles over the Danube—the Empress Maria Theresa would plan her itinerary to arrive in Linz in May, just as the fruit trees were about to bloom. No matter when you come, be sure to try some of those fruits in a Linzertorte (a filling of brandy-flavored apricots, raspberries, or plums under a latticed pastry crust), a treat as satisfyingly rich and co-pious as the scenic wonders of the Danube Valley itself.

Pleasures and Pastimes

Abbeys

Although castles galore dot the area—ranging from crumbling moun-taintop ruins to wonderfully restored edifices replete with gargoyles—the real gems in these environs are the abbeys, majestic relics of an era when bishops were as wealthy and as influential as kings. The great-est are Melk, Klosterneuburg, Kremsmünster, St. Florian, and Göttweig, all of which have breathlessly imposing scope and elegance.

Bicycling

The trail alongside the Danube must be one of the great bicycle routes of the world. For much of the way (the exception being the Korneuburg–Krems stretch) you can bike along either side of the river. Some small hotels will even arrange to pick up you and your bike from the cycle path. You'll find bicycle rentals at most riverside towns and at rail stations. The terrain around Linz is relatively level, and within the city there are 89 km (55 mi) of marked cycle routes. In the areas of Eferding, St. Florian, through the Enns River valley, and around Steyr, the territory, with its gentle hills and special routes, is generally good for cycling.

Dining

Wherever possible, restaurants capitalize on the river view, and alfresco dining overlooking the Danube is one of the region's unsurpassed de-lights. Simple *Gasthäuser* are everywhere, but better dining is more often found in country inns. The cuisine is basically Austrian, although desserts are often brilliant local inventions, including the celebrated Linz-ertorte and Linzer Augen, jam-filled cookies with three "eyes" in the top cookie.

Wine is very much the thing in the lower part of the Weinviertel, par-ticularly on the north bank of the Danube in the Wachau region. Here you'll find many of Austria's best white wines, slightly dry and with a touch of fruity taste. In some of the smaller villages, you can sample the vintner's successes right in his cellars. Restaurants, from sophisti-cated and stylish to plain and homey, are often rated by their wine offerings as much as by their chef's creations.

CATEGORY	COST*
$$$$	over €20
$$$	€15–€20
$$	€10–€15
$	under €10

per person for a main course at dinner

Hiking

You could hardly ask for better hiking country: from the level ground of the Danube Valley hills rise on both sides, giving great views when you reach the upper levels. There are *Wanderwege* (marked hiking paths) virtually everywhere; local tourist offices have maps and route details. Around Linz you might retrace the route of the Linz–Budweis horse-drawn tramway, Continental Europe's first railway, or trek from one castle to another. You can hike in the Mühlviertel from Freistadt to Grein and even arrange to get your pack transferred from hotel to hotel.

Lodging

Accommodation options range from castle-hotels, where you'll be treated like royalty, to quieter but elegant, usually family-run country inns, to standard city hotels in Linz. The region is compact, so you can easily stay in one place and drive to a nearby locale to try a different restaurant. Rates understandably reflect the quality of service and amenities and usually include breakfast, which may range from a fast to a feast. Summers are never too hot, and it cools off delightfully at night, so most hotels don't need air-conditioning.

Some hotels offer half-board, with dinner in addition to buffet breakfast (although most $$$$ hotels will charge extra for breakfast). The half-board room rate is usually an extra €15–€30 per person. Occasionally quoted room rates for hotels already include half-board accommodations, though a "discounted" rate is usually offered if you prefer not to take the evening meal. Inquire when booking. Many hotels offer in-room phones and TV (some feature satellite or cable programming). Room rates include taxes and service, and usually breakfast—although you should always ask about the latter.

CATEGORY	COST*
$$$$	over €175
$$$	€125–€175
$$	€75–€125
$	under €75

All prices are for a standard double room in high season and include breakfast and dinner if half-board plan is offered.

Exploring the Danube Valley

Although much of the river is tightly wedged between steep hills rising from a narrow valley, the north and south banks of the Danube present differing vistas. The hills to the north are terraced so that the vineyards can catch the sun; to the south, the orchards, occasional meadows, and shadowed hills are just as visually appealing if less dramatic. Upstream from the Wachau region the valley broadens, giving way to farmlands and the industrial city of Linz straddling the river.

Great Itineraries

The Wachau section of the Danube Valley is a favorite outing for Viennese seeking a pleasant Sunday drive and a glass or two of good wine, but for foreign sojourners to treat the region this casually would cause them to miss some of Austria's greatest treasures. Once there, castles and abbeys beckon, picturesque villages beg to be explored, and the vine-covered wine gardens prove nearly irresistible.

Numbers in the text correspond to numbers in the margin and on the Lower Danube Valley, Upper Danube Valley, and Linz maps.

IF YOU HAVE 3 DAYS

Start out early from Vienna, planning for a stop to explore the medieval center of **Krems** ③. The Vinotek Und's eponymous Kloster will give you a good idea of the regions's best wines. From Krems, you can scoot across the river to visit Stift Göttweig at **Göttweig** ㊷ or you can leave it until the return trip. Along the northern, Krems side of the Danube, spend a night in a former cloister, now an elegant hotel, in 🏨 **Dürnstein** ⑤, in the shadow of the ruined castle where Richard the Lion-Hearted was imprisoned. An early-morning climb up to the ruin or a jog along the Danube shoreline will reward you with great views. Take time to explore Dürnstein before heading west along the Danube, crossing over to 🏨 **Melk** ㊵, rated one of the greatest abbeys in Europe.

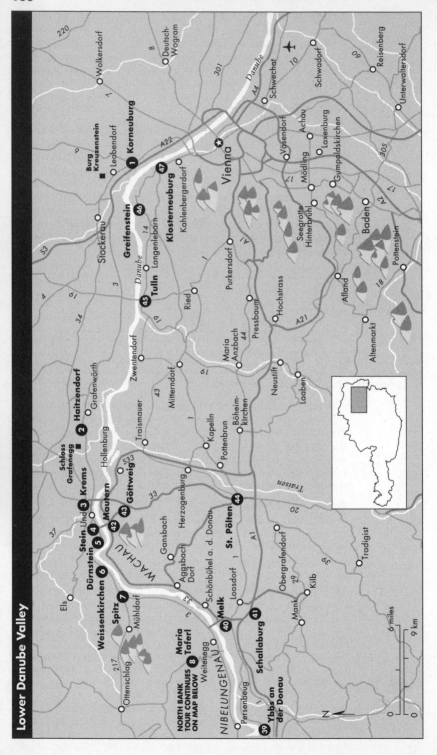

Lower Danube Valley

220

Wolkersdorf

Deutsch-Wagram

8

301

Danube

A4

Schwechat

Schwadorf

09

Reisenberg

Unterwaltersdorf

1

Korneuburg

Leobendorf

Burg Kreuzenstein

Stockerau

A22

1

47 Klosterneuburg

Kahlenbergerdorf

Vienna

Vösendorf

Achau

Laxenburg

Mödling

Gumpoldskirchen

17

A2

Baden

17

Pottenstein

Greifenstein **46**

14

Danube

Langenlebarn

Tulln **45**

19

Ried

1

A1

Purkersdorf

Hochstrass

Gießhübl

Seegrotte Hinterbrühl

Alland

18

Altenmarkt

S3

9

3

S33

Haitzendorf **2**

Grafenwörth

Gold

34

Hollenburg

Traismauer

Zwentendorf

43

Mitterndorf

44

Maria Anzbach

19

Pressbaum

A21

Neustift

Laaben

4

9

19

Schloss Grafenegg

Krems

Göttweig **3**

S33

Kapelln

Böheim-kirchen

Traisen

Pottenbrun

Herzogenburg

33

44

20

St. Pölten

Tradigist

37

Stein Und **3**

Dürnstein **4** **42**

5

Weissenkirchen **6**

Spitz **7**

Els

Mühldorf

WACHAU

Mautern

43

Gansbach

Aggsbach Dorf

Schönbühel a. d. Donau

Loosdorf

1

Melk

40

Schallaburg **41**

Obergrafendorf

29

Kilb

Mank

39

217

Oftenschlag

Maria Taferl **8**

Weitenegg

NIBELUNGENAU

NORTH BANK TOUR CONTINUES ON MAP BELOW

Persenbeug

Ybbs an der Donau **39**

N

6 miles

9 km

0

0

This is high baroque at its most glorious. Follow the river road back east to ⊡ **Göttweig** ㊸ and have lunch on the terrace at the abbey. The abbey's baroque chapel is breathtaking. Continuing eastward, follow the river as closely as possible (signs indicate Zwentendorf and Tulln) to **Klosterneuburg** ㊼, an imposing abbey that was once the seat of the powerful Babenburger kings, and onward to Vienna.

IF YOU HAVE 5 DAYS

A more leisurely schedule would follow the same basic route but permit a visit at either **Burg Kreuzenstein,** near **Korneuburg** ① or **Schloss Grafenegg,** near **Haitzendorf** ②, before stopping in **Krems** ③ and **Weinkolleg Kloster Und,** and overnighting in ⊡ **Dürnstein** ⑤. Spend the morning exploring Dürnstein, including the colorfully restored baroque Stiftskirche. In the afternoon, discover the wine villages of **Weissenkirchen** ⑥ and **Spitz** ⑦. Plan on two overnights in ⊡ **Linz** ⑪–㉖, to tour the city itself and to fit in a side trip across the river north to the walled city of **Freistadt** ㉗, and then southeast to **Kefermarkt** ㉘ to view the 42-ft-high intricately carved, wooden winged altar dating from 1497. On Day 4, take in **St. Florian** ㉜ and **Kremsmünster** ㉝, both southeast of Linz and south of the Danube; then proceed east to ⊡ **Melk** ㊵. The fifth day will be full, but start with the Melk abbey, then continue east to the abbey at **Göttweig** ㊸, and move onward to **Klosterneuburg** ㊼.

IF YOU HAVE 7 DAYS

Additional time allows for a far better acquaintance with this region. Located to the northwest of the Wachau, the Mühlviertel—the mill region north of Linz—turned out thousands of yards of linen from flax grown in the neighboring fields in the 19th century. You might follow the "textile trail," which takes you to museums tracing this bit of history. On your way along the northern Danube bank, visit the fascinating theater in **Grein** ⑨ and view the curious chancel in the church at **Baumgartenberg** ⑩. From ⊡ **Linz** ⑪–㉖, take trips upriver to **Eferding** ㉙, **Hartkirchen** ㉚, and **Aschach** ㉛, and south to ⊡ **Steyr** ㉟—you might also consider an overnight in this charming medieval city with its vast central square framed with pastel facades. From Steyr, attractive back roads will bring you to the town of **Waidhofen an der Ybbs** ㊳, parts of whose walls date from the Turkish invasion of the 1600s. Rather than trying to pack three abbeys into one day, spread out the pleasures, dining in **Mautern** ㊷ and overnighting in ⊡ **Tulln** ㊺ before heading on to **Klosterneuburg** ㊼ and, finally, returning to Vienna.

When to Tour the Danube Valley

The Wachau—both north and south Danube banks—is packed wall-to-wall with crowds in late April to early May, but of course there's a reason: apricot and apple trees are in glorious blossom, and bright orange poppies blanket the fields. Others prefer the chilly early- to mid-autumn days, when a blue haze curtains the vineyards. Throughout the region, winter is drab. Seasons notwithstanding, crowds jam the abbey at Melk; you're best off going first thing in the morning, before the tour buses arrive, or at midday, when the throngs have receded.

THE WACHAU: NORTH BANK OF THE DANUBE

Unquestionably the loveliest stretches of the Danube's Austrian course run from the outskirts of Vienna, through the narrow defiles of the Wachau to the Nibelungengau—the region where the mystical race of dwarfs, the Nibelungs, are supposed to have settled, at least for a while. If you're taking the tour by train, take Streetcar D to Vienna's

Upper Danube Valley

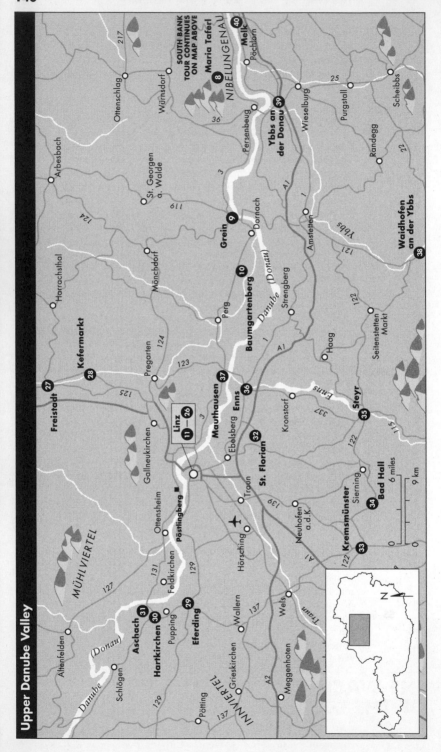

SOUTH BANK
TOUR CONTINUES
ON MAP ABOVE

NIBELUNGENAU

Maria Taferl **8**

Melk **40**
Pöchlarn

Ottenschlag

Würnsdorf

St. Georgen
a. Walde

Arbesbach

124

217

36

Persenbeug

Wieselburg

25

Purgstall

Scheibbs

Randegg

22

Ybbs an
der Donau **39**

3

Horrachsthal

Mönchdorf

611

Grein **9**

Dornach

Amstetten

1

Ybbs

Waidhofen
an der Ybbs **38**

Kefermarkt

124

Perg

Baumgartenberg **10**

Danube (Donau)

Strengberg

121

122

Freistadt **27**

Kefermarkt **28**

Pregarten

123

124

125

Mauthausen **37**

Enns **36**

A1

1

Haag

Seitenstetten
Markt

Gallneukirchen

Linz
11 — 26

Ebelsberg

St. Florian **32**

Kronstorf

Enns

Steyr **35**

337

122

115

Ottensheim

Pöstlingberg

3

Traun

139

Neuhofen
a.d.K.

Sierning

Bad Hall **34**

6 miles

9 km

Kremsmünster **33**

122

A1

MÜHLVIERTEL

127

Feldkirchen

131

129

Hörsching

Wallern

137

Wels

Traun

Aschach **31**

Harkirchen **30**

Pupping

Eferding **29**

Altenfelden

Schlögen

Donau

(Donau)

129

Pötting

137

Grieskirchen

INNVIERTEL

A2

Meggenhofen

N

Franz Josef Bahnhof, for your departure point. If you're driving, the trickiest part may be getting out of Vienna. Follow signs to Prague to get across the Danube, but once across, avoid the right-hand exit marked Prague—which leads to the autobahn—and continue ahead, following signs for Prager Strasse and turning left at the traffic light. Prager Strasse (Route 3) heads toward Langenzersdorf and Korneuburg.

Korneuburg

❶ *18 km (11¼ mi) northwest of Vienna.*

Until recently, Korneuburg was the center of Austrian shipbuilding, where river passenger ships, barges, and transfer cranes were built to order for Russia, among other customers. Stop for a look at the imposing neo-Gothic city hall (1864), which dominates the central square and towers over the town.

★ Atop a hillside 3 km (2 mi) beyond Korneuburg along Route 3 sits **Burg Kreuzenstein,** a castle with fairy-tale turrets and towers. Using old elements and Gothic and Romanesque bits and pieces brought to this site of a previously destroyed castle, Count Wilczek built Kreuzenstein between 1879 and 1908 to house his collection of late-Gothic art objects. You'll see rooms full of armaments, the festival and banquet halls, library, chapel, even the kitchens. It is possible to reach Kreuzenstein via the suburban train (S-Bahn) to Leobendorf, followed by a ¾-hour hike up to the castle. ✉ *Leobendorf bei Korneuburg,* ☎ 02262/66102. 🎟 €5.81. ☉ *Apr.–Oct., daily 10–4, guided tour on the hr.*

Haitzendorf

❷ *51 km (38½ mi) west of Korneuburg.*

The tiny farming community of Haitzendorf (to reach it from Korneuburg, take Route 3, 33 km/21 mi past Stockerau, then turn right at Graftenwörth) is landmarked by a church dating from the 14th century. In early summer, the vast strawberry fields surrounding the town yield a delicious harvest, which you can pick yourself.

★ A lush meadow and woodland area also surrounds the best-known site, the turreted **Schloss Grafenegg.** The moated Renaissance castle dating from 1533 was stormed by the Swedes in 1645 and rebuilt from 1840 to 1873 in the English Gothic Revival style. Greatly damaged during the 1945–55 occupation, it was extensively restored in the 1980s. Look for such fascinating details as the gargoyle waterspouts, and don't miss the chapel. ☎ 02735/2205–0, 🌐 www.grafenegg.com. 🎟 €5. ☉ *Mid-Apr.–Oct., Tues.–Sun. 10–5.*

Dining and Lodging

$$–$$$ ✕🏨 **Mörwald.** Just past the manicured lawns of Schloss Grafenegg,
★ this elegant tavern offers classic Austrian dishes with a fresh slant. The menu is seasonal, and may include Waldviertler duck with asparagus and *Schupfnudeln* (Austrian-style gnocchi), or grilled *Saiblingsfilet* (char) with tomato and zucchini risotto. Owner Toni Mörwald has his own winery, and a glass of his golden Gelbe Muskateller or sauvignon blanc provides the perfect accompaniment. In summer dine in the sunny garden under hunter-green umbrellas and linden trees. Mörwald also has a few attractive, comfortably furnished rooms upstairs that are in the $ category. ✉ *A–3485, Haitzendorf,* ☎ 02735/2616–0, 📠 02735/2616–60, 🌐 *www.moerwald.at. 9 rooms. Restaurant; no a/c. AE, DC, MC, V. Closed Mon. and Jan.–Feb.*

Krems

★ ❸   *12 km (7 mi) west of Haitzendorf, 80 km (50 mi) northwest of Vienna,*
        26 km (16¼ mi) north of St. Pölten.

Krems marks the beginning (when traveling upstream) of the Wachau
section of the Danube. The town is closely tied to Austrian history;
here the ruling Babenbergs set up a dukedom in 1120, and the earliest Austrian coin was struck here in 1130. In the Middle Ages, Krems
looked after the iron trade while neighboring Stein traded in salt and
wine, and over the years Krems became a center of culture and art.
Today the area is the heart of a thriving wine production, and narrow
streets, a Renaissance Rathaus, a parish church that is one of the oldest in Lower Austria, and a pedestrian zone make Krems an attractive
city to wander through.

Newly opened in 2001 (with Robert Crumb, the renowned comic-strip
artist, at the ribbon-cutting ceremony), the **Karikaturmuseum** (Caricature Museum) houses more than 250 works of cartoon art from the
20th century to the present, including a large collection of English-
language political satire and caricature. ⊠ *Steiner Landstr. 3a,* ☎
02732/908020, WEB *www.karikaturmuseum.* ⬚ €7.26. ⊗ *Daily 10–6.*

A 14th-century former Dominican cloister, farther along the street, now
serves as the **Weinstadt Museum Krems,** a wine museum that holds occasional tastings. ⊠ *Körnermarkt 14,* ☎ *02732/801–567,* WEB *www.*
weinstadtmuseum.at. ⬚ €3.60. ⊗ *Mar.–Nov., Tues.–Sun. 10–6.*

Dining and Lodging

$$$ ✕ **Zum Kaiser von Österreich.** At this landmark in the Old City dis-
trict, you'll find excellent regional cuisine along with an outstanding
wine selection (some of these vintages come from the backyard). The
inside rooms are bright and pleasant, and the outside tables in sum-
mer are even more inviting. Owner-chef Haidinger learned his skills
at Bacher, across the Danube in Mautern, so look for fish dishes along
with specialties such as potato soup and roast shoulder of lamb with
scalloped potatoes. ⊠ *Körnermarkt 9,* ☎ *02732/86001,* FAX *02732/*
86001–4. AE, DC, MC, V. Closed Mon. and last 2 wks in June.

$$ ✕🏨 **Am Förthof.** An inn has existed on the riverside site of this modern hotel for hundreds of years. The rooms are comfortable and bal-
conied; those in front have a view of the Danube and Göttweig Abbey
across the river (as well as the heavy traffic on the road directly below
your window). The dining room, and in summer the inviting courtyard garden, offer good regional cuisine; the chef's ambitions occasionally
surpass his achievements, but the sumptuous breakfasts are an assured culinary experience. ⊠ *Förthofer Donaulände 8, A–3500,* ☎
02732/83345 or 02732/81348, FAX *02732/83345–40. 16 rooms with*
bath. Restaurant, minibars, pool, sauna, Internet, no-smoking rooms;
no a/c. AE, DC, MC, V. Closed. Jan.–Feb.

$ ✕🏨 **Alte Post.** You're allowed to drive into the pedestrian zone to this
romantic house in the heart of the Old Town, next to the Steinener Tor
(Stone Gate). The rooms are in comfortable country style (full baths
are scarce), but the real draw here is dining on regional specialties or
sipping a glass of the local wine in the arcaded Renaissance courtyard.
The staff is friendly, and cyclists are welcome. ⊠ *Obere Landstr. 32,*
A–3500 Krems, ☎ *02732/82276–0,* FAX *02732/84396,* WEB *www.*
hotelaltepost-krems.at. 23 rooms, 9 with bath. Restaurant; no a/c. No
credit cards. Closed Jan.–mid-Mar.

En Route   Just outside the Krems Altstadt, in a beautifully restored Capuchin clois-
★   ter in the tiny town of Und, is the **Weinkolleg Kloster Und.** The building also houses the tourist office and a small wine museum, where you

can taste (and buy) more than 100 Austrian wines. ⊠ *Undstr. 6, Krems-Stein,* ☎ *02732/73073–0,* 𝖥𝖠𝖷 *02732/73074–85.* ≣ *€13 for unlimited tasting, €7 for 6 tastes, €1 and up per glass.* ☉ *Daily 11–7. Closed Dec. 23–mid-Mar.*

Stein

❹ *5 km (3 mi) east of Krems.*

A frozen-in-time hamlet that has, over the years, become virtually a suburb of the adjacent city of Krems, Stein is dotted with lovely 16th-century houses, many on the town's main street, Steinlanderstrasse. The 14th-century **Minoritenkirche,** just off the main street in the pedestrian zone, now serves as a museum with changing exhibits. A few steps beyond the Minoritenkirche, an imposing square Gothic tower identifies the 15th-century **St. Nicholas parish church,** whoše altar painting and ceiling frescoes were done by Kremser Schmidt. The upper part of the Gothic charnel house (1462), squeezed between the church and the hillside, has been converted to housing. Notice, too, the many architecturally interesting houses, among them the former tollhouse, which has rich Renaissance frescoes. Stein was the birthplace of Ludwig Köchel, the cataloger of Mozart's works, still referred to by their Köchel numbers.

Dürnstein

❺ *4 km (2½ mi) west of Stein, 90 km (56 mi) northwest of Vienna, 34 km (21¼ mi) northeast of Melk.*

If a beauty contest were held among the towns along the Wachau Danube, chances are Dürnstein would be the winner, hands down—as you'll see when you arrive along with droves of tourists. The town is small; leave the car at one end and walk the narrow streets. The trick is to overnight here—when the day-trippers depart, the storybook spell of the town returns. The top night to be here is the summer solstice, when hundreds of boats bearing torches and candles sail down the river here at twilight to honor the longest day of the year—a breathtaking sight best enjoyed from the town and hotel terraces over the Danube. In October or November, the grape harvest from the surrounding hills are gathered by volunteers from villages throughout the valley—locals garnish their front doors with straw wreaths if they can offer tastes of the new wine, as members of the local wine cooperative, the Winzergenossenschaft Wachau.

Set among terraced vineyards, the town is landmarked by its gloriously baroque **Stiftskirche,** dating from the early 1700s, which sits on a cliff overlooking the river—this cloister church's combination of luminous blue facade and stylish baroque tower is considered the most beautiful of its kind in Austria. After taking in the Stiftskirche, head up the hill, climbing 500 ft above the town, to the famous **Richard the Lion-Hearted Castle** where Leopold V held Richard the Lion-Hearted of England, captured on his way back home from the Crusades. In the tower of this castle, Richard was imprisoned (1192–93) until being located by Blondel, the faithful minnesinger. It's said that Blondel was able to find his imprisoned king when he heard his master's voice completing the verse of a song Blondel was singing aloud; Leopold turned his prisoner over to the emperor, Henry VI, who held him for months longer until the ransom was paid by Richard's mother, Eleanor of Aquitaine. The rather steep 30-minute climb to the ruins will earn you a breathtaking view up and down the Danube Valley and over the hills to the south.

Dining and Lodging

$$$ ✕ **Loibnerhof.** It's hard to imagine a more idyllic frame for a memorable
★   meal, especially if the weather is fine and tables are set out in the invit-
      ingly fragrant apple orchard. The kitchen offers inventive variations on
      regional themes: Wachauer fish soup, crispy roast duck, and various grilled
      fish or lamb specialties. The house is famous for its *Butterschnitzel*, an
      exquisite variation on the theme of ground meat (this one's panfried veal
      with a touch of pork). To reach Loibnerhof, look for the Unterloiben
      exit a mile east of Dürnstein. ⊠ *Unterloiben 7,* ☎ *02732/82890–0,* ⅁⅄
      02732/82890–3. DC, MC, V. Closed Mon.–Tues. and mid-Jan.–mid-Feb.

$$$$ ✕⊞ **Schloss Dürnstein.** Once the preserve of the princes of Starhem-
★   berg, this 17th-century early baroque castle, on a rocky terrace with
      exquisite views over the Danube, is one of the most famous hotels in
      Austria. Its classic elegance and comfort have been enjoyed by the ilk
      of King Juan Carlos of Spain, Prince Hirohito of Japan, Rudolf
      Nureyev, and a bevy of other celebs. The best guest rooms look onto
      the river, but all are elegantly decorated, some in grand baroque or
      French Empire style. Biedermeier armoires, ceramic stoves, and coun-
      try antiques grace public rooms. The restaurant is cozily nestled under
      coved ceilings—half-board is standard and a good value, but not re-
      quired. The kitchen matches the quality of the excellent wines from
      the area, and the tables set outside on the large stone balcony over-
      looking the river make dining here a memorable experience, with pike
      perch from the Danube, Waldviertler beef, or roast pheasant stuffed
      with apricots among the menu's delights. Even if you don't stay at
      the hotel, it's worth a stop for lunch or a leisurely afternoon Wachauer
      torte and coffee. ⊠ *A–3601,* ☎ *02711/212,* ⅁⅄ *02711/351,* ⓦⓔⓑ *www.
      schloss.at. 37 rooms. Restaurant, minibars, 2 pools (1 indoor), gym,
      sauna, bar, Internet; no a/c. AE, DC, MC, V. Closed Nov.–Mar.*

$$$ ✕⊞ **Richard Löwenherz.** The impressive, vaulted reception rooms of
★   this former convent are beautifully furnished with antiques, reflecting
      the personal warmth and care of the family management. The invit-
      ing open fire, stone floors, grandfather clock, and bowls of fresh roses
      make this one of the most romantic of the Romantik Hotels group.
      Though all rooms are spacious and comfortable, the balconied guest
      rooms in the newer part of the house have more modern furnishings.
      Wander through the grounds among the roses, oleanders, and fig trees,
      all set against the dramatic backdrop of 600-year-old stone walls. The
      outstanding restaurant is known for its local wines and regional spe-
      cialties, such as crispy duck with dumplings and red cabbage. In sum-
      mer, dine on the terrace under maple and chestnut trees, and admire
      the lushly wooded hills and languid Danube. ⊠ *A–3601,* ☎ *02711/
      222,* ⅁⅄ *02711/222–18,* ⓦⓔⓑ *www.loewenherz.cc. 38 rooms. Restau-
      rant, minibars, pool, bar; no a/c. AE, DC, MC, V. Closed Nov.–Mar.*

$$ ⊞ **Sänger Blondel.** Behind the sunny yellow facade is a friendly, tradi-
     tional hotel that has been in the same family since 1729. The simply fur-
     nished, country-style rooms are of medium size and have attractive
     paneling and antique decorations. The staff is particularly helpful and
     can suggest excursions in the area. The hotel's restaurant serves hearty
     Austrian food, and offers zither music on Thursday evenings. In summer,
     meals are served in the pretty courtyard under a huge chestnut tree. ⊠
     No. 64, A–3601, ☎ *02711/253–0,* ⅁⅄ *02711/253–7. 16 rooms. Restau-
     rant; no a/c. MC, V. Closed mid-Nov.–early-Mar. and 1 wk in early July.*

Weissenkirchen

❻ *5 km (3 mi) west of Dürnstein, 22 km (14 mi) northeast of Melk.*

Tucked among vineyards, just around a bend in the Danube, is Weis-
senkirchen, a picturesque town that was fortified against the Turks in

1531. A fire in 1793 laid waste to much of the town, but the 15th-century parish church of **Maria Himmelfahrt,** built on earlier foundations, largely survived. The south nave dates from 1300, the middle nave from 1439, the chapel from 1460. The Madonna on the triumphal arch goes back to the Danube school of about 1520; the baroque touches date from 1736; and to complete the picture, the rococo organ was installed in 1777.

On the Marktplatz, check out the 15th-century **Wachaumuseum** (Wachau museum), which has a charming Renaissance arcaded courtyard. The building now contains many paintings by Kremser Schmidt. ⊠ *Marktpl.,* ☎ *02715/2268.* 🎫 *€2.20.* ☉ *Apr.–Oct., Mon.–Sat. 10–1 and 4–6.*

Dining and Lodging

$$$ ✕ **Jamek.** The Jamek family's country inn on the Danube is well known throughout Austria, and though Josef and Edeltraud have handed over the management to their daughter, the quality remains the same. You dine either in one of several rooms tastefully decorated with 19th-century touches, or outdoors in the shady garden. Start with the vegetable torte gratin, then go on to lightly fried *Zanderfilet* (pike perch) on a bed of garlicky spinach, or pork cutlet with fried dumplings. Don't miss the house specialty, the surprisingly light chocolate cake with whipped cream and chocolate sauce. Wines are from the nearby family vineyards. Jamek is located just west of Weissenkirchen in Joching. ⊠ *Joching 45,* ☎ *02715/2235,* 𝐅𝐀𝐗 *02715/2235–22. Reservations essential. DC, MC, V.* ☉ *Lunch only Mon.–Thurs., Fri.–Sat. 11:30–11. Closed Sun. and mid-Dec.–mid-Feb.*

$$–$$$ ✕ **Gasthaus Erwin Schwarz.** Natives will tell you this is the best
★ restaurant in the area, offering delicious regional cooking in a former farmhouse and butcher shop. There is virtually nothing in the village of Nöhagen, which is 7 km (4½ mi) north of Weissenkirchen, yet people come from miles around to dine here. The restaurant raises its own animals, and all produce is grown on the premises. You're in luck if the succulent crispy duck with *Rotkraut* (red cabbage) and dumplings is on the menu. For information on the pleasant drive to this countryside spot, see the En Route below. ⊠ *Nöhagen 13,* ☎ *02717/8209. No credit cards. Closed Mon.–Tues., and Mon.–Thurs. Nov.–mid-Apr.*

$$$ 🏩 **Raffelsbergerhof.** This lovely Renaissance building (1574), once a shipmaster's house, has been tastefully converted into a hotel with every comfort. The friendly family management and peaceful surroundings make this a good lodging choice. Guest rooms, with beautiful original wooden floors, are furnished with charming country pieces, pretty fabrics, and fresh flowers, and most have sitting areas. Baths are modern and well equipped. The buffet breakfast is excellent. There's an extra charge of €5 for stays of only one night. ⊠ *A–3610,* ☎ *02715/2201,* 𝐅𝐀𝐗 *02715/2201–27. 15 rooms. Minibars, Internet; no a/c. MC, V. Closed Nov.–Easter.*

En Route One of the prettiest drives in the Wachau leads from Weissenkirchen to the renowned Gasthaus Erwin Schwarz in Nöhagen. From the main entrance to the town of Weissenkirchen, follow the road (Route L7094) north through the village, veering to your right and continuing upward. Soon the village gives way to a forested incline, after which you'll emerge into a verdant landscape of soft-contoured hills and vineyards and an occasional old farmhouse, passing through Weinzierl on Route L7090 on your way north to Nöhagen. From Nöhagen, take Route L7040 east toward Reichau, then to sleepy, rambling Senftenberg ("Mustard Mountain") with its romantic castle ruin perched above the town. A few kilometers east of Senftenberg, change to Route 218, going northeast to Langenlois. From here there will be signs to Vienna or back to Krems.

Spitz

❼ *5 km (3 mi) southwest of Weissenkirchen, 17 km (10½ mi) northeast of Melk.*

Picturesque Spitz is off the main road and set back from the Danube, sitting like a jewel in the surrounding vineyards and hills. One vineyard, the "Thousand Bucket Hill" is so called for the amount of wine it is said to produce in a good year. A number of interesting houses in Spitz go back to the 16th and 17th centuries. The late-Gothic 15th-century **parish church** contains Kremser Schmidt's altar painting of the martyrdom of St. Mauritius. Note the carved wood statues of Christ and the 12 apostles, dating from 1380, on the organ loft. Just beyond Spitz and above the road is the ruin of the **castle Hinterhaus,** to which you can climb.

Lodging

$–$$$ 🏰 **Burg Oberranna.** About 7 km (4½ mi) beyond the village of Mühldorf, directly west of Spitz, stands this well-preserved castle-hotel, surrounded by a double wall and dry moat. The original structure dates from the early 12th century, and the St. George chapel possibly even earlier. Some of the charming antiques-filled suites include a kitchenette and sitting room. This is a great base for hiking and also perfect for those who just want to get away. ⊠ *Ober-Ranna 1, A–3622 Mühldorf,* ☎ *02713/8221,* FAX *02713/8366. 5 rooms, 7 suites. Café, kitchenettes; no a/c. AE, V. Closed Nov.–Apr.*

En Route   The vistas are mainly of the other side of the Danube, looking across at Schönbühel and Melk, as you follow a back road via Jauerling and Maria Laach to Route 3 at Aggsbach. Shortly after Weitenegg the Wachau ends, and you come into the part of the Danube Valley known as the **Nibelungenau,** where the Nibelungs—who inspired the great saga *Das Nibelungenlied,* source of Wagner's *Ring*—are supposed to have settled for a spell. If you have always thought of the Nibelungs as a mythical race of dwarfs known only to old German legends and Wagner, dismiss that idea. The Nibelungs actually existed, though not as Wagner describes them, and this area was one of their stomping grounds.

Maria Taferl

❽ *49 km (31 mi) southwest of Spitz, 13 km (8 mi) west of Melk, 7½ km (4¾ mi) northeast of Persenbeug/Ybbs an der Donau.*

Crowning a hill on the north bank is the two-towered **Maria Taferl Basilica,** a pilgrimage church with a spectacular outlook. It's a bit touristy, but the church and the view are worth the side trip.

About 5 km (3 mi) up a back road is **Schloss Artstetten,** a massive square castle with four round defense towers at its corners. This is the burial place of Archduke Franz Ferdinand and his wife, Sophie, whose double assassination in 1914 in Sarajevo was one of the immediate causes of World War I. ⊠ *Artstetten,* ☎ *07413/8302,* WEB *www.schloss-artstetten. at.* 🎫 *€5.80.* ☉ *Apr.–Oct., daily 9–5:30.*

Lodging

$$–$$$ 🏰 **Krone–Kaiserhof.** Two hotels under the same family management share each other's luxurious facilities. The Krone looks out over the Danube Valley, and the Kaiserhof has views of the nearby baroque pilgrimage church. Both have rooms done a bit slickly in country style,

and the restaurants are popular. Cyclists staying overnight will be picked up free at Marbach or Klein Pöchlarn landing stations on the Danube. ☒ *A–3672,* ☎ *07413/6355–0,* ℻ *07413/6355–83,* ⓦₑᵦ *www. hotel-schachner.at. 72 rooms. 2 restaurants, café, miniature golf, 2 pools (1 indoor), sauna, waterskiing, bar; no a/c. AE, DC, MC, V. Closed Jan.–Feb., Nov.–Dec.*

Grein

❾ *32 km (20 mi) west of Maria Taferl, 20 km (12 mi) west of Persen- beug/Ybbs an der Donau.*

Set above the Danube, Grein is a picture-book town complete with castle. The river bend below, known for years as the "place where death resides," was one of the river's most hazardous stretches until the reefs were blasted away in the late 1700s. Take time to see the intimate rococo **Stadttheater** in the town hall, built in 1790 and still occasionally used for concerts or plays. ☒ *Rathaus,* ☎ *07268/7055,* ⓦₑᵦ *www.oberoesterreich.at/grein.* ☒ *€2.50.* ⊘ *Apr.–Oct., tours daily at 9, 11, 1:30, and 4.*

Baumgartenberg

❿ *11 km (7 mi) west of Grein, 17½ km (11 mi) east of Mauthausen.*

The small village of Baumgartenberg is worth a visit for its ornate baroque **parish church.** Note the lavish stucco-work and exquisitely carved 17th-century pews—and the unusual pulpit supported by a tree trunk. The church is the only reminder of a once-famed Cistercian abbey, founded in 1141 by Otto von Machland, that once stood here. Outside the town is the picturesque **castle of Klam,** which used to belong to Swedish playwright August Strindberg; it now contains a small museum.

LINZ

130 km (81¼ mi) east of Salzburg, 185 km (115½ mi) west of Vienna.

Linz, the capital of Upper Austria—set where the Traun River flows into the Danube—has a fascinating Old City core and an active cultural life. In 1832 it had a horse-drawn train to Czechoslovakia that functioned as the first rail line on the Continent. Once known as the "Rich Town of the River Markets" because of its importance as a medieval trading post, it is today the center of Austrian steel and chemical production, both started by the Germans in 1938. Linz is also a leader in computer technology—every September the city hosts the internationally renowned Ars Electronica Festival, designed to promote artists, scientists, and the latest technical gadgets. A city where past and present collide, Linz has Austria's largest medieval square and is now address to one of the country's most modern multipurpose halls, the Brucknerhaus, which is used for concerts and conventions.

With the city's modern economic success, Linz's attractions for tourists have been generally overlooked. Nevertheless, Linz can cast a spell, thanks to the beautiful old houses on the Hauptplatz; a baroque cathedral with twin towers and a fine organ over which composer Anton Bruckner once presided; and its "city mountain," the Pöstlingberg, with a unique railway line to the top. Extensive redevelopment, ongoing restoration, and the creation of traffic-free zones continue to transform Linz. The heart of the city—the Altstadt (Old City)—has been turned into a pedestrian zone; either leave your car at your hotel or use the

Linz

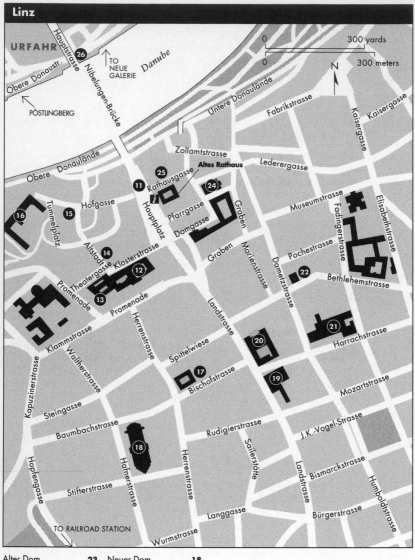

URFAHR

Hauptstrasse

26

Obere Donaustr.

TO NEUE GALERIE

Nibelungen-Brücke

Danube

0 ___ 300 yards

0 ___ 300 meters

N

PÖSTLINGBERG

Untere Donaulände

Fabrikstrasse

Kaisergasse

Kaisergasse

Obere Donaulände

Zollamtstrasse

Altes Rathaus

Rathausgasse

Lederergasse

25

11

i

24

Pfarrgasse

Museumstrasse

Fadingerstrasse

Elisabethstrasse

16

Tunnelplatz

15

Hofgasse

Hauptplatz

Domgasse

Graben

Pochestrasse

Altstadt

14

Theatergasse

Klosterstrasse

12

Graben

Graben

Marienstrasse

Dametzstrasse

22

Bethlehemstrasse

Promenade

13

Promenade

Herrenstrasse

Landstrasse

21

Harrachstrasse

Klammstrasse

Walherstrasse

Spittelwiese

20

Kapuzinerstrasse

Steingasse

17

Bischofstrasse

19

Mozartstrasse

Baumbachstrasse

Rudigierstrasse

J.K.-Vogel-Strasse

Hopfengasse

18

Hafnerstrasse

Herrenstrasse

Sailerstätte

Landstrasse

Bismarckstrasse

Humboldtstrasse

Stifterstrasse

TO RAILROAD STATION

Langgasse

Bürgerstrasse

Wurmstrasse

huge parking garage under the main square in the center of town. Distances are not great, and you can take in the highlights in the course of a two-hour walking tour.

A Good Walk

The center of the Old City is the Hauptplatz, with its pretty pastel town houses. Dominating the square is the **Pillar to the Holy Trinity** ⑪, erected in 1723 in gratitude for Linz's survival after threats of war, fire, and the dreaded plague. Head down Klostergasse to the **Minoritenkirche** ⑫, which is worth a stop to inspect the church's rococo interior before visiting the adjacent **Landhaus** ⑬, a rambling Renaissance building with two inner courtyards. In the arcaded courtyard is the Fountain of the Planets, with Jupiter as the crowning glory.

At No. 20 Klostergasse is the **Mozart Haus** ⑭, where Mozart stayed as a guest of the Count of Thun and composed the Linz Symphony in his spare time. Turn right at the corner onto Altstadtgasse. At No. 10 is the **Kremsmünstererhaus** ⑮, with its turrets and onion domes, where Emperor Friedrich III supposedly died in August 1493. Turn left from Altstadtgasse onto Hofgasse (one of the prettiest corners in the city), and climb the quaint narrow street that leads up to the Rudolfstor, one of the entrances to **Schlossmuseum Linz** (Linz Castle) ⑯. Since its early days as a prime fortress on the Danube, it has served as a hospital, army barracks, and even a prison, before becoming a provincial museum. The view from the castle promontory is one of the most impressive in Linz. Walk through the castle grounds to the end of the parking lot and turn left, going through the archway to the **Martinskirche,** one of the oldest churches in Austria, with its nave dating from 799.

Go back along Römerstrasse, which veers right down the hill. At the bottom it becomes the Promenade. Go straight on the Promenade, following it around to the left, then turn right onto Herrenstrasse. Where Bichofstrasse meets Herrenstrasse is the **Bischofshof** ⑰, which was built between 1721 and 1726 for the Kremsmünster monastery and is still the seat of the bishop of Linz. The west end of Bischofstrasse angles onto Baumbachstrasse, the site of the **Neuer Dom** ⑱, a massive 19th-century cathedral capable of holding 20,000 worshipers. Note the Linz Window, depicting the history of Linz, before heading back to Herrenstrasse.

Turn right and shortly afterward left onto Rudigierstrasse. Follow this to Landstrasse, where you'll make another left. Two baroque churches are located here, that of the **Karmelitenkloster** ⑲, modeled after St. Joseph's in Prague, and down the street the **Ursulinenkirche** ⑳. Between these two churches is Harrachstrasse, which holds another baroque gem, the **Heilegen Kreuz** ㉑, a seminary church, located shortly after you cross Dametzgasse. After inspecting the high altar by Hildebrandt, backtrack along Harrachstrasse to Dametzstrasse, where you'll turn right. At the corner of Dametzstrasse and Bethlehemstrasse is the **Nordico** ㉒, the city museum, which was originally an early 17th-century town house used by the Kremsmünster monastery for nearly 200 years as a Jesuit training center for young Scandinavian men. Now it houses a collection that ranges from archaeological finds to the Biedermeier era.

Keep going along Dametzstrasse until you reach the Graben, where you turn left and walk for a short while before turning right on Domgasse. Here is the **Alter Dom** ㉓, the old city cathedral where Anton Bruckner played the organ for 12 years, beginning in 1856. From here follow Domgasse around to the **Stadtpfarrkirche** ㉔, near the intersection to Kollegiumgasse. This was originally a Romanesque basilica before being rebuilt in the baroque style in the mid-17th century. In the entrance hall and approach to the tower staircase you can see Gothic cross-ribbing on the vaulted ceiling.

Go left from the church onto Kollegiumgasse, then left into the Pfarrplatz. From the northwest edge of the square, head down Rathausgasse to No. 5, the last stop on the walking tour, the **Kepler Haus** ㉕, home of astronomer Johannes Kepler. He lived here with his family for 10 years, beginning in 1612. More than 100 years later, Linz's first printing shop was established here. Rathausgasse leads into the Hauptplatz, the starting point of the tour.

TIMING

Of course the best time to visit Linz is between May and September, but fortunately the main tourist attractions are open year-round. Touring the Old City takes two to three hours, depending on how many of the sights you stop to visit. If you're pressed for time, head straight for Linz Castle. You'll pass through the loveliest parts of the city, and from the heights of the castle grounds you'll be able to enjoy stupendous views of the Danube.

Numbers in the text correspond to numbers in the margin and on the Linz map.

Sights to See

㉓ **Alter Dom** (Old Cathedral). Hidden away off the Graben, a narrow side street off the Taubenmarkt above the Hauptplatz, is this baroque gem (1669–78), whose striking feature is the single nave together with the side altars. Anton Bruckner was organist here from 1856 to 1868. ⊙ *Daily 7–7.*

Altes Rathaus (Old City Hall). Located at the lower end of the main square, the original 1513 building was mostly destroyed by fire and replaced in 1658–59. Its octagonal corner turret and lunar clock, as well as some vaulted rooms, remain, and you can detect traces of the original Renaissance structure on the Rathausgasse facade. The present exterior dates from 1824. The approach from Rathausgasse 5, opposite the Kepler Haus, leads through a fine, arcaded courtyard. On the facade here you'll spot portraits of Emperor Friedrich III, the mayors Hoffmandl and Prunner, the astronomer Johannes Kepler, and the composer Anton Bruckner. ⊠ *Hauptpl.*

㉖ **Ars Electronica Museum.** Just across the Nibelungen Bridge from the Hauptplatz, this futuristic museum allows visitors to try out all kinds of modern technology gadgets. Ever thought you could water a "telegarden" through the services of a robot? On the cyberdeck, you can be suspended aloft in a special flight suit and determine your own flight movements, and the virtual reality "cave" lets you experience, with the aid of 3-D glasses, the sensation of flying over Renaissance cathedrals, speeding through a labyrinth of underground tunnels, or entering a painting. Instructions for all exhibits are also in English. ⊠ *Hauptstr. 2,* ☎ *0732/72720,* WEB *www.aec.at.* ⊠ *€6.* ⊙ *Wed.–Sun. 10–6.*

⑰ **Bischofshof** (Bishop's Residence). At the intersection of Herrenstrasse and Bischofstrasse is this impressive mansion, which dates from 1721. Graced by a fine wrought-iron gateway, this remains the city's most important baroque secular building. The design is by Jakob Prandtauer, the architectural genius responsible for the glorious Melk and St. Florian abbeys.

㉑ **Heilegen Kreuz.** This former seminary church from 1723 is a beautiful yellow-and-white baroque treasure with an elliptical dome designed by Johann Lukas von Hildebrandt, who also designed its high altar. ⊠ *Harrachstr. 7,* ☎ *0732/771205.* ⊙ *Daily 7–5.*

⑲ **Karmelitenkloster.** This magnificent baroque church on Landstrasse was modeled on St. Joseph's in Prague. ✉ *Landstr. 33,* ☎ *0732/770217.* ⏱ *Daily 7–11:45 and 3–6:15.*

Ⓒ **Märchengrotte (Fairy-tale Grotto) Railroad.** Trains run through a colorful imaginary world at the top of the **Pöstlingberg.** It is entertaining for the rest of the family, as well as the kids. This may be closed for renovation in 2003. ☎ *0732/3400–7506,* WEB *www.linzag.at.* 🎫 *€4.* ⏱ *Apr. and mid-Sept.–mid–Nov., daily 10–5; May–mid-Sept., weekdays 10–6, weekends 10–4.*

㉕ **Kepler Haus.** The astronomer Johannes Kepler lived here from 1612 to 1622; Linz's first printing shop was established in this house in 1745. The interior is closed to the public. ✉ *Rathausgasse 5.*

⑮ **Kremsmünstererhaus.** Emperor Friedrich III is said to have died here in 1493. The building was done over in Renaissance style in 1578–80, and a story was added in 1616, with two turrets and onion domes. There's a memorial room to the emperor here; his heart is entombed in the Linz parish church, but the rest of him is in St. Stephen's cathedral in Vienna. The traditional rooms now house one of Linz's best restaurants, the Kremsmünsterer Stuben. ✉ *Altstadt 10.*

⑬ **Landhaus.** The early Renaissance monastery adjoining the **Minoritenkirche** is now the Landhaus, with its distinctive tower, seat of the provincial government. Look inside to see the arcaded courtyard with the Planet Fountain and the Hall of Stone on the first floor, above the barrel-vaulted hall on the ground floor; for a more extensive look at the interior, inquire at the local tourist office about their scheduled guided tours. The beautiful Renaissance doorway (1570) is of red marble. ✉ *Klosterstr. 7.*

⑫ **Minoritenkirche.** Situated at the end of Klosterstrasse, this church was once part of a monastery. The present building dates from 1752 to 1758 and has a delightful rococo interior with side altar paintings by Kremser Schmidt and a main altar by Bartolomeo Altomonte. ✉ *Klosterstr. 7,* ☎ *0732/7720–1364.* 🎫 *Free.* ⏱ *Nov.–Mar., daily 8–11* AM; *Apr.–Oct., daily 8–4.*

⑭ **Mozart Haus.** This three-story Renaissance town house, actually the Thun Palace, has a later baroque facade and portal. Mozart arrived here in 1783 with his wife to meet an especially impatient patron (Mozart was late by 14 days). Because the composer forgot to bring any symphonies along with him, he set about writing one and completed the sublime Linz Symphony in the space of four days. The palace now houses private apartments, but the courtyard can be viewed (entering from Altstadt 17, around the corner). ✉ *Klosterg. 20.*

Neue Galerie. Across the river in the Urfahr district is one of Austria's best modern art museums. The fine collection is well balanced, featuring mainly contemporary international and Austrian artists. Sometime in 2003 the museum will have a new name, Lentos, and will move to a new location south of the Danube on the riverbank, next to the Nibelungen Bridge; check with the tourist office for details. ✉ *Blütenstr. 15, Urfahr,* ☎ *0732/7070–3601,* WEB *www.neuegalerie.linz.at.* 🎫 *€5.* ⏱ *Mon.–Wed. and Fri. 10–6, Thurs. 10–10, Sat. 10–1.*

⑱ **Neuer Dom** (New Cathedral). In 1862 the bishop of Linz engaged one of the architects of Cologne cathedral to develop a design for a cathedral in neo-Gothic French-cathedral style and modestly ordered that its tower not be higher than that of St. Stephen's in Vienna. The result was the massive 400-ft tower, shorter than St. Stephen's by a scant

6½ ft. The cathedral contains gorgeous stained-glass windows. ⊠ *Herrenstr. 26,* ☎ *0732/777885.* 🎟 *Free.* ⊘ *Mon.–Sat. 7:30–7, Sun. 8–7.*

㉒ Nordico. At the corner of Dametzstrasse and Bethlehemstrasse, you'll find the city museum, dating from 1610. Its collection follows local history from pre-Roman times to the mid-1880s. ⊠ *Dametzstr. 23,* ☎ *0732/7070–1912.* 🎟 *€3.63.* ⊘ *Weekdays 9–6, weekends 2–5.*

⑪ Pillar to the Holy Trinity. One of the symbols of Linz is the 65-ft baroque column in the center of the Hauptplatz square. Completed in 1723 of white Salzburg marble, the memorial offers thanks by an earthly trinity—the provincial estates, city council, and local citizenry—for deliverance from the threats of war (1704), fire (1712), and plague (1713). From March through October there's a flea market here each Saturday (except holidays), from 7 to 2.

Pöstlingberg. With a glass of chilled white wine in hand, drink in the grand vista over Linz and the Danube from one of the flower-hung restaurants located at the top of Linz's "city mountain." At the summit is the **Church of Sieben Schmerzen Mariens,** an immense and splendidly opulent twin-towered baroque pilgrimage church (1748), visible for miles as a Linz landmark. Also on the mountain is the **Märchengrotte (Fairy-tale Grotto) Railroad.** An electric railway, the **Pöstlingbergbahn,** provides a scenic ride up the mountain. To reach the base station for the railway, take Streetcar 3 across the river to Urfahr, Linz's left bank. Note the railway's unusual switches, necessary because the car-wheel flanges ride the outside of the rails rather than the (usual) inside. When the line was built in 1898, it boasted the steepest incline of any noncog railway in Europe. In summer, the old open-bench cars are used. On a clear day the view at the top takes in a good deal of Upper Austria south of the Danube, with a long chain of the Austrian Alps visible on the horizon. ☎ *0732/7801–7002,* 🌐 *www.linzag.at.* 🎟 *Round-trip €3.20, combined ticket with Tram 3 €5 (combination tickets available only at Tourist Information).* ⊘ *Daily, every 20 min (Sun. morning every 30 min) 5:40 AM–8:20 PM.*

★ ⑯ Schlossmuseum Linz (Linz Castle). The massive four-story building on Tummelplatz was rebuilt by Friedrich III around 1477, literally on top of a castle that dated from 799. Note the **Friedrichstor** (the Friedrich Gate), with the same *A.E.I.O.U.* monogram also found in Krems, and the two interior courtyards. This is widely known as one of the best provincial museums in the country. The interior of the castle is well worth a visit, with a 17th-century inlaid walnut portal from Schloss Hartheim, historical musical instruments including Beethoven's *Hammerklavier* (fortepiano), re-creations of rooms from 19th-century Austrian homes, fine 19th-century portraits and landscapes by Dutch and Austrian artists, as well as weaponry, coins, and ceramics. ⊠ *Tummelpl. 10,* ☎ *0732/774482–84,* 🌐 *www.landesgalerie.at.* 🎟 *€5.10.* ⊘ *Tues.–Fri. 9–6, weekends 10–5.*

㉔ Stadtpfarrkirche. This city parish church dates from 1286 and was rebuilt in baroque style in 1648. The tomb in the right wall of the chancel contains Friedrich III's heart. The ceiling frescoes are by Altomonte, and the figure of Johann Nepomuk (a local saint) in the chancel is by Georg Raphael Donner, with grand decoration supplied by the master designer Hildebrandt. ⊠ *Pfarrpl. 4,* ☎ *0732/7761–200.* ⊘ *Daily 8–6.*

⑳ Ursulinenkirche. The towers at this baroque church are one of the identifying symbols of Linz. Inside is a blaze of gold and crystal ornamentation. Note the Madonna figure wearing a hooded Carmelite cloak with huge pockets, used to collect alms for the poor. *Landstr. 31,* ☎ *0732/7610–3151.* ⊘ *Daily 7:30–6.*

Dining and Lodging

$$$$ ✕ **Kremsmünsterer Stuben.** In a historic town house in the heart of the Altstadt you'll find an attractive wood-paneled restaurant that loses some of its time-burnished appeal by its clinical, "operation-room" lighting. The food, however, leaves nothing to be desired, and portions are plentiful. The menu is imaginative, with delicious seasonal items to choose from, such as radicchio cream soup, artichoke lasagne with sage pesto, and sea bream stuffed with pumpkin. ✉ *Altstadt 10,* ☎ *0732/782111,* ℻ *0732/7821112. Reservations essential. AE, DC, MC, V. Closed Sun., 2 wks in Jan., and 2 wks in Aug. No lunch Sat. and Mon.*

$$$ ✕ **Donautal.** Fish is the main event at this quaint old house perched above the Danube—even the warm, fresh rolls come in a fish shape. Green-striped banquette tables offer gorgeous views of the river, and there's a terrace for dining in fine weather. The menu offers such choices as grilled *Saibling* (char) served simply with lemon and capers, or crispy Zanderfilet with gnocchi in a paprika sauce. You can also get fried chicken (*Backhendl*), or vegetarian pasta. Desserts are delicious here, from the simple vanilla ice-cream sundae with chocolate sauce to caramel cannelloni stuffed with praline ice cream. Donautal is about five minutes from the Alstadt by taxi. It's also possible to walk, though it could be hazardous at night because of traffic. ✉ *Obere Donaulände 105,* ☎ *0732/795566,* ℻ *07327/795566–7. Reservations essential. AE, DC, MC, V (credit cards not allowed on Sun. or holidays). Closed Sun. night, Mon.*

$$ ✕ **Goldenes Schiff.** Four generations of the Rauscher family have served traditional Austrian dishes in this rambling yellow house across the river (and about a 10-minute walk) from the Altstadt. The rustic, cozy rooms have stone walls and vaulted ceilings, and the old-fashioned kitchen proudly showcases a stone oven, which turns out delectable *Schweinsbraten* (pork sausages) and roast duck. Vegetarian dishes are always offered. Be sure to finish with homemade apple strudel. It's particularly charming to eat here in nice weather, when tables are set out by the river with stunning views of the Altstadt. ✉ *Ottensheimerstr. 74,* ☎ *0732/739879,* ℻ *0732/715420. AE, DC, MC, V. Closed Mon.– Tues. and 2 wks around late Sept. or early Oct.*

$$ ✕ **Verdi Einkehr.** The trendy, less pricey bistro (Austrian-style) ac-
★ companiment to Verdi—Linz's favored dinner restaurant—Verdi Einkehr shares the same house and kitchen. The rooms are done in rustic chic, with stone fireplaces, chintz-covered chairs, and lots of polished wood. There is also a terrace for summer dining. Choose from guinea fowl with Venetian-style gnocchi in a balsamic sauce, crispy strips of chicken breast in a wild mushroom sauce with butter noodles, or a *Saiblingschnitzel* (golden-fried char), served with lime radicchio risotto. If you don't have a car, you'll need a taxi to get here. It's set in Lichtenberg, about 3 km (2 mi) north of the center, off Leonfelderstrasse. You must specify that you want to be seated in the Einkehr. ✉ *Pachmayrstr. 137,* ☎ *0732/733005,* ℻ *07327/733005–4. Reservations essential. DC, MC, V. Closed Sun., no lunch.*

$ ✕ **Traxlmayr.** Proud with the patina of age, this is one of Austria's great
★ old-tradition coffeehouses. You can linger all day over a single cup of coffee, reading the papers (*Herald Tribune* included) in their bentwood holders, and then have a light meal. In winter it's extremely smoky, but in summer you can sit outside on the terrace and watch passersby. Ask for the specialty, Linzertorte (almond cake with jam), with your coffee. ✉ *Promenade 16,* ☎ *0732/773353. No credit cards. Closed Sun.*

$$$ ⊡ **Arcotel Nike.** Next door to the Brucknerhaus concert hall, the Arcotel Nike is a good 10-minute walk from the Altstadt. Rooms in this modern high-rise on the banks of the Danube are smallish, and though lacking charm, they're comfortable and well equipped. Ask for a river view. There's also a generous breakfast buffet. ⊠ *Untere Donaulände 9, A–4020,* ☎ *0732/76260,* FAX *0732/76262,* WEB *www.arcotel.at. 176 rooms. 2 restaurants, minibars, indoor pool, gym, 2 bars, Internet, meeting rooms, parking (fee). AE, DC, MC, V.*

$$ ⊡ **Drei Mohren.** Facing the Landhaus Park and in the very heart of the
★ city center, this pretty, family-owned hotel occupies three 16th-century buildings. Some rooms are beautifully decorated in regal blue and gold with large, state-of-the art baths, whereas others are smaller and more modestly furnished. The elegant drawing room offers card tables, wing-back chairs, and a fireplace. Breakfast is substantial, and there is 24-hour room service for drinks. There is limited space for free parking. ⊠ *Promenade 17, A–4020,* ☎ *0732/772626–0,* FAX *0732/ 772626–6. 22 rooms. Bar; no a/c. AE, DC, MC, V.*

$$ ⊡ **Wolfinger.** A 500-year-old former nunnery, the centrally located Wolfinger has been a hostelry since the late 1700s. Some rooms have real charm, with vaulted ceilings and antique headboards; others are furnished with a mixture of kitsch and modern pieces. Those in the front are less quiet but offer a view of city activities. Baths are satisfactory. Rooms without bath are in the $ category. ⊠ *Hauptpl. 19, A–4020,* ☎ *0732/773291–0,* FAX *0732/773291–55,* WEB *www.austria-classic-hotels.at/wolfinger. 45 rooms, 4 without bath. Parking (fee); no a/c. AE, DC, MC, V.*

$ ⊡ **Zum Schwarzen Bären.** The "Black Bear" is a fine, traditional house in the center of the Old City, a block from the pedestrian zone, and incidentally was the birthplace of the renowned tenor Richard Tauber (1891–1948). Rooms on the first floor are the best, with imaginative brick-lined baths. Upper-floor rooms are plainer, but plans are under way for more renovation. ⊠ *Herrenstr. 9–11, A–4020,* ☎ *0732/ 772477–0,* FAX *0732/772477–47. 35 rooms with bath. Restaurant, bar, parking (fee); no a/c. MC, V.*

Nightlife and the Arts

Linz is far livelier than even most Austrians realize. The local population is friendlier than those of either Vienna or Salzburg, and much less cliquish. Nor has Linz lagged behind other Austrian cities in developing its own hot section, known as the Bermuda Triangle. Around the narrow streets of the Old City (Klosterstrasse, Altstadt, Hofgasse) are dozens of fascinating small bars and lounges; as you explore, you'll probably meet some Linzers who can direct you to the current "in" location.

THE ARTS

The **Linz opera company** is talented and often willing to mount venturesome works and productions. Most performances are in the Landestheater, with some in the Brucknerhaus.

The tourist office's monthly booklet "Was ist los in Linz und Oberösterreich" ("What's On in Linz and Upper Austria") will give you details of theater and concerts. Two **ticket agencies** are Linzer Kartenbüro (⊠ Herrenstr. 4, ☎ 0732/778800) and **Kartenbüro Pirngruber** (⊠ Landstr. 34, ☎ 0732/772833, FAX 0732/772833–76).

Concerts and recitals are held in the **Brucknerhaus,** the modern hall on the bank of the Danube. From mid-September to early October, it's the center of the International Bruckner Festival. In mid-June the hall hosts the biggest multimedia event in the area, the Ars Electronica, a musical and laser-show spectacle. ⊠ *Untere Donaulände 7,* ☎ *0732/775230,* FAX *0732/7612–201.* ☉ *Box office weekdays 9–6, Sat. 9–noon.*

A good starting point, where both the young and the older will feel comfortable, is the bar **S'Linzerl** (⊠ Hofberg 5), which is open Monday–Saturday 9 PM–3 AM.

The Linz **casino,** with roulette, blackjack, poker, and slot machines, is in the Hotel Schillerpark; the casino complex includes a bar and the Rouge et Noir restaurant. A passport is required for admission. ⊠ *Rainerstr. 2–4,* ☎ *0732/654487–0,* FAX *0732/654487–24.* ▣ €*18.89 (includes 5* €*3.63 tokens).* ☉ *Daily noon–3* AM.

For the young crowd there are several choices for popular late-night clubs. One of the most frequented is **Sassi** (⊠ Spittelwiese 8, ☎ 0732/787850), in the Taubenmarkt Arkade shopping mall on the pedestrian Landstrasse, which is noted for, set behind the bar, its pyramid of champagne bottles that can be reached only by stepladder. Open Monday to Thursday 10 AM to 2 AM, Saturday 9 AM to 4 AM, and Sunday 1 PM to 1 AM, the modern bar also offers soup, sandwiches, and light pasta dishes. **Josef Stadtbräu** (⊠ Landstr. 49, ☎ 0732/773165) is another hopping establishment with its own home-brewed beer on tap, light snacks, or hearty regional dishes, open every day from 10 AM until the wee hours.

Shopping

Linz is a good place to shop; prices are generally lower than those in resorts and the larger cities, and selections are varied. The major shops are found in the main square and the adjoining side streets, in the old quarter to the west of the main square, in the pedestrian zone of the Landstrasse and its side streets, and in the Hauptstrasse of Urfahr, over the Nibelungen Bridge across the Danube.

For local handmade goods and good-quality souvenirs, try **O. Ö. Heimatwerk** (⊠ Landstr. 31, ☎ 0732/773376–0), where you'll find silver, pewter, ceramics, fabrics, and some clothing. Everything from clothing to china is sold at the **Flea Market,** open March–mid-November, Saturday 7–2, on the Hauptplatz (main square). Check with the tourist office about other flea markets. At the state-run **Dorotheum auction house** (⊠ Fabrikstr. 26, ☎ 0732/773132–0), auctions take place the first Wednesday of the month at 2 PM. The Dorotheum is open weekdays from 9 to 5.

For antiques, head for the Old City and these shops on the side streets around the main square. **Günther Begsteiger** (⊠ Bischofstr. 15, ☎ 0732/779127) sells gorgeous old jewelry and furniture. **Otto Buchinger** (⊠ Bethlehemstr. 5, ☎ 0732/770117) is the place to go for modern graphic drawings and 19th-century furniture and artworks. **Richard Kirchmayr** (⊠ Bischofstr. 3a, ☎ 0732/797711) has a tempting collection of paintings and furniture. **Kunst-Haus Dr. Pastl** (⊠ Wischerstr. 26, ☎ 0699/117221–44) is known throughout Linz for the great selection of sculpture and 18th-century paintings, ceramics, and porcelain.

There are two superior places in the city center to shop for elegant jewelry at reasonable prices: **Lucas Drobny** (⊠ Herrenstr. 20, ☎ 0732/779218) and **Wild** (⊠ Landstr. 49, ☎ 0732/774105–0). For nice, less costly jewelry and souvenirs, go to **Egger Peter** (⊠ Graben 24, ☎ 0732/774670).

Outdoor Activities and Sports

Buy tickets for sports events at **Kartenbüro Pirngruber** (⊠ Landstr. 34, ☎ 0732/772833, FAX 0732/772833–76). The office is open weekdays 9–6 and Saturday 9–5.

BICYCLING

Cyclists appreciate the relatively level terrain around Linz, and within the city there are 89 km (55 mi) of marked cycle routes. Get the brochure *Cycling in Linz* from the tourist office. You can rent a bike through **LILO Bahnhof** (⊠ Coulinstr. 30, ☎ 0732/600703).

GOLF

Fairly close to Linz is the 9-hole, par-72 **Golfclub St. Oswald-Freistadt** (⊠ Promenade 22, St. Oswald, ☎ 07945/7938). The 18-hole, par-72 **Böhmerwald Golfpark** (⊠ Seitelschlag 50, Raiffeisenpl. 1, Ulrichsberg, ☎ 07288/8200) is near Linz. East of Linz is the relatively new 18-hole, par-71 **Linzer Golf Club Mühlviertel** (⊠ Am Luftenberg 1a, Luftenberg, ☎ 07237/3893), playable April–November.

ICE-SKATING

Linz is an ice-skating city. From late October to early March there's outdoor skating at the city rink. Check with Tourist Information for the times the rink is open. Skating is also available late September to April at the adjoining indoor sports complex, the **Eishalle,** Wednesday 9–noon, Saturday 2–5 and 6–9, and Sunday 9–noon, 2–5, and 6–9. Hockey and skating competitions are also held in the Eishalle. ⊠ *Untere Donaulände 11,* ☎ 0732/776508–31.

SOCCER

Soccer matches are played in Linz in the **Stadion** (⊠ Roseggerstr. 41, corner of Ziegeleistr., ☎ 0732/657311).

TENNIS

Tennis matches and other sports events are held at the **Stadthalle** (☎ 0732/660680).

WATER SPORTS

The Danube is not suitable for swimming, but here are alternatives. The closest swimming is at **Pleschinger Lake**; to get there, take Tram 1, 2, or 3 to Reindlstrasse and then Bus 33 to the lake. This is a pleasant spot for family swimming, although it tends to be crowded on sunny, warm weekends. The **Kral Waterskiing School** (⊠ Talg. 14, at Ottensheimerstr., ☎ 0732/731494) offers waterskiing and other water sports.

EXCURSIONS FROM LINZ

Many travelers find Linz the most practical point of departure for visits to the Mühlviertel and the Gothic and baroque sights found in the towns of St. Florian, Kremsmünster, and Steyr, although Steyr certainly merits an overnight itself. North of Linz toward Freistadt and the Czech border, the Mühlviertel (a "mill district" now in the agricultural, not industrial, sense) is made up of meadows and gentle wooded hills interspersed with towns whose appearance has changed little since the Middle Ages. To the west of Linz, south of the Danube, lies the Innviertel, named for the Inn River (which forms the border with Germany before it joins the Danube), a region of broad fields and meadows, and enormous woodland tracts, ideal for cycling, hiking, and riding. To the south, the hilly landscape introduces the foothills of the Austrian Alps.

Freistadt

★ ㉗ *41 km (26 mi) northeast of Linz.*

Located in the eastern part of the Mühlviertel, Freistadt developed as a border defense city on the salt route into Bohemia (now the Czech Republic), which accounts for the wall, towers, and gates, still wonderfully preserved today. To get to Freistadt, cross the Danube to Linz-Urfahr and turn right onto Freistädter Strasse (Route 125/E55).

A walk around the wall gives an impression of how a city in the Middle Ages was conceived and defended; it takes about a half hour. Look at the late-Gothic **Linzertor** (the Linz Gate), with its steep, wedge-shape roof, and the **Böhmertor,** on the opposite wall, leading to the Czech Republic. The city's **central square,** aglow with pastel facades, is virtually the same as it was 400 years ago; only the parked cars belie the picture of antiquity. Pause for a local beer; the town's first brewery dates from 1573. The 15th-century parish church of **St. Catherine's** was redone in baroque style in the 17th century but retains its slender tower, whose unusual balconies have railings on all four sides.

The late-Gothic castle to the northeast of the square now houses the **Mühlviertel Heimathaus** (district museum); the display of painted glass in the chapel and the hand tools in the 163-ft tower are especially interesting. ☎ 07942/72274. ◪ €2.40. ☉ *Daily 9–noon and 2–5.*

Centering on Freistadt is a historical road called the **Museumstrasse,** which takes you to points of interest from the glory days of the Mühlviertel, when this area was famous for its mills. Among places to stop and visit are historical mills, a former dye-works museum, and a leather-working museum. Contact the Mühlviertel Tourist Office in Linz (☞ Visitor Information *in* Danube Valley A to Z) for information.

A fun excursion for kids and grown-ups alike is the **Pferdeeisenbahn,** which is the Austrian version of an old stagecoach ride. You'll travel by horse-drawn carriage along the back roads, stopping for meals and at a hotel for the night. Contact the Mühlviertel Tourist Office in Linz (☞ Visitor Information *in* Danube Valley A to Z) for information.

Dining and Lodging

$ ✕🛏 **Zum Goldenen Adler.** Here you'll be in another 600-year-old house; it has been run by the same family since 1807, so tradition runs strong. The medium-size rooms are modern yet full of country charm; hotel service is exceptionally accommodating. The garden contains a piece of the old city wall as background and is a delightful oasis. The restaurant is known for regional specialties such as *Böhmisches Bierfleisch* (beef cooked in beer). The desserts are outstanding. ✉ *Salzg. 1, A–4240,* ☎ *07942/72112-0,* 🖷 *07942/72112-44,* 🌐 *www.hotels-freistadt.at. 37 rooms. Restaurant, pool, gym, sauna, bar; no a/c. AE, DC, MC, V.*

Kefermarkt

㉘ *9 km (5½ mi) south of Freistadt.*

From Freistadt, you can get to Kefermarkt either via marked back roads or by turning east off Route 125/E14. Both towns can be visited on a loop excursion from Linz. The late-Gothic **Church of St. Wolfgang** has one of Austria's great art treasures, a 42-ft-high winged altar intricately carved from linden wood, commissioned by Christoph von Zelking and completed in 1497. So masterly is the carving that it has been ascribed to famous 15th-century sculptors Veit Stoss and Michael Pacher, but most historians now attribute it to Jürg Huber and Martin Kriechbaum. Some figures, such as the St. Christopher, are true masterpieces of northern Renaissance sculpture. The church also has some impressive 16th-century frescoes.

Eferding

㉙ *25 km (16 mi) west of Linz.*

Eferding, a centuries-old community with an attractive town square, lies west of Linz. You can easily drive the 25 km (16 mi) on Route 129, but the more adventurous method is via the **LILO** (Linzer Lokalbahn) interurban railway from Coulinstrasse 30 (☎ 0732/654376), near the main rail station.

In Eferding, the double door in the south wall of the 15th-century **Church of St. Hippolyte** is a gem of late-Gothic stonecutting, with the Madonna and Child above flanked by Saints Hippolyte and Agyd. Inside, note the Gothic altar with its five reliefs and the statues of Saints Wolfgang and Martin. Visit the **Spitalskirche** (built in 1325) and note the Gothic frescoes in the Magdalen chapel, which date from about 1430.

Dining and Lodging

$$$ ✕ **Dannerbauer.** Two kilometers (1 mi) north of Eferding, on the road
★   to Aschach and directly on the Danube, is one of the area's best restaurants. It serves many species of fish—some you probably never heard of—to your taste: poached, grilled, broiled, or fried. Many of the fish come from the river; some are raised in the house ponds, to ensure freshness. There are meat dishes, too, and game in season, and the soups (try the nettle soup) are excellent. The place has a pleasant outlook with lots of windows. ⊠ *Brandstatt bei Eferding,* ☎ *07272/2471. AE, DC. Closed Mon.–Tues., Mar.–Apr., and early Nov.–early Feb.*

$ ⌂ **Zum Goldenen Kreuz.** The golden facade indicates a typical country-style hotel, simple and with the appealing charm of a family-run establishment. You'll sleep under fluffy feather-bed coverlets. The restaurant is known for its good regional cuisine, and there are occasional specialty weeks. ⊠ *Schmiedstr. 29, A–4070,* ☎ *07272/ 4247–0,* ☒ *07272/4249. 21 rooms. Restaurant; no a/c. AE, DC, MC. Closed Christmas wk.*

Hartkirchen

㉚ *12 km (7 mi) north of Eferding, 26 km (16¼ mi) northwest of Linz.*

The **parish church** at Hartkirchen is worth a visit to see fine baroque wall and ceiling frescoes, dated 1750, that create the illusion of space and depth. To reach Hartkirchen, take Route 130 north from Eferding to Pupping and continue 3 km (2 mi).

Aschach

㉛ *2 km (1 mi) north of Hartkirchen, 21 km (13¼ mi) northwest of Linz.*

Aschach, a small village that was once a river toll station, is the birthplace of Leonard Paminger, one of the most noted 16th-century Austrian composers. Still well preserved are several gabled-roof burghers' houses, a castle, and a late-Gothic church. Less intact is the castle, now semi-ruined, that once belonged to the counts of Harrach, located near the town.

Lodging

$–$$ ⌂ **Faust Schlössl.** As you enter Aschach you're struck by the glimpse
★   of this golden castle perched high on a hill on the opposite bank of the Danube. Rumor has it that the place is haunted by the Devil, who is said to have built it in a single night for Dr. Faustus. Nowadays the converted castle offers pleasantly decorated rooms with comfortable chairs, good reading lamps, well-designed bathrooms, and great views. Its popular restaurant offers good, traditional Austrian cooking, and in nice weather tables are set on the terrace facing stunning views of the river. This is an ideal place to stop if you're biking between Passau and Vienna. ⊠ *Oberlandshaag 2, A–4082 Feldkirchen,* ☎ *07233/ 7402–0,* ☒ *07233/7402–40. 15 rooms. Restaurant, pool, fishing, bicycles; no a/c. AE, DC, MC, V. Closed Jan.*

St. Florian

★ ② *13 km (8 mi) southeast of Linz.*

St. Florian is best known for the great Augustinian abbey, considered among the finest baroque buildings in Austria. Composer Anton Bruckner (1824–96) was organist here for 10 years and is buried in the abbey. From Linz, you can drive south through Kleinmünchen and Ebelsberg to St. Florian, or for a more romantic approach try the **Florianer Bahn,** a resurrected electric interurban tram line, which runs museum streetcars on Sundays and holidays from May to early July, and from mid-August until mid-October, 6 km (4 mi) from Pichling to St. Florian (☎ 0732/387778); streetcars depart at 10, 1:30, and 3.

Guided tours of **Stift St. Florian** (St. Florian Abbey) include a magnificent figural gate encompassing all three stories, a large and elegant staircase leading to the upper floors, the imperial suite, and one of the great masterworks of the Austrian baroque, Jakob Prandtauer's **Eagle Fountain courtyard,** with its richly sculpted figures. In the splendid **abbey church,** where the ornate surroundings are somewhat in contrast to Bruckner's music, the Krismann organ (1770–74) is one of the largest and best of its period. Another highlight is the **Altdorfer Gallery,** which contains several masterworks by Albrecht Altdorfer, the leading master of the 16th-century Danube School and ranked with Dürer and Grunewald as one of the greatest northern painters. ⊠ *Stiftstr. 1,* ☎ *07224/8902–0,* FAX *07224/8902–23,* WEB *www.stift-st-florian.at.* ⌑ *€5.* ⊙ *1½-hr tour Apr.–Oct., daily at 10, 11, 2, 3, and 4. Call ahead for other bookings.*

Nightlife and the Arts

Summer concerts are held from June to August at the Kremsmünster and St. Florian abbeys; for tickets, contact Oberösterreichische Stiftskonzerte (⊠ Domgasse 12, ☎ 0732/776127, WEB www.stiftskonzerte.at). A series of **concerts** on the Bruckner organ are given in the church of St. Florian from mid-May–mid-October at 2:30 every day except Tuesday and Saturday for €2.40 (☎ 07224/8902). Also look for the St. Florian choir boys' (*Sängerknaben*) annual Christmas concert. For details check (WEB www.florianer.at).

Kremsmünster

③ *36 km (22½ mi) south of Linz.*

The vast Benedictine **Stift Kremsmünster** was established in 777 and remains one of the most important abbeys in Austria. Most travelers arrive here by taking Route 139 (or the train) heading southwest from Linz. Inside the church is the Gothic memorial tomb of Gunther, killed by a wild boar, whose father, Tassilo, duke of Bavaria (and nemesis of Charlemagne), vowed to build the abbey on the site. Centuries later, the initial structures were replaced in the grand baroque manner, including the extraordinary tower. Magnificent rooms include the Kaisersaal and the frescoed library with more than 100,000 volumes, many of them manuscripts. On one side of the Prälatenhof courtyard are Jakob Prandtauer's elegant fish basins, complete with sculpted saints holding squirming denizens of the deep, and opposite is the Abteitrakt, whose art collection includes the Tassilo Chalice, from about 765. The seven-story observatory (*Sternwarte*) houses an early museum of science. ☎ *07583/5275–151,* WEB *www.tiscover.com/kremsmuenster.* ⌑ *Rooms and art gallery €4.80, observatory and tour €5.10.* ⊙ *Rooms and art gallery tour (minimum 5 people) Easter–Oct., daily at 10, 11, 2, 3, and 4; Nov.–Easter, Tues.–Sun. at 11 and 2. Observatory tour (minimum 5 people) May–Oct., daily at 10 and 2.*

Schloss Kremsegg has a collection of rare musical instruments, mostly brass, with plans for a woodwind and folk music section in the future. ⊠ *Kremseggerstr. 59*, ☎ *07583/52470*, 🖷 *07583/6830.* 🎫 €*5.* ☉ *Apr.– Oct., daily 10–5. Open in winter by appointment.*

$$$ ✕ **Gasthof Moser.** North of Kremsmünster on Highway 139 in the vil-
★   lage of Neuhofen, the Moser is known throughout the countryside for its good cooking. Built in 1640, it retains a time-stained ambience with its vaulted ceilings, curving, thick white walls, and dark wood. The menu ranges from old standards like turkey cordon bleu to the innovative cannelloni stuffed with Zanderfilet on a bed of roast zucchini and toma- toes. ⊠ *Marktpl. 9, A–4501 Neuhofen an der Krems*, ☎ *07227/4229*, 🖷 *07227/42294. Reservations essential. V. Closed Mon. and 1st 2 wks of Aug. No dinner Sun.*

Bad Hall

③④ *9 km (5½ mi) southeast of Kremsmünster, 36 km (22 mi) south of Linz.*

Bad Hall is a curious relic from earlier days when "taking the cure" was in vogue in Europe. It's still a spa and its saline-iodine waters are pre- scribed for internal and external complaints, but you can also enjoy the town for its turn-of-the-20th-century frills and houses. Since those on the cure need amusement between treatments, the town lays on numerous sports offerings—during warm weather, there are especially excellent opportunities for golf and tennis—and an operetta festival in summer.

Dining and Lodging

$$ ✕ **Forsthof.** Located between Bad Hall and Steyr in the village of Siern- ing on Highway 122, this bustling, popular restaurant is reminiscent of a large, venerable farmhouse, with lots of cozy rooms. The kitchen prides itself on good home-style cooking, and local specialties might include turkey breast in a paprika sauce or *Pfandl*, a hearty skillet dish of pork fillet with spinach spätzle and cheese gratiné. ⊠ *Neustr. 29, A–4522 Sierning*, ☎ *07259/23190*, 🖷 *07259/2319–66. AE, DC, MC, V. No dinner Sun.*

$$$ 🏨 **Schlosshotel Feyregg.** Exclusive and charming, this baroque castle
★   just outside town was once the elegant summer residence of an abbot. The comfortable, spacious guest rooms are a tribute to the Biedermeier style, and the period knickknacks scattered throughout add to the over- all feeling of being a guest in a treasured home rather than a hotel. Baths are modern and filled with light. The township's golf course is within an easy stroll. This is an ideal base for exploring the monasteries in the area. ⊠ *A–4540*, ☎ *07258/2591. 11 rooms. No credit cards.*

Steyr

★ ③⑤ *18 km (11 mi) east of Bad Hall, 40 km (25 mi) south of Linz. If you travel to Steyr from Kremsmünster, follow Route 139 until it joins Route 122 and take the road another 17 km (10½ mi).*

Steyr is one of Austria's best-kept secrets, a stunning Gothic market town that watches over the confluence of the Steyr and Enns rivers. Today the main square is lined with baroque facades, many with rococo trim, all complemented by the castle that sits above. The Bummerlhaus at No. 32, in its present form dating from 1497, has a late-Gothic look. On the Enns side, steps and narrow passageways lead down to the river.

In Steyr you are close to the heart of Bruckner country. He composed his Sixth Symphony in the parish house here, and there is a Bruckner room in the Meserhaus, where he composed his "sonorous music to con- found celestial spheres." Schubert also lived here for a time. So many of the houses are worthy of attention that you will need to take your time and explore. Given the quaintness of the town center, you'd hardly guess that in 1894 Steyr had Europe's first electric street lighting.

The **Steyrertalbahn** (☎ 07252/7102), a narrow-gauge vintage railroad, wanders 17 km (10½ mi) from Steyr through the countryside on weekends June–September, and on selected weekends in December.

The **Museum Industrielle Arbeitswelt** (industrial museum), set in former riverside factories, is a reminder of the era when Steyr was a major center of ironmaking and armaments production; hunting arms are still produced here, but the major output is powerful motors for BMW cars, including those assembled in the United States. ✉ *Wehrgrabeng. 7,* ☎ *07252/77351.* 🎫 *€4.75.* ☉ *Early Mar.–Dec. 21, Tues.–Sun. 9–5.*

Dining and Lodging

$$$ ✕ **Rahofer.** You'll have to search for this popular restaurant, which is
★ hidden away at the end of one of the passageways off the main square. Inside it's warm and cozy with dark-wood accents and candlelight. The focus here is Italian, from the Tuscan bread and olives that are brought to your table on your arrival to the selection of fresh pastas and lightly prepared meat and fish dishes. Individual pizzas are baked to perfection with a thin, crispy crust and toppings ranging from arugula and shaved Parmesan to tuna and capers. ✉ *Stadtpl. 9,* ☎ *07252/54606. MC, V. Closed Sun.–Mon.*

$$ ✕🏨 **Minichmayr.** From this traditional hotel the view alone—out over the confluence of the Enns and Steyr rivers, up and across to Schloss Lamberg—will make your stay memorable. Bedrooms have recently been renovated with faux Biedermeier furnishings, complementing the charm of the building's exterior and public rooms. Try to get a room on the river side. The restaurant offers light cuisine, specializing in fresh fish. The grilled trout with almond butter is especially good. The hotel is one of the Romantik Hotels group. ✉ *Haratzmüllerstr. 1–3, A–4400,* ☎ *07252/53410–0,* 📠 *07252/48202–55,* 🌐 *www.tiscover.com/minichmayr. 47 rooms. Restaurant, gym, sauna, bicycles, bar, no-smoking rooms; no a/c. AE, DC, MC, V.*

$$ ✕🏨 **Mader/Zu den Drei Rosen.** In this very old family-run hotel with small but pleasant modern rooms you're right on the attractive town square. The restaurant offers solid local and traditional fare, with outdoor dining in a delightful garden area within the ancient courtyard. ✉ *Stadtpl. 36, A–4400,* ☎ *07252/53358–0,* 📠 *07252/53358–6,* 🌐 *www.mader.at. 62 rooms. Restaurant; no a/c. AE, DC, MC, V.*

THE WACHAU: SOUTH BANK OF THE DANUBE

The gentle countryside south of the Danube and east of Linz is crossed by rivers that rise in the Alps and eventually feed the Danube. Little evidence remains today, in this prosperous country of light industry and agriculture, that the area was heavily fought over in the final days of World War II. From 1945 to 1955 the River Enns marked the border between the western (United States, British, and French) and eastern (Russian) occupation zones.

Enns

36 *20 km (12 mi) southeast of Linz.*

Enns has been continuously settled since at least AD 50; the Romans set up a major encampment shortly after that date. Contemporary Enns is dominated by the 184-ft-high city tower (1565–68) that stands in the town square. A number of Gothic buildings in the center have Renaissance or baroque facades.

Visit the **Basilika St. Laurenz,** built on the foundations of a far earlier church, west of the town center, to view the glass-encased archaeological discoveries. And outside, look for the baroque carved-wood Pontius Pilate disguised as a Turk, alongside a bound Christ, on the balcony of the old sanctuary.

Guided tours (☎ 07223/82777) of the town's highlights, starting at the tower, are available daily for a minimum of three people at 10:30, May–mid-September.

Lodging

$$ ▣ **Lauriacum.** You might overlook this plain contemporary building, set as it is among baroque gems in the center of town, but it's the best place to stay. The bright rooms offer modern comfort, and the quiet garden is a welcoming spot. ⊠ *Wiener Str. 5–7, A–4470,* ☎ *07223/ 82315,* ⟰ *07223/82332–29. 30 rooms. Restaurant, café, sauna, bar; no a/c. MC, V.*

Mauthausen

㊲ *14 km (8½ mi) southeast of Linz, 6 km (4 mi) north of Enns.*

Adolf Hitler had the **Mauthausen Konzentrationslager,** the main concentration camp in Austria, built here along the bank of the Danube in the town of the same name. From Linz, follow signs to Enns and Perg, and then to the EHEMALIGE KZ DENKMAL, the concentration-camp memorial. The pretty town of Mauthausen was selected as the site for a concentration camp because of the granite quarries nearby, which would provide material needed for the grandiose buildings projected in Hitler's "Führer cities." The grim, gray fortress was opened in August 1938 for male prisoners (including children), and the conditions under which they labored were severe even by SS standards. More than 125,000 people lost their lives here before the camp was liberated by the American army in May 1945. The site includes a small museum and memorials, as well as a bookstore. ⊠ *Erinnerungsstr. 1, A–4310,* ☎ *07238/2269 or 07238/3696,* ⟰ *07238/2269–40,* 🌐 *www.mauthausen-memorial.gv.at.* ▣ *€1.82.* ⊙ *Feb.–Mar. and Oct.– Dec. 15, daily 8–4 (last admission 3 PM); Apr.–Sept., daily 8–6 (last admission 5 PM).*

Waidhofen an der Ybbs

㊳ *30 km (18 mi) east of Steyr.*

Waidhofen an der Ybbs is well worth a slight detour from the more traveled routes. This picturesque river town developed early as an industrial center, turning Styrian iron ore into swords, knives, sickles, and scythes. These weapons proved successful in the defense against the invading Turks in 1532; marking the decisive moment of victory, the hands on the north side of the town tower clock remain at 12:45. In 1871, Baron Rothschild bought the collapsing castle and assigned Friedrich Schmidt, architect of Vienna's City Hall, to rebuild it in neo-Gothic style. Stroll around the two squares in the Altstadt to see the Gothic and baroque houses and to the Graben on the edge of the Old City for the delightful Biedermeier houses and churches and chapels. From Enns, take the A1 autobahn or Route 1 east to just before Amstetten, where Route 121 cuts south, paralleling the Ybbs River and the branch rail line for about 25 km (16 mi).

Ybbs an der Donau

③⑨ *69 km (43 mi) east of Linz.*

Floods and fires have left their mark on Ybbs an der Donau, but many 16th-century houses remain, their courtyards vine covered and shaded. The parish church of **St. Laurence** has interesting old tombstones, a gorgeous gilt organ, and a Mount of Olives scene with clay figures dating from 1450. To get to Ybbs an der Donau from Waidhofen an der Ybbs, make your way back to the Danube via Routes 31 and 22 east, then take Route 25 north through the beer-brewing town of Wieselburg.

Melk

★ **④⓪** *22 km (13 mi) east of Ybbs an der Donau, 18 km (11 mi) west of St. Pölten, 33 km (20¼ mi) southwest of Krems.*

The ideal time to approach the magnificent abbey of Melk is mid- to late afternoon, when the sun sets the abbey's ornate baroque yellow facade aglow. As one heads eastward paralleling the Danube, the abbey, shining on its promontory above the river, comes into view—unquestionably one of the most impressive sights in all Austria. The glories of the abbey tend to overshadow the town—located along Route 1—but the riverside village of Melk itself is worth exploring. A self-guided tour (in English, from the tourist office) will head you toward the highlights and the best spots from which to photograph the abbey.

By any standard, ★**Stift Melk** (Melk Abbey) is a baroque-era masterpiece. Part palace, part monastery, part opera set, Melk is a magnificent vision thanks greatly to the upward-reaching twin towers, capped with baroque helmets and cradling a 208-ft-high dome, and a roof bristling with baroque statuary. Symmetry here beyond the towers and dome would be misplaced, and much of the abbey's charm is because of the way the early architects were forced to fit the building to the rocky outcrop that forms its base. The Benedictine abbey's history actually extends back to the 11th century, as it was established in 1089. The glorious building you see today is architect Jakob Prandtauer's reconstruction, completed in 1736, in which some earlier elements are incorporated; two years later a great fire nearly totally destroyed the abbey and it had to be rebuilt. A tour of the building includes the main public rooms: a magnificent library, with more than 90,000 books, nearly 2,000 manuscripts, and a superb ceiling fresco by the master Paul Troger; the marble hall, whose windows on three sides enhance the ceiling frescoes; the glorious spiral staircase; and the church of Saints Peter and Paul, an exquisite example of the baroque style. Call to find out if tours in English will be offered on a specific day. The **Stiftsrestaurant,** which is closed November–April, offers standard fare, but the abbey's excellent wines elevate a simple meal to a lofty experience—particularly on a sunny day on the terrace. ✉ *Abt Berthold Dietmayr-Str. 1,* ☎ *02752/ 555–225,* ☎ *02752/555–226,* ⓦ *www.stiftmelk.at.* ☞ *€6.18; with tour €7.63.* ⊙ *End of Mar.–Apr. and Oct., daily 9–5 (ticket office closes at 4); May–Sept., daily 9–6 (ticket office closes at 5).*

Dining and Lodging

$$–$$$ ✕⊡ **Stadt Melk.** Nestled below the golden abbey in the center of the
★ village square, this elegant restaurant has been well known ever since the Duke and Duchess of Windsor dined here long ago. Though the decor is decidedly Biedermeier, the food is nouvelle Austrian, and may include duck in a honey glaze or chicken breast stuffed with leeks and accompanied by corn and potato croquettes. There are also 16 rather plain bedrooms upstairs, if you don't feel like driving on. ✉ *Hauptpl.*

1, A–3390, ☎ *02752/52475,* FAX *02752/52475–19. 16 rooms. AE, DC, MC, V. Closed Nov., Jan.–Feb.*

$$　🏨 **Hotel zur Post.** Here in the center of town you're in a typical village hotel with the traditional friendliness of family management. The rooms are nothing fancy, though comfortable, and the restaurant offers solid, standard fare. ✉ *Linzer Str. 1, A–3390,* ☎ *02752/52345,* FAX *02752/ 52345–50. 27 rooms. Restaurant; no a/c. MC, V. Closed Jan.–Feb.*

Schallaburg

④①　*6 km (4 mi) south of Melk.*

From Melk, take a road south marked to Mank to arrive at the restored **Schloss Schallaburg** (dating from 1573), a castle featuring an imposing two-story arcaded courtyard that is held to be the area's finest example of Renaissance architecture. Its ornate, warm brown terra-cotta decoration is unusual. The yard once served as a jousting court. Many centuries have left their mark on the castle: inside, the Romanesque living quarters give way to an ornate Gothic chapel. The castle now houses changing special exhibits. ✉ *3382 Schloss Schallaburg,* ☎ *02754/6317,* FAX *02754/ 631755,* WEB *www.noel.gv.at/service/k/k1/schalla.htm.* 🎟 *€6.50.* ⊙ *Late Apr.–late Oct., daily 10–5 (last admission 1 hr before closing).*

En Route　To return to the Wachau from Schallaburg, head back toward Melk and take Route 33 along the south bank. This route, attractive any time of year, is spectacular (and thus heavily traveled) in early spring, when apricot and apple trees burst into glorious bloom. Among the palette of photogenic pleasures is **Schönbühel an der Donau,** whose unbelievably picturesque castle, perched on a cliff overlooking the Danube, is unfortunately not open to visitors. Past the village of Aggsbachdorf you'll spot, on a hill to your right, the romantic ruin of 13th-century Aggstein Castle, reportedly the lair of pirates who preyed on river traffic.

Mautern

④②　*34 km (21 mi) northeast of Melk, 1 km (½ mi) south of Stein.*

Mautern, opposite Krems, was a Roman encampment mentioned in the tales of the Nibelungs. The old houses and the castle are attractive, but contemporary Mautern is known for one of Austria's top restaurants, in an inn run by Lisl Wagner-Bacher; another culinary landmark—also excellent—is run by her brother and sister.

Dining and Lodging

$$$$　✕🏨 **Landhaus Bacher.** This is one of Austria's best restaurants,
　★　elegant but entirely lacking in pretension. The innovative style of Lisl Wagner-Bacher, the top female chef in the country, is constantly changing, but lamb and fish dishes are always present. For starters, try the potato soup with truffles, served in a huge, hollowed-out potato, or the fresh cheese ravioli in an artichoke ragout. Dining in the garden in summer enhances the experience. For an added treat, stay overnight in a Laura Ashley–decorated bedroom in the 10-room guest house (in the $$–$$$ category). It's on the riverbank opposite Krems. ✉ *Südtirolerpl. 208,* ☎ *02732/82937–0 or 02732/85429,* FAX *02732/74337,* WEB *www.landhaus-bacher.at. Reservations essential. DC, V. Closed Mon.– Tues. and Jan. 7–end of Feb.*

Göttweig

④③　*4 km (2½ mi) south of Mautern, 7 km (4½ mi) south of Krems.*

　★　You're certain to spot **Stift Göttweig** (Göttweig Abbey) as you come along the riverside road: the vast Benedictine abbey high above the Danube

Valley watches over the gateway to the Wachau. To reach it, cross the river from Krems in the direction of Mautern and then follow signs to Stift Göttweig. Göttweig's exterior was redone in the mid-1700s in the classical style, which you'll note from the columns, balcony, and relatively plain side towers. Inside, it is a monument to baroque art, with marvelous ornate decoration against the gold, brown, and blue. The stained-glass windows behind the high altar date from the mid-1400s. The public rooms of the abbey are splendid, particularly the Kaiserzimmer (Emperor's Rooms), in which Napoléon stayed in 1809, reached via the elegant Emperor's Staircase. ☒ *Furth bei Göttweig,* ☎ *02732/ 85581–231,* WEB *www.stiftgoettweig.or.at.* ☞ *€5.* ☉ *June–early Sept., daily 10–6; guided tours at 11 and 3; rest of year by appointment.*

Dining

$$–$$$ ★ ✕ **Schickh.** This rambling yellow restaurant, tucked away next to a brook and among lovely old trees below the north side of Göttweig Abbey, is worth looking for. Chef Christian Schickh creates new versions of traditional Austrian dishes while his sister Eva makes sure everything runs smoothly. Seasonal choices might include creamy *Bärlauch* (wild wood garlic) soup, organic Waldviertler duck and homemade dumplings, or delicately seasoned fried chicken. Be sure to save room for the house dessert, *Cremeschnitte,* a light cream pastry. There's a handful of agreeable guest rooms in the $ category available for overnighters. To reach Schickh, cross the river from Krems in the direction of Mautern and Furth bei Göttweig, continuing on a couple of kilometers to the tiny village of Klein Wien. ☒ *Klein-Wien 2, Furth bei Göttweig,* ☎ *02736/ 7218–0,* FAX *02736/7218–7,* WEB *www.schickh.at. Reservations essential. MC, V. Closed Wed.–Thurs. and mid-Jan.–Mar.*

St. Pölten

🄊 *18 km (11 mi) south of Göttweig, 65 km (40¼ mi) west of Vienna.*

St. Pölten, Lower Austria's capital to the south of the Danube, is a busy industrial and commercial center, but still worth a detour 20 km (12½ mi) to the south of the main stretch of the Wachau. The old municipal center, now mainly a pedestrian zone, shows a distinctly baroque face. The originally Romanesque cathedral on Domplatz has a rich baroque interior; the rococo Franciscan church at the north end of the Rathausplatz has four altar paintings by Kremser Schmidt.

Dining and Lodging

$$$ ✕ **Galerie.** Mellow furnishings lend an old-fashioned grandmotherly air to this popular restaurant, a favorite with locals. In contrast to the antiques, the kitchen strives—generally successfully—for a nouvelle approach to fine Austrian standards like pork fillet and turkey breast. ☒ *Fuhrmanng. 1,* ☎ *02742/351305. AE, DC, MC, V. Closed Sun.–Mon. and 2 wks around Easter.*

$$ 🏨 **Metropol.** Slick modern styling marks this modern hotel on the edge of the pedestrian zone at the heart of the Old City. Rooms are comfortable, if rather uniform. ☒ *Schillerpl. 1, A–3100,* ☎ *02742/ 70700–0,* FAX *02742/70700–133. 87 rooms. Restaurant, sauna, bar, parking (fee); no a/c. AE, DC, MC, V.*

OFF THE BEATEN PATH — **HERZOGENBURG –** The great Augustinian monastery of Herzogenburg is 11 km (6½ mi) north of St. Pölten (take Wiener Strasse/Route 1 out of St. Pölten heading east for 12 km, or 8 mi, to Kapelln; then turn left to Herzogenburg). The present buildings date mainly from the mid-1700s. Fischer von Erlach was among the architects who designed the abbey. The church, dedicated to Saints George and Stephen, is wonderfully baroque, with exquisitely decorated ceilings. ☎ *02782/83112–35,*

WEB *www.herzogenburg.at/stift.* ⌨ *€5.* ⏱ *1-hr tour Apr.–Oct., daily
9–noon and 1–5 on the hr.*

En Route Small rural villages abound on the south bank plain, some quaint, some
typical. From St. Pölten, head north on Route S33 or the parallel road,
marked to Traismauer, and pick up Route 43 east. If you're ready for back
roads (too well marked for you to lose your way), cut off to the left to Ober-
bierbaum and then proceed on to Zwentendorf (there's a fascinating
"black" Madonna in the side chapel of the parish church here). If you follow Route 43, it will land you on Route 1 at Mitterndorf; drive east and
after 4 km (2½ mi), turn left off Route 1 onto Route 19, marked for Tulln.

Tulln

🄸 *41 km (24½ mi) northeast of St. Pölten, 42 km (26¼ mi) west of Vienna.*

At Tulln you'll spot a number of charming baroque touches in the attractive main square. There's an **Egon Schiele Museum** to honor the great
modern artist (1890–1918), who was born here; the museum showing
a selection of his works is in the one-time district prison, with a reconstruction of the cell in which Schiele—accused of producing "pornog-
raphy"—was locked up in 1912. ✉ *Donaulände 28,* ☎ *02272/64570.*
⌨ *€2.90, more for special exhibits.* ⏱ *Tues.–Sun. 9–noon and 2–6.*

A former **Minorite cloister** now houses a complex of museums. Among
the more interesting are the **Limesmuseum,** which recalls the early Roman
settlements in the area, and the **Landesfeuerwehrmuseum,** document-
ing rural fire fighting. Also look inside the well-preserved, late-baroque
(1750) Minorite church next door. ✉ *Limesmuseum: Marc-Aurel-
Park 1b; Landesfeuerwehrmuseum: Minoritenpl. 2,* ☎ *02272/61915
or 02272/65922.* ⌨ *Each museum €2.15.* ⏱ *Limesmuseum: Tues.–
Sun., 9–noon and 2–6; Landesfeuerwehrmuseum: Sun. 9–noon.*

Dining and Lodging

$$ ✕ **Zur Sonne.** Just a five-minute walk from the Tulln train station, this
★ upscale Gasthaus owned by the Sodoma family gets so much buzz about
its delicious Italian and nouvelle Austrian cuisine that people come all
the way from Vienna to eat here. Elegant yet unpretentious, Zur Sonne
has high ceilings, large windows, and fresh flowers. The seasonally chang-
ing menu may include *Saibling* (char) lasagne with garden vegetables,
organic pork in a creamy mushroom cabbage sauce with *Erdäpfelpuffer*
(hash browns), or saltimbocca of chicken breast with herb risotto. Aus-
trian wines by the glass are very reasonable. Make sure to end your
meal with the homemade apple strudel, which comes warm out of the
oven. It's a 20-minute train ride from the Heiligenstadt or Franz Josef
stations in Vienna. ✉ *Bahnhofstr. 48,* ☎ *02272/64616. Reservations
essential. No credit cards. Closed Sun.–Mon.*

$$ 🛏 **Zur Rossmühle.** From the abundant greenery of the reception area
to the table settings in the dining room, you'll find pleasing little
touches in this attractively situated hotel on the town square. The rooms
are done in grand-old yet brand-new baroque. Take lunch in the courtyard garden; here, as in the more formal dining room, you'll be offered
Austrian standards. ✉ *Hauptpl. 12–13, A–3430,* ☎ *02272/62411,* FAX
*02272/62411–33. 55 rooms. Restaurant, sauna, horseback riding,
bar; no a/c. AE, DC, MC, V.*

Greifenstein

🄸 *10 km (6½ mi) northeast of Tulln.*

Greifenstein is east of Tulln along Route 14; turn left at St. Andrä-
Wördern and stay along the Danube's south bank. Atop the hill at

Greifenstein, yet another **castle** with spectacular views looks up the Danube and across to Stockerau. Its earliest parts date from 1135, but most of it stems from a thorough but romantic renovation in 1818. The view is worth the climb, even when the castle and inexpensive restaurant are closed. ⊠ *Kostersitzg. 5,* ☎ *02242/32353.* ☑ *€1.82.* ☉ *Mar.– Oct., weekends noon–5.*

Klosterneuburg

⑥ *13 km (8 mi) northwest of Vienna.*

The great Augustinian abbey **Stift Klosterneuburg** dominates the town. The structure has undergone many changes since the abbey was established in 1114, most recently in 1892, when Friedrich Schmidt, architect of Vienna's City Hall, added neo-Gothic embellishments to its two identifying towers. Klosterneuburg was unusual in that until 1568 it housed both men's and women's religious orders. In the abbey church, look for the carved-wood choir loft and oratory and the large 17th-century organ. Among Klosterneuburg's treasures are the beautifully enameled 1181 Verdun Altar in the Leopold Chapel, stained-glass windows from the 14th and 15th centuries, Romanesque candelabra from the 12th century, and gorgeous ceiling frescoes in the great marble hall. In an adjacent outbuilding there's a huge wine cask over which people slide; the exercise, called *Fasslrutsch'n,* is indulged in during the Leopoldiweinkost, the wine tasting around St. Leopold's Day, November 15. The **Stiftskeller,** with its atmospheric underground rooms, serves standard Austrian fare and wine bearing the Klosterneuberg label. ⊠ *Stiftspl. 1,* ☎ *02243/411–0,* WEB *www. stift-klosterneuburg.at.* ☑ *€5.09.* ☉ *1-hr tour Mon.–Sat. on the hour, 10–5.*

The new **Sammlung Essl** contemporary art museum, somewhat alarmingly resembling a sports center from the outside, was designed by Heinz Tesar to showcase works created after 1945. The permanent collection includes works by such regional artists as Hermann Nietsch and Arnulf Rainer, and changing exhibitions focus on contemporary artists, including Nam June Paik. The emphasis here is on "new," including special evening concerts highlighting various modern composers' work. To get to the Sammlung Essl museum, take the U-4 to Heiligenstadt, then transfer to Bus 239 to Klosterneuberg. ⊠ *An der Donau–Au 1,* ☎ *0800/232–800,* FAX *02243/370–5022,* WEB *www.sammlung-essl.at.* ☑ *€6.* ☉ *Tues.–Sun. 10–7, Wed. 10–9.*

OFF THE BEATEN PATH | **KAHLENBERGERDORF** – Near Klosterneuburg and just off the road tucked under the Leopoldsberg promontory is the charming small vintners' village of Kahlenbergerdorf, an excellent spot to stop and sample the local wines. You're just outside the Vienna city limits here, which accounts for the crowds (of Viennese, not international tourists) on weekends.

DANUBE VALLEY A TO Z

To research prices, get advice from other travelers, and book travel arrangements, visit www.fodors.com

AIR TRAVEL

Linz is served mainly by Austrian Airlines, Lufthansa, Swissair, and Tyrolean. Regular flights connect with Vienna, Amsterdam, Berlin, Düsseldorf, Frankfurt, Paris, Stuttgart, and Zürich.

AIRPORTS

The Linz airport is in Hörsching, about 12 km (7½ mi) southwest of the city. Buses run between the airport and the main train station according to flight schedules.

➤ AIRPORT INFORMATION: **Linz airport** (☎ 07221/600–123).

BIKE TRAVEL

For details on the scenic Danube river route, ask for the folder "Danube Cycle Track" (in English, from Tourist Office of Lower Austria). The brochure "Radfahren" is in German, but lists contact numbers for cycle rentals throughout Austria. You can rent a bike in Linz, or you can rent a bike privately in Kremsmünster at Tenniscenter Stadlhuber.

➤ BIKE MAPS: **Tourist Office of Lower Austria** (✉ ☎ 01/53610–6200, FAX 01/53610–6060).

➤ BIKE RENTALS: **LILO Bahnhof** (✉ Coulinstr. 30, ☎ 0732/600703). **Tenniscenter Stadlhuber** (☎ 07583/7498–0).

BOAT AND FERRY TRAVEL

Large riverboats with sleeping accommodations ply the route between Vienna and Linz and between Passau on the German border and Linz from late spring to early fall. Smaller day boats go between Vienna and the Wachau Valley, and there you can change to local boats that crisscross the river between the colorful towns.

Bridges across the river are few along this stretch, so boats provide essential transportation; service is frequent enough that you can cross the river, visit a town, catch a bus or the next boat to the next town, and cross the river farther up- or downstream. You can take a day trip from Vienna and explore one of the stops, such as Krems, Dürnstein, or Melk. Boats run from May to late September.

There are two boat companies that ply the Danube: the Blue Danube Schiffahrt/DDSG and the Brandner Schiffahrt.

➤ BOAT AND FERRY INFORMATION: **Blue Danube Schiffahrt/DDSG** (✉ Friedrichstr. 7, A–1043 Vienna, ☎ 01/588–800, FAX 01/58880–440, WEB www.ddsg-blue-danube.at). **Brandner Schiffahrt** (✉ Ufer 50, A–3313 Wallsee, ☎ 07433/2590–0, WEB www.brandner.at).

BUS TRAVEL

If you link them together, bus routes will get you to the main points in this region and even to the hilltop castles and monasteries, assuming you have the time. If you coordinate your schedule to arrive at a point by train or boat, you can usually make reasonable bus connections to outlying destinations. You can book bus tours in Vienna or Linz by calling central bus information, listed below.

➤ BUS INFORMATION: **Central bus information**(☎ 01/71101).

CAR RENTALS

Cars can be rented at the airports in Vienna (☞ Vienna A to Z) or Linz. Linz contacts are listed below.

➤ MAJOR AGENCIES: **Avis** (✉ Europapl. 5–9, ☎ 0732/662881). **Europcar** (✉ Wienerstr. 91, ☎ 0732/6000–91). **Hertz** (✉ Bürgerstr. 19, ☎ 0732/784841–0).

CAR TRAVEL

A car is certainly the most comfortable way to see this region, as it conveniently enables you to pursue the byways. The main route along the north bank is Route 3; along the south bank, there's a choice between the autobahn Route A1 and a collection of lesser but good roads.

A car is certainly the most hassle-free way to get around. Roads are good and well marked, and you can switch over to the A1 autobahn, which parallels the general east–west course of the route (☞ Car Travel *in* Smart Travel Tips A to Z).

EMERGENCIES
If you need a doctor and speak no German, ask your hotel how best to obtain assistance.
➤ EMERGENCY SERVICES: **Ambulance** (☎ 144). **Fire** (☎ 122). **Police** (☎ 133).

OUTDOOR ACTIVITIES AND SPORTS
CANOEING
The Danube is fast and tricky, so you're best off sticking to the calmer waters back of the power dams (at Pöchlarn, above Melk, and near Grein). You can also canoe on an arm of the Danube near Ottensheim, about 8 km (5 mi) west of Linz. There are a couple of places to rent canoes, which are listed below.
➤ CONTACTS: **Ruderverein Donau** (Heilhamerweg 2, Linz, ☎ 0732/736250). **Ruderverein Ister-Sparkasse** (Am Winterhafen 19, Linz, ☎ 0732/774888).

FISHING
In the streams and lakes of the area around Linz, you can fly-cast for rainbow and brook trout and troll for pike and carp. Check with the town tourist offices about licenses and fishing rights for river trolling and fly-casting in Aggsbach-Markt, Dürnstein, Emmersdorf, Grein, Klein-Pöchlarn, Krems, Mautern, Mauthausen, Persenbeug–Gottsdorf, Pöchlarn, Schönbühel/Aggsbachdorf, Spitz, Waidhofen/Ybbs, and Ybbs.

HIKING
Local tourist offices have maps and route details of the fabulous trails in the area. For information on the Mühlviertel from Freistadt to Grein, call the number listed below.
➤ CONTACTS: **Mühlviertel Touristik** (☎ 0732/735020).

TOURS
Tours out of Vienna take you to Melk and back by bus and boat in eight hours, with a stop at Dürnstein. Bus tours operate year-round except as noted, but the boat runs only April–October. There are a couple of reputable operators, listed below.
➤ FEES AND SCHEDULES: **Cityrama Sightseeing** (✉ Börseg. 1, ☎ 01/534–130, FAX 01/534–1328). **Vienna Sightseeing Tours** (✉ Stelzhammerg. 4/11, ☎ 01/712–4683-0, FAX 01/714–1141).

TRAIN TRAVEL
Rail lines parallel the north and south banks of the Danube. Fast services from Vienna run as far as Stockerau; beyond that, service is less frequent. The main east–west line from Vienna to Linz closely follows the south bank for much of its route. Fast trains connect German cities via Passau with Linz.

All the larger towns and cities in the region can be reached by train, but the train misses the Wachau Valley along the Danube's south bank. The rail line on the north side of the river clings to the bank in places; service is infrequent. You can combine rail and boat transportation along this route, taking the train upstream and crisscrossing your way back on the river. From Linz, the delightful LILO (Linzer Lokalbahn) interurban line makes the run up to Eferding. A charming narrow-gauge line meanders south to Waidhofen an der Ybbs.
➤ TRAIN INFORMATION: **LILO** (☎ 0732/654376). **ÖBB—Österreichisches Bundesbahn** (☎ 05/1717).

TRAVEL AGENCIES

In Linz, there are several leading travel agencies.

➤ LOCAL AGENT REFERRALS: **American Express** (✉ Bürgerstr. 14, ☎ 0732/669013, FAX 0732/655334). **Kuoni** (✉ Hauptpl. 14, ☎ 0732/771301, FAX 0732/775338). **Oberösterreichisches Landesreisebüro** (✉ Hauptpl. 9, ☎ 0732/771061–0, FAX 0732/771061–49).

VISITOR INFORMATION

For general information on the area, check with the district tourist offices: Lower Austria, Upper Austria, Linz, Mühlviertel, and Wachau. In Linz you can pick up the latest *Guests Magazine* in English as well as German.

Most towns have a local *Fremdenverkehrsamt* (tourist office); these are listed below by town name.

➤ TOURIST INFORMATION: **Dürnstein** (✉ Parkpl. Ost, A–3601, ☎ 02711/219, FAX 02711/442, WEB www.duernstein.at). **Eferding** (✉ Stadtpl. 31, A–4070, ☎ 07272/5555–160, FAX 07272/5555–161). **Freistadt** (✉ Hauptpl. 12, A–4240, ☎ 07942/72974, FAX 07942/73207). **Grein** (✉ Stadtpl. 7, A–4360, ☎ 07268/7055, WEB www.oberoesterreich.at/grein). **Klosterneuburg** (✉ Niedermarkt 4, A–3400, ☎ 02243/32038, FAX 02243/26773, WEB www.klosterneuburg.net/tourismus). **Krems/Stein** (✉ Undstr. 6, A–3500, ☎ 02732/82676, FAX 02732/70011). **Linz** (✉ Hauptpl. 1, A–4020 Linz, ☎ 0732/7070–1777, FAX 0732/772873, WEB www.linz.at). **Lower Austria** (✉ Niederösterreich Werbung GMBH, Fischhof 3/3, A-1010 Vienna, ☎ 01/53610–6200, FAX 01/53610–6060). **Melk** (✉ Babenbergerstr. 1, A–3390, ☎ 02752/52307–410, FAX 02752/52307–490). **Mühlviertel** (✉ Blütenstr. 8, A–4040 Linz, ☎ 0732/735020, FAX 0732/712400). **Pöchlarn** (✉ Regensburger Str. 11, A–3380, ☎ 02757/2310–30, FAX 02757/2310–66). **St. Pölten** (✉ Rathauspl. 1, A–3100, ☎ 02742/353354, FAX 02742/333–2819). **Steyr** (✉ Stadtpl. 27, A–4400, ☎ 07252/53229–0, FAX 07252/53229–15). **Tulln** (✉ Minoritenpl. 2, A–3430, ☎ 02272/65836, FAX 02272/65838, WEB www.tulln.at). **Upper Austria** (✉ Schillerstr. 50, A–4010 Linz, ☎ 0732/771264, FAX 0732/71807120). **Wachau** (✉ Undstr. 6, A–3500 Krems, ☎ 02732/85620, FAX 02732/87471, WEB www.wachau.at). **Waidhofen an der Ybbs** (✉ Freisingerberg 2, A–3340, ☎ 07442/511255, FAX 07442/51199, WEB www.waidhofen.at). **Weissenkirchen** (✉ Donaulände 262, A–3610, ☎ 02715/2600, FAX 02715/2600–16, WEB www.weissenkirchen-wachau.at).

WORDS AND PHRASES

Austrian German is not entirely the same as the German spoken in Germany. Several food names are different, as well as a few basic phrases.

Umlauts have no similar sound in English. An ä is pronounced as "eh." An äu or eu is pronounced as "oy". An ö is pronounced by making your lips like an "O" while trying to say "E" and a ü is pronounced by making your lips like a "U" and trying to say "E".

Consonants are pronounced as follows:

CH is like a hard H, almost like a soft clearing of the throat.

J is pronounced as Y.

Rs are rolled.

ß, which is written "ss" in this book, is pronouced as double S.

S is pronounced as Z.

V is pronounced as F.

W is pronounced as V.

Z is pronounced as TS.

An asterisk (*) denotes common usage in Austria.

English	German	Pronunciation
Basics		
Yes/no	Ja/nein	yah/nine
Please	Bitte	**bit**-uh
May I?	Darf ich?	darf isch?
Thank you (very much)	Danke (vielen Dank)	**dahn**-kuh (**fee**-len dahnk)
You're welcome	Bitte, gern geschehen	**bit**-uh, gairn ge**shay**-un
Excuse me	Entschuldigen Sie	ent-**shool**-di-gen zee
What? (What did you say?)	Wie, bitte?	vee, **bit**-uh?
Can you tell me?	Können Sie mir sagen?	kunnen zee meer **sah**-gen?
Do you know ____?	Wissen Sie ____?	**viss**-en zee
I'm sorry	Es tut mir leid.	es toot meer lite
Good day	Guten Tag	**goo**-ten tahk
Goodbye	Auf Wiedersehen	owf **vee**-der-zane
Good morning	Guten Morgen	**goo**-ten **mor**-gen
Good evening	Guten Abend	**goo**-ten **ah**-bend
Good night	Gute Nacht	**goo**-tuh nahkt
Mr./Mrs.	Herr/Frau	hair/frow
Miss	Fräulein	**froy**-line
Pleased to meet you	Sehr erfreut.	zair air-**froyt**
How are you?	Wie geht es Ihnen?	vee **gate** es **ee**-nen?
Very well, thanks.	Sehr gut, danke.	sair goot, **dahn**-kuh
And you?	Und Ihnen?	oont **ee**-nen?
Hi!	*Servus!	**sair**-voos

Days of the Week

Sunday	Sonntag	**zohn**-tahk
Monday	Montag	**moan**-tahk
Tuesday	Dienstag	**deens**-tahk
Wednesday	Mittwoch	**mitt**-voak
Thursday	Donnerstag	**doe**-ners-tahk
Friday	Freitag	**fry**-tahk
Saturday	Samstag	**zahm**-stahk

Useful Phrases

Do you speak English?	Sprechen Sie Englisch?	**shprek**-hun zee **eng**-glisch?
I don't speak German.	Ich spreche kein Deutsch.	isch **shprek**-uh kine doych
Please speak slowly.	Bitte sprechen Sie langsam.	**bit**-uh **shprek**-en zee **lahng**-zahm
I don't understand	Ich verstehe nicht	isch fair-**shtay**-uh nicht
I understand	Ich verstehe	isch fair-**shtay**-uh
I don't know	Ich weiss nicht	isch vice nicht
Excuse me/sorry	Entschuldigen Sie	ent-**shool**-di-gen zee
I am American/ British	Ich bin Ameri-kaner(in)/Eng-länder(in)	isch bin a-mer-i-**kahn**-er(in)/**eng**-len-der(in)
What is your name?	Wie heissen Sie?	vee **high**-sen zee
My name is ...	ich heiße ...	isch **high**-suh
What time is it?	Wieviel Uhr ist es? *Wie spät ist es?	**vee**-feel oor ist es **vee** shpate ist es
It is one, two, three ... o'clock.	Es ist ein, zwei, drei ... Uhr.	es ist ine, tsvy, dry ... oor
Yes, please/	Ja, bitte/	yah **bi**-tuh/
No, thank you	Nein, danke	**nine** dahng-kuh
How?	Wie?	vee
When?	Wann? (as conjunction, als)	vahn (ahls)
This/next week	Diese/nächste Woche	**dee**-zuh/**nehks**-tuh **vo**-kuh
This/next year	Dieses/nächstes Jahr	**dee**-zuz/**nehks**-tuhs yahr
Yesterday/today/ tomorrow	Gestern/heute/ morgen	**geh**-stern/**hoy**-tuh/**mor**-gen
This morning/ afternoon	Heute morgen/ nachmittag	**hoy**-tuh **mor**-gen/**nahk**-mit-tahk
Tonight	Heute Nacht	**hoy**-tuh nahkt
What is it?	Was ist es?	**vahss** ist es
Why?	Warum?	vah-**rum**
Who/whom?	Wer/wen?	vair/vehn
Who is it?	Wer ist da?	vair ist dah

I'd like to have . . .	Ich hätte gerne . . .	isch **het**-uh gairn
a room	ein Zimmer	ine **tsim**-er
the key	den Schlüssel	den **shluh**-sul
a newspaper	eine Zeitung	i-nuh **tsy**-toong
a stamp	eine Briefmarke	i-nuh **breef**-mark-uh
a map	eine Karte	i-nuh **cart**-uh
I'd like to buy . . .	ich möchte . . . kaufen	isch **merhk**-tuh **cow**-fen
cigarettes	Zigaretten	tzig-ah-**ret**-ten
I'd like to exchange . . .	Ich möchte . . . wechseln	isch **merhk**-tuh . . . **vex**-eln/
dollars to schillings	Dollars in Schillinge	dohl-lars in **shil**-ling-uh
pounds to schillings	Pfunde in Schillinge	pfoonde in **shil**-ling-uh
How much is it?	Wieviel kostet das?	**vee**-feel **cost**-et dahss?
It's expensive/ cheap	Es ist teuer/billig	es ist **toy**-uh/**bill**-ig
A little/a lot	ein wenig/sehr	ine **vay**-nig/zair
More/less	mehr/weniger	mair/**vay**-nig-er
Enough/too much/ too little	genug/zuviel/ zu wenig	geh-**noog**/tsoo-**feel**/ tsoo **vay**-nig
I am ill/sick	Ich bin krank	isch bin krahnk
I need . . .	Ich brauche . . .	isch **brow**-khuh
a doctor	einen Arzt	I-nen artst
the police	die Polizei	dee po-lee-**tsai**
help	Hilfe	**hilf**-uh
Fire!	Feuer!	**foy**-er
Caution/Look out!	Achtung!/Vorsicht!	**ahk**-tung/**for**-zicht
Is this bus/train/ subway going to . . . ?	Fährt dieser Bus/ dieser Zug/ diese U-Bahn nach . . . ?	fayrt **deez**er buhs/ **deez**-er tsook/ **deez**-uh **oo**-bahn nahk . . .
Where is . . .	Wo ist . . .	**vo** ist
the train station?	der Bahnhof?	dare **bahn**-hof
the subway station?	die U-Bahn- Station?	dee **oo**-bahn- **staht**-sion
the bus stop?	die Bushaltestelle?	dee **booss**-hahlt-uh- **shtel**-uh
the airport?	der Flugplatz? *der Flughafen?	dare **floog**-plats dare **floog**-hafen
the hospital?	das Krankenhaus?	dahs **krahnk**-en- house
the elevator?	der Aufzug?	dare **owf**-tsoog
the telephone?	das Telefon?	dahs te-le-**fone**
the rest room?	die Toilette?	dee twah-**let**-uh
open/closed	offen/geschlossen	**off**-en/ge-**schloss**-en
left/right	links/rechts	links/**recktz**
straight ahead	geradeaus	geh-**rah**-day-owws
is it near/far?	ist es in der Nähe/ist es weit?	ist es in dare **nay**-uh? ist es vite?

MENU GUIDE

English	German
Entrées	Hauptspeisen
Homemade	Hausgemacht
Lunch	Mittagsessen
Dinner	Abendessen
Dessert	Nachspeisen
At your choice	Önach Wahl
Soup of the day	Tagessuppe
Appetizers	Vorspeisen

Breakfast

Bread	Brot
Butter	Butter
Eggs	Eier
Hot	Heiss
Cold	Kalt
Caffeine-free coffee	Café Hag
Jam	Marmelade
Milk	Milch
Juice	Saft
Bacon	Speck
Lemon	Zitrone
Sugar	Zucker

Soups

Stew	Eintopf
Goulash soup	Gulaschsuppe
Chicken soup	Hühnersuppe
Potato soup	Kartoffelsuppe
Liver dumpling soup	Leberknödelsuppe
Onion soup	Zwiebelsuppe

Fish and Seafood

Trout	Forelle
Prawns	Garnele
Halibut	Heilbutt
Lobster	Hummer
Crab	Krabbe
Salmon	Lachs
Squid	Tintenfisch
Tuna	Thunfisch
Turbot	Steinbutt

Meats

Veal	Kalb
Lamb	Lamm
Beef	Rindfleisch
Pork	Schwein

Game and Poultry

Duck	Ente
Pheasant	Fasan

Goose	Gans
Chicken	Hühner
Rabbit	Kaninchen
Venison	Reh
Turkey	Truthahn
Quail	Wachtel

Vegetables and Side Dishes

Red cabbage	Rotkraut
Cauliflower	Karfiol
Beans	Bohnen
Button mushrooms	Champignons
Peas	Erbsen
Cucumber	Gurke
Cabbage	Kohl
Lettuce	Blattsalat
Potatoes	Kartoffeln
Dumplings	Knödel
French fries	Pommes frites

Fruits

Apple	Apfel
Orange	Orangen
Apricot	Marillen
Blueberry	Heidelbeere
Strawberry	Erdbeere
Raspberry	Himbeere
Cherry	Kirsche
Cranberry	Preiselbeere
Grapes	Trauben
Pear	Birne
Peach	Pfirsich

Desserts

Cheese	Käse
Crepes	Palatschinken
Soufflé	Auflauf
Ice cream	Eis
Cake	Torte

Drinks

Tap water	Leitungswasser
With/without water	Mit/ohne wasser
Straight	Pur
Non-alcoholic	Alkoholfrei
A large/small dark beer	Ein Krügel/Seidel Dunkles
A large/small light beer	Ein Krügel/Seidel Helles
Draft beer	Vom Fass
Sparkling wine	Sekt
White wine	Weisswein
Red wine	Rotwein
Wine with mineral water	Gespritz

INDEX